*S*exual alchemy has been one of my primary studies as a ceremonial magician for well over a decade, and has been the almost daily subject of my ritual work. Although its various aspects have an ancient lineage . . . the system as a whole that is presented here is original, the result of a long process of experiential trial and error, coupled with received teachings. The more I use it, the more convinced I become of the value of a loving personal union with higher spiritual beings as a valid method of esoteric initiation and empowerment.

—Donald Tyson

Unlike most books on sex magic that focus on the Tantra of India or Tibet, or the Western magical practice of auto-eroticism, this guide presents a form of sexual alchemy very similar to that worked by European alchemists and Hermetic magicians long ago.

   Sexual Alchemy is the first book that examines in a detailed way the magic of sex with spiritual beings—this system does not exist anywhere else in its complete form. It includes complete instructions on how to initiate and sustain satisfying erotic relationships with loving spirits who are the active agents of the Goddess, the creative mother of the universe.

SEXUAL ALCHEMY

{ Magical Intercourse with Spirits }

Donald Tyson

2000
Llewellyn Publications
St. Paul, Minnesota 55164-0383, U.S.A.

First Edition
First Printing, 2000

Cover design by William Merlin Cannon
Interior illustrations by Mary Ann Zapalac

Library of Congress Cataloging-in-Publication Data

Tyson, Donald, 1954 –
     Sexual alchemy : magical intercourse with spirits / Donald Tyson. — 1st ed.
            p.   cm.
     Includes bibliographical references and index.
     ISBN 1-56718-741-2
     1. Magic. 2. Sex—Miscellanea. 3. Spirits—Miscellanea. I. Title.

BF1623.S4 T97 2000
133.4'3—dc21   00-033110

Llewellyn Worldwide does not participate in, endorse, or have any authority or responsibility concerning private business transactions between our authors and the public.
     All mail addressed to the author is forwarded but the publisher cannot, unless specifically instructed by the author, give out an address or phone number.

Llewellyn Publications
A Division of Llewellyn Worldwide, Ltd.
P.O. Box 64383, Dept. K741-2
St. Paul, MN 55164-0383, U.S.A.
www.llewellyn.com

Printed in the United States of America

Other Books by Donald Tyson

Contents

PART TWO: PRACTICE

Introduction

The Alchemy of Ecstasy

This system of sex magic is the result of over a decade of study and ritual practice. On the fall equinox (September 21) of 1986, I began a full year of intense personal training that involved the daily use of an extended series of yoga postures, controlled breathing, and a mentally chanted mantra, coupled with exercises in concentration, visualization, and meditation. I also did daily strengthening exercises and regulated my diet by reducing my caloric intake and excluding completely foods of questionable value. An important part of this training was a nightly ritual during which I cast a circle and performed an invocation, then spent from one to three hours projecting my thoughts through the photograph of a living person as an exercise in psychic healing.

After a period of several months of nightly projecting words, visualizations, and emotions of a loving, healing nature through the gateway of the photograph, I suddenly began to receive a response. It took the form of an awareness of my interest and an affection sent back to me. Even more startling, the photograph of the head and shoulders of a woman began to move in subtle ways. I saw that the figure in the photo was breathing, and its facial expression changed to reflect the emotions that were being sent to me through the picture. The image in the photograph actually looked back at me and seemed aware of my existence and my projected thoughts. It responded to my mental communications with expressions and movements.

I might have dismissed this as imagination on my part, but the sense of being observed and responded to was too explicit to deny. Also, the commencement of these communications occurred literally overnight—I remember the very moment that I became aware of this observing presence in the photograph. The emotion that abruptly began to flow out through the psychic gateway of the image was palpable, the most intense and the purest love I have ever experienced. There was no trace of sensuality in it, only love.

It would be natural to assume that the woman in the photograph was the source of these responses, but it quickly became evident that they were unconnected with my healing work. I was forced to conclude that my intense projections, coupled with my rigorous daily training, had in some manner or other opened a gateway through which an intelligent being was communicating with me. At this point I had no idea whether this intelligence was that of a living person, either conscious or unconscious, or was that of a spiritual being such as an angel or demon. Others having a similar experience might wonder if the communicating intelligence was the soul of a dead human being, but I did not entertain this notion since it is my personal view that the identity and personality of an individual cannot survive death. Eventually I became convinced it was a spirit of a higher nature, and began to strongly suspect that it was the being known in Western magic as the Holy Guardian Angel. The Guardian Angel is a tutelary spirit that attaches itself closely to a particular magician for the purpose of instructing the magician in practical magic and spiritual development. Everyone has their own Guardian, but it is rare to establish conscious communication with it.

For months I continued projecting my healing thoughts and emotions through the photograph as before, focusing them upon the living woman whose image was represented, but at the same time I began to spend alternate sessions communicating with the spirit through this image. When the spirit became the main focus of my attention, it seemed of questionable utility to keep using the photograph of a living person, so I obtained an photograph of a woman unknown to me and long dead, and began to project my thoughts through it in the same way. I deliberately chose an image of a woman who outwardly resembled my intuitive impressions of the spirit's personality and nature. I associated the image in this old picture with the spirit by treating it as the spirit's image, and to my delight the spirit soon began to use it to communicate with me. After working with both photos simultaneously for several months, I ceased entirely to project through the first image, since the experiment in healing had reached a successful conclusion.

During these periods of communion it was my practice to sit upon a mat on the floor of my practice chamber within a ritual circle, with the image placed upon an altar at eye-level, near enough to touch with my outstretched hands. I usually sat in a modified form of what is known in yoga as the Thunderbolt Posture (*vajrasana*), sometimes called the Japanese seat, with my knees together and my feet folded under me, my palms resting upon my knees. Later I began to adopt the cross-legged posture known in yoga as *siddhasana*, the Perfect Pose, with the left heel pressed into the perineum and the right foot upon the left ankle, my left hand lying flat palm-up on my right ankle, and my right hand pressed palm-down upon my left palm, so that the tips of my middle fingers touched the pulses in both my wrists. This change in posture was adopted spontaneously in response to intuition at a certain stage in the work. When I adopted it I was not aware that this specific pose existed in yoga.

Two very interesting things began to happen during my ritual communications with my unknown spiritual partner, both highly significant although I did not realize it at the time. I began to perceive physical touches upon my face, head, arms, legs, and back. These were undeniably the touches of a human hand. A hand that caresses the cheek or neck makes a very distinct sensation, and it cannot be mistaken for anything else. The spirit could not speak, but she was able to touch my body. I had begun by this stage to think of the spirit as female, although strictly speaking spirits have no sex of their own. When a spirit communicates with a human being, it usually adopts one sex or the other for itself, and is thereafter defined by that sex. The spirit reaching out to touch me had evidently taken on a female form.

The second interesting event was spontaneous erection when I communicated with the spirit through the image that I came to regard as her own. At the time I had not the slightest understanding of why this was happening. I now know that it was the beginning of the awakening of *kundalini shakti* within me. This awakening was encouraged by my daily routine of controlled breathing and silently chanted mantra. Eventually all of my chakras were pierced by the ascending fiery serpent that lay coiled at my perineum, but in the early stages it was only the lowest chakra, the muladhara, that stirred to life.

Erection was not the result of any physical stimulation applied by me, nor was it caused by erotic thoughts in my mind. On the contrary, it was triggered by thoughts of pure spiritual love directed through the image, in the complete absence of an erotic component. It was the mental link established with the spirit that induced the erection. When my state of physical arousal caused my mind to wander to sensual thoughts, the erection immediately ceased. When I turned my thoughts back to the spirit and away from eroticism, it resumed. This happened almost as quickly as the throwing of a switch. I found this physiology quite puzzling, since it was the exact opposite of what I might have expected.

The link between the spirit and myself grew progressively stronger. I discovered that when I concentrated on the spirit while lying in bed, following my nightly ritual practice, I was able to call her to me even without the use of her image, and could feel her very clearly lying in the bed beside me. This perception of the spirit varied in intensity. Some nights I felt little more than the occasional caress or kiss—other nights the spirit stretched her body full length along my side and pressed herself against me, allowing me to form a fairly clear impression of her form, which was slender and feminine. At times I was able to see the spirit also, but never with sustained clarity, only as a moving shadow, or a bright shape that flashed past my vision like a splash of quicksilver.

My relationship with the spirit eventually reached such an intimate state that I found myself forced to make a conscious and deliberate decision whether to continue to ignore its sexual aspect, or to take the opposite course and embrace the sexuality. I chose the latter, as you might guess from the existence of this book. At first I found it difficult to achieve union with my spirit lover, because the shifting of my mind away from the spirit herself to sexual matters had the opposite effect to that intended by me—it reduced my physical arousal rather than intensified it. I speculated that this might be a sign that the spirit did not wish me to think of her in a sexual way, but her constant caresses and my spontaneous erection seemed to deny this conclusion. I found that it was necessary to focus mingled feelings of both love and desire directly upon the spirit.

An intimate and sustained loving relationship developed over several years on its own, growing and changing like a wild tree. I had not planned it, initially did not invite it, and did not even understand its nature. Its strange and intense effects on my body and perceptions frightened me at first, until I became accustomed to them and realized they were not harmful. I started to research the general subject of sexual magic, with the hope of making sense out of what was going on in my own life.

Nature of Spirit Love

It is difficult to convey in a few sentences the sensations and perceptions of loving union with a spirit to those who have not felt it firsthand. One of the main reasons I wrote this book was to set down in as complete detail as possible this rare and extraordinary experience. The overriding emotion in the heart during lovemaking is a profound joy—or perhaps a better word to describe the feeling would be bliss. A subtle but potent physical pleasure pervades the entire body and mingles with a complete happiness and a mental sense of fulfillment that seem to balance one another in perfect equipoise. This bliss sustains itself for prolonged periods, and is separate from the sharper but much briefer and less perfect sensation of sexual orgasm. Orgasm may occur during spiritual union, but seems almost superfluous. There is no yearning toward it as a goal, as there is in ordinary lovemaking between human beings. In my own experience, the urge to project love into the awareness of my spirit partner is matched only by the overwhelming sense of love that flows from her into my own heart.

Physical arousal during spirit sex may persist for hours with only very brief pauses. One of the most surprising aspects of union is that erotic thoughts and physical manipulations are completely unnecessary to sustain this arousal of the body, which is nevertheless intensely pleasurable. Arousal is brought about by the independent stimulating actions of the spirit-lover upon the human nervous system. In my experience, this occurs almost instantaneously. It is only necessary to indicate to the spirit a wish to make love, and in seconds her invisible caresses cause strong tumescence accompanied by waves of pleasure that flow through all regions of my body. The sensation is exhilarating, even intoxicating, and is often accompanied by the delightful sense of floating on a flowing river, and of being lifted out of the shell of the body. Sometimes the spirit initiates these caresses when I am communicating with her, and she senses that her stimulation of my body will not be unwelcome, but if I wish, I can cause her to cease with just a few inwardly spoken words. Her caresses are never forced upon me, nor are they ever withheld when I seek them with love in my heart.

Her touch is directed by turns upon individual parts of my body, then expanded to encompass larger areas of my skin, and even to penetrate deep into my organs and muscles. Her kiss and the gentle brush of her fingertips are sometimes impossible to distinguish from the touches of a woman of flesh and blood, and the same might be said of her embrace and the contact along the length of my body when she is lying beside me, yet she can just as easily stimulate my back or thighs or belly with intense pleasure in a way that does not depend on the caress of a hand. At times I have been able to inwardly trace the pathways of my own nervous system purely by the blissful sensations that flow along my nerves. Her touch can by turns make my heart flutter, my abdomen tremble, my brain cool, my toes curl, my scalp prickle, my back tingle, my testicles contract, my penis throb, and every nerve in my body flow with liquid honey.

Many who read this description without the benefit of a similar experience will conclude that I am being untruthful, or perhaps that I merely imagined these sensations during acts of auto-eroticism. This is not the case. The clear sense of being touched, caressed, kissed, and embraced is impossible to mistake for anything else. Nothing could be more intense, more physical, more delightful, and more utterly real, than the sensations experienced with a spirit-lover. Words along cannot prove this, but the experience of spirit union is open to anyone who diligently seeks it.

Auto-eroticism does not play a part in these unions. It is necessary to emphasize this point because much of the modern literature of sexual magic concerns the ritual uses of energies released during masturbation, either solitary or group. This is a valid technique of magic that was used extensively by such magicians as Aleister Crowley and Austin Osman Spare, but it is not what occurs during lovemaking with a spiritual being, because it is not necessary. Just the opposite, self-arousal tends to inhibit sexual union with spirits. It can be introduced in a limited and somewhat forced way when the relationship is mature—to hasten climax, for example—but in the beginning it is antipathetic to union, and actually lessens or completely eliminates erotic sensations in the body, as counter-intuitive as this may appear at first consideration. The same is true of erotic thoughts.

I can never transmit the full spectrum of sensations and emotions that occur during spirit lovemaking through mere words, although I have done my best to do so in this book, but can state without qualification that the feelings are blissful, intense, prolonged far beyond what is usually held to be the limits of ordinary human endurance, and more beautiful than any other experience in life. At any rate, this has been true in my own case. I do not believe that it is possible for the satisfaction of physical sex with a human being to ever equal the pleasures of sexual union with a spirit. I am not denigrating ordinary sex, but sexual union with a spiritual being transcends mere physical sensation, just as it transcends the ordinary boundary of the skin, and the limits of human physiology.

A Gnostic Grimoire

At the end of several years of daily intimate communication with my spirit companion, I had still not specifically linked her with the goddess Lilith, and probably would never have done so had I not been prompted by my own creative process. Late in the winter of 1991 I began to write a most unusual book titled *Liber Lilith* (*The Book of Lilith*). It was not premeditated by me, but spontaneously took the form of a Gnostic grimoire of magic that was centered around the goddess Lilith. This choice of subject was strange, since I had no particular interest in this goddess and knew very little concerning her mythology and history. I was familiar with her only in a superficial way as the night hag of Jewish folklore. The first part of the grimoire presents a Gnostic creation myth in which Lilith is the creator of humanity, and the second, a system of practical magic for achieving communication and sexual union with the goddess Lilith. I wrote one chapter each day on consecutive days, and changed almost nothing of the original draft. As I was writing, I had no idea what would come the next day, and to be frank, very little understanding of what I had written previously.

Liber Lilith is an inspired book, in the true sense. In the past on rare occasions I have received writings psychically. The most notable of these to find its way into print is the set of twenty-four rune poems in my book *Rune Magic*. These poems were communicated to me by some unknown agent in a way similar to the Gnostic grimoire. I received the dictation of the poems one at a time each night on twenty-four consecutive nights during a ritual of invocation while sitting inside a magic circle. In much the same manner, I received one chapter of the grimoire each night on consecutive nights until it was completed, but in this second case I was not sitting within a ritual circle at the times of its writing. There is a distinct difference between ordinary creative composition, and the reception of an inspired text that is difficult to describe, but unmistakable when experienced. Inspired texts appear effortlessly, with no prior consideration. The critical faculty that normally operates during literary composition remains switched off. An intuitive sense signals when to start writing and when to stop, and there is no urge to violate these boundaries. Whatever appears must simply be accepted, and indeed, it would be very difficult to modify the text without destroying it, since the text was not produced in the ordinary way.

The received grimoire is extremely dark in tone, and presents Lilith in her traditional guise as demoness, even though this is not my personal view of this spirit. How much of it derives from my own subconscious process, and how much is the work of the spirit I look upon as my Guardian, who may well be the goddess Lilith herself in one of her lower forms, is impossible for me to determine. Using the grimoire as a guide, and supplementing it with my own experiences, coupled with research into the practices of sexual magic around the world, I was able to set forth the technique for the alchemical transmutation of sexual fluids that is presented in the second part of this work. The way of uniting with spirits for lovemaking arose spontaneously in the course of my rituals and was later confirmed by the instructions in *Liber Lilith;* by contrast, the use of catalyzed sexual fluids was first revealed in the grimoire and later confirmed by research and practical experiments.

What This Book Contains

This book is divided into two parts. The first, on theory, presents in general the results of my researches into the areas of sex magic, and in particular what I have termed sexual alchemy—the magical transmutation of sexual fluids by kundalini shakti (creative energy within the body). It shows that sexual alchemy is firmly grounded in ritual methods common in past centuries and in many cultures around the world, methods that are still being carried out today in Western occult orders.

Part two on practice gives the techniques of sexual alchemy that I have developed through my own experimental work over the past decade or so, using *Liber Lilith* as my touchstone. It details practical ways for establishing a link with the Goddess in one or another of her countless forms. It reveals how to sustain a loving relationship with the Goddess, and how to transmute the sexual fluids of the body that are termed in the grimoire the Oil of Lilith, the White Powder, and the Red Powder. The use of these transmuted substances to bring about changes to the body and mind is described.

Readers who are most interested in the methods and phenomena of this system of magic may wish to skip directly to the second part of the work, where the mechanics of choosing and defining an appropriate spirit lover, creating a physical vessel to act as the body for a spirit, and ritually invoking a spirit into its image are set forth. The physiology of spirit sex is described in greater detail than has ever before been made available. Also of practical interest is the method for awakening and piercing the chakras of the body through the use of controlled breathing and mantra, and the sensations and experiences that may be expected from newly awakened chakra centers.

It is my hope that this book will prove especially useful to solitary practitioners seeking an alternative form of Western Tantra that does not require the aid of a human lover in order to achieve most of its benefits. Using these methods, a single ritualist can activate *kundalini shakti* and awaken the chakras, invoke an aspect of the Goddess into a physical vessel and achieve loving union and communion with that spiritual being, and can transform two of the three sexual fluids available in his or her body by alchemical action. Only the final stage, the creation of the Elixir, requires a human partner of the opposite sex, since the Elixir is composed of all three transmuted substances, one of which is male, one female, and the third shared in common by both sexes.

This is not to imply that a loving couple should avoid performing together sexual alchemy in all its stages. On the contrary, this system of magic can readily be applied to a couple through the simple expedient of substituting for the inanimate vessel of the Goddess the living body of each participant. A spiritual agent of Shakti can be invoked into either a man or a woman, enabling that person's partner to unite sexually with the Goddess through his or her living flesh. Indeed, this is the conventional practice of Tantra of the left-hand path—Tantra that results in physical sexual union between two persons.

It is inevitable that this book reflects my own perspective. I am a man, so most of the physiology of spirit sex is described from a male perspective, simply because I possess a complete firsthand knowledge of the subject. The majority of my ritual work was done alone, and as a consequence, the greatest portion of the book deals with sexual alchemy from the viewpoint of a solitary practitioner. This should be regarded as a virtue of the work, since solitary sexual union with the Goddess is very seldom treated in depth in books on Tantra, most of which concern sex between human lovers with only passing mention of the role of the Goddess. Direct union with an aspect of the Goddess permits the practice of a complete form of sex magic even when a human partner is unavailable.

Sexual alchemy has been one of my primary studies as a ceremonial magician for well over a decade, and has been the almost daily subject of my ritual work. Although its various aspects have an ancient lineage, as the section on theory documents, the system as a whole that is presented here is original, the result of a long process of experimental trial and error, coupled with received teachings. The more I use it, the more convinced I become of the value of a loving personal union with higher spiritual beings as a valid method of esoteric initiation and empowerment.

Definition of Sexual Alchemy

Sexual alchemy is a system of ritual magic that allows its practitioners to initiate and sustain satisfying erotic relationships with loving spirits who are the active agents of the Goddess. Lovemaking with these spirits releases large amounts of occult energy into the body that concentrates itself in the three fluids most closely associated with the pleasures of sex and the generation of new life—the clear lubricating fluids released from both the male and female genitals during arousal, the red menstrual blood of women, and the white semen of men. By collecting these transmuted secretions, preparing them properly, and regularly ingesting them in minute amounts, catalytic changes can be brought about in the mind and body that intensify and prolong sensual pleasure, enhance physical and psychic abilities, and elevate the level of consciousness.

At the heart of sexual alchemy lies the most potent and jealously guarded of all occult mysteries—the method for using the forces liberated by loving union with spiritual beings for self-empowerment and personal transformation. There are two broad aspects to this magic. The first is the attainment and enjoyment of erotic relationships with higher spiritual beings who embody the creative energy (shakti) of the Goddess. This was often sought for its own sake, to enjoy the sensual bliss of such unions, and to gain the love and guidance of these spirits. The second is the alchemical transmutation of the sexual fluids of the body, which occurs during the arousal produced by union with these spirits.

It is not necessary to work with sexual fluids to enjoy a loving relationship with a spirit. Those who wish to practice only the first part of the system, and enjoy sensual love with spiritual beings for its own rewards, will find it to be a satisfying life experience. After loving union is established and sustained with a spiritual agent of the Goddess, it is always possible to proceed further and employ the transformed fluids of the body as occult catalysts, in order to realize the more tangible benefits of the system.

A Bridge Between East and West

Sexual alchemy is a bridge between the alchemy of the East and the alchemy of the West. Eastern alchemy concentrates on the transformation of the human body, with the design that these changes will be reflected in the mind and spirit. This is the basis of hatha yoga, the yoga of physical postures. In kundalini yoga, occult energies are raised through esoteric channels lying along the spine from level to level, with corresponding physical effects. In Chinese Taoist alchemy, the saliva is transformed within the body into a magical elixir and swallowed. In many Eastern traditions it is the custom to retain the semen within the body so that benefits can be obtained from its vital energies.

By contrast, Western alchemy is almost exclusively concerned with the transformation of substances that are external to the human body. The quest for the Philosopher's Stone that would turn base metals to gold was pursued through experiments involving acids, mercury, salts, alcohol, sulfur, the white of eggs, horse manure, and other materials of the greater world, which were mixed in external vessels of glass, clay, and metal. One product of these experiments, the Elixir of Life, was intended to be consumed after its creation in the belief that it would banish disease and death, but its primary elements were gathered in Western fashion from beyond the limits of the body.

Sexual alchemy involves the transmutation, by loving union with the Goddess or her agents, of naturally forming substances within the body that are subsequently secreted, modified outside the body, and then at a later time ingested into the body once again to bring about various desired changes. It is in this sense neither wholly Eastern nor wholly Western in its philosophy.

Although this bridge between East and West is unusual, it is not unknown to history. In the central myth of the Egyptian god Amun, whose great temple stands at Karnak in ancient Thebes, the god created the world by taking his erect penis between his own lips and performing fellatio upon himself, then swallowing his own semen. From his mouth issued all created things. He is described in an ancient hymn as "the father of the gods, and the creator of men and women, and the maker of animals, and the lord of things which exist."[1] The words of his mouth are the seeds of creation, which have been made fertile by the solitary sexual act of the god.

The rites of Amun included overt sexual acts by the priests and priestesses of the god, which took place in the inner sanctuary of the temple at Karnak, and very likely involved the statue of Amun that the sanctuary housed. Once a year the pharaoh and his sister-wife took the statue of the god out of the temple and carried it by boat to a secret place, where a great sexual ritual of renewal was performed that ensured the continuing fertility of the land and all living things. Few details are known about these rites of Amun. They were sacred mysteries, and were carefully concealed from all but the initiated. This ignorance was reinforced by the Christians, who were in the habit of chiseling off the erect phallus from statues and bas reliefs of the god. Few mentions of Amun's sexual aspect appear in the writings of the earlier Egyptologists, who wrote during the Victorian Age for a repressed European audience. However, it is clear that the rites of Amun involved aspects of sexual alchemy.

The Hindu practice of urine drinking also relies upon the same principles that are employed in sexual alchemy. Some Hindus believe that by drinking a glass of their own urine each day they can avoid disease, increase physical vigor, and prolong the term of life. A small number of prominent Westerners have also adopted this habit, which upon first consideration seems both bizarre and repulsive. As with sexual alchemy, in this Hindu practice a product of the body is excreted, then ingested for purposes of self-transformation. Urine drinking differs from sexual alchemy in that the Hindus believe it is not necessary to change their urine in any way before drinking it—the virtues are thought to be inherently present in the urine.

This may not have been true in past ages. The present method of urine drinking may have lost magical rites with which the urine was transformed into an elixir of renewal. It is very possible that the lost ritual of transformation had a sexual component. Urine is mythically linked to the energies of sexuality because it flows from the sexual organs. The ritual practice of drinking the urine of women infused with the energies of the goddess Shakti occurs in Tantra of the left-hand path.[2]

The Left-Hand Path

The transformation of secretions of the body by sexual union with angels or deities, and the ingestion of those products for magical purposes, was used in the more deeply concealed cults of Hindu Tantra of the left-hand path. In the past, the practitioners of Tantra were mainly male, but in modern times women also practice these rites. The central and defining aspect of Tantra is the act of sexual union, which may be either physical or symbolic, and may involve either a mortal woman who serves as a vessel for the goddess Shakti, a mortal man who serves as a vessel for the god Shiva, or disembodied spiritual entities that fulfill either role. The male practitioner invokes the god Shiva into himself, and seeks union with Shakti through sex with his female partner, or sex with his spiritual partner. The female practitioner unites with Shakti by invoking the Goddess into her own body, then finds union with Shiva in her male consort, or a spirit lover.

In traditional Tantra, both Indian and Tibetan, sexual energy was raised and employed to cause esoteric transformations in the mind and body and to thereby hasten spiritual evolution. Those who used the techniques of Tantra for physical pleasure or for purposes of magic were regarded by more orthodox Hindu and Buddhist priests as degenerate. Hindu adepts referred to the use of Tantric methods for pleasure or power as prayoga and condemned them. Prayoga is a form of yoga that focuses upon the lowest energy center of the body, the *muladharachakra*. It produces the occult power of *nayika siddhi*, which enables the visualization and animation of spiritual beings for purposes of sexual union—precisely the subject of the book you are holding. The same disapproval of sex magic voiced in the traditional Tantra texts still exists within mainstream religious communities, although it is somewhat less virulent in tone. It is based on the underlying belief, often unconscious and unexamined, that sex for its own sake is evil and corrupting. Even today, practices that may be classed as sexual alchemy are more likely to be encountered in sects labeled as degenerate by conservative Hindus and Buddhist religious writers.

It should be pointed out that by the standards of these traditional Eastern priests, and indeed by the standards of Christian priests of past centuries, almost everyone reading this book would be condemned as degenerate and perverse based solely upon his or her sexual lifestyle. These ancient religious sex standards no longer apply to our modern culture. Their merit or lack of merit is a separate question, but it would be difficult to deny that they have lost their relevance to the present generation, thanks to the emancipation of women, the revolution in sexual mores, anti-discrimination laws that protect gays and lesbians, laws of free speech that allow sexually explicit publications, abortion rights, availability of contraception, and a number of other social milestones that have taken place over the past half-dozen decades or so. Few persons today would attempt to live up to the sexual standards of the Middle Ages, and by the same token few enlightened individuals today would condemn many of the traditional practices of prayoga as evil or degenerate.

The term "left-hand" is a code phrase for Tantra rituals that include physical intercourse. In right-hand Tantra, the female assistant who is present to embody and represent the shakti (energy) of the great Goddess sits on the right side of the practitioner, and intercourse is symbolic; in left-hand Tantra the living vessel of the goddess Shakti sits on the left hand of the practitioner, and actual physical sex occurs. As indicated above, until very recently left-hand Tantra was flatly condemned by practitioners of the right-hand path as perverse and degenerate. By the same token, prayoga was condemned by practitioners of left-hand Tantra, who sought to use erotic physical union with human vessels of the Goddess only as a means of spiritual evolution. Left-hand Tantrists regarded the employment of their methods for the attainment of magic power, or the enjoyment of sensual pleasure, as an insult to Shakti, and as a stumbling block on the path to *samadhi* (enlightenment). Magic has always been concerned mainly with the attainment of personal power, whether this power is used for spiritual growth or merely for social gain. This secular purpose of magic is one of the primary reasons it was universally condemned by traditional religious teachings of both East and West.

It is important to understand that when a person (traditionally most often a woman) was used in the rituals of Tantra to embody the energy and to act as a focus for the Goddess-power of Shakti, sexual union, whether physical or symbolic, actually occurred between the male practitioner and the deity. The woman herself was regarded merely as an instrument by Hindu adepts. Prostitutes trained in Tantra were favored because of their knowledge of sex and their freedom from false modesty. Adepts also employed their wives in this role, but the use of a prostitute had the advantage of creating an emotional detachment between the adept and the woman chosen as the living vessel of Shakti.

Since the partner who embodies the power of Shakti is only a vessel for that occult energy, it is possible to achieve union with the deity directly in her spiritual, noncorporeal form. This is somewhat more difficult, but when achieved is ultimately more useful and liberating. The practitioner can never be denied union with the Goddess when he or she is able to unite sexually with Shakti in her disembodied male or female forms. Though the human physical vessel of Shakti aids male Tantrists in first establishing communication with the deity, a living partner can become a crutch that prolongs an unnecessary dependence upon physical flesh. Similarly, a female Tantrist does not really need a man to embody Shiva, but can unite directly with the god in his spiritual form.

Loving the Goddess

In order to grasp the relationship between Shakti, Shiva, Lilith, and Samael, which plays so important a part in this book, it is necessary to clearly understand the nature of the Goddess, who is the embodiment of the underlying creative energy of the universe. The spirits who come in male and female shapes to serve as loving partners in this magic are all aspects of the single creative Goddess whose limitless power pervades all things. She travels under many names in diverse cultures, and wears many faces around the world. She is the virgin bride of the spirit and the heavenly mother of gods and humans, yet at the same time the eternal mistress of sensual pleasure and queen of all sorceries. Her names are too numerous to reckon. Egyptians knew her as Isis, the Sumerians as Ishtar, the Greeks as Cybele, the Romans as Rhea, the Gnostics as Barbelo, the Christians as Mary, the Jews as the Matronit.

The best all-encompassing name for the Goddess is that used by the Hindus, who call her Shakti, a word that simply means *power*. The Goddess is energy in all its expressions, but she is especially evident in the creative life-force that is most concentrated and active during sexual arousal and lovemaking. When this life-force is employed to engender new life, it is ruled by the divine-mother aspect of the Goddess; but when it is used for other purposes both exalted and base, it is ruled by the pleasure-seeking aspect of the Goddess, who in ancient times was often described as a harlot, because the ancients associated prostitution with sex purely for pleasure.

There are actually three phases of the Goddess, which I will call the Virgin, the Matron, and the Crone. The Virgin has not yet attained her sexual maturity. The

Matron is able to bear children. The Crone has exceeded her child-bearing years. The three are distinguished by the stages of childhood, maturity and old age, and in a magical sense by the process of menstruation. The Virgin has yet to menstruate, the Matron is actively menstruating and thus fertile, and the Crone has passed through menopause. We are concerned in this book with the sexually active middle stage of the Goddess, which has two sides, the Mother and the Lover.

Sexual alchemy deals with the sensual, pleasure-seeking Lover aspect of this fertile phase of the Goddess, since it teaches the use of active sexual energy for purposes other than the physical conception of human offspring. The three major religions of Western culture—Christianity, Islam, and Judaism—have in the past for the most part looked upon this use of sexual energy for enjoyment or for practical magic as an abuse, and often characterize this aspect of Shakti in a negative way. To a lesser extent this is also true of mainstream Eastern faiths such as Buddhism. Most entrenched religions seek to limit sexual expression and focus it on the engendering of children within a social contract accepted by the religion—usually monogamous marriage. The use of sexual energy for spiritual growth, though sometimes tolerated in a limited and controlled context, was popularly regarded as abnormal and suspicious behavior.

In Jewish folklore this sensual side of Shakti has been reduced to the level of the night demoness Lilith, a spirit who may be traced back to a type of ancient Sumerian demon. In popular legend Lilith was fabled to be a female spirit who could reveal herself as a beautiful young woman or a withered crone at her pleasure, who visited sleeping men and gave them erotic dreams, and very interestingly, who had the power of life or death over newborn infants. She is represented in the Talmud as a winged demoness with a woman's face who sexually arouses men to steal their semen so that she can use it to engender demons. In the *Midrash* she is portrayed as the first woman created by God, who defied the authority of Adam by wishing to lie on top when they made love. The Jewish Kabbalists, with their deep understanding of both practical magic and mystical philosophy, elevated Lilith to the infernal throne and made her Queen of Hell.

In modern times, an effort is being made to rescue Lilith from her demonic ghetto and exalt her as the goddess of sexual liberation. Lilith represents for her modern worshippers the freedom to experience and enjoy sexuality for its own sake, or for any reason that has nothing to do with the conception of corporeal children. This includes the use of sexual energy for works of practical magic or spiritual enlightenment, or to enhance psychic or physical abilities. In this sense, the sensual aspect of Shakti may be referred to as Lilith, and the spirits who serve as her sexual agents as the Sons and

Daughters of Lilith. According to the Kabbalah, the consort of Lilith is Samael, a male spirit viewed by most traditional Jewish Kabbalists as roughly equivalent to the Christian Satan. Another less common but subtle Kabbalistic doctrine states that Samael is Lilith herself in her masculine aspect. Thus the male manifestation of Shakti in her role of erotic lover may be called Samael.

The Lilith who represents the sexual liberation of modern women is not the same spirit as the Lilith reviled in Jewish folklore as the murderess of infants, even though they bear the same name. One is an enlightened goddess, the other an evil night hag. The identity of a spirit is determined by the qualities and actions attributed to it, not solely by its name. Over time, the qualities of a spiritual being can change so drastically that it becomes, in effect, a separate entity. This has occurred countless times throughout history. An example is the Syrian goddess of love and fertility, Ashtoreth, who in Christian demon lore became the mighty duke of hell, Astaroth. The Syrian goddess was not transformed into Astaroth—she continued to exist while the Christian demonologists created their demon with the collective power of their imaginations. Ashtoreth the goddess of love and Astaroth the demon are distinct beings who exist simultaneously.

It is important to avoid confusion on this matter. There is only one creative Goddess, but that Goddess has countless names and forms of expression both male and female. These are like small streams that flow out of a larger river, each with its own unique shape or identity, yet all composed of the same river water. They may also be thought of as different masks which the Goddess wears, or as children of the Goddess, but they are all constituted of the same fundamental nature, all shakti. Higher masks in turn have lower masks which express their individual qualities. The Goddess or Shakti, in her totality as the fundamental creative principle of being, divides into a female (Shakti) and male (Shiva) principle. Shakti considered in a narrower sense as the female creative principle further subdivides into deities that are sexually immature, sexually active and sexually dormant. The class of sexually active deities who represent the loving face of Shakti further subdivides into those devoted to sex for the creation of children, and those concerned with sex for pleasure or power. The class of deities concerned with sex for pleasure or power subdivides into the two broad categories of feminine and masculine. It is into this last division that Lilith and Samael fall. Other divisions exist, but it is the thread outlined that leads from Shakti and Shiva to Lilith and Samael.

It is not that Lilith and Samael are evil, but merely that they are deities whose natures are fundamentally erotic, and whose sexual energies are directed for personal gain or pleasure. This led them to be maligned as evil by Jewish religious teachers, and to be saddled with all the wicked qualities of human nature, simply because there was an unconscious equation made between sexuality for pleasure and evil. Even in modern times, this equation exists deep in the minds of many persons. Samael and Lilith are capable of wicked acts, but their basic nature does not require them to do evil, contrary to the teachings of Jewish legend and conservative Jewish Kabbalists. Like magic itself, these shadowy deities can be used to achieve constructive personal goals.

The fundamental oneness of Shakti and Shiva is the highest concept of Hindu Tantra doctrine. Similarly, the essential unity of Lilith and Samael is among the most subtle and elevated teachings of the traditional Kabbalah. It is a difficult concept for many persons to attain, because we are accustomed to making an absolute distinction between one goddess and another, and between goddesses and gods. However, accepting the principle, the various sexual unions with spirits male or female in appearance, described in this book, may all be viewed as unions with Lilith, who is a higher mask of the sensual, erotic side of the fertile Goddess. Female practitioners who use this magic to unite with Samael or some other male spirit embodying shakti force should bear in mind that they are uniting with Lilith in one of her masculine forms. Even those practitioners who seek to unite directly with Shakti herself are only able to unite with a mask of the Goddess, since her essential nature is too exalted to perceive or comprehend without the aid of a lower vessel to contain it.

These animate vessels through which we enjoy sexual union with Lilith may be either wholly spirit, or invoked spiritual entities who have temporarily entered the flesh of human beings, as occurs in the rituals of traditional Tantra. Hence, the sex described in this book is of two general classes: either sex between a single human being and a spiritual being who is a male or female aspect of Lilith; or sex between two human beings, one or both of whom has invoked a spirit into the body. By far the greater part of this book is devoted to sex between a single human being and a discarnate spirit, and the products of that union, but sexual alchemy is not limited to this form of union.

Anti-sexuality of Mainstream Religions

Sexuality lies at the heart of all the ancient mystery traditions, but in past generations this fact was seldom openly admitted. Usually it is passed over in silence, or hinted at with poetic imagery. Sometimes details slipped out when one sect was maligned and defamed by another. It has not helped the dissemination of this knowledge that the four great religions of the world, Christianity, Buddhism, Islam, and Judaism, are all puritanical in their attitude towards sex. It is no accident that they are also all patri-archal, composed of institutions of male priests who worship God in a male form.

The hysterical condemnations of sex for pleasure in the traditional scriptures and commentaries of these religions, coupled with the sanctions against women, particu-larly in connection with their menstrual cycle, stem from an underlying fear by the male priests of the magical power of female sexuality. All of the prohibitions against sexual things are attempts to control the power that women inherently possess over men. The power of sex was looked upon as a threat to the authority which the priests of the major religions exerted over the thoughts and behavior of their male members. Since women controlled sex for pleasure through prostitution and even within the confines of marriage, women were also vilified unless they adhered wholeheartedly to religious laws concerning sex.

The extreme attitude towards sexuality exhibited by the early Church Fathers was a reaction away from the celebration of sex, both secular and religious, that they saw all around them in the larger and stronger pagan communities. Origen went so far as to cut off his own penis with a knife. The explanation he gave was that he wished to be able to preach the Gospels to women without the distraction of erotic thoughts. The apostle Paul wrote: "It is good for a man not to touch a woman."[3] In the Biblical book Revelation the elect of humanity with the name of God written on their fore-heads are said to be "they which were not defiled with women; for they are virgins."[4]

The incredibly virulent diatribe against women and lovemaking that occupies verses 148–170 of the ancient Buddhist text known as the *Precious Garland,* written around the first century B.C. by the Indian pandet Nagarjuna, illustrates the intensely puritanical attitude in traditional Buddhism that opposed the dissemination of Tantra teachings on mystical sexuality. While it was probably not the sole view of women held by ancient Buddhists, this text exerted a profound and far-reaching influence on subsequent Buddhist attitudes. The body of a woman is presented by Nagarjuna not as a precious and beautiful expression of the Goddess, but as a rotting bag of filth:

> 156.
> Why should you lust desirously for this
> While recognizing it as a filthy form
> Produced by a seed whose essence is filth,
> A mixture of blood and semen?

157.

He who lies on the filthy mass
Covered by skin moistened with
Those fluids, merely lies
On top of a woman's bladder.[5]

From the wording of the two verses quoted from this diatribe, it may be that Nagarjuna intended to caution Buddhist monks specifically against the left-hand path of sexual ecstasy. The combined mention of blood (undoubtedly menstrual blood) and semen is significant. No one knows where the Eastern tradition of Tantra began, but some form of sex magic must have been in existence in India at the time of the Buddha. Nagarjuna would have been aware of its allure to young monks.

The power of menstrual blood in magic is that, symbolically, it slays life. While the menses flow forth from the body, no new life may be engendered in the womb. When the menses stop flowing in their regular lunar cycle, it is a sign of pregnancy. Therefore, religious texts dictate that a man may not make love to a woman during her period of menstruation because his seed will fall upon her blood and perish. The power of menstrual blood to cause death is greater than the power of semen to cause life. Pregnancy controls women and transforms them into docile instruments in the service of God. Freedom from pregnancy allows women to use the innate power of sex, which they control, to dominate men. This perception underlies all the ancient taboos against menstrual blood and menstruating women.

In Islam women have always been forbidden to uncover their charms to any but intimate family members. It is written in the Koran:

> And speak unto the believing women, that they restrain their eyes, and preserve their modesty, and discover not their ornaments, except what necessarily appeareth thereof: and let them throw their veils over their bosoms, and not show their ornaments, unless to their husbands, or their fathers, or their husband's fathers, or their sons, or their husband's sons, or their brothers, or their brother's sons, or their sister's sons, or their women, or the captives which their right hand shall possess, or unto such men as attend them, and have no need of women, or unto children, who distinguish not the nakedness of women.[6]

In other words, they must cover themselves up from all men who might be tempted to have sexual relations with them except their husbands. There is also a strong stricture against having sex with women during menstruation: "They will ask thee also concerning the courses of women: Answer, They are a pollution: therefore separate yourselves from women in their courses, and go not near them until they be cleansed."[7] These directives against women were intended to limit both the sexual and occult powers of women. Any form of worship that involved the adoration of women as the incarnation of the Goddess would have been anathema to conservative Islamics.

The commandments against uncovering the nakedness of women is even stronger in traditional Judaism than it is in Islam. In ultra-orthodox households not even the husband should look upon the nakedness of his wife—sex is carried out in the dark and beneath the sheets. Sex for any other purpose than the conception of children—that is to say, sex conducted in such a way that conception is deliberately avoided—is considered sinful. The religious law of Judaism views menstruating women as unclean, and not to be touched by a man: "And if a women have an issue, and her issue in her flesh be blood, she shall be put apart seven days; and whosoever toucheth her shall be unclean until the even."[8] In the Old Testament blood is usually the repository of the life-force, but menstrual blood is the repository of death.

Sex Rites in Religion

In the same way that women were feared and reviled because of their sexual power, the gods and goddesses of the ancient pagan world who presided over sexual rites became the objects of virulent propaganda designed to reduce them to the level of infernal demons. The incorporation of sexual ecstasy into religious observances, particularly when such ecstasy was provoked by an incorporeal being such as an angel, was outwardly condemned by mainstream Christians, Buddhists, Islamics, and Jews alike. Paradoxically, it has always been practiced by esoteric Christians, Buddhists, Islamics, and Jews, but practiced only in secret.

The guardians of these religious mysteries considered them too dangerous to reveal to the uninitiated. Again and again in ancient texts you will encounter the statement that information is being deliberately omitted, and those who wish to know these forbidden matters must learn them by oral teaching from an initiated master of the tradition. This concealment has been greatly aided by religious censorship concerning all things that involve unconventional sexual experiences. Because both the esoteric sects themselves and the orthodox religious hierarchies conspired to conceal rites of sexual ecstasy, we possess few details.

For example, most of what is known about the sexual mysteries of the Gnostics is the result of attempts to slander them by the early Fathers of the Christian Church. Eusebius wrote that the Gnostics "practised unspeakable incest with mothers and sisters and took part in wicked food."[9] This "wicked food" is presumed by commentators to mean the corpses of sacrificed infants, but more likely refers to semen or other products of the body associated with sexuality. We have very few details about the actual ritual practices of the Gnostics, as opposed to their philosophical beliefs, because these were cult secrets. What little information that appeared in their writings was lost when zealous Christian monks hunted up and destroyed the Gnostic books. We can only be sure that they sometimes used sex magic in their worship.

The same double barrier of deliberate secrecy from within and censorship from without prevents us from understanding fully what went on in the inner sanctuary of the medieval Christian religious order of the Knights Templar. The practices of the Templars may have involved homosexual rites and techniques of sexual alchemy, but the details, if they were ever known outside the ranks of the Templars themselves, were vigorously suppressed, and malicious slanders inserted into the official records in their place.

Sex in Modern Magic

Those who believe strongly on religious grounds that all types of sex are sinful when performed outside of marriage, or for purposes that preclude the engendering of children, will not practice the techniques described in this book. Those who follow the traditional teachings of the major religions will not practice ritual magic in any form, sexual or otherwise, since magic is condemned in various scriptures as a crime punishable by death. However, readers who regard themselves as sexually liberated, and are not disposed to allow the long-dead authorities of patriarchal religions to tell them what do for their own pleasure or personal benefit, must make their own judgements about the morality of this form of magic.

In making this judgment, it is important to consider two factors. First, sexual alchemy does not involve harm to either human beings or to spirits, directly or indirectly. Second, there is no coercion involved in bringing about a union between a human and a spirit. The practitioner of sexual alchemy invites with love and friendship an agent of the Goddess to enjoy sexual union. If the spirit declines the invitation, that is the end of the matter. The union is freely entered into by both parties, and either party is equally free to end the union at any time. Lovemaking is enjoyed under the gaze of the Goddess, and with her complete approval. Only if the Goddess participates in the union will the products of sexual alchemy become charged with occult virtue, and act as catalytic substances to increase physical and psychic abilities. There is no way to force the participation of the Goddess—it must be invited with love.

A prejudice still exists among the more conservative practitioners of Western magic about the morality of sexual relations with spiritual beings. To a large extent, this view is a carryover from the Victorian era, when any kind of sex was looked upon with suspicion. Most of the magic practiced in the modern world, at least among English-speaking nations, has descended from the system of the Hermetic Order of the Golden Dawn, an English Rosicrucian society dedicated to the teaching of Hermetic philosophy and ceremonial magic. Although the original Golden Dawn became moribund around the beginning of the First World War, its members continued to teach the Golden Dawn system of magic in various forms for decades. In this way, it spread far and wide, and in its dissemination many of its Victorian attitudes were carried along with it.

We know that sexual union with spirits was at least discussed in the higher rank of the Golden Dawn thanks to an 1895 correspondence between Moïna Mathers, the wife of the leader of the Order, and her friend Annie Horniman, who supplied Mathers with money to support his occult activities and helped run the Order in London. Horniman wrote to Mrs. Mathers asking her about the propriety and advisability of sex with elementals. Apparently the question of sex and procreation between human beings and spirits was an ongoing matter of discussion within the Golden Dawn, and was known generally as the Elemental Theory. Moïna Mathers' reply illustrates very well her own attitude toward sex in general, and sex with spirits in particular:

> Knowing as yet only something of the composition of the human being (as a Theor. Adept), you are really not in a position to give an opinion on these subjects; so that if one of these uncomfortable cases that have been discussed as to elemental or human sexual connection (which I think with all other sexual connections are *beastly*) came up you would have to refer the question to a member of a much higher grade than Theor. Adept.
>
> Any *much* higher grade (one who understands the subject a little better) would be willing to take the responsibility. In your illogical letter you say that Elementals forming part of your composition has not a bearing on the subject—if Elementals form a considerable part of you, they are not so

incongruous to the human as you imply, and this theory bears strongly on the subject for their connection between a human and elemental is not so far removed from the usual one.

When I first heard of this theory it gave me a shock, but not such a horrible one as that which I had when I was young, about the human connection. Child or no, a natural thing should not upset one so. I remember that my horror of human beings for a while was so great that I could not look at my own mother without violent dislike—and loathing.

I have always chosen as well as 'SRMD' [Mathers, her husband] to have nothing whatever to do with any sexual connection—we have both kept perfectly clean I know, as regards the human, the elemental, and any other thing whatever.

I have tried, and I think succeeded, never to allow myself to think of any subject in that direction, and I think having been pretty well tested, personally as well as from one's own position in G.D., we are competent to give an opinion. To return to the Elementals, the story of Melusina, Undine, and others you will know of all refer to marriages between human and elemental and you think them probably very charming stories, because they have a halo of poetry round them. As to exaggeration in you, you distinctly have a fad as regards sexual subjects, and you know it is a dangerous one to have.[10]

During the Victorian age, Moïna Mathers' complete abstinence from sex of any kind, even within the bounds of her marriage, would have been considered an admirable achievement, but today we would be much more inclined to look upon Annie Horniman's interest in sexual matters as normal and healthy. Two things are obvious from this letter. Sexual unions with spirits were known in the Golden Dawn, and very probably practiced by some members; and the leaders of the Order were complete prudes on the subject of sex. This puritanical viewpoint finds its way subtly into Golden Dawn documents, most of which were written by Mathers, and many of these documents are still studied and used today. But the puritanical view is completely alien to the modern attitude that sex is not only natural and healthy, but to be enjoyed.

To be sure, not every member of the original Golden Dawn was puritanical about sex. Aleister Crowley, who went on to found his own occult order, and later became the head of the Ordo Templi Orientis, had no sexual inhibitions. But most of the members agreed with the prevalent Victorian ideal, at least in principle, and reflected this belief in their writings and teachings. For example, Dion Fortune, the founder of the Society of the Inner Light, was a member of the Golden Dawn when it was headed by Moïna Mathers after her husband's death. In one of her many books about ritual occultism, Fortune wrote: "There are also certain techniques of sex and blood magic which, though they may be harmless enough among primitive peoples, are certainly out of place among civilized ones, and are only resorted to for the sake of a debased sensationalism."[11] We can clearly detect in this statement Victorian prejudices against race as well as sex. A. E. Waite, another prominent member of the Golden Dawn who headed an offshoot of the Order, and who wrote many books on occultism, held similar views in public, although he kept a mistress in private.

The same prudery and hypocrisy is found in the teachings of Theosophists of the Victorian era. Madame Blavatsky, the founder of the Theosophical movement who endured two brief, failed marriages, wrote: "Worse than this; for, whoever indulges after having pledged himself to occultism, in the gratification of a terrestrial love or lust, must feel an almost immediate result; that of being irresistibly dragged from the impersonal divine state down to the lower plane of matter. Sensual, or even mental self-gratification, involves the immediate loss of the powers of spiritual discernment, the voice of the Master can no longer be distinguished from that of one's passions or even that of a Dugpa; the right from wrong; sound morality from mere casuistry."[12] Dugpa was Blavatsky's favorite term for a black magician who followed the left-hand path of sex magic.

As a consequence of the Victorian era aversion to sex in any form, texts on practical magic written by original Golden Dawn members and Theosophists flatly condemn sex with spirits, and this view is sometimes carried forward by the subsequent generation of writers, who have based their opinions and practices on the beliefs of their teachers. The promulgation through the popular literature of Western occultism of this view that sex and magic do not mix, that sex inevitably leads to black magic, exerts its influence even today on the minds of those approaching the study of magic for the first time. The vague sense that it is somehow dangerous has replaced the belief that it is immoral.

Is Spirit Communication Dangerous?

The alleged dangers of spirit contact are not confined to sexual unions with spirits, but are often supposed to befall anyone who enters into a close communion with a spiritual being without adopting the accepted ritual safeguards. Precisely what those dangers entail is not always made clear, but obsession and madness are usually cited as the most likely pitfalls. Concerning intimate contact with elemental spirits, Dion Fortune wrote:

> And there is also an involuntary relationship, very often, between those people who are naturally psychic without training and quite spontaneously come into touch with other beings. The effect of this is seldom wholesome. It has the effect of unbalancing them. It is a too intensely stimulating contact. Elementals are of a pure type, composed of one Element only, whichever that may be, whereas a human being is a mixture of all. So they are too potent a stimulus to that one Element in our own being, which is very apt to throw a human being off his balance, lure him to follow it and abandon his human ways. He is 'taken by the fairies,' or what we should call a pathology. You can see the thought control withdrawing from the physical vehicle. They hear the call of the fairies, and only an empty shell remains, insane.[13]

During the nineteenth century thousands of psychically gifted individuals began to receive spirit communications and became trance mediums as spiritualism grew from an oddity in the Fox family to a social phenomenon that swept across Europe and America. They hosted countless séances, voluntarily allowed themselves to be possessed by spirits of all sorts, and produced apports and physical manifestations such as ectoplasmic forms. Although many were undoubtedly frauds, many others were genuine. From Fortune's ominous warning we might expect to learn that the majority of them became insane or committed suicide, but this is not the case. I have seen no evidence whatsoever that suggests that the incidence of insanity was any higher in spirit mediums than in the general population. The same might be observed about spirit channelers in the late twentieth century. There is no indication that they became mad or catatonic at a rate higher than that of the social norm. Contact with spirits, whether elementals or other types, is not in itself a danger.

The key distinction is that trance mediums and channelers not only accept spirit communication voluntarily, they actively seek it out for their own purposes. Fortune was writing about involuntary relationships, and here there exists evidence of danger of a psychological nature in those rare instances when a hurtful spirit tries to intrude itself into the mind of a person with a natural susceptibility. When a malicious or demonic spirit attempts to forcibly possess the body of a mediumistic person who has no knowledge of ritual safeguards, against the will of that person, the spirit can generate intense fear that is centered around a loss of self-control. It can even, in the most extreme cases, displace human consciousness and assume voluntary control of the body. This is a very uncommon occurrence, and it is doubtful if the avoidance of occult matters decreases its frequency. Despite all the apocryphal tales of unwitting souls becoming possessed after using the Ouija board, there is no solid evidence that demonic possession is any more common among students of magic or spiritualism than among the general population.

Why trance mediums, channelers, and ritual magicians who seek out voluntary union with spirits are not possessed more frequently by malicious spirits is a matter that can only be conjectured. Perhaps the very process of inviting benevolent spirits to come near and communicate makes it more difficult for malevolent spirits to force their way into perception and seize control of the body. Perhaps by virtue of having been attracted with harmonious thoughts and congenial symbols, friendly spirits are given a priority of place, and are able to displace and exclude unfriendly spirits that have not been invited or encouraged to approach. If so, the regular invitation of good spirits actually serves to protect a medium against the intrusions of evil spirits.

In my opinion, the threat of mental illness or possession is virtually nil when engaged in sexual alchemy, statistically no higher than when playing tennis. This view is based on over a decade of almost daily contact with spiritual beings, and an exhaustive study of the literature concerning possession, spiritualism, ritual invocation, and evocation. The nature of sexual alchemy itself precludes the involuntary intrusion of malicious spirits. When seeking a spirit as a lover, first the spirit is selected or defined, and then it is actively and consciously called. It is summoned by means of names, symbols and objects in harmony with its specific nature, always with an attitude of love and respect. All of these factors serve to exclude the appearance of a malicious, unwanted spirit.

As additional safeguards, in the early stages of practice the spirit lover is always invoked into a physical vessel that serves as its manifest body, where it can be easily contained should this prove necessary, and invocation occurs within the bounds of a magic circle in the context of a specific ritual. As a result, the spirit finds it difficult to extend itself beyond the vessel that acts as its material body, or beyond the physical limits of the circle and the temporal limits of the ritual, unless specifically invited to do so by the practitioner. Once the personality of the spirit becomes better known, these barriers can be relaxed, but it is wise as a general policy to maintain them in the first few weeks of communion with a spirit. The use of two basic magical defenses, the hardening of the aura and the ritual of banishing by pentagram, are incorporated into the ritual method of sexual alchemy to add another layer of security.

Why Bother with Spirit Sex?

Loving relationships with spiritual beings can be the most joyous, pleasurable and rewarding experience in life. There is nothing inherently dangerous, or perverse, or evil, about sex with a spirit. Just the opposite. A study of historical accounts and ancient legends, as well as years of personal interaction with spirits, have led me to conclude that loving and erotic unions with angels and lesser beings such as elementals are a precious gift that should be cherished with the highest feelings of respect and gratitude by those who are fortunate enough to enjoy them. The crucial feature of these relationships is love. Spirits who seek sexual union with human beings solely for the emotions and physical sensations sex generates tend to be lower or infernal beings, but spirits who establish long-term personal relationships with humans that are centered around love, caring, and mutual respect are of a higher and more complex nature. These spirits are also more powerful magically, which makes their good wishes and desire to help their human lovers of greater significant in a practical sense.

Love is all important. It is the existence of love in the heart when seeking a relationship with a spirit that insures that the spirit who responds will be of a type capable of compassion and friendship as well as amorous feelings of desire. The continuing love between a spirit and a human being will sustain the union over months or even years despite all vicissitudes of fortune and changes of circumstance. Love causes the spirit in such a relationship to use its esoteric abilities in whatever ways are possible to insure the happiness and prosperity of its lover—the spirit truly becomes the guardian of its lover. Finally, and most important of all, love invokes the Goddess herself and allows union with the spirit to be simultaneously union with Shakti. The loving radiance of Shakti filling the vessel of the spirit insures that it is not simply an empty shell or husk, and transforms the sexual fluids of the human body emitted during spirit love into alchemical substances of great potency that can be used to achieve personal health and spiritual evolution. There is no higher form of love, because love of Shakti is love of the Creator.

Part One

~

Theory

{ 1 }

Spirit Sex
in Magic and Religion

The Ayami and the Syvén

The concept of inducing sexual intercourse with spirits appears to ultimately descend from the subjective experiences of shamanism. That sex with spirits is a genuine physiological phenomenon and not a contrived fantasy is indicated by its appearance throughout the world and at all periods in human history. More often, coition occurs spontaneously, so far as the human is concerned—it is not necessary for a human being to seek intercourse with a god, an angel, or a demon for such intercourse to happen. However, once sexual union was understood to be possible between humans and spirits, it began to be deliberately cultivated by human beings for its sensual pleasures and for the supposed benefits it conferred.

In the shamanic tradition of Siberia, there are two classes of spirits that have sex with shamans, those who teach and those who serve. Among the Goldi people these spirits were known as the *ayami* and the *syvén*. The ayami is the tutelary familiar who appears to the shaman at the beginning of his training and remains with him throughout his life. Often the coming of the ayami is the event that determines a shamanic vocation. It is not necessary for the shaman to seek out his ayami—she comes to him. Where the tradition of shamanism is well established, the young shaman is not surprised by her coming, and on the contrary expects and anticipates it.

A Twenty-eight Inch Lover

One Goldi shaman described his ayami as a very beautiful woman with black hair that hung down to her shoulders, who was dressed in the ordinary female attire of the tribe. The features of this spirit were normal, although sometimes the ayami reveals herself with a face that is white on one side and red on the other. Perfectly formed in every way, she was only twenty-eight inches tall. The spirit told the shaman that she was the ayami of his ancestors who had taught them all their healing and magic, and now she was come to teach him and make him into a shaman. She said to him:

> I love you, I have no husband now, you will be my husband and I shall be a wife unto you. I shall give you assistant spirits. You are to heal with their aid, and I shall teach and help you myself. Food will come to us from the people. . . . If you will not obey me, so much the worse for you. I shall kill you.[1]

After making the shaman an offer he could not refuse, she remained faithful to him throughout his life. The shaman related that he slept with his ayami "as with my own wife." His ayami lived by herself in a hut on a mountain, but often changed her residence, along with her physical form. Sometimes she appeared to the shaman as an old woman, sometimes as a wolf terrible to look upon, and sometimes as a winged tiger. In this last form she carried his soul mounted upon her back to distant lands.

The ayami gave the shaman three lesser spirit aids who appeared in the forms of a panther, a bear, and a tiger. These came to the shaman in dreams and appeared instantly when he summoned them. If they were slow to approach or obey his instructions, his ayami would appear and command them. These lesser spirits are among the class of helping spirits (*syvén*) referred to above. Both the ayami and the syvén entered the body of the shaman in the form of "smoke or vapour" to possess him, in order to gift him with oracular speech. During possession the spirits partook of ritual food offerings (*sukdu*) and drank pig's blood, the drinking of which was forbidden to all except shamans, without the awareness of the shaman.

The Celestial Wife

The ayami was known in Siberian shamanism generally as the celestial wife. There were also male spirits who had sexual relations with female shamans. Presumably these would fulfill the role of celestial husband. One shamaness was observed to become sexually aroused during her rite of initiation.[2] Sexual arousal was not an inevitable and invariable part of the initiatory rite of Siberian shamanism, but it was a common component.

Among the Buryat, shamanism began when the soul of a male candidate was carried into the sky by the spirit of an ancestor. The shaman was taken to the Center of the World, where he had sexual union with the nine daughters of Solboni, the god of the dawn. These nine goddesses were only worshipped by shamans, who made offerings to them. After his instruction, the soul of the shaman met his future celestial wife among the heavens and made love to her.

Among the Teleut people, every shaman has a celestial wife who dwells in the seventh heaven. When his soul first ascends, she meets him and asks him to stay with her. She prepares a heavenly banquet for her future husband and woos him with love songs, telling him that he cannot go on because the "road to the sky has been blocked." The shaman refuses to eat the food of the banquet, and declares his determination to press forward, saying, "We shall go up the tapti and give praise to the full moon."[3] The *tapti* is the spiral groove that winds up the shamanic tree, which represents the axis of the world.

The sexual imagery is obvious. When urine is emitted from the penis, the stream will often twist itself into a spiral form, which would suggest to an observer lacking a knowledge of anatomy that the urethra itself is spiral. Sperm is symbolically linked to the Moon by its pearly opalescent whiteness. Climbing the tapti is equivalent to ejaculation. The reason the shaman refuses to eat from the banquet table is the belief, which also exists in European fairy lore, that to eat the food of the spirits is to be lost in their world forever.

This myth has a particular significance for me personally. While engaged in my year of intense training, mentioned in the introduction, I once dreamed that I climbed a tall, naked stump in a clearing in the forest and stood balanced precariously in nervous exaltation on its tip. The stump was so ancient and weathered, its bark had long ago fallen away, and the spiral grain of its wood had worn into deep grooves that gave hand and foot holds in its side, allowing it to be climbed. In the dream my body was naked and hairy, so primitive that it was almost apelike. This dream was clearly shamanic, but I experienced it years before I had ever heard of the climbing of the shamanic tree, or the tapti.

Among the Yakut people there is a myth that young celestial spirits, who are the children of the Sun and Moon, descend to the earth to marry mortal women. This myth echoes the Hebrew fable recorded in the Book of Enoch of the descent to earth of the rebellious angels, or Watchers, for the purpose of enjoying the sexual favors of the daughters of men. Even as the fallen angels teach forbidden wisdom in return for sexual pleasure with mortal women, so do the ayami of the shamans instruct their husbands (or wives) in secret techniques of magic and healing in return for their love. It is worth noting that sex is said to be had not with the "masters and mistresses" of heaven and the underworld by the shaman, but with the "sons and daughters" of these supreme gods.[4]

The bond between a shaman and his ayami was a genuine love bond, not merely a union of convenience. The ayami often became jealous if her husband showed interest in mortal women. However, this seems not to have been a common problem. Mortal sex could not begin to compare with spirit sex. The shamans of the Teleut declare to their celestial brides: "My wife on earth is not fit to pour water on thy hands." The Yakut say that after a young man has been visited by a spirit lover, he no longer approaches girls and may remain a bachelor for life. A married man who has the same experience may become impotent toward his wife.

The Currency of Spirit Sex

These visitations by amorous spirits were not confined to shamans, but might happen to any man or woman. In the common occurrence of spirit sex, the intention on the part of the spirit was personal. They were interested in sex or affection. In the case of the spirit guide or ayami the bond was recognized from the outset as binding for life and dedicated to a higher purpose—the teaching of secret shamanic knowledge about healing and magic, the conveyance of obedient lesser spirits (syvén) to serve the shaman in his vocation, and the awakening of occult powers within the soul of the shaman. The shaman and his ayami were business partners as well as sexual partners.

The currency exchanged within this partnership was sexual potency—in Tantric terms, *shakti*. As I mentioned in the introduction, Shakti, the name of the great Mother Goddess, literally means "power." It is convenient to apply the terms of Tantra in a more universal way, since it is in Tantra texts that the relationship between humans, sexual energy and spirits is most clearly expressed. Spirits are capable of arousing human sexuality. They are able to do this with or without the consent of the human being involved. The reason spirits arouse humans is that they derive some immediate, fundamental benefit from the sexual currents stirred up inside the human body. This is usually described as pleasure, and undoubtedly spirits experience pleasure in sex with human beings, but I believe their motivation is even more fundamental.

The basis of human sexual energy (kundalini shakti) acts as a kind of nourishment for spiritual beings and allows spirits to fix and maintain their forms and personal identities. In the same way that the act of sex between a man and a woman fixes the identity of the engendered child, at least potentially, so does the act of sex between a human and a spirit have the potential use of fixing or manifesting a specific, enduring shape and personality on the astral level. This creative energy may be used by the spirit lover to solidify its own form and sense of self; or it may engender a completely new spirit that is the child of the human and spirit couple.

Dion Fortune mentioned this phenomenon in her book *Applied Magic,* though she does not explicitly mention a sexual connection: "They [elemental spirits] seek as initiators those who have got a spiritual nature; the initiated man is the initiator of the Elemental being: Humans take them as pupils and help them develop their 'sparks' of individual consciousness. In return for this service the Elemental beings perform services for the magician. We read of these as familiar spirits."[5]

Magical Powers

The benefits of spirit love need not all be on the side of the spirit. Sexual power, provoked and sustained by the spirit, can be used by the human lover to awaken what are called in yoga siddhis (magical powers). Patanjali, author of the Yoga Sutras (third century B.C.), wrote that these are eight in number: 1) *anima*—the ability to become tiny; 2) *mahima*—the ability to become enormous; 3) *laghima*—the ability to grow lighter than air; 4) *garima*—the ability to become very heavy; 5) *prapti*—the ability to obtain any desired possession; 6) *prakamya*—the ability to obtain any desired purpose; 7) *ishatwam*—the ability to control any person or thing; 8) *vashitwa*—the ability to control any situation.

Many other occult abilities mentioned in traditional texts might be added to the *ashata siddhis* of Patanjali, such as the ability to read the minds of others, the ability to project the astral body, the ability to scry unknown matters, the ability to ignite fires psychically, the ability to see and hear spirits, the ability to seem invisible, the ability to travel with extraordinary swiftness from place to place, the ability to generate internal body heat, and so on. These powers were looked upon by orthodox Hindus as black magic, and all were regarded as distractions in the search for *samadhi,* the Hindu version of the Buddhist enlightenment.

Famous Spirit Marriages of Ancient Times

In return for the pleasure and benefits of sex with a human being, a spirit was willing to teach his or her human lover occult secrets and difficult arts and sciences, to prognosticate future events, to warn of impending dangers, and to provide protection in times of need. In the classical age these unions sometimes assumed the status of legal marriages. One of the most famous of these was the marriage between King Numa of Rome and the water nymph Egeria, who was one of the Carmenae, a class of prophetic spirits worshipped in very early times at Rome. They were linked by the Roman writer Varro with hydromancy, or water divination.

Legend says that King Numa was in the habit of going alone at night to a small clump of trees that concealed a grotto or cave from which issued a spring. It was located near the Porta Capena in the southern wall of the old city of Rome. Here he met his celestial wife Egeria, and enjoyed lovemaking with her. She instructed him in the sacred laws that he later instituted over his people. The sacred mysteries that Egeria revealed to him, he recorded in a set of books, which after his death were burned by order of the Senate. Numa's long reign (716–673 B.C.) was renowned for its peace and prosperity, and was the happiest period in the entire history of Rome.

One of the greatest love stories in the literature of ancient Rome involved the union of the mortal woman Psyche and the god Cupid, son of Venus, to whom she was betrothed by an oracle of Apollo. Cupid came to her unseen in the darkness, although she was able to hear his voice and feel "his eyes, his hands, and his ears." He gave her his love, a palace, great wealth, and spirit servants to meet all her needs, on the single condition that she never try to see him:

> Then came her unknowne husband and lay with her: and after that hee had made a perfect consummation of the marriage, he rose in the morning before day, and departed. Soone after came her invisible servants, and presented to her such things as were necessary for her defloration.[6]

Of course Psyche broke her promise and looked upon the naked body of Cupid while the god lay asleep. At once he flew away, and she was only reunited with him after a series of long and bitter ordeals. A condition or vow that must be honored by the human partner, with a penalty of immediate divorce for its violation, is a very common feature of marriages between spirits and human beings in myth and folklore.

Marriages between spirits and humans are found throughout the folklore of Europe. The fairies were renown for their lust and love of mortal men and women. Fairies were understood to be a race of immortal, invisible beings who lived in the same hills and valleys as mortals, but in a universe that is slightly out of phase with our own. At special times such as twilight and on certain nights of the year such as June 21, the midsummer's night of Shakespeare, the barrier between the fairy world and the mortal world becomes thin. Then fairies and mortals easily meet and fall in love. Sometimes mortals simply encounter fairies by chance during the day when they pass by sacred hills, groves, or springs.

Don Diego Lopez, Lord of Biscay, met a fairy on a hill in the forest while out hunting wild boar. He was so enamored of her beauty, he married her, in spite of the fact that one of her feet was in the form of a cloven hoof. She bore him two children. Elinas, the king of Albania, was also out hunting when he stopped at a spring to drink. He heard singing, and discovered the fairy woman Pressina. They were soon wed, and she bore him three daughters which she carried back with her to fairyland. One of the daughters, Melusina, had the appearance of a normal woman six days of the week, but on Saturday became a serpent from the waist downward. She married Raymond, Count of Lusignan, and made him rich and powerful through her magic. Several noble houses of France claim a direct descent from this fairy wife.

These semi-historical legends should not be dismissed as mere fables, but studied for the insights they give into the reality of spirit love. Details of these accounts may appear quaint or grotesque to the modern mind, but the legends are founded upon the actual occurrence of sexual unions between mortals and spirits, which were recognized to exist by ancient chroniclers.

Raped by Angels

In the formal partnership of a shaman with his ayami, which was solemnized with a ritual that was very similar to a regular wedding ceremony, it was understood that there would be give and take. Both the spirit and the human would benefit from the sexual energy generated by their loving union. Unfortunately, when spirits chose to unite with individuals not magically gifted, they often did so with no intention of giving equal payment for services rendered.

The ancient world is filled with stories of spirit rapists. The gods of the Greeks, especially Zeus, were notorious for this crime, which was regarded as part of their divine prerogative. The rapes committed by Zeus on mortal women usually engendered heroes—men born of mortal women who are semi-divine. The intercourse, which was probably rape in the beginning, committed by the Watchers of heaven on the daughters of men in the Book of Enoch had a similar result. They gave rise to the "mighty men which were of old, men of renown," who are mentioned in Genesis. In the esoteric Jewish system of philosophy known as the Kabbalah, these semi-divine heroes are called Aishim, or Men of God—that is to say, men of the gods (*elohim*).

Spirit Seductresses

Female spirits were just as unscrupulous as their male counterparts (which is not surprising, since spirits are androgynous, potentially able to assume a male or female form). Men traveling through India at night had to contend with the voracious predations of a sexual vampire known as the *churreyl*, said to be the spirit of a woman who had died in childbirth. The churreyl was fabled to literally suck out the life energies of her entranced lover while performing fellatio. A more attractive Indian tree spirit was the *yukshee*, who was beautiful and voluptuous. So great were her sexual appetites, she rendered her exhausted lovers impotent. The *pishauchees* caused men to have wet dreams.

Ancient Persian men were forced to contend with *drujes*, spirits in female form who delighted in leading their lovers into perversion, agony, and destruction. The Greeks and Romans fought off the embraces of *lamias*, who, in addition to stealing the seed of men, drank the blood of small infants. Russian travelers were stalked in the forests and farmlands by the beautiful *poludnitsa*, who took lewd joy in copulating with men. The *upierzyca* was a Ukrainian spirit who came to the beds of youths during the Full Moon and consumed them with passion. The *rusalki* of Slavic nations had burning green eyes and caused the men in her embrace to die in ecstasy. A kind of Slavic undine, or water spirit, known as the *vodyanoi* lured lustful men into the water to drown them.

In the modern Western world we are more familiar with the night hag, who comes to squat upon the chest of a man who sleeps alone for the purpose of provoking in him sexual dreams, usually of a perverted nature (perhaps because desires regarded by the sleeper as forbidden evoke a more intense physiological response). In Jewish mythology this hag is known as Grandmother Lilith. At first, folktales assert, Lilith comes in the shape of a beautiful young woman. After the spirit is sure of her prey, she reveals herself as a horrible devouring monster which has many of the characteristics of the Hindu goddess Kali. When the hag is upon the chest, most men find it impossible to move or cry out. Occasionally she sits upon the face of her captive lover and stifles his breath.

Incubus and Succubus

In Christian folklore the male spirit who comes to rape women is called an *incubus*, while the female spirit who seduces sperm out of men is known as a *succubus*. In the opinion of the majority of medieval demonologists, incubus and succubus are two forms of a single tempting spirit who steals the semen from men while in a female form, then carries it to women and assumes a male form to impregnate them with the stolen seed. In this way demonic offspring are generated.

Merlin was believed to be the product of a similar type of union. His greatest power, the ability to predict the future, descended from his spirit father, who was variously regarded as a pagan god, a fallen angel, or Lucifer himself. According to one legend, Merlin would have been the Antichrist had not a clever priest baptized him as an infant. The Antichrist was to be born from a union between a mortal woman and an incubus. Thus the halflings of spirit and human parents, who in biblical and classical times were regarded as heroes, came in medieval Christianity to be regarded as foul fiends.

The vast majority of Judeo-Christian folklore concerning sexual unions with spirits is negative. Such unions were viewed as temptations of the Adversary or as manifestations of witchcraft. The condemnation of sex with spirits was part of a broader censure against all forms of spirit communication, and indeed of magic in general. Theurgy, the highest and most sacred art of the ancient pagan world, was slandered and reviled as devil worship by both rabbis and priests, who resorted to the vilest propaganda their suppressed imaginations could fabricate in an attempt to throw it into disrepute. This relentless campaign to revile and discredit all dealings with spirits, and in particular sexual dealings, must be borne in mind while reading Jewish and Christian accounts of spirit love. They are never impartial.

Sara and Asmodeus

The story of Sara, which occurs in the apocryphal Book of Tobit, is probably the most famous case of obsession by an incubus. Sara, the daughter of Raguel, is upbraided by her father's maids because, they say, she has been married to seven husbands in succession who were all killed by the demon Asmodeus on their wedding nights before they had the opportunity to consummate, and therefore legitimize, their marriages with her. "Dost thou not know, said they, that thou hast strangled thine husbands?" At this accusation Sara becomes distraught and contemplates suicide, but decides against it on the consideration that such an act would bring disgrace upon her father.

Sara prays to God, saying, "Thou knowest, Lord, that I am pure from all sin with man, and that I never polluted my name, nor the name of my father."[7]

Asmodeus is the fallen angel or demon of lust in Jewish mythology. It was his appointed office to tempt mankind to perverse and unlawful acts of desire. He is described in the *Malleus Maleficarum* as "the very devil of Fornication, and the chief of that abomination."[8] The implication of Raguel's maids is not explicitly stated, but is very clear—they are accusing Sara of carrying on a consensual affair with the demon Asmodeus, who has jealously murdered her husbands before they had the opportunity to cuckold him.

Sara does not deny that Asmodeus comes to her bed. Her impulse to commit suicide is strong evidence that the maids are correct on this matter. In her prayer to God she asserts that she is "pure from all sin with man," but says nothing about demons. This curious wording might be interpreted as a clever bit of sophistry, but Sara also says, "I never polluted my name," which suggests that even though Asmodeus comes to her bed each night, she has thus far refused to have sexual relations with the demon.

Strange Case of the Amorous Incubus

In Christian accounts, the experiences of a woman who suffered the embrace of an incubus were not always unpleasant, but might become so if she resisted her lover. Ludovico Maria Sinistrari (1622–1701), for the past two centuries regarded as the leading authority on sexual unions between humans and demons, relates in his *Demoniality* the story of a woman named Hieronyma, a native of the Italian city of Pavia, who for several years was tormented by the poltergeist tricks of an amorous incubus. Sinistrari himself was a witness of the ongoing affair. His account offers insights into the nature of spirit love, although it is distorted by religious superstitions and prejudices.

After receiving and eating a mysterious cake for which she had not paid, and therefore had no right to eat, Hieronyma began to suffer the loving advances of a spirit.

> The next night, whilst in bed with her husband, and both were fast asleep, she suddenly woke up at the sound of a very small voice, something like a shrill hissing, whispering in her ears, yet with great distinctness, and inquiring whether "the cake had been to her taste?" The good woman, thoroughly frightened, began to guard herself with the sign of the cross and repeatedly called upon the Names of Jesus and Mary. "Be not afraid," said the voice, "I mean you no harm; quite the reverse: I am prepared to do anything to please you; I am captivated by your beauty, and desire nothing more than to enjoy your sweet

embraces." Whereupon she felt somebody kissing her cheeks, so lightly, so softly, that she might have fancied being stroked by the finest feather-down. She resisted without giving any answer, confidently repeating over and over again the Names of Jesus and Mary, and crossing herself most devoutly. The tempter kept on thus for nearly half an hour, when he withdrew.[9]

The incubus would not take no for an answer. When Hieronyma persisted in repulsing him, he began to appear to her in the form of a handsome young man with golden hair, a flaxen beard, and sea-green eyes. He was dressed like a Spaniard. He even appeared to her while she was in the company of others, whispering loving words into her ear and kissing her hand, but only she was able to see or hear him—to everyone else the incubus remained invisible.

This gentle persuasion continued for several months. When the lady would not relent, the spirit began to steal valuables from her and beat her. The blows raised livid bruises on her face and body, but these only persisted for a day or two then quickly faded. More alarmingly, the incubus took to snatching Hieronyma's infant child away from her arms when she was breastfeeding it, and hiding it upon the roof of the house, or on the edge of the gutter. The child was never injured.

The spirit played all the common tricks of poltergeists, upsetting the furniture, throwing around pots and pans, smashing dishes. One night it built a wall of flag-stones around the bed of the sleeping woman and her long-suffering husband. In the morning they found themselves unable to leave the bed without the aid of a ladder. Another time when the husband was having a few friends over for dinner, the spirit caused the entire dining table, along with the feast and dishes laid upon it, to vanish into thin air, then later restored it with a loud crash, but set with different dishes.

After several months of this sort of nonsense, Hieronyma made a vow to St. Bernardine that she would wear the holy robe of his religious order every day for a full year if the saint would rid her of the incubus. The next day, as she was about to enter the church to pray, the robe was stripped from her body and whisked away on the wind, leaving her in the crowded street completely naked.

There is no neat ending to this fascinating eyewitness account of poor Hieronyma's tribulations. Sinistrari relates that after several years, when she steadfastly refused to accept his advances, the incubus finally became less and less forward, until at last he left the woman, and she was able to enjoy the embraces of her husband in peace.

The Conclusions of Sinistrari

From the fact that incubi and succubi appear to be immune from exorcism, which he himself on a number of occasions observed firsthand, Sinistrari reached the interesting conclusion that incubi and succubi were not infernal demons of hell. He pointed out that the incubus does not actually tempt a woman to damn her soul, as the Devil was supposed to do, but merely to have sex with him.

> Besides, the Evil Spirits, the incorporeal Demons who copulate with Sorceresses and Witches, constrain them to Demon worship, to the adjuration of the Catholic Faith, to the commission of enchantments, magic, and foul crimes, as preliminary conditions to the infamous intercourse, as has been above stated; now, Incubi endeavour nothing of the kind: they are therefore not Evil spirits. . . . Now, if the evil Demons, subdued by our Lord Jesus Christ, are stricken with fear by His Name, the Cross and the holy things; if, on the other hand, the good Angels rejoice at those same things, without however inciting men to sin or offend God, whilst the Incubi, without having any dread of the holy things, provoke to sin, it is clear that they are neither evil Demons nor good Angels; but it is clear also that they are not men, though endowed with reason. What then should they be?[10]

Sinistrari speculated that the incubus and succubus were beings of a rank intermediate between angels and humans. In lusting after men and women, they pollute themselves, even as a man is degraded by coitus with a beast; on the contrary, a man or a woman who has sex with an incubus or a succubus is elevated and exalted.

> From all that has been concluded above, it is therefore clear that there are such Demons, Succubi and Incubi, endowed with senses and subject to the passions thereof, as has been shown; who are born through generation and die through corruption, who are capable of salvation and damnation, more noble than man, by reason of the greater subtilty of their bodies, and who, when having intercourse with humankind, male or female, fall into the same sin as man when copulating with a beast, which is inferior to him. . . . But, when copulating with an Incubus, it is quite the reverse: for the Incubus, by reason of his rational and immortal spirit, is equal to man; and, by reason of his body, more noble because more subtile, so he is more perfect and more dignified than man. Consequently, when having intercourse with an Incubus, man does not degrade, but rather dignifies, his nature.[11]

This is a remarkably bold assertion for a Franciscan monk born in 1622, who served as Consultor to the Supreme Tribunal of the Most Holy Inquisition. Sinistrari was undoubtedly uncomfortable with it, but he had the courage to follow his own logical process to its inevitable conclusion. However, it is no accident that the manuscript of *Demoniality* remained unpublished and lost to the world until discovered in the possession of a London collector in 1872. It was first printed at Paris three years later. Sinistrari could never have published it during his lifetime.

If such spirits do degrade their nature by having sex with humans, it is a voluntary degradation on their part. They usually come to men and woman unsought, so no accusation of tempting the spirits to sin can be leveled at their human partners, anymore than we would accuse a beast of tempting the passion of a man who copulates with it.

The Moral of Being Tailed

I find myself wondering what might have happened had Hieronyma accepted the spirit as her lover on the first night and kept her mouth shut about the relationship, rather than giving in to her religious hysteria. The incubus told her that he was willing to do anything to please her. Had she received him into her embrace, the spirit perhaps would have revealed many occult secrets to her, and awakened in her mind and body esoteric perceptions and abilities that she could scarcely have dreamed possible. He would perhaps have given her pleasures far beyond anything her husband was capable of providing.

The Church preached that intercourse with spirits was a sin, therefore Hieronyma was determined to avoid it regardless of the cost. She was also determined to be faithful to her husband, and evidently regarded sex with an incubus as equivalent to adultery. We must respect the choice of this good, pious woman, but I tend to question her wisdom on purely pragmatic grounds.

It was necessary to dwell for a time upon the spirits who rape and pervert humans because such spirits do exist, have always existed, and will always exist. They come unsought to anyone who takes their fancy. They do not persist in bothering those who are knowledgeable in the techniques of ritual magic and communing with spirits of various degrees. Magicians are quite capable of controlling such beings, or banishing them in the unlikely event that such a course of action seems desirable. The spirits know this. They search out easier prey.

The nature of a visiting spirit is often conditioned by the mind of the person it visits. Those who are suppressed, superstitious, fearful and unhappy are far more likely to find themselves subject to the forced affections of incubi and succubi than are ritual occultists. To a magician, a spirit is an everyday visitor, a friend, a colleague, a servant, a lover, and so on depending on the nature of the spirit. To a nervous, devout Christian a spirit is likely to be a terrifying and monstrous enemy intent on perversion, lust, and destruction. The thought is father to the deed.

The Witch's Familiar

Spirit rapists exist, but in my judgment based on the literature of these events they are no more common in the general population of spirits than human rapists are in the general population of humans. It was the mania concerning the lustful incubus and the evil witch with her demon familiar, sweeping through Europe in the fifteenth and sixteenth centuries, that provoked so many genuine reports of obsession by incubi and succubi. Those good Church women who spent hours each day gossiping over the juicy details of the latest witch trial were, in effect, begging to be obsessed and possessed by hurtful spirits. Some of them had their unconscious wishes fulfilled.

I should mention that possession occurs when a spirit appears to enter and take control of the body. Most often the conscious identity, or soul, of the person possessed is displaced during the event, which is usually of finite duration. The experience is similar to deep dreamless sleep. Less often, the consciousness remains present during possession, but is unable to control its body. Obsession occurs when a spirit persists in making its presence known to a human being, either by appearing to the sight, or whispering or shouting into the ear, or caressing or striking the skin, or generating other sensory impressions directly or indirectly. By this definition, sex with spirits is a form of obsession.

According to the biased and corrupt testimony of the witch trials, there were two types of spirit sex enjoyed by witches. The first was the sex a witch was often supposed to have with her demon familiar. Usually the familiar was portrayed in the form of a pet animal. Cats were very popular scapegoats. Superstitious persecution and destruction of cats during the Middle Ages was in no small measure responsible for the spread of plague. In a sense, witch and cat had their revenge upon their persecutors. And a terrible revenge it was! Millions died from the plague-infected fleas carried on rats that more cats in the port towns might have kept under control.

Witchcraft is a form of shamanism. It evolved out of the folk practices of rural cunning men and wise women, who had acquired their art through hereditary lore. The animal familiar of the witch was a material instrument through which the spirit familiar, a kind of helpful spirit or syvén, to use the shamanic term, expressed itself to the witch. The Inquisition of the Christian Church sought to subvert and pervert the nature and purpose of witchcraft to suit its own insane view of the world, and to a great extent it succeeded. The familiar of the witch became a demon of hell in the eyes of the common people.

Not much is known about genuine witchcraft in Europe during the period of the witch burnings. However, it is quite likely that wise women practicing pagan forms of folk magic did have sexual intercourse with familiar spirits, though probably not with the animals that sometimes may have served as physical hosts for those spirits. Familiar spirits were capable of entering into the body of the witch, just as the ayami and syvén entered into the body of the shaman. They were not bound to animal hosts. The sheer number of accounts of intercourse between accused witches and spirits at the witch trials, coupled with the regularity of this form of union in shamanism, suggests that witches had sex with familiars on occassion, but there is no way to guess how commonly it occurred.

The Devil as a Lover

The other form of spirit sex that formed a topic of interest at the witch trials was coitus between the witch (usually a woman during the period known as the witch mania) and Satan himself. In the same way that nuns symbolically married Christ, witches were believed to wed the Devil. It was held by the Church that they swore obedience to him, allowed him full access to their bodies for his pleasure, and remained faithful to him throughout their lives.

Under torture, accused witches testified that Satan came to their beds, usually in the form of a man with swarthy skin and dark hair and eyes, sometimes as a black man, and sometimes as a large black dog or a goat. His lovemaking was rough and often painful. He preferred his sex doggy style, and enjoyed anal intercourse. Most accused witches denied that they derived any pleasure from his caresses, although this posture may have been motivated from fear that if they admitted pleasure in the arms of the Devil, their torture and eventual execution would be made more horrible. A minority of women interrogated as witches testified that the Devil's lovemaking was highly pleasurable.

Some said the penis of Satan (or Lucifer, or Beelzebub—these were considered to be different princes of hell in medieval demonology, but were nonetheless often confused together) was as small as a finger; others testified that it was so thick, it hurt them to receive it into their bodies. It sometimes became swollen at the tip and could not be withdrawn. Often the Devil's prick was said to be cold as ice, rock hard, or covered with scales that expanded as it was withdrawn on each back stroke to rip flesh from the walls of the witch's vagina. Accused witches claimed that they often bled after intercourse. Paradoxically, in a few accounts the Devil's penis was said to be fiery, but this may have been similar to the fiery cold of dry ice.

Not content with endowing Satan with a huge instrument, the demonologists of the Inquisition asserted that he possessed a double penis. In this way he could perform vaginal and anal penetration on a witch simultaneously for her greater degradation. It was even claimed that he had three tools, one of which was extremely long so that the witch could perform fellatio on the Prince of Hell while filled in both nether orifices. The French artist Felicien Rops illustrated this remarkable anatomical feature of the Devil in several of his engravings.[12]

In the opinion of the Church, Satan gained no sensual satisfaction from his copulation with men and women in both sexes and various forms. Since he is an angel, without a corporeal body, and is not constituted to reproduce sexually, it was assumed that he could not derive pleasure from sex. Therefore he and his demons committed sexual acts for the sole purpose of leading humans into sin and damnation. At first, the writers of the Church asserted, Satan came to witches in the form of an attractive young man and spoke soft words of love. Later he became increasingly cruel. To insure that the witch felt her own damnation to be irredeemable, and ceased to pray or look for salvation from Christ, he took care to induce her to commit the most perverse of sexual acts.

Love in the Convent

At the same time that poor rural women were being burned alive for confessing under torture to sexual relations with familiars and the Devil, monks and nuns were committing essentially identical acts with spirits in the privacy and security of their cloisters. Usually they were wise enough to maintain a discreet silence about their spirit lovers, but sometimes they were observed in the sexual act (the spirits were usually invisible to others). Then they would claim that their lover was Jesus, Mary, an angel, or a saint. Saint Mechtildis reported a visitation by Christ: "He kissed my hand, pressed me to Him, whispered to me to give Him my love, and I surrendered my all to Him and in return tasted of His divine essence."[13]

Other nuns were not so fortunate as Mechtildis. Sinistrari relates the case of a nun who was observed by one of her holy sisters to lock herself into her cell each day after dinner. Suspicion aroused, the spying nun went into an adjoining cell and listened with her ear to the wall. She heard the sounds of two voices conversing in subdued tones, and the creak of a bed accompanied by groans and sighs. The spy alerted her abbess, who came to listen. At first they suspected the sister was making lesbian love with another nun, but had to drop this idea when they found all the nuns of the convent accounted for at the times of the assignations. After gathering evidence, one day when the sounds of lovemaking were emanating from the locked cell, the abbess pounded on the door and demanded that it be opened. When the sister in the cell eventually opened the door, the cell was found to be otherwise empty.

Temporarily frustrated, the abbess allowed the matter to drop. The spy was more persistent. She contrived to bore a hole through the wall of the suspected sister's cell. Through this peephole she saw the suspected nun making love with an attractive young man. She called the abbess and other sisters to witness the proceedings. By the time they got the cell door open the male lover had vanished into thin air. The amorous sister continued to deny everything until threatened with torture, at which point she at last confessed that she had been sleeping with an incubus.

The Private Life of Joan of Arc

Sometimes the authorities had political reasons for not believing that the connection between pious individuals and angels was approved by God. Joan of Arc claimed to see the angels in corporeal form. At her trial for heresy her accusers tried to trick her into admitting that she had committed sexual acts with these angels, but Joan adroitly eluded their questions, without ever actually denying the accusation:

> *Question:* Has she kissed St. Michael and St. Catherine?
> *Answer:* Yes.
> *Question:* Do they smell pleasant?
> *Answer:* It's good to know they smell pleasant.
> *Question:* In embracing them, does she ever feel any warmth or
>   anything else?
> *Answer:* It is not possible for me to embrace them without feeling or
>   touching them.

Question: What part has she embraced, the upper or lower?
 Answer: It is more decorous to embrace them above rather than below.
Question: Was St. Michael nude?
 Answer: Do you think then that God has nothing to clothe him with?[14]

The reference to the smell of the angels has to do with the belief that demons carried with them a stench of excrement, whereas saints and angels exuded an odor of sanctity that resembled the scent of roses or lilacs. As intent as the English-led court had been to demonstrate that the spirits from whom she received her instructions were demons, the French later became even more determined to demonstrate that these spirits were holy angels. In 1920 Joan was canonized as a saint.

Whether a spirit was perceived to be an angel or a demon often depended on the social climate of the region, the moment in history, and the political power of the person accused. In pagan times sexual relationships and formalized marriages between human beings and spirits were looked upon as fortunate unions, on the grounds that such spirits were higher beings than man, and therefore to have connection with them was to be elevated and favored by the gods. Under Christianity the gods of love such as Pan, Bacchus, Aphrodite and Priapus, and the spirits of nature such as the fawns, satyrs, dryads and nymphs, were all condemned as demons. Therefore no sexual connection with them could be other than damnable—at best a pollution, at worst an heretical act.

The God of the Templars

This was the fate that overtook the Order of the Knights Templar, a religious order founded in 1119 to safeguard pilgrims on their journeys to the Holy Land. Its primary center was established at Jerusalem on the site now occupied by the Dome of the Rock. The Templars were initiates of a secret society that over the centuries developed its own esoteric beliefs and practices. These may have been Gnostic in nature, and were certainly influenced by Eastern beliefs and practices. There is evidence to suggest that they included sexual magic of a homosexual kind.

What actually went on in the secret chambers of the Templars is lost to history, and the confessions extracted from the knights under torture are suspect. Initiation seems to have involved the denial of Christ, spitting upon the cross, and a ceremony that took place in a locked room. In this room the initiate partially disrobed, then received kisses from his fellow knights on various parts of his body. "One of the knights examined, Guischard de Marzici, said he remembered the reception of Hugh de Marhaud, of the diocese of Lyons, whom he saw taken into a small room, which was closed up so that no one could see or hear what took place within; but that when, after some time, he was let out, he was very pale, and looked as though he were troubled and amazed."[15]

The Templars worshipped an idol in the form of a brazen or gilded head called Baphomet. This is variously described as an statue in metal or wood of a bearded face with blazing eyes. Sometimes the head is said to have possessed two faces, or three. Sometimes it was a full human figure, but with four feet—two in front and two behind. These may have been different representations of the same deity. One knight upon being shown the image for the first time was told, "You must adore this as your saviour, and the saviour of the order of the Temple."

The idol was believed to have the power of making the knights rich, and of causing trees to flourish and the earth to become fruitful. They were said to anoint it with the fat of murdered infants, and to touch cords to it and then wear them around their waists to gain the benefit of its magical potency. Almost certainly the head was oracular, and was probably connected with the numerous legends of prophetic brazen heads so popular during the Middle Ages. It was the residence for a tutelary spirit of the Templars, which the Knights credited for their wealth and power.

I am inclined to speculate that the head was the focus for a ritual of god-making acquired by the Templars from Eastern sources, and that sexual magic was used to empower it. It is more likely that the head was anointed with semen than with the fat of murdered babies. Semen may be regarded as the fat of murdered babies, in a symbolic sense, since when it is spilled outside the womb it cannot generate new life. It is white like fat. This symbolism was used by Aleister Crowley, most notably in interpreting a line from his spirit-inspired *Book of the Law*, dictated to him by his Holy Guardian Angel. The line reads: "Sacrifice cattle little and big: after a child."[16]

The Templars were also accused of adoring a demon in the shape of a giant cat, although one testimony says that it was a calf, which seems more probable. Along with the cat appeared "devils in the shape of women." It is possible that these were women paid to perform offices similar to the shaktis of Tantric worship. Or they may have been *houris*, succubi spirits in the form of beautiful women that are supposed in Moslem folklore to have sex with the faithful in Paradise.

The Jinn of Islam

Among the common people of the Moslem world, sexual connection with a spirit was considered a fortunate omen, particularly to a boy who had just reached puberty.

Most favorable of all was when the first nocturnal emission of semen experienced by a boy was provoked by a jinni during the ten days of El-Mohurrum (New Year Festival of the Shiite sect). Some young Islamic men deliberately delayed marriage to prolong relations with spirit lovers. One ascetic holy man claimed to have maintained a sexual relationship with the same *jinneeyeh* (evil spirit) for more than forty years.[17]

Women were equally enamored of their incubi lovers. Islamic women who had experienced coitus with spirits reported that the act often left them exhausted (a statement that parallels the testimony of European accused witches), that the seed of the jinn was black in color and icy cold (the coldness of the Devil's seed was frequently reported in the witch trials), and that virgins who copulated with *jinn* did not lose their hymens (a fact also observed by European demonologists). So respectable was the practice of spirit love in the Islamic world, at least among the laboring classes, that it was socially correct to greet a woman with the salutation, "May God copulate with thee! May a thousand huge-membered virile jinn have carnal knowledge of thee!"[18]

Sex in Modern Spiritualism

In the nineteenth century spirit mediums frequently reported sexual feelings during contacts with certain spirits, who due to the puritanical outlook of the day were reviled as evil and perverse. Ectoplasm, a mysterious substance usually characterized as viscous, sticky or slimy in its fully materialized form, that came out of the body of the medium and took the shapes of faces or other body parts of spiritual beings, sometimes emanated from the vagina of female mediums, suggesting that it was based upon the occult sexual energy of kundalini shakti. There is a famous photograph of the medium Mina Crandon (1883–1941) extruding an ectoplasmic hand and arm from her pelvic region.[19] It illustrates the underlying connection in spiritualism between spirit energy and human sexual energy.

The investigator of psychic phenomena, Dr. Hereward Carrington, noted this connection in a paper read before the First International Congress for Psychical Research at Copenhagen in 1921, in which he mentioned "the observation made in the cases of [the mediums] Kathleen Goligher and Eva C. which show that the plasma which is materialized, frequently issues from the genitals."[20] In the same paper Carrington made mention of "the teachings and practices of the Yogis India, who have written at great length upon the connection between sexual energies and the higher ecstatic states, and of the conversion of the former into the latter," showing that he had a least a passing acquaintance with Tantra.

Female mediums sometimes experienced sexual climax at the height of their manifestations:

> These speculations have, I believe, been amply verified by certain recent investigations, wherein it has been shown that (in the case of a celebrated European medium) the production of a physical phenomenon of exceptional violence has been coincidental with a true orgasm. From many accounts it seems probable that the same was frequently true in the case of Eusapia Paladino, and was doubtless the case with other mediums also.[21]

Often the onset of a talent for mediumship is announced by the persistent appearance of poltergeist events. As is the case with poltergeist activity generally, the obsessing spirits turn their energies upon the psychic with whom they are associated, sometimes causing bruises, welts, cuts in the skin, or stigmata of various kinds. The psychic is troubled by loud noises, voices, pinches, slaps, and other events. "Mediumship often develops from Poltergeist phenomena: from a ferocious persecution to make the sensitive a medium against his will."[22]

Poltergeists

Sinistrari and other Church demonologists noted the occurrence of *poltergeist* events in connection with visitations of incubi and succubi centuries ago. It is a common belief among modern parapsychologists that poltergeist phenomena are generated by human sexuality. A poltergeist (German for "noisy ghost") is a spirit that moves furniture, smashes dishes, knocks pictures off the walls, and otherwise makes a nuisance of itself. Poltergeists almost always reveal themselves in the close proximity of a girl or boy just attaining puberty. As the child grows older and finds normal outlets for sexual energy the poltergeist happenings usually cease.

There has been a futile attempt in parapsychology to deny the existence of a spirit agent in poltergeist activities. They are put down as spontaneous occurrences of telekinesis, a postulated power of the human mind to move things at a distance that has never been proven to exist. Parapsychologists generally dodge the question of how human sexuality enters into the equation. The ancient and obvious explanation, that poltergeists are incubi and succubi feeding off of the sexual energies of adolescents, is never presented.

There seems good reason to suppose that the malicious poltergeists and the benevolent household spirits, who are called by various names in different cultures, are the same class of spirit, which draws upon human sexual energy to accomplish its ends. In Russia these benevolent spirits were known as *domovoy*, and were believed to perform common household tasks and to watch protectively over the sleeping inhabitants of the house. In Germany they were called *kobolds*, in England *brownies*. I suspect they seldom if ever manifest themselves in houses that do not contain a child approaching adolescence, although a woman recently widowed, a celibate priest or nun, or an unmarried individual of adult age may sometimes generate the same necessary sexual energies.

UFO Abductions

Since the 1940s a new form of spirit manifestation has arisen that bears a technological mask. Many thousands of otherwise sane and normal individuals have reported seeing strange lights and shapes moving through the sky or landing upon the ground. Some have even reported curious unearthly beings of various shapes and natures. The latest aspect of this cultural happening consists of assertions by a small number of persons that they have been abducted by these beings against their will, taken to an otherworldly place, and sexually violated with instruments.

If we assume for a moment that the beings responsible for these abductions and sexual assaults are not living creatures from distant star systems, but spirits intent on interacting with human beings in a sexual way, these stories begin to reveal familiar details. The inability of some abductees to move while being sexually penetrated is similar to the inability of a person to throw off the night hag after waking from an erotic nightmare. The coldness of the instruments is similar to the icy sensation of the Devil's penis. The theft of semen or ova by supposed aliens is analogous to the theft of semen by medieval demons, and the reason stated is similar in both cases—the engendering of offspring who are half-human and half-alien (or half-spirit).

To regard the UFO phenomenon as a modern form of spirit apparition is not to rob it of its interest or significance. We are left with the fascinating question as to why beings so different from us have spent so much time and energy communicating with and interacting with humanity over a span of so many millennia. As important as spirits can sometimes become to human beings, evidently human beings are even more important to at least a percentage of spirits. They seem intent upon teaching us something, or deriving something of value from us, perhaps both. The destinies of humans and spirits appear to be inextricably intertwined.

Intellectual Gangsterism

In the modern Western world carnal union with spirits has ceased to be a matter for religion and instead become a subject for medicine and clinical psychology. This has had two significant effects on the general perception of the phenomenon.

On the one hand, by placing it into the hands of physicians, spirit sex is relegated to the status of a disease that must be cured. Such relationships with spirits, angels, and gods are regarded as breakdowns in the normal functioning of the flesh, imbalances of body chemistry that can often be successfully treated with drugs.

On the other hand, by regarding sex with spirits as a psychological disorder of the mind, it can be dismissed as a mere fantasy or illusion, probably induced by some childhood trauma, that has no value to or significance in the so-called real world. The view is that once a person who is under the "illusion" that he or she is having sex with a spirit has been successfully counseled, the aberrant notion will simply fade away like a forgotten dream.

The determination to cast sex with spirits as a disease of the flesh or an aberration of the mind is driven by an intense fear of what has been misleadingly classed as the supernatural. Modern man, perhaps because he cannot understand and control them, is utterly terrified by spirits. He responds by trying to ignore them, by mocking them, by vilifying them and associating them with taboos and crimes, and by classifying them as a disease to be cured. Even the word "supernatural" has been shaped by this impulse, driven by terror, to thrust magic and spirits out of the commonly shared experience of humanity.

Spirits in all their forms are a natural, and indeed an inescapable, part of life. Despite all the efforts of scientific materialism to deny them existence they continue to be seen, heard, smelled, touched, and from time to time loved. Spirits persist in modern life in the form of UFO aliens because they are real. Sexual intercourse with angels and other spiritual beings continues to occur because it is real. To rigorously deny and ridicule the existence of an entire class of beings whose existence has been acknowledged in all cultures from the dawn of recorded history is a form of intellectual gangsterism that is inevitably doomed to fail.

{ 2 }

The Great Mother Goddess

The Ocean of Shakti

Spirits are engendered by *shakti*, which at root means creative or birth energy. It is the primal potency that permits and enables being. In Hinduism this creative energy is personified as a mother goddess.

> Before creation this world was devoid of sun, moon, and stars, and without day and night. There was no fire and no distinction of directions. The Brahmanda was then destitute of sound, touch, and the like, etc., devoid of other force, and full of darkness. Then but that one eternal Brahman [ultimate reality] of whom the Shrutis speak, and the Prakriti [source of Nature], who is existence, consciousness, and bliss, alone existed.
>
> She is pure, full of knowledge, beyond the reach of speech, perpetual, immaculate, unapproachable by even yogis, all-pervading, untroubled, eternally blissful, subtle, and devoid of all such properties as heaviness, lightness, and the like.
>
> Subsequently, when that Anandamayi [full-of-delight] became desirous to create in order to manifest Her own play of bliss, that supreme Prakriti, though in truth formless, at once assumed a form by the strength of Her own will.

That Devi [goddess] with form was of the colour of crushed collyrium, Her face was fair and as charming as a full-blown lotus. She had four arms, fiery eyes, disheveled hair, and full and erect breasts. She was naked as space, terrific, and seated on a lion.[1]

Shakti is neither male nor female, and is capable of manifesting in either sex or in androgynous forms. She is usually represented as a goddess because it is the womb that gives form to formlessness and brings forth new life. Also, it is the mother that nurtures life in all its forms.

Whatever form She may assume in Her aspect with attributes is but Her form. That Shakti alone who grants enjoyment, salvation, and devotion, is in all such forms. Now the Sadhaka [practitioner] may, if he so desires, know Her as Vishnu, Krishna, Shiva, and Rama, or as Kali, Tara, Radha, Durga, Sita, and Lakshmi, or please himself by calling Her mother, father, friend, and well-wisher. It does not matter whether the Vaishnava considers Her as Vishnu in the form of Shakti, or the Shakta considers Her as Shakti in the form of Vishnu. When we sink into the ocean of Her substance, which is Chit-shakti, forgetful of all differences of masculinity and femininity appertaining to forms, then Krishnashakti, Shivashakti, or Kalishakti, and all other Shaktis, will be mingled into one by the waves of that ocean.[2]

Soul of the World

In the philosophy of ancient Greece and Rome, Shakti was known as the Soul of the World, the first created being that animates and gives form to the body of the cosmos. All manifest things exist within and are expressions of the Soul of the World. As is true of the Hindu philosophers when they speak of Shakti, the Greek philosopher Plato commonly referred to the Soul of the World as feminine, yet clearly recognized that this deity is neither male nor female in her essential nature.

And the same argument applies to the universal nature which receives all bodies—that must be always called the same, for, inasmuch as she always receives all things, she never departs at all from her own nature and never, in any way or at any time, assumes a form like that of any of the things which enter into her; she is the natural recipient of all impressions, and is stirred and informed by them, and appears different from time to time by reason of them.[3]

It is striking to note how similar the descriptions of the Soul of the World in Plato are to the descriptions of Shakti in the Tantra texts. There is one important difference, however. Plato always distinguishes the Soul of the World from the supreme creative source, the "best of causes," which he describes as unknowable but characterizes as male, even as he characterizes the Soul of the World, the "fairest of creations," as female. In the highest understanding of Shakti, no distinction is made between Shakti and Brahma, the supreme creative cause. Consequently, in the ancient Tantric philosophy of the East the supreme godhead is regarded as either female or neuter, whereas in the ancient philosophy of the West it is male or neuter.

The Goddess with Attributes

Only philosophers of the highest attainment are capable of worshipping Shakti as an abstract potential. The rest of us must give the Goddess some sort of quality or identity before we can relate to her in any meaningful way.

Shakti herself teaches in one of the Hindu *shastras* (sacred texts) that she must be experienced through her forms before she can be approached in her formless reality:

> None can comprehend my subtle form without first having duly meditated on my gross form. The sight of this subtle form releases Jiva [consciousness] from the bonds of Sangsara [transitory world], and gives him Nirvana Samadhi [ecstasy of liberation]. For this reason a Sadhaka who desires liberation must first seek refuge in my gross forms, and then, having by Kriyayoga duly worshipped these forms slowly and step by step, think of My supreme, unwasting, subtle form.[4]

Kriya yoga is the system of yoga described in the first half of the teachings of Patanjali. It involves the observance of rites and ritual actions for the purpose of weakening the five *kleshas* (afflictions), which are: *avidya* (ignorance), *asmita* (egotism), *raga* (desire), *dwesha* (hatred), and *abhinivesha* (possessiveness). The distinction made in the quotation is between the worship of Shakti with attributes and the worship of Shakti without attributes. It is generally agreed that Shakti must be worshipped as a goddess with a name and a shape before she can be approached in her formless reality. It is not a sign of weakness or intellectual inferiority to worship Shakti with attributes, merely a pragmatic recognition of the inherent limitations of human consciousness.

The Cult of Cybele

The Goddess appears in many guises throughout the mythological history of the human race. All of the great mother goddesses are manifest aspects of Shakti. In ancient Greece and Rome she was worshipped as Cybele, originally a Phrygian goddess of the caverns of the earth who became identified with Rhea, the wife of Cronus. The Romans called her the Great Mother, and regarded her as the mother of all the gods. She was also known as *Mater Turrita* because she wore a square crown in the shape of a turreted city fortification.

Her worshippers in Phrygia, the Corybantes, paraded through the streets to the piping of flutes and the beating of drums, dancing themselves into an ecstatic trance during which they lashed themselves on the upper body with whips and cut themselves with knives and swords until their blood flowed forth in profusion. Cybele was a fertility goddess. One of her rites involved the ritual castration of her priests. This was done in memory of Attis the Phrygian, a mythic lover of Cybele who, when he sought to marry another lover, was driven insane by the goddess and made to castrate himself so that he bled to death.

It may seem strange that castration occurs in connection with a fertility goddess, but by castrating themselves the priests of Cybele symbolically devoted all of their sexual energy to the goddess, rather than expending it in more normal pursuits. The divine ecstasy of the Corybantes was driven by their suppressed sexual energies, released through flagellation and similar types of ritual self-injury. During their trance the physical punishment of their bodies generated pleasure rather than pain. It was their way of making love to Cybele. It sometimes induced an oracular state in which prophecies were uttered.

Isis the Beloved

Existing in Greece, Rome, and Egypt alongside the frenzied processions of Cybele, the cult of Isis offered a more gentle way to worship the Goddess. Isis is the ancient Egyptian goddess of magic, the faithful wife of Osiris and the mother of Horus. It is clear that Isis was recognized by the Greeks and Romans as a form of Shakti, and Osiris as a form of Shiva, by a remark made by Plutarch, who says of these gods: "Whatever there is in nature that is fair and good exists entirely because of them, inasmuch as Osiris contributes the origins, and Isis receives them and distributes them."[5] This is quite close to the usual Hindu understanding of Shiva as the initial creative spark and Shakti as the womb that gives form and brings forth.

The priests of Isis shaved their heads and bodies and remained celibate to signal their personal devotion to her. Osiris, the husband of Isis, was castrated by his brother Set, and it was Isis who restored his penis by creating a replica through her magic. The symbolism of castration, which occurs in the myths of Cybele and Isis,[6] stands in both cases for the devotion of sexual energy to worship, although the gentle and contemplative worship of Isis was very different from the frenzied and abandoned worship of Cybele. By magically re-creating the penis of Osiris, Isis demonstrated that its sexual energies were hers to command and control. Through the celibate worship of her priests, the Goddess is voluntarily granted complete command over their sexual function. All of their latent love-energies are given to her. This transmutation of sexual energy (kundalini shakti) yields magical powers (siddhis).

This is the real reason that Catholic priests adore Mary, the mother of God, and remain celibate. The true purpose for celibacy within the Christian Church has been hidden for so many centuries that it is almost completely forgotten by the priests themselves. There is agreement among Christian historians that the cult of Mary, or Mariolotry, is a direct descendent of the cult of Isis in Rome and Egypt. Similarly, the celibacy of Christian priests is based upon the celibacy of the priests of Isis. The custom was probably instituted at the urging of priests of Isis after their conversion to Christianity.

On the connection between the Roman worship of Isis and the Catholic adoration of Mary, James Frazer wrote:

> We need not wonder, then, that in a period of decadence, when traditional faiths were shaken, when systems clashed, when men's minds were disquieted, when the fabric of the empire itself, once deemed eternal, began to show ominous rents and fissures, the serene figure of Isis with her spiritual calm, her gracious promise of immortality, should have appeared to many like a star in a stormy sky, and should have roused in their breasts a rapture of devotion not unlike that which was paid in the Middle Ages to the Virgin Mary. Indeed her stately ritual, with its shaven and tonsured priests, its matins and vespers, its tinkling music, its baptism and aspersions of holy water, its solemn processions, its jewelled images of the Mother of God, presented many points of similarity to the pomps and ceremonies of Catholicism. The resemblance need not be purely accidental. Ancient Egypt may have contributed its share to the gorgeous symbolism of the Catholic Church, as well as to the pale abstractions of theology. Certainly in art the figure of Isis suckling the infant Horus is so like that of the Madonna and child that it has sometimes received the adoration of

ignorant Christians. And to Isis in her later character of patroness of mariners the Virgin Mary perhaps owes her beautiful epithet of *Stella Maris*, "Star of the Sea," under which she is adored by tempest-tossed sailors.[7]

Cybele and Isis are completely different in their natures and in the manners of their worship, yet both express aspects of the Goddess. Shakti is neither Cybele nor Isis—she is both Cybele and Isis at the same moment, along with numerous other mother goddesses of the ancient world. This may be a difficult concept for modern worshippers, who are accustomed to regarding God as a single, immutable identity (although they disagree as to the nature of this identity), but it was clearly understood by the priests of Isis at Rome. Lucius Apuleius, who lived during the second century, is best known for his novel *The Golden Ass*, but he was also an anointed priest of Isis. In his novel he describes a visitation of the Goddess, who speaks the following:

> I am she that is the naturall mother of all things, mistresse and governesse of all the Elements, the initiall progeny of worlds, chiefe of powers divine, Queene of heaven, the principall of the Gods celestiall, the light of the goddesses: at my will the planets of the ayre, the wholesome winds of the Seas, and the silences of hell be disposed; my name, my divinity is adored throughout all the world in divers manners, in variable customes and in many names, for the Phrygians call me the mother of the Gods: the Athenians, Minerva: the Cyprians, Venus: the Candians, Diana: the Sicilians, Proserpina: the Eleusians, Ceres: some Juno, other Bellona, other Hecate: and principally the Aethiopians which dwell in the Orient, and the Aegyptians which are excellent in all kind of ancient doctrine, and by their proper ceremonies accustome to worship mee, doe call mee Queene Isis.[8]

The Queen of Heaven

Mary is an earthly incarnation of the Queen of Heaven just as Jesus is an earthly incarnation of the heavenly Christ, or Messiah. The Queen of Heaven is described in the New Testament book of Revelation, even though she is not explicitly called by this name: "And there appeared a great wonder in heaven; a woman clothed with the sun, and the moon under her feet, and upon her head a crown of twelve stars."[9] Since she is said to be the mother of "a man-child, who was to rule all nations with a rod of iron" and who was "caught up unto God, and to his throne," she can only be Mary, since the "man-child" is obviously Jesus.

The only explicit mention of the Queen of Heaven in the Bible occurs in Jeremiah, where her worship "in the cities of Judah, and in the streets of Jerusalem" is condemned by the prophet. Even though the god of the Hebrews is completely masculine in all the Old Testament descriptions, the Goddess survived in Judaism from ancient to modern times in the form of the Matronit (matron), who in the literature of the Kabbalah is described as the wife of God, and as the Shekhina (imminent presence of God) who is personified as a goddess and a lover of holy men. Although it is seldom explicitly stated, there is frequent implication that the love of the Shekhina for her worshippers can assume a sexual expression.

The Goddess among the Gnostics

The Matronit and the Shekhina echo the two forms of the Goddess that occur within the cults of Gnosticism. This will not come as a surprise when we consider the profound influence Gnostic doctrines, particularly those of the Jewish Gnostics, had on the doctrines of the Kabbalah. The Gnostics recognized Shakti as the supreme mother goddess of heaven, whose children are the stars. In this role she was called Barbelo (virgin) by the Barbelo Gnostics. Barbelo is similar in many respects to the Matronit. The Gnostics also recognized a form of the Goddess that voluntarily descended to Earth, where she was trapped in the forgetfulness of matter. This second form of the Goddess was more youthful and sexually active, and was characterized as either a maiden or a whore. Descending as an innocent virgin, she was forced into prostitution by the Archons. She was called by various names, among them Helena (torch) by the Simonian Gnostics, and the Light Maiden, but most commonly appears under the name Sophia (wisdom). Sophia is very much like the Kabbalistic concept of the Shekhina.

It should be noted that the symbolism of the serpent played an important part in Gnostic myths and worship, particularly in earlier cults such as that of the Ophites. In Gnosticism it is the serpent who frees mankind from the tyranny of the chief archon, Yaldabaoth. In Gnostic doctrines Yaldabaoth is paradoxically both Satan (Samael) and Jehovah (IHVH) of the Old Testament. The serpent gives Adam and Eve the gift of gnosis or wisdom, which awakens them to their true divine state and liberates them from their bondage in Eden.

In the Gnostic text *The Apocryphon of John*, the serpent in the Garden, who in this text is replaced by the form of an eagle, is Sophia herself. Thus spiritual gnosis is a gift to humanity from the Goddess: "I appeared in the form of an eagle on the tree of knowledge, which is the Epinoia [intention] from the foreknowledge of the pure light, that I might teach them and awaken them out of the depth of sleep. For they were both in a fallen state and they recognized their nakedness. The Epinoia appeared to them as a light (and) she awakened their thinking."[10]

The serpent appears here as an eagle to indicate that sexual energy has been alchemically transmuted into spiritual energy (in one myth of the phoenix, the phoenix is reborn from a small worm). The serpent generally symbolizes sexual energy, and also wisdom—the two are linked. In Gnosticism, sexual energy was used deliberately to produce spiritual transcendence.

The Gnostics regarded marriage and procreation as evil, or at least as activities valueless to their own spiritual evolution, because they looked upon the physical body as a prison. They did not wish to trap more souls in cells of flesh. As a result, Gnostic sects tended to split into two types, those that advocated strict celibacy, and those that freely employed prostitutes in a ritualistic way. This is an inevitable outcome of redirecting sexual energy away from the propagation of the species to the generation of magical powers and spiritual wisdom. The physical side of sex must either be completely suppressed and turned inward, or deliberately channeled and controlled in such a way that no offspring result and the energy of orgasm can be put to other uses. Catholic priests chose the first path, Tantric yogis the second, and Gnostics split over the question, some sects avoiding physical sex while others used it deliberately to advance their spiritual evolution.

Goddess of the Witches

In modern witchcraft, or Wicca, which is an attempt to revive the pre-Christian nature worship of Europe, Shakti is usually known simply as the Goddess. Individual groups sometimes invoke her in her forms with attributes, such as Diana and Cerridwen and Hecate, but there is a general understanding that these are only masks for the Goddess, who assumes many forms and names to suit her various purposes. The Goddess is closely identified in Wicca with Mother Nature. The Horned God of Wicca, who appears in English folklore under various distinct names such as Herne the Hunter, Robin Goodfellow,[11] and the Green Man, is an expression of the masculine seminal power of Shiva.

In some covens strenuous efforts are made to balance the Goddess and the Horned God during ceremonial worship, but the high priestess of the coven, who is during rituals an incarnate vessel for the Goddess energy (shakti) often takes the more active, central role in the circle. It is through the high priestess that occult force is channeled during works of ritual magic. It is the customary practice of Gardnerian witches to perform witchcraft "skyclad," or naked. This undoubtedly heightens sexual tension, and is probably quite useful in empowering works of magic with shakti energy. For practical reasons, such as performing rituals in public places, or outdoors during winter, Wiccan covens not a part of the Gardnarian tradition often do not work skyclad.

One of the more interesting details of Wiccan initiation is the fivefold kiss. This is delivered by the high priestess to the naked initiate upon the feet, knees, pubic region, breast and mouth. When the mouth is kissed, the priestess presses her own naked body full length upon the body of the initiate. It is worth noting that the initiate is bound and blindfolded during this kiss. Both bondage and blindfolding are intended to create a symbolic state of sexual impotence, which is lifted once the initiate enters the coven (see the description of the Blindragon, page 42). The direction of the kiss traces the ascending route of spiritualized Kundalini energy up the body to the head.

Another interesting aspect of modern Gardnerian witchcraft is ritual flagellation. As mentioned above, this played a central role in the worship of Cybele, and in other Mystery traditions of the ancient world. In the third grade of Alexandrian witchcraft initiation is completed by an act of sexual intercourse within the magic circle in the presence of the coven. The man and woman initiated into this grade are said to represent the conjunction of the Sun and Moon. The members of the coven turn their backs upon the couple during intercourse.

The Gaea Theory

Over the past few decades science has contributed to the Western concept of Shakti through the Gaea theory. This states that the entire Earth is a single living organism that has over many millions of years gradually transformed the global environment to suit its own needs. This theory explains the existence of high concentrations of oxygen in the atmosphere. Before life came into being, there was only a trace amount of oxygen in the air. The living ecosystem itself generated the free oxygen we now take for granted as a byproduct of its life processes, then used that oxygen as the basis for its own evolution of oxygen-dependent organisms such as human beings. The Gaea theory is an elaboration in materialistic terms on the Platonic concept of the Soul of the World.

One consequence of the Gaea theory is that every living organism is not only an offspring of the Goddess, but part of the body of the Goddess. Gaea is able to regulate the health of her body dynamically, just as we can regulate our sensations of heat and cold, hunger and thirst. For example, when a large meteorite impacts the Earth, eliminating the majority of species, Gaea is able to expand herself into the liberated ecological strata by evolving many entirely new species, for the purpose of restoring the stability and harmony of the entire ecosystem.

In the future should the human race ever become a major destabilizing factor on the balance of the ecosystem (and there are many signs that this time is not far away) Gaea will react to eliminate the destabilizing influence. Mother Nature will turn against her destructive offspring, humanity, and destroy us in order to maintain her own health, just as the human body eventually reacts to the presence of damaged and putrefying tissue by eliminating it. The failure of new antibacterial drugs to combat old diseases and infectious agents, as well as the failure of pesticides to eliminate insect infestations, are subtle indications that Gaea is already beginning to respond in a hostile way to her own disease, the human race.

The Dark Goddess

Not every aspect of Shakti is life-affirming. The Goddess has power over all forms, both to bring them forth and to destroy them. Whenever anything is created, the act of creation changes the form of what existed previously, and in this sense destroys it. Creation and destruction always exist together. Whether a change of form is regarded as creative or destructive largely depends upon the attitude of the observer. When we burn a log of wood in the stove, we create warmth along with ash and smoke. These same products are generated when we burn a house to the ground, but burning a house is more apt to be regarded as a destructive act. In general it may be observed that creative acts usually, but not always, involve the accumulation and concentration of energy. Destructive acts usually involve the dispersal of energy.

Many of the forms with attributes of Shakti are goddesses of the dead, the underworld, destruction, and black magic. This is an important factor in our consideration because frequently in literature, mythology, and folklore it is these dark aspects of the Goddess that are most closely linked to human sexuality, particularly sexuality that has as its goal the attainment of pleasure rather than the procreation of offspring.

Hecate of the Crossroads

For the Greeks, the dark face of Shakti was most completely expressed by Hecate, the lunar goddess of witches and black magic. Originally Hecate was probably a

Thracean Moon goddess. Hesiod asserted that she was the daughter of the Titans Perses and Asteria. Hecate had three heads, those of a lion, a dog, and a mare, which accorded with the three phases of the Moon. Her sacred beast was the dog, her sacred place the crossroads. At the end of each month the Greeks set out food at crossroads as an offering to her, to turn aside her wrath. Dogs and black female lambs were sacrificed in her honor. Her spectral appearance was accompanied by the howling of dogs. She taught sorcery and commanded the spirits of the underworld to work her will upon the Earth. She had the power to bestow upon or withhold from mortals any gift they desired.

Hecate was invoked by sorcerers when they had dealings with the underworld or wished to work evil magic. One of these was the induction of uncontrollable sexual desire in the heart of a previously indifferent person. This was accomplished through love charms or philters such as the infamous *hippomanes* created under the authority of Hecate. The hippomanes was described by ancient Roman writers as a small lump of matter found on the forehead of a newly born colt which the mother horse immediately consumed, or alternatively as the sexual secretions of a mare in heat. The connection of the mare with Hecate is significant. The mare is also linked with nightmares, particularly those of a disagreeable sexual nature.

Some authorities asserted that Hecate was the companion of Persephone, wife of Hades and queen of hell. Later Greek writers identified Hecate with Persephone. Hecate was said to rule the underworld as Persephone (to the Romans, Proserpina), the surface of the Earth as Artemis (Diana), fatal goddess of the hunt, and the heavens as Selene (Luna). All three are Moon goddesses. There is always a very strong connection between Shakti in her female aspects and the Moon, just as there is a link between the creative spark or seed (*bindu*), Shiva, and the Sun.

Lilith

In Jewish folklore and in the texts of the Kabbalah, the dark shadow aspect of Shakti is Lilith, who was also known by such titles as the Old One, the Harsh Husk, the Mother of Demons, the Woman of Harlotry, the Convolute Serpent, and the Northerner. Lilith was portrayed as the mother of all demons, which she gave birth to after stealing the semen of men who slept alone and impregnating herself with it. She induced spontaneous emission in her lovers by causing them to experience erotic dreams. She was also believed to provoke abortions and to strangle infants in their cribs. The Jews blamed her for what we now call sudden infant death syndrome, or crib death.

It was not that the Lilith of Jewish folklore hated children, but rather that they belonged to her, to do with as she saw fit. Sometimes she came to play with them. When Lilith appeared invisibly beside a crib to play with a baby, it was believed that its parents could be alerted to her presence by the smile on the baby's face. It was then necessary to tap the baby on the nose to break the fascination of the goddess, which otherwise might prove fatal to the infant. This was particularly true should Lilith decide to kiss the child. Its life would then be drawn out through its lips into the goddess.

According to some more materialistic fables, Lilith came to young children in the form of an owl and drank their blood. This story was based upon an ancient Greek superstition that screech owls were night hags who sometimes sucked the blood of children. The Romans called these hags *stirges*. "With their beaks they are said to tear the entrails of the sucklings, and they have their maws distended with the blood which they have swallowed."[12]

Grandmother Lilith and Lilith the Maiden

Sometimes Lilith is divided into two goddesses. The first is Grandmother Lilith, the Ancient One, who is mainly concerned with the birthing and nurturing of demons, inducing abortions and still births, and causing crib deaths. Grandmother Lilith is the night hag in her most horrible aspect. She is the dark reflection of the Matronit, and appears in European folklore as the evil fairy godmother. She is also called Lilith the Great, and is said to be the consort of the demon Samael.

The second form of Lilith is Naamah, who in the Bible was the sister of Tubal-cain, "an instructor of every artificer in brass and iron."[13] In the literature of the Kabbalah, Naamah was transformed into a beautiful seductress who comes to the beds of men sleeping alone and makes love to them. At first she appears as the most beautiful woman imaginable. According to the Zohar she adorns herself as a prostitute and stands waiting for her victim at a crossroads. Her hair is long and rose-red. Her cheeks are lily-white and tinged with pink. She wears earrings and necklaces and paints her lips. Her dress is scarlet.

After she has captured the affection of her victim and induced him to commit sin, she appears as a giant and savage demoness who in many ways bears a striking resemblance to Kali, the Hindu goddess of destruction. She stands before her lover clothed in flame, her body full of eyes, a drawn sword in her hand that drips poison from its tip. She kills him and carries him off to hell. Naamah is the shadow equivalent to the

Shekhina. She is also called Little Lilith and Lilith the Maiden, and is said to be the consort of the demon Ashmodai.

With Naamah the emphasis is on the sexual act and its pleasures. She is the beautiful houri of forbidden lust, and embodies the enormous power of sexual energy to corrupt and seduce, as well as to give joy. With Grandmother Lilith, the emphasis is on the unnatural offspring born of unions between spirits and humans. Lilith the Great embodies the power of sexual energy to create and bring forth into manifest being, a power that can be perverted to produce monsters. She is referred to in Kabbalistic writings as the Alien Crown because she usurps the place of the Matronit on the throne of heaven. She is sexual energy used for creative purposes not sanctioned by the holy torah.

Both goddesses are aspects of Lilith, just as both the Matronit and the Shekhina are two forms of the same shakti energy. Thus Lilith in her undifferentiated aspect as both the mother of demons and the seducer of human beings is an excellent expression of the chaotic or destructive reflection of shakti (Kalishakti). In Jewish folklore, all sexual pleasure that is enjoyed for its own sake in the embrace of spirits falls under the command and control of Lilith, or her daughter Naamah, since all such unions are unlawful.

Sometimes Lilith is divided into four demon queens who are set over the four quarters of the Earth. Lilith, who is often called the Northerner, rules Rome, which stands for the northern quarter. Naamah rules Damascus, which stands for the eastern quarter. Mahalath (or Rahab) rules Egypt, which stands for the southern quarter. Igrat (or Agrath, or Agrat) rules Salamanca, which stands for the western quarter. The four demon queens are merely various aspects of Lilith acting to seduce human beings in different parts of the world.

Sex and Sin

To understand why Lilith is portrayed in such a completely negative way in Jewish folklore, it must be borne in mind that until the last few decades sex outside the bounds of marriage for any reason was considered sinful and unlawful by most Western cultures and religions. Even sex within the bounds of marriage was looked upon as a sin if it was committed purely for the purposes of sensual gratification, or if it involved variations of technique that were considered perverse or criminal. Such acts as fellatio, anal intercourse, masturbation, and even intercourse that was conducted naked in daylight or with a lamp burning were condemned as damnable acts. Any attempt to have sex without conceiving a child was regarded as a form of abortion. All types of abortion were looked upon as the blackest of crimes.

For this reason, sexual pleasure enjoyed with a spiritual being for its own sake was automatically classed as evil, and was grouped with aspects of Shakti that have to do with the underworld, black magic, poisoning and other crimes. Sex with a woman of flesh and blood was also looked upon as evil when it occurred outside the marriage bond or when it was entered into purely for purposes of pleasure. Since sex with spirits could not engender lawful offspring, the usual assumption was that it was invariably unlawful.

The single exception occurred when the Shekhina (divine presence) made love to a holy man or woman. This occurrence was implicitly recognized in the Kabbalah and in Christian mysticism, but was seldom openly discussed. Holy rabbis might receive ecstasy in the embrace of the Shekhina. Devout nuns might lie in the marriage bed with their heavenly spouse, Jesus, and monks might share a similar bliss in the arms of Mary, or more commonly, also with Jesus. Descriptions of the kiss and the embrace of Christ are usually interpreted in a symbolic way, but in my opinion they should be interpreted literally in most cases. It is only the materialistic mindset of modern times which, because it disallows the very existence of spirits, dictates that all such liaisons must be poetic fantasies.

There is a certain amount of hypocrisy and ambivalence here. When the Shekhina came to a holy Kabbalist, she might induce an ecstatic state that had as one of its features sexual pleasure—this is implied in Kabbalistic texts but never clearly stated. The pleasure was regarded as a reward for extreme piety and correct worship. On the other hand, if Lilith or Naamah came to the bed of an ordinary man or woman and made love to that person with the person's consent, it was regarded by Kabbalists as a damnable sin. The actions of the goddess and the human being involved are the same in both cases. Whether or not the action is good or evil depends upon the intention of the human and the spirit.

When Jesus came to Saint Theresa and placed a mark upon her, it was perceived as a sign of her blessedness in the eyes of the Church:

> On another occasion, Jesus Christ appeared before her, and, putting his right hand, printed with the nail, into her hand, said, "See this nail print. It is the sign of My marriage contract with you. Ere long you shall be my bride, and nothing shall separate you from the love of God your Savior." . . . Being at mass on St. Paul's Day, Christ manifested Himself to her in His human form,

but His body was glorified. This intercourse continued for three years, when a seraph came with a flaming dart and pierced her to the heart.[14]

On the other hand, if Satan came to a woman later accused of witchcraft and placed his mark upon her, then made love to her, it was looked upon by the doctors of the Holy Inquisition as a sure sign of her damnation. Guazzo tells a local fable of a twelve-year-old girl who was taken out to gather rushes by her witch mother, whereupon she was introduced to a "strange man" who was probably the Devil in disguise:

> The girl was made to swear an oath to this man, and he marked her on the brow with his nail as a sign of her new allegiance, and then he lay with her in the sight of her mother. The mother in her turn offered herself to be defiled by him in the daughter's presence.[15]

The mark made upon the brow of the girl by the fingernail (talon) of the spirit whom the Inquisitors assumed to be the Devil has the same purpose as the mark made upon the palm of St. Theresa by the spirit she assumed to be Jesus. It is a blood pact between the female and the spirit as a token of their marriage, which is subsequently consummated. In the case of the witches, sex is had with both mother and daughter because both are wedded to the spirit. Apart from the fact that the sex of the witches is held in the open, and is thus sinful in the eyes of the Church, there is little material difference between the two unions. One is holy and one is blasphemous mainly because of the presumed intentions of the lovers.

This distinction also exists in Tantra. Yogis who seek carnal union with the Goddess or her daughters merely for sensual pleasure rather than for spiritual evolution are condemned as black magicians. They practice Prayoga, the visualization and animation of spirits for the purpose of sexual union. The underlying assumption of this censure is that all sexual pleasure for its own sake is unlawful. The traditional belief was that a good yogi should employ sexual energy only for a higher spiritual purpose, just as a good householder should employ sexual union with his wife only for the engendering of children.

This is an important distinction to understand because the book you are presently reading is essentially a manual of Prayoga, in the sense that it advocates pleasurable erotic union with spirits for the purpose of personal empowerment. In past centuries this purpose would be have been regarded as evil, or at least valueless, by most mystics and religious teachers. In the modern world, where sex for pleasure is accepted as a worthy goal it itself, Prayoga is more apt to be viewed with tolerance, and regarded as a legitimate pursuit.

Lilith and Samael

Kabbalists believed that Lilith could come to the beds of women and make love to them in the form of a male spirit, or incubus, who was usually called Samael. Samael is the Jewish equivalent to Satan. He is the lord of the underworld. Lilith is his consort. In the Kabbalah, Lilith has the ability to make love to human beings in a female or a male form. In one Kabbalistic text Lilith is identified with the Serpent who seduced Eve in the Garden of Eden: "And the Serpent, the Woman of Harlotry, incited and seduced Eve through the husks of Light which in itself is holiness."[16] The "Light" refers to the underlying energy of the goddess Kundalini, which may be employed for lawful or unlawful purposes. Kundalini is the personified manifestation of Shakti within the human body and always has a serpentine expression. The "husks" are demons. The "Woman of Harlotry" is another title for Lilith.

This is in perfect accord with the understanding of the nature of Shakti in the Tantric texts of India. Since Shakti expresses and enables all forms, she can just as easily manifest as a male spirit. The fact that Lilith shares this ability to come in either sex confirms that she is a genuine expression of Shakti.

The same understanding exists in the literature of the European demonologists, who believed that Satan could come to male witches in the form of a succubus, or to female witches in the form of an incubus, with equal ease. Concerning demons, who are usually understood in Christian theology to be mere extensions of the archdemon Satan himself, Guazzo writes: "They can therefore create the appearance of sex which is not naturally present, and show themselves to men in a female form, and to women in a masculine form, and lie with each accordingly."[17] The same phenomenon is being discussed, but Christian Europeans assumed that at root the seducing devil was masculine whereas Jewish Kabbalists assumed it to be at root feminine. The most profound of the Hindu pandits understood that it was neither.

The Blindragon

Later Kabbalists made a highly important distinction between dark or chaotic Shakti in her female aspect (Lilith), dark Shakti in her male aspect (Samael), and the underlying destructive energy of dark shakti (energy) itself, which they represented in the form of a great serpent or dragon. This is very similar to the representation of the power of Kundalini as a serpent in Hindu Tantra—so similar that it is tempting to assume that the Kabbalists borrowed from the Hindu Tantric texts. The serpent power of shakti in the Kabbalah is called the Blind Dragon or Blindragon. This serpent is described as an "intermediary groomsman" who lies between Samael and Lilith while they are copulating, and in fact actually enables their "adhesion and coupling."[18]

The Blindragon is credited with immense power for creation or destruction. It is castrated so that it cannot beget offspring of itself, lest these offspring destroy the world. About this great serpent is also written that had it been created whole and complete, it would have destroyed the world in a single minute. According to the Kabbalist Naftali Herz Bacharach, who wrote about the Blindragon in his *Valley of the King* (1648), the dragon is said to be blind to indicate that it is invisible—that is, without color. I tend to believe that the true reason for its blindness is probably the same as the reason for its castration, to limit its otherwise limitless power. Magic energy is projected through the eyes. It is perhaps only a coincidence that the penis is sometimes described in vernacular conversation as a "blind snake," but nevertheless an interesting coincidence.

In Tantra the human body has three esoteric channels connected with Shakti. A central channel called the *shushumna* runs straight up from the lowest of the chakras, the *muladhara*, which is the seat of sexual energy, to the highest quasi-chakra, the *sahasrara* or Thousand-petalled Lotus. The fiery serpent Kundalini is said to lie coiled three and one-half times at the base of the spine in, or just below, the muladhara, and to rise up this central tube to the sahasrara. Twined around the shushumna in a winding helix are two other channels, one that begins and ends on the left side of the body and is female, called the *ida,* and another that begins and ends on the right side and is male, called the *pingala*. The ida is associated with the Moon and with the lunar breath of the left nostril; the pingala is associated with the Sun and the solar breath of the right nostril.

A correspondence can be drawn between these three channels and the three persons of the trinity of hell in the Kabbalah. The Blindragon corresponds to the fiery serpent Kundalini who awakens with blind or unfocused sexual desire and ascends up the central shushumna. The ida and its lunar energies are related to dark Shakti in her female aspect, Lilith. The pingala and its solar energies are related to dark Shakti in her male aspect, Samael. Essentially the same triple relationship occurs in the magical and alchemical symbol of the caduceus of Hermes.

Lilith, the Liberator of Women

All created things, including all spirits, are the children of Shakti. All demons, who are spirits that commit acts considered unlawful by the mainstream religion, are the children of the dark reflection of Shakti, who in the Kabbalah is known as Lilith. In ancient and even fairly modern times, sexual acts that were unconventional or occurred outside of marriage were invariably considered evil. Sex solely for pleasure was sinful, even when is occurred within marriage. Therefore any spirit that aided or enabled sexual pleasure for its own sake was historically regarded as a demon, and a child of Lilith.

Since most men and women in the modern West do not regard sexual pleasure as inherently evil, we would not look upon a spirit of sexual pleasure as an evil spirit. The modern view of sex with spirits among those who have broken free of conventional religious morality is somewhat closer to the view of the ancient shamans with their ayami or spirit wives in heaven. Among modern Wiccans and pagans, sex with familiar spirits is increasingly regarded as not inherently sinful or evil, and perhaps useful for energizing works of magic.

Over the past few decades Lilith has been rehabilitated. This is especially true among feminist writers, who see Lilith as a goddess of woman's rights. Lilith represents sex outside of marriage, sex for pleasure, unconventional sexual techniques, sex as an instrument of power over men, as a tool of female liberation, and as an exaltation of the divine feminine. Lilith also stands for abortion rights, since she is mythically the first abortionist, and for birth control, since when a man makes love to Lilith his semen is spilled outside the womb. In this sense Lilith is the goddess of modern feminism.

{ 3 }

Tantra and Tao

Internal Alchemy

Eastern alchemy involves the transmutation of energies and substances within the human body. The body itself serves as the Hermetic vessel, and the fire of change is generated internally through prayers, meditations, visualizations, mantras, physical postures, controlled breathing, and other ritual observances. The internalization of the alchemical process in Eastern alchemy is the most important distinction that may be drawn between the traditional alchemy of Asia and Europe.

Although various forms of internal alchemy may be found throughout the nations of the Far East, the two main branches exist in India and China. Both have been influenced by the practices and beliefs of Buddhism, with the result that the systems overlap to a degree, yet they are distinct enough to be examined separately. Both systems of internal alchemy employ sexuality as an essential component.

The Eastern systems of internal alchemy differ from the sexual alchemy described in this book in that they generally do not involve the deliberate excretion of transmuted fluids of the body. Just the opposite is true—in most of the mainstream alchemical systems of the East, the semen is strenuously retained within the male body to conserve and transmute its energy. Exceptions to this rule are to be found in certain sects that emphasize the acquisition of magical powers above spiritual enlightenment, but the majority of the practitioners of the traditional Eastern alchemical systems condemn these sects as degenerate, perhaps in the belief that where ejaculation occurs, the goal must be sensual pleasure rather than spiritual growth.

In Hindu Tantra, ejaculation of the semen is usually permitted to occur after a prolonged period of sustained arousal, during which occult energies are generated and circulated throughout the body. Subsequent emission of the seed forms a type of sacrifice to the goddess Shakti. By contrast, in the Buddhist Tantra of India, Tibet, and other nations, ejaculation is for the most part avoided. The view is that when the seed is discharged, vitality is lost from the body. Sustained arousal generates occult power. By retaining the seed, this vitality is stored like electrical potential in a battery. Buddhists tend to believe that climax acts as a kind of short circuit in this process and frustrates its fulfillment.

This distinction is not absolute. It merely indicates a different philosophical emphasis concerning how the energies raised by sexual union with the Goddess should be manipulated. One Hindu sect advocates the oral consumption of the seed from the vagina of the *shakti* (human vessel of the Goddess) in order to reabsorb its power. In certain Buddhist practices the semen is emitted and consumed orally, or is reabsorbed directly into the penis after climax. This remarkable example of yogic muscular control causes the semen to be drawn backward through the urethra into the bladder.

The internal alchemy of India will be examined under the name of Tantra, and that of China will be referred to as Taoist alchemy. Although these terms are somewhat misleading, they are convenient for distinguishing the primary characteristics of each system.

Shakti and Shakta

In Hindu Tantra, the emphasis in placed upon the act of sexual union with the goddess Shakti, also known as Bhairavi (the Goddess) and Bhavani or Parvati in her role as wife of the god Shiva (also spelled Siva). When the union is of a symbolic nature and does not involve physical sex, it is said to be of the right-hand path (*dakshina marg*). When the union with Shakti involves actual sexual congress, it is said to be of the left-hand path (*vama marg*).

It is common to regard the term "left-hand path" as synonymous with evil. This arises from the traditional association in Western culture of the left side, and particularly the left hand, with darkness, the unconscious, and the Devil. The Latin word for the left hand is *sinister*. This connotation may be unwarranted in connection with Tantra. The term "left-hand path" stems from the Tantric practice of seating the woman who assists in the ritual and represents the Goddess on the left side of the practitioner when the sexual act is to be physically consummated, but on the right side when the sexual act is to be symbolic.[1]

Tantra literally means "loom" or "warp of the loom"—the framework or basis of doctrine. It is a broad term. By its own internal definition Tantra is the collection of religious writings (*shastra*) revealed by the god Shiva to serve as the scriptural guide during the fourth and present age of Kali (Kaliyuga).[2] Many works of Tantra have nothing to do with sexuality. However over the past century or so Tantra has come to mean specifically those texts that teach the worship of the Goddess in her various forms through sexual practices, either symbolic or actual. In Tantra the yogi courts and adores Shakti as a lover. He is called a *shakta*. During lovemaking, he conceives himself as an embodiment of the god Shiva, and his partner as an embodiment of the wife of Shiva, Bhavani, or Parvati.

Bhavani is the same as the great mother goddess Shakti, whose forms are innumerable. "She changes and transforms herself into a thousand shapes, and appears sometimes as a man and sometimes as a woman."[3] Shakti is able to appear in a male form because the Goddess is the essential power of all manifestation. She causes things to be, and is present in the things that have being. The power of Shiva, by contrast, is one of abstract conception. He is the seed that initiates the process of life, but is not himself the process or its product. In the diagram known as the Shri Yantra, which is the most important of all images dedicated to Shakti, Shiva is represented by the small dot (*bindu*) in the center of the downward-pointing triangle.

Yantra literally means instrument or tool. It is the symbol through which communication is established with the divinity who forms the object of worship. The worshipper first meditates upon the deity, then arouses the god or goddess within his or her own body, then projects this awakened deity into the yantra with the aid of mantras (sounds) and mudras (gestures). The yantra thus is quickened with the living awareness of the deity, who as a result may be welcomed and worshipped. A similar technique is employed to awaken a physical image of a deity such as a statue.

An important distinction must be made between yantras and mandalas. A mandala is an occult symbol, generally four-sided with a circular center, that may be used in the worship of any god or goddess, whereas a yantra is a symbol specific to a single deity. The Shri Yantra is devoted only to Shakti, and should not be used in the invocation of any other goddess.

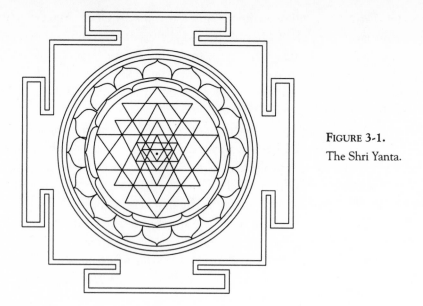

FIGURE 3-1.
The Shri Yanta.

The Five M's

The Hindu Tantra ritual involves the use of five *makaras* or sacraments. These are: *matsya* (fish), *mamsa* (meat), *madya* (wine), *mudra* (grain), and *maithuna* (copulation). In this context mudra does not mean ritual hand gestures, but parched grain fashioned into the shape of paddies or cakes, then fried. The Western equivalent is bread.

These are called the *pancatattva* (five elements) or, because all five words begin with the letter M, *pancamakara* (five M's). They were of three types, the literal (where "wine" means wine), the substitutional (where "wine" means something else, such as coconut milk), and the symbolic (where "wine" means the intoxication of transcendent awareness).

> For the worship of S'akti, the Pancatattva are declared to be essential. Without the Pancatattva in one form or another S'aktipuja [Goddess worship] cannot be performed (*Mahanirvana*, V. 23-24). The reason of this is that those who worship S'akti, worship Divinity as Creatrix and in the form of the universe. If She appears as and in natural function, She must be worshipped therewith, otherwise, as the Tantra cited says, worship is fruitless. The Mother

of the Universe must be worshipped with these five elements, namely, wine, meat, fish, grain and woman, or their substitutes.[4]

Partaking of some of these things is a violation of orthodox Hindu worship. Wine is forbidden to devout Hindus at all times. Eating anything is forbidden shortly before or during rituals, since they are directed to conduct their worship on an empty stomach. Beef is forbidden under all circumstances, yet it is often beef that forms the meat consumed during Tantric worship. Sex is definitely forbidden during worship.

The deliberate violation of sacred taboos during Tantric worship serves two functions. It liberates the mind from the constraints of conventional thinking and enables a fresh interpretation of the experience of worship. It is also an acceptance of the fact that the approach of Tantra to worship is to use those desires in human nature that are normally considered vices and impediments as instruments of salvation. This was always recognized as a path fraught with danger and liable to abuse:

> Let us consider what most contributes to the fall of a man, making him forget his duty, sink into sin and die an early death. First among these are wine and women, fish, meat, Mudra and accessories. By these things men have lost their manhood. S'iva then desires to employ these very poisons in order to eradicate the poison in the human system. Poison is the antidote for poison. This is the right treatment for those who long for drink or lust for women. The physician must, however, be an experienced one. If there be a mistake as to the application, the patient is likely to die. S'iva has said that the way of Kulacara is as difficult as it is to walk on the edge of a sword or to hold a wild tiger.[5]

The text quoted above was written for male readers, so "women" should be understood to signify sexual pleasure for its own sake. The author of the text asserts that Tantra is necessary in this degenerate Kaliyuga, which is the final age of the present cycle of the world. By one calculation, each cycle of 24,000 celestial years has an ascending and descending arc of 12,000 celestial years, and in each arc are four ages, each briefer and less exalted than the last: Satyayuga (4,800), Tretayuga (3,600), Dwaparayuga (2,400) and Kaliyuga (1,200). A celestial year is equal to 360 human years. The current age of Kali is dominated by lust. This is difficult to control because of the prevalence of ignorance. Because desire for sex cannot be suppressed in most individuals, its power may be used in worship. Through the controlled use of lust, lust is eventually overcome, and enlightenment attained.

Worship of the Goddess

Group worship takes place within a magic circle, called a chakra (chakra literally means "wheel"), that is formed out of the seated bodies of the Sadhakas (male worshippers) and Sadhikas (female worshippers). The shakti is seated on the left side of the Sadhaka. A Lord of the Chakra (Cakresvara) presides over the ritual, sitting with his own shakti in the center of the circle. There are various different kinds of chakra, and these produce different effects on the worshippers.

Traditionally, the woman who assumed the role of shakti was the wife of the practitioner. This was thought to reduce the likelihood that sexual worship would be undertaken for motives of mere sensual pleasure, or a desire for novel sexual experiences. An exception was made when the Sadhaka was unmarried, or his wife was incapable of sexual union. Then it was considered permissible to take another woman as his shakti. These substitutes were ordinarily chosen from the ranks of prostitutes or temple dancers. These women knew what was expected of them and were expert in the physical arts of love.

It is important to understand that the bond between a Sadhaka and his shakti is not casual. It was considered to be a lifetime commitment. Woodroffe wrote: "The proper rule, I am told, is that the relationship with such a S'akti should be of a permanent character; it being indeed held that a S'akti who is abandoned by the Sadhaka takes away with her the latter's merit (Punya). The position of such a S'akti may be described as a wife 'in religion' for the Sadhaka."[6] It was thought essential that the shakti be of similar intelligence and occupy the same plane of spiritual evolution. She must have an equal degree of skill in ritual as the Sadhaka.

A distinction was made between a shakti who was to be worshipped as the Goddess incarnate and a shakti who represented some lesser female aspect of the Goddess, and might be united with sexually. As a substitute for sexual intercourse it was considered permissible to worship the feet of the Goddess.

> I may observe that because there is a S'akti in the Cakra it does not follow that there is sexual intercourse, which, when it occurs in the worship of householders, ordinarily takes place outside the Cakra. S'aktis are of two kinds—those who are enjoyed (Bhogya S'akti) and those who are worshipped only (Pujya) as earthly representatives of the Supreme Mother of all. Those who yield to desire, even in thought, as regards the latter commit the sin of incest with their mother. Similarly, there is a widespread practice amongst all Saktas of worship of Virgins (Kumaripuja)—a very beautiful ceremony.[7]

Dust from the Feet

In some sects at least, the "feet" of the Goddess seems to have been a euphemism for the vulva, just as in ancient Greece the "thigh" was a code word for the penis (Pythagoras is fabled to have gone about showing those he took a fancy to his "golden thigh"[8]). The feet of the Goddess specifically refers to the muladhara chakra of the human body, which is located at the perineum between the genitals and the anus. The muladhara is the residence of Kundalini, she who is Shakti in the microcosm.

Even where intercourse was not held with the shakti, the products of her genitals—urine, sexual fluid, and menstrual blood—were sometimes gathered and used for magical purposes within the Kalacakra, the circle or cult that worshipped the Goddess in the form of Kali the Destroyer. The "feet" of the Goddess are said in one commentary to be "like soft cotton" and "colored red with dyed cotton."[9] Mention is made of "red dust" which covers the "feet" of Shakti. Kenneth Grant interprets this to mean "the dust of the Feet of the Mother that manifests in the menstrual effluvia of the second and third day's periodic flow."[10]

The urine of the shakti was collected and drunk for a variety of occult purposes, including the curing of disease, the stimulation of occult faculties and the awakening and raising of Kundalini up the central channel (*shushumna*) of the body. It was one of the substitutes for *madya*, the wine of pancatattva worship. Her feces were sometimes burned to a white ash and spread upon her body. These ashes were ritually washed off the feet of the shakti during worship and mixed with wine in a special consecrated chalice, then consumed by the Sadhakas.[11]

Perhaps the most valued of the genital secretions of the shakti was the clear fluid produced during sexual arousal. This was permitted to drip from the vulva of the shakti while she maintained one of several ritual postures within the chakra, and was collected upon a bhurja leaf laid beneath her for this purpose. In order to maintain the purity of this supreme elixir, the shakti was never touched. "If the *suvasini* is so much as touched during this transcendental state, the fluids are darkened and become venomous."[12]

Needless to say, the magical manipulation of bodily secretions is one of the darkest and most closely hidden aspects of Tantra worship. It is commonly referred to only obliquely, if at all.

> There are some things the ordinary man looks upon as 'unclean' and, as long as he does so, to offer such a thing [to the Goddess] would be an offence. But,

if to his 'equal eye' these things are not so, they might be given. Thus the Vira-sadhana of the *S'akta Tantra* makes ritual use of what will appear to most to be impure and repulsive substances. This (as the *Jnanarnava Tantra* says) is done to accustom the worshipper not to see impurity in them but to regard them as all else, as manifestation of Divinity. He is taught that there is nothing impure in itself in natural functions though they be made, by misuse or abuse, the instruments of impurity.[13]

Union with Shakti

Although it was common in Hindu Tantra to worship the Goddess as virgin or mother, sexual intercourse did occur, and sometimes assumed curious forms that might in more conservative quarters be classed as orgiastic or degenerate. During group sexual rites, where the shakti was selected for each Sadhaka at random by a form of lot drawing that involved the garments of the women, intercourse occurred even when a man drew the bodice or jacket of his own mother or sister. This indicates that in some forms of Tantra the distinction between the shakti of the Goddess and the shakti of her devas was not respected, and that ritual intercourse was practiced with the Mother Goddess herself, through her human female representatives, by her male worshippers.

> A Pandit friend tells me that the Siddhamalarahasya describes a rite (Cuda-cakra) in which fifty Siddha Viras go with fifty S'aktis, each man getting his companion by lot by selecting one out of a heap of the S'akti's jackets (Cuda). His S'akti is the woman to whom the jacket belongs. In the Snehacakra (Love Cakra), the Siddha Viras pair with the S'aktis according as they have a liking for them. Anandabhuvanayoga is another unknown rite performed with not less than three and not more than one hundred and eight S'aktis who surround the Vira. He unites with one S'akti (Bhogya S'akti) and touches the rest. In the Urna Cakra (Urna = spider's web) the Viras sit in pairs tied to one another with cloths.[14]

Very possibly the cloths were stained with menstrual blood. It is also likely that in the rite of Anandabhuvanayoga the shaktis were stimulated to the point of repeated orgasm by the hands of the Vira. As Woodroffe correctly observes, these rites were intended to generate magic power rather than to serve primarily as worship. They did not form the regular observances of Tantra, but were extraordinary exceptions conducted for specific purposes. For example, the Cudacakra was done to insure success for the rajas in imminent military battles.

Kundalini Shakti

On the level of the microcosm or human body, the goal of Hindu Tantra is the awakening of Kundalini Shakti in the lowest energy wheel, the muladhara chakra, and her elevation through the esoteric channel known as the shushumna to the sahasrara region at the crown of the head, where she unites with Shiva and showers down the nectar of bliss. Kundalini is also known by such descriptive titles as the serpent power and the fire snake. She is conceived in the form of a fiery serpent that lies coiled in three and one-half turns near the base of the spine at the perineum.

Worship of Shakti awakens the fiery serpent of Kundalini. The awakening of Kundalini is signaled by spontaneous tumescence in the sexual organs. In men the penis becomes erect. In women the same erection takes place in the clitoris, and the labia become more prominent. The sexual organs of both men and women secrete copious amounts of fluids whose mundane purpose is lubrication during coitus.

Kundalini is awakened by controlled breathing exercises accompanied by rhythmic contraction of the anal sphincter while seated in certain yoga postures believed to facilitate the purpose. Mantra, the repetition of certain significant words or sounds, is also employed, along with visualization of various forms of the Goddess and her occult symbols such as the Shri Yantra. There is an elaborate structure of mantras and visual symbolism for raising the serpent power.

Kundalini is Shakti manifesting herself within the human body. Kundalini is conceived as both an esoteric energy and a goddess. She is not a goddess that dwells within the human body, but Shakti expressing herself through the human body with the organs and energies of the human body. Kundalini Shakti is present in both men and women.

Chakras of the Microcosm

Kundalini yoga has its own occult physiology. In the process of raising the serpent power up the shushumna, which corresponds roughly with the spinal column, a series of knots or ganglia must be pierced. These blockages along the shushumna are known as chakras, but should not be confused with the chakras, or ritual circles, of pancatattva worship.

There are various numbers given for the chakras of the human body, which are believed to lie in other places besides along the spinal column, but those through which Kundalini passes on her journey to the crown of the head are the most important. These are usually said to be six in number. The crown of the head is linked to the god Shiva, and is known as the sahasrara. It is not, strictly speaking, a chakra, but the place where Kundalini Shakti unites with Shiva.

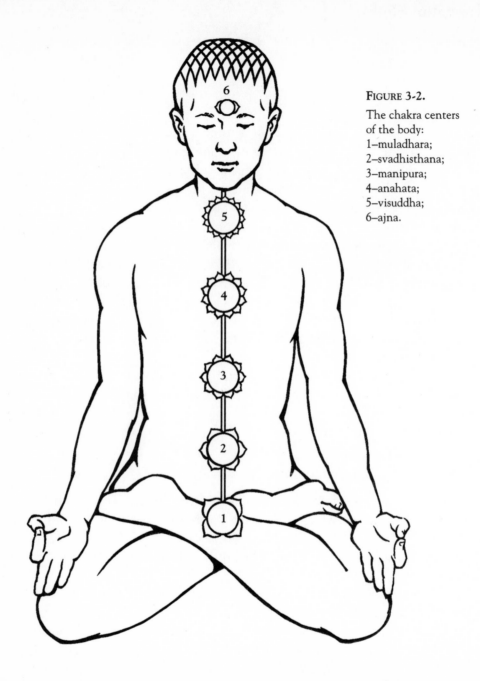

FIGURE 3-2.

The chakra centers
of the body:
1–muladhara;
2–svadhisthana;
3–manipura;
4–anahata;
5–visuddha;
6–ajna.

The lowest chakra is the muladhara. It is located at the perineum and is the dwelling place of sleeping Kundalini. The second chakra is the svadhisthana, located in the pelvic region at the level of the genitals. The third chakra is the manipura, located in the abdomen. The fourth is the anahata chakra, located at the level of the heart. The fifth is the visuddha chakra, located at the base of the throat. The sixth is the ajna chakra, located between the eyebrows (see Figure 3-2 at left).

Muladhara is described as a closed lotus with its petals turned downward when Kundalini lies sleeping. When the Goddess awakens, this lotus expands and glows a dull red color with a bright scarlet center. The lotus turns its petals upward. As Kundalini ascends, she encounters the barriers of the chakras, which only become perceptible in resisting her progress. The piercing of each chakra may cause pain and even temporary illness. Sometimes Kundalini leaps or bypasses a chakra that is difficult to pierce. When at last the head of the fiery serpent touches the base of the skull, bliss both physical and spiritual is experienced.

In my own rituals I have succeeded in piercing all of the chakras, and can state from personal experience that they are arranged in a row up the center of the torso, and located near the front of the body—they are not located on the spine itself. I have never experienced their successive upward piercing in order, as though Kundalini were climbing the rungs of a ladder, but have felt them become active individually, as well as in pairs and trines. There is no awareness of the chakras until they become active, but when active it is impossible to remain unaware of them, since they produce powerful and distinct sensations.

The muladhara feels like a tight, hard knot in the perineum, about the size of a Ping-Pong ball. Svadhisthana is felt as a drawing or pulling below the surface of the pubic triangle. Manipura produces a very curious feeling in the lower abdomen, a kind of sucking pit, as though a fist were being pressed down into the base of the belly to make a hollow. The awakening of anahata causes the heart to palpitate and sometimes to skip beats—the heart almost seems to flutter like a trapped bird. Visuddha shows its presence as a tightness and tickling at the base of the throat, which has at times evoked from me a very dry cough. Ajna is a difficult feeling to describe, but feels something like a fingertip pressed gentle against the forehead between the eyebrows from the inside of the head, a kind of tension or pulling. The initial stimulation of sahasrara is accompanied by a pricking exactly in the center of the top of the skull. This pricking is very localized—it covers an area no larger than the head of a nail. The entire scalp on the top of the head feels tightly stretched, almost as though a tight rubber shower cap were on the head. I have also felt a distinct coolness on the surface of my brain when sahasrara is stimulated.

Tantra in Buddhism

In the Buddhist Tantra of India and Tibet, sexual union with a living shakti is seldom used. Instead, various deities are visualized within mandalas and the chakras of the body. Historically, Buddhism has had a strongly puritanical strain running through its teachings. It has preferred to distance itself from sexual acts, and teaches that the semen should not be ejaculated during arousal generated during meditations. "Buddhist Tantra lays little stress on the lowest lotus, knows no Kundalini, and prefers to omit the lotus behind the genitals."[15]

In theory Buddhism is atheistic, and does not recognize a supreme deity, or group of deities, to be worshipped, but rather seeks to manipulate anthropomorphic forms of different aspects of mind. Its gods, spirits, and demons are viewed as illusions, but instead of denying their existence Buddhists seek to use these supernatural beings to achieve enlightenment. In practice, the average devout, poorly educated Buddhist perceives the gods in a way that is very similar, if not identical, to that of his Hindu neighbor. I refer here to living Buddhism, as practiced by ordinary men and women in the East, not the style of intellectual Buddhism that has become popular among well-educated Westerners.

For at least three hundred years the Tantric beliefs and practices of Hindus and Buddhists have been merged together, so that it is very difficult to draw precise distinctions between them. This division is made more difficult by the multiplicity of beliefs and cults in both religions. In Tibet, the goddess Green Tara appears to have fulfilled the role of Shakti in her sexual aspect, and White Tara that of Shakti in her benign mother aspect. Tantric practices in Tibet are further complicated by the influence of the shamanic Bon religion, which existed in Tibet before the coming of Buddhism, and undoubtedly possessed its own sexual mysteries.

Taoist Alchemy

The internal alchemy of China found expression in Taoist alchemy. When this began, around the fourth century B.C., it had the same two goals familiar to us from Western alchemy—the manufacture of gold and the Elixir of eternal life. Chinese alchemy relied on external materials in its early centuries of development, and in fact was virtually identical in its approach and procedures to Western alchemy. It was even held in the same disdain by lawmakers as an art of trickery and deceit. In 144 B.C. the making of gold by alchemical means was forbidden by the Chinese emperor on the grounds that it promoted dishonesty.

By the sixth century the pursuit of gold had been forgotten, and Taoist alchemy had turned all its efforts inward in an attempt to create the Elixir. The terms of conventional external alchemy were retained, but were reapplied to different occult parts and energies of the human body. The body itself became the Hermetic vessel. As is so often the case with ancient texts, the writers assumed all their readers to be male. Consequently, the description that follows applies to the male practitioner, but female readers should understand that the same techniques can be applied, with minor and obvious modifications, to their own practice.

Taoist alchemy is based on the belief that there is a life-force that is responsible for health and longevity. This force manifests itself most plainly as sexual desire and procreation. In men, it is naturally concentrated in the semen. When semen is emitted, some of this life-force is lost. The goal of Taoist alchemy is to retain the semen within the body and transmute it into vitality, for the purposes of better health and longer life. This is accomplished by circulating the generative force within the body until it is sublimated into vitality.

There are striking similarities in the description of the circulation of the generative force and the raising of Kundalini. It is clear that the same fundamental psycho-physiological process is at work in both cases. Both involve sexual arousal. Both are based on raising an internal force upward along the central core of the body from the genital region to the head. In both cases this is accomplished in successive stages.

Generative force is accumulated by the curious practice of gathering saliva in the mouth until the mouth is full and swallowing it. This is accomplished by straightening the neck as you swallow. It is asserted that unless this is done, the saliva will not form the proper type of generative force, and will have a harmful effect on the body. An increase in the generative force promotes erection of the penis. It is only when the penis is erect that the force may be circulated and transmuted.

Those who are old and have difficulty experiencing spontaneous erection are instructed to use masturbation to erect the penis, but this is not carried on to the point of ejaculation. Another approach is to practice the alchemical circulation of the generative force when erection occurs in sleep—presumably the practitioner is expected to wake up, or to arrange to be awakened, at the proper hour, the hour of *tsu* (midnight). Following the principles of Yin and Yang, the first half of the day (midnight to noon) is positive or Yang, while the second half of the day (noon to midnight) is negative or Yin. The alchemist Lu K'uan Yü writes: "It is important to avail oneself of this moment when the penis stands to gather the generative force for sublimation, for the gathering of it during the negative half of the day is ineffective."[16]

Generative force is accumulated in the cauldron, a region in the abdomen just below the navel and toward the back of the body. Blood that circulates to the cauldron is changed into this generative force. Saliva swallowed in the proper manner also creates this force in the cauldron. The cauldron is heated by means of an inner fire that is lit in the stove below it in the region of the genitals. This is ignited by reg-ulated breaths. By drawing air deeply into the lower abdomen, pressure is applied to the stove, igniting the fire and heating the cauldron.

It is important not to confuse the energy in the air, called *ch'i,* with the generative energy inherent in the body. Teachings existed based upon the accumulation of ch'i through breathing exercises, and the transmutation of this energy into the vital alchem-ical agent, but these are said to be false teachings.[17] The force undergoing transmutation cannot be drawn into the body from the outside, but is already present within the body in the region of the stove. It can, however, be strengthened by accumulating ch'i.

Circulation of the Generative Force

When the breath is drawn in and pressed downward upon the lower abdomen, both the fire in the stove and the generative force in the cauldron rise along a channel that extends up the region of the spine to the head. This back channel is called the chan-nel of control (*tu mo*). When the breath is exhaled, the generative force is allowed to descend down a channel in the front of the body that runs through the face, chest and abdomen. The front channel is called the channel of function (*jen mo*).

This whole process is known as circulating the generative force in microcosmic orbit. Each orbit purifies the force a little more. The orbit begins at the base of the spine (first gate), ascends to between the kidneys (second gate), and from there to the back of the head (third gate), from where it moves on to an occult cavity in the brain. From the brain it is allowed to descend down the front of the body.

Readers familiar with the writings of Israel Regardie may notice that this circula-tion of the vital force up the back and down the front of the body is very similar to a technique Regardie described in his expanded version of the Golden Dawn ritual of the Middle Pillar. Regardie believed the circulation of light in the Middle Pillar Exer-cise to be of immense value and to possess "infinite possibilities."[18] Regardie's circula-tion of light is described, in a more limited way, in the documents of the Golden Dawn. It is unlikely that S. L. MacGregor Mathers, the leader of the Golden Dawn who was the creator of most of its magical methods, deliberately imitated the Taoist technique. This suggests that there is a real physiological mechanism at work in the microcosmic orbiting of subtle forces in the body.

After the generative force has circulated for a number of times, it is purified and changed into the alchemical agent. The cauldron, which is not fixed but mobile along the central column of the body, rises to the level of the solar plexus. Here it is called the middle cauldron. Within the middle cauldron the alchemical agent is transmuted into vitality. In Taoist alchemical terminology this vitality is known as

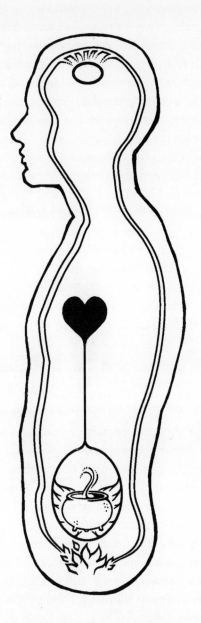

FIGURE 3-3.
Circulation of the generative force in Taoist alchemy.

lead. When the vitality has been purified in the middle cauldron, the cauldron rises to the brain, where it is known as the precious cauldron. Here vitality is transmuted into spirit. In alchemical terminology, this spirit is known as mercury.

To restore the transmuted generative force, the inner fire is circulated up the back channel and down the front channel of the body with the aid of controlled breaths. As the fire passes through four cardinal points in its orbit, it is sublimated. This is known as the inner copulation of the positive (Yang) and negative (Yin) principles. Spirit develops in the brain and a bright light manifests itself. This is the preparation of the golden Elixir. The spirit is forced down the central channel of the body, known as the thrusting channel, into the occult center below the navel.

Through the use of the breath the transmuted agents are forced up and down the central thrusting channel between the brain and the lower center, in the process becoming ever more refined and potent, until at last "the heavenly gate at the top of the head" is forced open, and the spirit is able to leave the body entirely to inhabit "countless bodies in space."[19] The opening of the crown of the skull is another aspect of Taoist alchemy that appears in Hindu and Buddhist Tantra. There is a technique in yoga for actually inducing a small fissure in the scalp at the top of the head solely through meditative practices, without the application of any physical instrument. As a sign of success, the guru (teacher) inserts a blade of grass into the newly opened fissure, where it stands upright from the shaven skull of the chela (disciple).

Distinction Between Tantra and Taoist Alchemy

Little or no attention is paid to the Goddess in Taoist alchemy. Yet she is implicitly present, since without her to cause arousal and the erection of the penis the fundamental beginning of the alchemical practice could not be successfully completed. However, the approach of Taoist alchemy is not to rejoice in the arousal generated by the Goddess, as is the case in Hindu Tantra, but to seek to completely invert and transmute it into spiritual energy.

Taoist alchemy seeks to "turn back the flow of generative force to fortify the body so that it will be restored to its original condition before puberty and cause the penis to cease standing during sleep and to retract."[20] The expression of sexuality in the body, particularly by erection and ejaculation, is perceived as debilitating and destructive, to be frustrated by any means. At those times when the alchemist cannot resist sexual climax, he is directed to press hard at the base of his penis to seal the "mortal gate" so that the semen is not emitted from the body.

In Hindu Tantra, the Goddess Shakti is externalized and worshipped in the form of a mortal woman with sexual congress that frequently climaxes with emission of the semen. In some sects, the semen and other sexual secretions of the body of the shakti and the Sadhaka may be reabsorbed orally. In Buddhist Tantra the Goddess is internalized. Imagined union may be held with lesser spiritual beings, variously known as *dakinis* or *yoginis*, but Kundalini Shakti is never worshipped and ejaculation is avoided even though sexual pleasure may be prolonged and intense. In Taoist alchemy, arousal of the penis is perceived to be a necessary evil and merely a means to an end—dangerous and to be minimized because it may result in unintentional emission with a consequent loss of generative force.

Although the attitude and methods of Taoist alchemy differ from those of Tantra, both Hindu and Buddhist, as do its intermediate goals, the ultimate goal is the same—to transmute sexual energy into spiritual energy. It is clear from this brief summary that a single underlying mechanism is at work in both esoteric systems. Sexual alchemy relies upon this basic physiological response, which is universal, but emphasizes different aspects of it, one of which is a satisfying physical and emotional relationship with a spiritual being. The pursuit of pleasure through loving sexual union with spirits (known in Hindu Tantra under the name Prayoga) was condemned by orthodox Tantrists and Taoists alike, but was not an uncommon experience, and was by no means universally abhorred.

{ 4 }

Sex in Western Alchemy

Origin of Alchemy

The fundamental purpose of all forms of alchemy is transmutation. The word "alchemy" means the art of changing of one substance into another substance (Arab: *al-kimia*—"the transmutation," sometimes rendered the "Egyptian art" because the Egyptians were renowned for their alchemy). Western alchemy was driven by the efforts of natural philosophers to change common or base metals into silver and gold. They sought this transmutation mainly for the purpose of making themselves wealthy and powerful, and used external physical instruments and substances. Their efforts, continued over many centuries, laid the basis for modern chemistry.

Several fables exist that pretend to relate the origins of alchemy. By one account, it descends from the teachings of the Graeco-Egyptian god Hermes Trismegistus, who was a god of wisdom credited with many inventions, among them cards, dice, gambling, writing, and numbers. In the Middle Ages alchemy became known as the Hermetic art. The common term "hermetically sealed" comes from the practice of alchemists of putting the graphic symbol, or seal, of Hermes upon their vessels.

Another legend, which is more significant in the context of sexual alchemy, states that alchemy was one of the forbidden arts taught to the sons of the women who were taken in lust by the rebellious angels of heaven, who had descended to the Earth in order to obtain sexual congress with these mortal women. This is related in the third century by the alchemical writer Zosimus of Panopolis. The legend is based upon Genesis 6:4—"There were giants in the earth in those days: and also after that, when the sons of God came in unto the daughters of men, and they bare children to them, the same became mighty men where were of old, men of renown."

Because the half-human and half-angel offspring of the unions between mortal women and the fallen angels were children of the angels, the angels sought to pass on to them a legacy of knowledge. One of the forbidden subjects taught by the angels was alchemy, if we are to believe Zosimus and other writers who adhere to this account. It was to punish mankind for the abuse of these forbidden secret arts that God caused the Flood.

The magical instruction of mankind by the fallen angels is mentioned in the Book of Enoch, which states:

> And Azazel taught men to make swords, and knives, and shields, and breast-plates, and made known to them the metals (of the earth) and the art of working them, and bracelets, and ornaments, and the use of antimony, and the beautifying of the eyelids, and all kinds of costly stones, and all coloring tinctures. And there arose much godlessness, and they committed fornication, and they were led astray, and became corrupt in all their ways. Semjaza taught enchantments, and root-cuttings, Armaros the resolving of enchantments, Baraqijal (taught) astrology, Kokabel the constellations, Ezeqeel the knowledge of the clouds (Araqiel the signs of the earth, Shamsiel the signs of the sun), and Sariel the course of the moon.[1]

Faux Alchemy

Azazel was one of the leaders of the rebel angels. In some portions of the text he is identified as the supreme leader. It may be that the "working" of metals included alchemical transformation, since "coloring tinctures" are mentioned. One of the main purposes of early alchemy was to impart a golden color to silver, or alloys of silver, to be worked into jewelry, with the intent that it should be mistaken for genuine gold. Another aspect of early Graeco-Egyptian alchemy was the coloring of semiprecious stones to simulate precious stones of greater value, and the heightening of color and concealing of flaws in gems so that they could be sold for a greater price.

These questionable practices gave alchemy a bad reputation. The Egyptians were masters at imitating costly metals, minerals such as turquoise and lapis lazuli, enameling, and gem stones that were used in the construction of jewelry and other ornaments. Some of their secrets have baffled chemists and artisans to the present day. It was as a criminal art of false appearance that alchemy first became notorious among the Greeks and Romans who lived beside and traded with the Egyptians in the great city of Alexandria.

The Angelic Connection

Even though alchemy was usually regarded as a purely physical art of deception by the Egyptians, Greeks, and Romans, the ancient connection between congress with spirits and the acquisition of the power of transmutation cannot be overlooked. It suggests that as early as before the time of the Cæsars, alchemy may have had a higher, esoteric purpose, although this esoteric aspect of the art was never openly described.

It is significant that from earliest mentions alchemy has been linked to the fallen angels. The knowledge of transmutation and other secrets are usually represented as payments given by the angels in return for the pleasure of sexual union with human beings. However, it is reasonable to speculate that something more important than pleasure was involved, and that the fallen angels were compensating mankind for esoteric energies generated by the act of human-angel sex, energies that can be generated in no other manner. This biblical fable is an allegory concerning the underlying nature of the relationship that exists between human and spirit lovers.

The Magic of Babylon

Toward the end of the fourth century a shift of emphasis occurred in the way the general population perceived alchemy. Prior to this, it had been known as an art of deception that could be used to simulate the false appearance of costly jewels and precious metals. It gradually came to be viewed as an occult art by which base metals might be transmuted into genuine silver and gold.

This change of attitude was probably inspired by mystical teachings that made their way westward from Babylon. The astrological glyphs for the seven wandering bodies of the heavens began to be used as symbols for the common metals around this period. The importance of observing astrological times in alchemical operations came to be generally recognized. The Greek alchemist pseudo-Democritus claimed to have studied the art under Ostanes the Mede. The practices of the Persian Magi were mentioned by other authorities such as Zosimus and Synesius.

Theory of Transmutation

A theory was developed to account for transmutation. All substances were said to be composed of a *prima materia* or first matter, which was differentiated into all the substances in the world by various overlying impurities that obscured its essential nature. After removing these imposed qualities from the first matter, alchemists hoped to use it in the creation of gold or silver by imposing the desired qualities that would yield the substance they sought.

The purified prima materia was treated with modified sulfur (or sulfur and arsenic) to produce either the White or the Red Powder. The White Powder was credited with the power of transmuting base metal into silver. The Red Powder was believed to transmute base metal into gold. In theory, any material might be changed into gold, but the transformation was easiest when it involved a substance that was already very similar to gold in its qualities. Thus, alchemists might employ the White Powder with copper to create silver, and the Red Powder with mercury or silver to create gold.

Stages of the Alchemical Process

Details of the alchemical operation vary greatly from author to author, and from century to century, but the overall process involved three main phases: the blackening, the whitening, and the reddening of the material contained in the alchemical vessel (*vas Hermetis*). In earliest times there were four stages, but the third stage, known as the yellowing, which formed a transition from the white to the red stage, was dropped during the fifteenth century.

The production of blackness (*negredo*) was necessary as a foundation for the work. This was achieved by separating the elements (*separatio*), then combining them in a union of opposites (*conjuctio*) that was conceived as the sexual union of male and female (*coitus*) which was sanctified as a kind of alchemical marriage (*matrimonium*). The sexual act brings about the death (*mortificatio*) of the product of the union. By corruption of the corpse (*putrefactio*) the desired blackness is at last obtained.

The chaotic black product (*massa confusa*) is then washed (*ablutio*) in the same way a corpse might be washed in preparation for burial. This ritual washing (*baptisma*) calls back the soul (*anima*) that was released by death, bringing about a resurrection of the corpse in a peacock's tail (*cauda pavonis*) of many colors (*omnes colores*). The metaphor is that of the risen phoenix reborn from its own dead body. The many colors merge into whiteness (*albedo*), which contains all colors. This is the White Powder (*tinctura alba*) or White Stone (*lapis albus*) that is the lunar condition, capable of transmuting lesser metals into silver.

To make the White Powder into the Red (*rubedo*), the alchemical vessel is heated to the highest possible intensity. This generates the Red Powder which has the ability to transmute silver, mercury, and lesser metals into pure gold.

The Philosopher's Stone

Some alchemists distinguished the White Powder of the Moon and the Red Powder of the Sun from the Philosopher's Stone, which they represented as the product of a "chymical wedding" between these opposite tinctures, the royal marriage of the Queen and King. This stage should not be confused with the conjunction of opposite elements that occurs during the generation of the blackness at the beginning of the alchemical work. The marriage of the White and Red powders is a royal marriage, the marriage of the elements a common marriage.

The Stone of the philosophers (*lapis philosophorum*) is often confused by alchemical writers with the Red Powder, and with the first matter (*prima materia*) that underlies it, and with the universal panacea or Elixir of Life (*elixir vitae*), which was also sometimes known as potable gold (*aurum potabile*) because it was drunk in liquid form. It is the Azoth, a word formed from the combination of the first and last letters in the Latin, Greek, and Hebrew alphabets—A plus Z, Alpha (A) plus Omega (Ω), Aleph (א) plus Tau (ת).

The Philosopher's Stone is even given the attributes of a living spiritual entity and called the God of the Earth (*Deus terrestris*) and the Son of the Macrocosm (*filius macrocosmi*). These two beings are more or less equivalent to Adam Kadmon and the Microprosopus of the Jewish mystical system known as the Kabbalah. Basically, they are two sides of the same coin. One is God descended into the world in a human form; the other is man ascended into heaven in a divine form.

As the literature of alchemy evolved over the centuries, it became increasingly mystical. Whereas in its beginning simple chemical operations alone were believed sufficient to create the Stone, in the Middle Ages prayers and personal observances were thought to be essential to success. Not just anyone could transmute, but only a man (there were few women alchemists) who had purified himself, in effect refining the prima materia in his own human nature. Alchemy could not be worked without the intimate spiritual involvement of the man who worked it.

The Stone, the Elixir, and the Homunculus

The two primary material works of medieval Western alchemy, the Philosopher's Stone of transmutation and the Elixir of eternal life, are similar in nature and were often confused in alchemical texts. However, there is an important distinction to be drawn between them. The Philosopher's Stone, a solid which may be subdivided into the White and Red powders, was believed able to transform macrocosmic physical substances—things in the larger outer world. The Elixir, which has a liquid form, was thought capable of transforming microcosmic human nature, both physical and spiritual. It cured disease, extended the term of life or made it eternal, and purified the soul.

The Elixir took effect when it was drunk. Although some believed that the Philosopher's Stone needed only to be touched to an object to transform it, the actual operation was somewhat more involved. A small portion of the Red Powder was mixed into the molten metal that was to undergo transmutation. It appears to have exerted a kind of catalytic action, and was capable of converting many thousands of times its own weight of base metal into gold. The more perfect the Stone, the more powerful its action.

It is important to notice that even though the alchemist participated in the purification of the prima materia with prayers, fasts, austerities, and ritual observances, he usually did not contribute any physical thing from his own body. The exception to this was in the creation of the homunculus, a small spiritual being in the form of a human child that was grown inside a sealed alchemical vessel from the semen of the alchemist. This was presumably procured through masturbation. The homunculus is an operation of genuine sexual alchemy, as I have defined the term in this work.

Sexual Imagery in Alchemy

Sexual imagery plays a key role in alchemical texts, which are filled with illustrations showing a woman and a man making love. These are symbolic representations of the union of the Moon and the Sun, the opposites of nature that are also represented in the White and Red powders. As mentioned above, coitus was one of the stages of alchemical transformation. In the *Rosarium Philosophorium*, an alchemical work published in 1550, below the image of a crowned man and women making love, with the Sun at the feet of the man and the Moon at the feet of the woman, occurs the following caption:

> O Luna, folded by my embrace,
> Be you as strong as I, as fair of face.
> O Sol, brightest of all lights known to men,
> And yet you need me, as the cock the hen.[2]

The prevalence of sexual imagery in alchemy raises a question as to how much of alchemical sex was symbolic and how much was physical on the part of the alchemist. The literature makes no explicit mention of sexual practices by the alchemist, but since ritualistic observances such as purifications and prayers were believed necessary, it is not beyond the bounds of speculation that some alchemists used sexual observances, either alone or in the company of a partner, to forward the progress of their experiments. Credence is lent to this notion by the use of semen in the making of the homunculus. It is possible that one of the secret ingredients of alchemy, never mentioned in any of the written texts, was the sexual ecstasy of the alchemist.

Nicholas Flammel and Perrenella

Nicholas Flammel, who was widely believed to have successfully created the Philosopher's Stone after a lifetime of searching, conducted his experiments in the company of his wife, Perrenella, and with her active help. If that help involved the raising of sexual energy, this may account for Flammel's success. Regarding the projection of the Red Powder upon mercury, Flammel wrote:

> I may speak it with truth, I have made it three times, with the help of Perrenella, who understood it as well as I, because she helped in my operations, and without doubt, if she would have enterprised to have done it alone, she had attained to the end and perfection thereof.[3]

This quotation suggests that if there is a sexual energy involved in the actual act of transmutation, it issues from the female, not the male. This would be in accord with Eastern philosophy, which personifies the creative power of nature as the goddess

Shakti, who alone can bring forth ideal forms into manifestation. The opposite masculine power of Shakta or Shiva is creative in an abstract or conceptual sense, but the fulfillment of the creative impulse that originates with Shiva can only be realized by the goddess Shakti.

The Marriage of Opposites

In the manufacture of the Philosopher's Stone, two sexes appear to be necessary. Concerning the alchemical stage of *coitus*, Flammel wrote:

> I made then to be painted here two bodies, one of a Male and another of a Female, to teach thee that in this second operation thou hast truly, but yet not perfectly, two natures, conjoined and married together, the Masculine and the Feminine; . . . whereof the one hath conceived by the other and by this conception it is turned into the body of the Male, and the Male into that of the Female; that is to say, they are made one only body, which is the Androgyne, or Hermaphrodite of the Ancients . . . which (if they be guided and governed wisely) can form an Embrion in the womb of the Vessel, and afterwards bring forth a most puissant King, invincible and incorruptible, because it will be an admirable quintessence.[4]

Flammel used images of himself and of his wife, Perrenella, to represent the male and female in his series of alchemical emblems, which he caused to be painted in 1413 upon an arch in St. Innocents churchyard in Paris. It may be that the sexual allusions are purely metaphorical. This is the usual interpretation of such imagery. However, it is possible that some spiritualized ritual sexual congress is intended.

The Elixir of Immortality

Flammel continued with this same sexual imagery in describing the creation of the Elixir of Life from the marriage of the White and Red powders, which he characterized as two dragons or sperms. Referring to an emblematic image that shows two dragons locked together in battle, or lovemaking, he wrote:

> Look well upon these two Dragons, for they are the true principles of beginnings of this Philosophy, which the sages have not dared to show to their own children. He which is undermost without wings, he is the fixed or the male; that which is uppermost is the volatile, or the female, black and obscure, which goes

about to get the domination for many months. The first is called Sulphur, or heat and dryness; and the latter Argent-vive [quicksilver], or cold and moisture; these are the Sun and the Moon of the Mercurial source, and sulphurous original, which, by continual fire, are adorned with royal habiliments; that, being united and afterwards changed into a quintessence, they may overcome everything Metallic, how solid, hard and strong soever it be. . . . These two sperms, saith Democritus, are not found upon the earth of the living; the same saith Avicen, but he addeth that they gather them from the dung, odour and rottenness of the Sun and Moon. O, happy are they that know how to gather them, for of them they afterwards make a treacle, which hath power over all grief, maladies, sorrows, infirmities and weaknesses, and which fighteth puissantly against death, lengthening the life, according to the permission of God, even to the time determined, triumphing over the miseries of this world, and filling a man with the riches thereof.[5]

Treacle was a medicinal preparation chiefly composed of the fat of serpents. In classical mythology serpents are credited with the power to restore life. The snake is the beast of Hermes. Seen coiled about his staff, called a caduceus, twin serpents have become the emblem of the modern medical profession. Flammel uses treacle as a metaphor for the Elixir, which is to be prepared from the "two sperms" not to be found "upon the earth of the living," yet paradoxically prepared from the "dung, odour and rottenness of the Sun and Moon."

Did Flammel Use Sexual Alchemy?

It is possible to interpret Flammel's imagery in purely chemical terms. This is the usual approach. The male dragon is viewed as some modified form of sulfur, and the female dragon as a preparation of quicksilver. However, there is another possible interpretation. If it is assumed that Flammel is speaking about sexual products of the human body, then the female dragon becomes menstrual blood and the male dragon semen. These are not common blood and semen, but blood and semen that have been refined and spiritualized so that, in the words of the alchemical writer pseudo-Democritus, they are "not found upon the earth of the living."

This explains how the two sperms can be at one and the same time spiritual, yet gathered from the "dung, odour and rottenness of the Sun and Moon." The sexual organs are united with the organs that excrete solid and liquid wastes from the human body. In ancient times this juxtaposition was seen as a mystery—why did God place the organs of generation, surely the most holy of all acts, together with the organs of excretion, the foulest function of the body? Semen and menstrual blood truly do spring from the "dung, odour and rottenness" of incarnate humanity.

Menstrual blood was regarded as the occult female equivalent of semen. It is red and semen is white, yet in uniting to form an alchemical hermaphrodite each is transmuted into the other, so that the red menstrual blood becomes the source of the White Powder, and the white semen becomes the source of the Red Powder. From this androgyne is born an "Embrion" or embryo in the "womb of the Vessel." This embryo may be the homunculus, the Philosopher's Stone, or the Elixir, depending upon the ultimate goal of the alchemical work.

If menstrual blood and semen are the two dragons of Flammel, it might explain his curious remark that the sages have not dared to show them "to their own children." Modesty would forbid such a disclosure. In the Bible children are expressly prohibited from uncovering the nakedness of their parents—this was the sin of Ham, who saw the nakedness of his father, Noah, and was cursed (Genesis 9:22–25). Biblical strictures would be taken seriously by the alchemists, if they were thought to have a bearing on the work.

"A Clear Tear"

The third primary substance of sexual alchemy, the clear lubricating oil that is generated from the sexual organs during arousal, also occurs in the symbolism of alchemy—at least, it is one possible interpretation for certain alchemical symbolism. The following passage from the *Recueil stéganographique* of Béroalde de Verville is highly suggestive in this context:

> If any man wish at times to change the drop of mastic, and by pressing it to cause a clear tear to issue from it, let him take care, and he will see in a fixed time, under the gentle pressure of the fire, a like substance issue from the philosophic matter; for as soon as its violet darkness is excited for the second time, it will stir up from it as it were a drop or flower or flame or pearl, or other likeness of a precious stone, which will be diversified until it runs out in very clear whiteness, which thereafter will be capable of clothing itself with the honour of beauteous rubies, or ethereal stones, which are the true fire of the soul and light of the philosophers.[6]

The sexual imagery in this passage may be unconscious, but it is certainly overt. In fact the "clear tear" that wells out of the "violet darkness" in response to a "gentle pressure" in "very clear whiteness" is an essential phenomenon of the physiology of sexual alchemy.

The description is very apt for the generation of the Oil of Lilith.

Alchemical Confusion

Menstrual blood and semen undoubtedly did form the ingredients of alchemical experiments from time to time, if only because so many diverse substances were employed in an effort to derive the prima materia, to the great frustration and disgust of some experimenters. The alchemist George Ripley wrote:

> I have tried all, the blood, the hair, the soul of Saturn, the marcassites, the *aes ustum*, the saffron of Mars, the scales and the dross of iron, litharge, antimony, all this is not worth a rotten fig. I have worked much to obtain the oil and water of silver, I have calcined this metal with a prepared salt, and without salt, with eau-de-vie; I have used the corrosive oils, but all this was useless. I have employed the oils, milk, wine, rennet, the sperm of the stars which fall on the earth, celandines, secundines, and an infinity of other things, and I have derived no advantage from them.[7]

Very much the same tone of frustration is displayed in the writing of Bernard Trévisan:

> And in truth I believe that those who have written their books parabolically and figuratively, in speaking of hair, of blood, of urine, of sperm, of herbs, of vegetables, of animals, of plants and of stones and minerals such as salts, alums, copperas, attraments, vitriols, borax and magnesia, and any stones and waters whatsoever; I believe, I say, that this has cost them nothing: or that they have taken no trouble: or that they are too cruel . . . for know that no book declares in true words, unless by parables, as signs. But Man must think and revise often the possible meaning of what they say, and must regard the operations by which Nature conducts her works.[8]

From these examples it will be obvious that no accepted alchemical formula existed upon which everyone agreed. Semen and menstrual blood were probably used by some alchemists in their chemical experiments, but it is very unlikely that they were transmuted into their spiritual essences by sexual ecstasy generated from a union between a human being and an angelic being, as is true in the operation of sexual alchemy described in this book. Flammel may have used this sexual technique in conjunction with his beloved wife, Perrenella, but if so he was one of very few Western alchemists to attempt it.

Meditation and Imagination in the Great Work

Yet human spirit as a necessary ingredient in the alchemical work was well understood. The alchemist must purify and transform his or her own nature before the first matter could be liberated from base substances. "Know that thou canst not have this science unless thou shalt purify thy mind before God, that is, wipe away all corruption from thy heart."[9] This process of purification and refinement was carried out by prayer and meditation (*meditatio*).

Meditation was a recognized stage in the work. It was defined as an inner dialogue with "someone unseen," who might be the alchemist's own higher nature, or God, or the good angel of the alchemist.[10] The alchemist, who is an essential ingredient in the work, must *become* the first matter in order to refine the first matter. Dorn wrote: "Thou wilt never make from other the One that thou seekest, except there first be made one thing of thyself."[11]

The bridge between purified human nature and the nature of the substance being worked upon by the alchemist was the imaginative faculty (*imaginatio*) of the alchemist. Imagination is defined by the alchemist Ruland as "the star in man, the celestial or supercelestial body."[12] Building on this definition, Carl Jung defined alchemical imagination as "a concentrated extract of the life forces, both physical and psychic."[13] For the alchemist, the realm of the mind and the realm of the physical world must merge and overlap. Only in this way can the purified spiritual fire of the alchemist act upon the base substances in the Hermetic vessel to purify them.

It can readily be seen that all of the essential ingredients for sexual alchemy existed in traditional Western alchemy, but it is unlike they were ever assembled together in a conscious way, although it is possible this was done by a few inspired individuals such as Nicholas Flammel, who had the advantage of working intimately for many years with his wife in pursuit of the Philosopher's Stone and the Elixir of Life.

{ 5 }

The Homunculus

"Spagyric" Substances of Paracelsus

The homunculus (literally "little man") is one of the primary, though seldom discussed, works of Western alchemy. In its most material form, alchemists believed that an actual child could be engendered and reared within an alchemical vessel, which served as its womb. This child was reported to be perfectly formed in all respects, but smaller than an ordinary human infant and more fragile in health.

Paracelsus (1493–1541) taught that an homunculus could be made by enclosing "spagyric" substances in a glass vessel and burying it in horse dung for forty days. Dung heaps were common before the advent of automobiles. They generate a low, constant heat from their natural decay. This heat was made use of by alchemists in their experiments. At the end of forty days something will stir in the vessel, a little transparent man without a body. He is reared by feeding him within the vessel each day for forty weeks on the "arcanum" of human blood. Blood was believed to carry the life force, which is the equivalent of shakti. At the end of this period a child will emerge that is perfect in all its proportions, but smaller than an ordinary child and requiring more care and attention in its physical education.[1]

The Opinions of Edward Kelley

By spagyric substances, a term coined by Paracelsus that he did not choose to explain, it is very likely that semen and perhaps menstrual blood are intended. Semen is strongly solar; menstrual blood is strongly lunar. A union of the Sun and Moon was believed necessary in the formation of the homunculus. This is clear from a chapter in the alchemist Edward Kelley's *The Theatre of Terrestrial Astronomy* titled "The Conjunction of Sun and Moon," which I will quote here in full:

> The ancient philosophers have enumerated several kinds of conjunction, but to avoid a vain prolixity I will affirm, upon the testimony of Marsilius Ficinus, that conjunction is union of separate qualities or an equation of principles, viz., Mercury and Sulphur, Sun and Moon, agent and patient, matter and form. When the virgin, or feminine, earth is thoroughly purified and purged from all superfluity, you must give it a husband meet for it; for when the male and female are joined together by means of the sperm, a generation must take place in the menstruum. The substance of Mercury is known to the Sages as the earth and matter in which the Sulphur of Nature is sown, that it may there putrefy, the earth being its womb. Here the female seed awaits that of the male, by means of which they are inseparably united, the one being hot and dry, and the other cold and moist; the heat and dryness of the male are tempered with the cold and moisture of the female, and, in due time, the matter will assume a specific form. For all action tends to the production of a form, being, as it is, an efficient principle.
>
> Opposition
> A very red Sun is pouring blood into an urinal. An old man is pouring blood out of another urinal, together with a winged child, into a third urinal, which stands on straw and contains the Moon lying on her back in blackish water. Near the Sun a jug is pouring white rays, or drops, into an urinal. On the hill stands a Phoenix, biting its breast, out of which drops blood, the same being drunk by its young. Beneath the rock a husbandman is scattering seed in his field.[2]

The white drops are semen, the two kinds of blood are ordinary blood and menstrual blood. The Moon lies on her back to indicate that she is sexually receptive. The phoenix on the hill is a symbol of rebirth. It usurps the mythic role of the pelican—the pelican was believed to nourish its chicks on its own blood, which it drew from its breast with its beak. The farmer sowing seeds indicates that this is a process

FIGURE 5-1.

Emblem from Kelley's *Theater of Terrestrial Astronomy.*

of sexual generation. The Earth itself, who is the Soul of the World and the Great Mother (Shakti), is the womb into which the seed is sown. The Moon lies in blackish water to indicate that a softening ("rotting" was the term used by farmers) of the seeds was necessary before they would germinate. In alchemy, this is the stage of the Great Work called putrefaction.

Kelley quotes several alchemical writers concerning the stage of conjunction in another of his works, *The Stone of the Philosophers:*

> Ascanius: "The conjunction of the two is like the union of husband and wife, from whose embrace results golden water."
> Anthology of Secrets: "Wed the red man to the white woman, and you have the whole Magistery."
> Hermes: "Join the male to the female in their own proper humidity, because there is no birth without union of male and female."
>
> . . .
>
> Avicenna: "Purify husband and wife separately, in order that they may unite more intimately; for if you do not purify them, they cannot love each other. By conjunction of the two natures you get a clear and lucid nature, which, when it ascends, becomes bright and serviceable."

. . .

Exposition of the Letter of King Alexander: "In this art you must wed the Sun and the Moon."

. . .

Senior: "I, the Sun, am hot and dry, and thou, the Moon, art cold and moist; when we are wedded together in a closed chamber, I will gently steal away thy soul."

. . .

Rosinus to Saratant: "When the Sun, my brother, for the love of me (silver) pours his sperm (i.e. his solar fatness) into the chamber (i.e. my Lunar body), namely, when we become one in a strong and complete complexion and union, the child of our wedded love will be born."[3]

The reference to "golden water," a product of the alchemical process, explains Kelley's use of the term "urinal" to describe his alchemical vessels in the previous quotation. The result of conjunction has the appearance of urine. The "red man" and the "white woman" are sulfur and quicksilver, respectively. Avicenna's reference to a "clear and lucid nature" explains why Paracelsus states that the homunculus is at first transparent and without a body. The statement by Rosinus that the Sun and Moon are brother and sister is quite common in alchemy. It stems from the extremely ancient notion that the offspring of a royal bloodline should intermarry to prevent the dilution and weakening of the divine element in their blood—all royal families were thought to have descended, at some distant time in the past, from deities. This is why the Pharaoh of Egypt married his own sister.

In alchemical works it is often difficult to determine whether the authors are using alchemical symbolism to disguise operations of human sexuality, or sexual symbolism to disguise operations of chemical alchemy. The general view is that references to sexual acts are to be interpreted in purely symbolic terms, but I believe this is a naive attitude. As I have tried to show in this work, there was a clear understanding in ancient times that magic power can be raised by the correct manipulation of human sexual energy.

In most works of alchemy it is quite obvious that the homunculus, or alchemical child, is merely a metaphor for a stage in the alchemical process. Other writers, such as Paracelsus, took the creation of the homunculus quite seriously as a material work in its own right, and regarded the creature created within the vessel as a living being. When attempts were made by alchemists to create a physical homunculus, it is quite likely that physical semen was used, and probably menstrual blood, which was often looked upon as the female counterpart of semen.

Spirit and Flesh

The narrow alchemical definition of homunculus is too restrictive to provide a full description of the concept. In its broader sense the term homunculus may be applied to any creature with a human form that is deliberately created by occult or magical means through the combined efforts of a human and a spiritual agency, and that possesses a material body or at least gives the perception of possessing a material body. By this definition any being of human shape created through the sexual intercourse of a human and a spirit is an homunculus. The homunculus may also be created by methods that on the surface do not appear to be overtly sexual, although they must always utilize shakti, or creative energy, which in human beings is always at root sexual (kundalini shakti).

It is not always clear whether angels, demons, and spirits have physical bodies, spiritual bodies, or spiritual bodies that accurately mimic physical bodies. This confusion is the result of the control spirits exercise over human perceptions. In biblical times angels were believed to possess bodies of flesh and blood. The ancient Egyptians thought their hungry ghosts—the precursors to the vampire of European legend—were physical. The incubi and succubi of medieval Europe were usually regarded as physical by those who experienced their lovemaking.

Even in the last few centuries, nature spirits such as elves, dwarfs, pixies, and fairies were considered to be physical beings by many country folk. Concerning the nature of fairies, a Scotsman testified at the beginning of the twentieth century: "I never saw any myself, and so cannot tell, but they must be spirits from all that the old people tell about them, or else how could they appear and disappear so suddenly? The old people said they didn't know if fairies were flesh and blood, or spirits. They saw them as men of more diminutive stature than our race."[4] The opinion that fairies were a physical race of humans, or human-like beings, is persistent. Even today some scholars believe that the genesis of the fairy legends was an indigenous race of human beings living in northwestern Europe before the coming of the Britons.

Similarly, the so-called Devil who presided over the Sabbats of witches was completely material, according to eyewitness testimonies recorded in the transcripts of European witch trials. Even assuming that some of these accounts extracted by threats and torture refer to actual gatherings, it is impossible to determine whether they refer to a living man impersonating the Horned God of the witches, or to a spiritual being who merely gives the impression of possessing a physical body.

Early vampire legends describe the vampire as a physical fiend, a kind of cannibalistic corpse. It is only in later legends that it becomes spiritualized. Even in modern times this process has not run its full course. In modern myth the vampire is still an animated corpse, albeit a corpse that can discard its materialism at will to become vapor, and a corpse that casts no reflection.

An aspect of this general vagueness concerning the solidity of supernatural beings is the ambiguity over whether the homunculus is completely physical, completely spiritual, or a strange and changeable mixture of the two. One of the most common fairy myths concerns the changeling, a fairy child substituted for a human child which through magic it is made to resemble, with the intention that the human mother shall nurture it. The changeling is in every outward way indistinguishable from the stolen human infant, who is taken to the land of fairy, but the tales say that it can be recognized by its fey actions. It laughs knowingly and gives sly looks, has a malicious temperament, a deeper than normal voice, a voracious appetite, and greater than human strength.

The changeling is really a sanitized form of the homunculus. It is an amalgam of human child and spirit child, but the sexual act that would be most likely to result in such a half-breed, a loving union between a human and a spirit, is never mentioned in the changeling myth. However, fairies are often supposed to have sexual relations with human beings, and even to marry them. Children are born of such unions, and entire bloodlines are said to have descended from the union between a mortal man and his fairy bride. The familiar figure of the wicked fairy godmother who comes to the crib of a newborn infant to curse it is another version of the Lilith of popular Jewish folklore, who is the mother of demons.

Lilith, the Goddess of Carnal Love

Lilith was supposed in Jewish folklore to have the power of life and death over any child born from a sexual union between husband and wife that took place under the light of a candle, or when the woman was completely naked, or at a time forbidden by Jewish law. Children engendered under these conditions were called oppressed souls. Indeed, any act or omission that renders sexual union less than completely sacred was believed to result in the fruit of that union falling under the power of Lilith.

If a husband lusted after his wife's naked body, or committed forbidden sexual acts, it was said that he permitted the spirit of Lilith to enter into the impregnated womb. Lilith of Jewish folklore is, among other things, the spirit of lust for its own sake. It goes without saying that any child born to a couple out of wedlock was thought to be a child of Lilith, since bastards could not be lawfully conceived.

This notion may seem incredibly quaint and ridiculous to us today, but it was universally believed until the last century that any strong thought or emotion in the mind of a man or women during lovemaking would impress itself on the engendered fetus. For example, it was superstitiously held that a woman frightened by a dog at the moment of her climax might very well have a child with hair growing all over its face. It was believed that if the father or mother grimaced in pleasure during lovemaking, a child born from their union would have ugly or twisted facial features.

Given these universal beliefs, it is not to be wondered at that lustful or perverse desires and fantasies during intercourse were thought to impress the child with a degenerate, sensual and lawless nature and make it a creature of Lilith. The same understanding existed within Christianity. In a form of sex magic sanctioned by the Church, good Catholics were often counseled to make love beneath a portrait of Jesus or the Virgin Mary, and to have religious thoughts in their minds during their mutual climax (which was believed necessary to mingle the male and female "sperms"). If they failed to do this, their engendered child might receive some imperfection from their sin and fall under the influence of the Devil.

In order to avoid such a fate, good Jews were counseled in the *Zohar* to concentrate the mind on the holiness of God during the hour of intercourse, and to recite a specific prayer that ends: "I hold on to the Holy One, Wrap myself in the King's holiness."[5] Then the husband was directed to cover his head and that of his wife for an hour, and to do this for the three days during which the attempt was made to engender a child. By another account this was to be done for thirty days, and after each sexual act, clean water was to be sprinkled around the marriage bed.

Lilith was believed to lie invisible between the sheets of the bed in which a husband and wife made love, waiting for any violation of religious law to bring forth her own child. She managed this by utilizing any stray "sparks" of the drops of semen that might escape being deposited within the womb of the wife. By sparks, the vital essence of spirit is intended. It is said of these children of Lilith, who are called *lilin*, that they "multiply like humans, eat and drink and die."[6] The implication is that this class of demon is born from mortal women, and is flesh and blood. Using the excess energies inherent in the sperm of the husband, Lilith projects some shadow of herself into the womb of the wife at the moment of conception, displacing or altering the "seed" of the wife. The name lilin was loosely applied to illegitimate offspring, on the principle that any child born out of wedlock must belong to Lilith, but even legitimate offspring could be lilin if their parents sinned when they were conceived.

Lilin, the Children of Lilith

In the Kabbalistic text titled *The Valley of the King* it is stated that the lilin and other types of demons engendered by Lilith from her union with mortal men first came into being when Adam had sex with Eve during her menstrual period. Menstrual blood is described, in typically misogynist terms, as "the filth and the impure seed of the Serpent who mounted Eve before Adam mounted her."[7] When Lilith witnessed the forbidden act of Adam, she "became strong in her husks" and forced herself upon him against his will, engendering many demons.

The importance of this symbolism cannot be too greatly stressed. Lilin, the offspring of Lilith and Adam that are (by implication) born from the womb of Eve, are the result of the mingled seeds of Adam, Eve (women were believed to emit a semen similar to a man's at the moment of their climax), and, in the form of Eve's menstrual blood, the seed of the Serpent. But we have already seen elsewhere that in the more esoteric and hidden teachings of the Kabbalah, the Serpent, who is usually said to be Samael, is another form of Lilith herself. Samael and Lilith are one in the Kabbalah, just as in Tantric doctrine Shakti and Shiva are at root both Shakti.

The distinction between Lilith and the Great Goddess is that Lilith is the Goddess in her aspect of mistress of sexual love and sensual pleasure. Since sexual pleasure for its own sake was considered in past centuries to be evil, sinful, and a violation of religious law, this placed Lilith into the role of wicked temptress and rebel against the will of God. However, her energy is still shakti. This is why in the literature of the Kabbalah it is stressed that she needs to use the "sparks" in the semen of human beings to accomplish her engenderings. Shakti energy is concentrated in semen, and is released by the sexual act.

It is interesting to imagine what the medieval Kabbalists would have made out of test-tube fertilization. The seed of man and woman are artificially brought together outside the womb, in a kind of alchemical vessel, then mechanically inserted into the womb of the mother. By traditional Jewish belief, any child of such a process must be lilin, since the act itself is unlawful, and allows ample opportunity for Lilith to cast her shadow over the fertilized ovum.

According to Jewish folklore, lilin can be recognized by their excessive hairiness (symbolic of their bestial nature), and paradoxically, by the bald patch on the crown of their heads. Probably lilin are said to be bald on their crowns because it was the practice of all good Jews to keep their heads covered. The resemblance between lilin and Christian monks, who shaved their crowns, may not be coincidence—priests and monks must often have seemed indistinguishable from demons in the eyes of the rabbis of medieval Europe.

Two Categories of Homunculus

For purposes of greater clarity, we may divide the homunculus into two categories that are based upon the nature of its engendering. Either it is a physical being of flesh and blood with a living human mother and a spirit father who is the masculine expression of Shakti, Lilith in her male form of Samael; or it is a spiritual being that at times may reside in a physical body or other object, or gives the sensory impression that it possesses a physical body, who has Lilith or one of her spirit daughters for a mother and a living human father. Both forms of homunculus are deliberately engendered by a sexual act. The names Lilith and Samael are here used as general terms to signify spirits who adopt either female or male forms to have sex with human beings for the purpose of generating unnatural offspring. Needless to say, when a male spirit lies with a woman to engender a physical child, the physical sperm of a living man is needed to give the child a body of flesh—the male spirit unites with a woman at the same time that she is making love with a living man.

Returning to the homunculus of Paracelsus, we see that it falls into the second category. It is engendered from the semen of the alchemist within the womb of the alchemical vessel, which is a little representation of the womb of the Goddess herself. Since it issues from the womb of a spirit, it must be essentially spiritual in its nature, even though it gives the appearance of having a physical body. A basic tenet of magic is that "like produces like." A spiritual mother will produce a spiritual child, a mother of flesh will produce a child of flesh.

However, since the actual vessel that supports the homunculus is made of glass, and it is fed on the arcanum of physical blood, the implication is that although it begins life as a purely spiritual creature it can be made to take on flesh gradually over the forty weeks of its nurturing. For this reason it is described as transparent when first engendered, but solid when released from the vessel.,

The Golem of Rabbi Loew

Another way to provide a spiritual homunculus with a physical body is to make one from physical substances. This occurred in the legend of the *golem*, a spiritual being of immense power created with Kabbalistic methods by Rabbi Judah Loew of Prague (circa 1525–1609) for the defense of the Jews living in that city. Rabbi Loew fashioned a man out of river clay and then used the authority of the divine names of God to breathe life into the statue, in a way analogous to the method used by God to breathe life into the clay body of Adam.

There are different versions of the golem legend, but according to the *Book of the Miracles of R. Loew,* published in Piotrkov in 1909, the Jews living in the Prague Ghetto were threatened by the rabble-rousing tactics and malicious libels of a Catholic priest named Thaddeus, who regularly preached in favor of the destruction of the Ghetto. Rabbi Loew was a leader of the Jews and a *Ba'al Shem* (Master of the Name), a practitioner of the magical Kabbalah. Concerned about the way public opinion was tending in the Christian community, Loew used his occult skills to obtain a dream oracle from God. The oracle instructed him to create a golem (Hebrew: embryo). The making of golems, or animated beings, from inanimate materials is one of the most ancient forms of Kabbalistic magic.

In the oracle, God delivered in ten Hebrew words the following message to Loew: "Create a Golem, kneed the clay, and thus you will destroy the plotters who want to tear Israel to pieces." Loew enlisted his son-in-law, Rabbi Katz, and his disciple, Rabbi Sason, to act as his assistants in the work. He revealed to them the oracle, and asserted that hidden within the Hebrew letters of the ten words was a "combination of names" by the power of which a golem might be animated. The magic required the involvement of the four elements acting in unison. He chose his son-in-law because Katz had been born with mastery over the element Fire, and his disciple because Sason had been born able to control the element Water. Loew himself had been born with power over the element Air. The element Earth was to be represented by the clay body of the golem.

Loew commanded his helpers to perform *tiqqunim,* or Kabbalistic meditations, for seven days in order to purify and strengthen their souls for the task ahead. When they were ready, at four hours after midnight they left the walled city of Prague and went down to the muddy bank of a nearby river. They found some moist clay and carefully shaped the form of a man three cubits (about five feet) in length lying on its back, paying particular attention to its face, hands, and feet. The three stood at the feet of the golem with their faces turned toward its face.

Loew ordered Katz, who had power over Fire, to walk seven times around the body of the golem in a clockwise direction while reciting a portion of the combination of Hebrew letters which Loew had earlier extracted, by Kabbalistic means, from the words of his dream oracle. Katz recited the set of letters at each circumambulation of the golem, so that when finished circling the clay figure he had said them seven times. The legend states that when Katz was finished, the body of the golem began to glow like hot embers.

Sason, who had power over Water, in his turn circumambulated the glowing form of the golem seven times clockwise. Each time around, he recited a different set of Hebrew letters given to him by Loew. When he was done and had returned to his place at the feet of the golem, moisture entered the figure from the air and extinguished its glow. The golem emitted steaming mist. When this cleared, the rabbis saw that it was now covered with the same amount of hair that might grow on the head and body of a man of thirty. There were fingernails on the tips of the golem's fingers.

Rabbi Loew himself, who had power over the element Air, walked seven times clockwise around the cooling golem, reciting a third set of mystic Hebrew letters seven times. The golem took on the color of a living human being. The three Kabbalists together stood at the feet of the figure and recited the biblical verse in unison: "And he breathed into his nostrils the breath of life, and the man became a living soul" (Genesis 2:7). The legend explains that it was necessary for all three to speak these words together because living breath contains not only air, but fire and water as well.

The golem opened his eyes in amazement. Rabbi Loew commanded him to stand up. The golem understood and obeyed, but could not speak because he was a mute. They dressed his naked body in the clothing and shoes "suitable for a servant of a court of law." At six in the morning, before the sun was up, four went back into Prague, where only three had come out. The golem was obedient to his creator Rabbi Loew, who explained to the golem that he must stay in the chamber of his law court and do the work of a servant of the court, but whenever Loew commanded, he must immediately perform whatever task was asked of him, even if it meant walking into fire or jumping from a tower or into a raging river. Because of his magical origins, the golem could not be injured by the four elements.

This is one form of the golem legend. We will probably never know the actual method used by Rabbi Loew to create the golem, if such a being ever was created by Loew or some other Master of the Name, but it may well have been similar to the method described. It likely involved the ten most sacred names of God that are connected with the ten Sephiroth on the Tree of the Kabbalah, and also the twelve permutations of Tetragrammaton, the supreme unutterable name of God. It may, as the legend indicates, have been enacted through the four elements, Fire, Water, Air and Earth.

For such an act to be successful, it would probably require that the Kabbalist involved emit his semen within the context of a ritual upon the physical matrix of clay from which the golem was to be formed. It would also be magically correct for menstrual blood to have been previously mixed into that clay. Probably a blood sacrifice of some sort would have been performed to energize the ritual. The semen and menstrual blood would have been sealed within the body of the golem, whereas the blood of the sacrifice would most likely have been spilled upon its head as a form of baptism.

In biblical times Jews regularly performed animal sacrifices upon their altars, then dashed the blood of the victim onto the altar stones. It was a universal belief in ancient magic that vital spiritual energy resides in blood. By dashing the blood of the sacrifice onto the altar, the person performing the rite offered the spiritual vitality of the beast as nourishment for the god (IHVH), or gods (Elohim), being worshipped. In the Old Testament, God is made to command explicitly that all blood be reserved exclusively for him (Genesis 9:4, Leviticus 7:27).

In the legend of the golem, the three Kabbalists stood at the feet of the golem. We may assume that Loew was in the middle, with Katz on his right side and Sason on his left. In the Kabbalah, the airy elemental letter Aleph is usually placed between fiery Shin and watery Mem—Aleph is known as the tongue of the balance. The left side is magically feminine, so Sason who commanded the feminine element Water would stand on Loew's left. Katz, who commanded masculine Fire, would stand on Loew's right, his masculine side. We do not know how the golem was oriented, but my guess is that the head of the golem pointed to the north.

The reclining man-sized clay statue became fiery hot when Rabbi Loew's disciple R. Katz, who possessed the power of the Fire element, recited a set of Kabbalistic letters provided by Loew that are connected with Fire. These letters were probably the three permutations or banners of Tetragrammaton that are begun with the letter Yod, which is the letter of fire—IHVH (יהוה), IHHV (יההו) and IVHH (יוהה). The figure sprouted hair and fingernails when Sason, the disciple who had the power of the Water element, recited seven times the banners of Tetragrammaton that begin with the letter Heh, which is the letter of the Name associated with Water—HVHI (הוהי), HVIH (הויה)and HHIV (ההיו). Finally Rabbi Loew himself spoke seven times the banners that begin with Vau, the letter of Air—VHIH (והיה), VHHI (וההי)and VIHH (ויהה).

It is not stated in the golem legend, but in my opinion it would be necessary for menstrual blood to be mixed into the clay of the riverbank to make it a suitable matrix of earth for the three higher elements, Fire, Water and Air. Possibly the raw clay was softened by the urine of the three men prior to its shaping. It would also be necessary for the three rabbis to masturbate into a cavity in the golem's body, probably the open mouth, which would afterwards be sealed. This would provide one reason why in the legend the golem remains mute. Another appropriate receptacle for the sperm of the rabbis would be a cavity formed in the top of the golem's head. Each rabbi would probably masturbate into the golem just before making his sevenfold circumambulation.

The power of shakti is essentially lunar, so the creation of the golem probably occurred in the predawn hours of a Monday morning. The reason the legend states that Rabbi Loew received ten words containing a combination of names of power is because the most holy names of God were said in the Kabbalah to be ten in number, and among these ten is the name Tetragrammaton (IHVH), which is permuted into twelve forms or banners that may be linked in sets of three with the four elements.

The legend states that ten years later, after the threat to the Jews of Prague was ended, Loew ordered the golem to go up into the attic of the synagogue and lie down on the floor. It is not explicitly mentioned how the golem was to lie, but from hints in the narrative we can determine that Loew instructed him to lie upon his face. At two hours after midnight Loew stood with his son-in-law Rabbi Katz and his disciple Rabbi on either side of him, as he had stood on the riverbank when the golem was formed, but this time they stood at the head of the golem. Each in turn walked around the golem seven times counterclockwise while reciting the same holy letters he had recited in the golem's formation, but this time the banners of the name were spoken in reverse. The way of doing this is not revealed in the legend. In my opinion, it involved inverting the locations of the first Heh and the second Heh in each banner—if so, we may presume that the first and second Heh in the name were pronounced slightly differently to allow this distinction to be made.

By reversing all the steps they had used in creating the golem, the creature was gradually deprived of vitality, and returned once again into a statue of inert clay. Loew stripped the clothes off the figure and ordered them burned, then hid the statue of the golem under a pile of holy books in the attic of the synagogue, and let it be known among his servants that his mute law clerk had run away during the night. He gave orders that nobody should enter the attic, and that no more old holy books should be stored there. The Jews thought this was to prevent the risk of fire, but the true purpose was to conceal the body of the golem. Loew confided to Katz, the supposed author of the legend, that at the final resurrection of the dead, the golem would arise "from the coupling of a man and a woman" just prior to the coming of the Messiah. This would occur through the actions of a Righteous One "in order to bring perfection to a very great and essential thing which is a deep secret."

Truth Behind the Golem Legend

This legend is not to be interpreted literally. However, it contains many symbolically accurate elements that reveal a great deal about the actual creation of an homunculus. Loew's golem, assuming that it actually did exist, would not have been a living, walking statue, but a statue infused by Kabbalistic magic with a living spirit, probably the spirit of a potent angel of God. The protection offered to the Jews of the city of Prague against their Jesuit enemies would have taken the form of magical punishments that manifested themselves as accidents, heart attacks, infections, sudden deaths, and diseases.

Loew would have consulted the spirit engendered within the golem to learn the plots of his Jesuit foes, and the golem would have communicated its messages, not with spoken words, but by means of subtle gestures perceptible to Loew, such as the twitch of a finger, the blink of an eye, and so on. It is possible that Loew was psychically sensitive enough to hear the voice of the golem within his own mind. By feeding the spirit of the golem on the arcanum of freshly spilled blood, or on the vitality of newly emitted semen, or both, Loew would have kept his creature strong.

It is important to understand that the homunculus created by Rabbi Loew was the spiritual being that resided within the clay statue of the golem, not the actual statue, which was nothing more than a pattern or matrix upon which that spirit could more easily form itself. In a similar way, the human body of flesh and blood is a matrix that allows the human spirit to express itself in the physical universe. Rabbi Loew was the father of his golem. Kabbalists would say that its mother was the divine Shekhina, if they regarded the act of its creation as lawful and holy; or the demoness Lilith, if they choose to regard Loew's act as black magic. In either case the underlying energy was shakti.

The offspring of human mothers and angelic fathers play an important part in the literature of the Bible. They appear prominently in both the beginning of the Old Testament and the end of the New Testament, at the creation of the world and its final destruction. In the book Genesis they are the offspring of mortal women and the fallen angels, who were set to watch over the Earth, but who became enamored of human females and lusted after them. The creation of these semi-divine heroes is more explicitly described in the Book of Enoch. They are roughly equivalent to the heroes of Greek mythology who had one mortal parent and one parent who was a nature spirit or deity.

In the book Revelation the homunculus is the Antichrist, he who is to be born of a mortal woman with (in Christian myth) Satan for a father. The parentage of the Antichrist is not explicitly stated in St. John's apocalyptic vision, but that he is to be the son of Satan was generally accepted by Christian theologians. As I mentioned elsewhere, the druid Merlin was believed by early Christian monks to have been born from the union of a demon with a mortal woman for the purpose of becoming the Antichrist, but according to legend the clever actions of a monk in baptizing the child were said to have changed his fate, and temporarily averted the end of the world.

Aleister Crowley and the Homunculus

Lest you think that my expanded definition is arbitrary, and that I am stretching the term "homunculus" too greatly when I apply it to the children of women and angels, the "mighty men which were of old" as the Bible calls them, and to the Antichrist, I should point out that the Antichrist was understood to be a form of homunculus by no less an authority than the magician and prophet Aleister Crowley.

What Lilith and other spirits caused the shakti energy of men and women to produce against their will and usually without their knowledge, Crowley tried to generate deliberately in order to fulfill the prophecy of his inspired *Book of the Law*. This brief document, possessing passages of poetic beauty, was dictated to Crowley by his guardian angel, Aiwass, in 1904. It describes the coming of the Aeon of Horus with war and destruction. The leading figure of the Aeon of Horus was identified by Crowley with the biblical Antichrist. From childhood Crowley had always considered himself to be the Great Beast of Revelation.

After receiving and accepting the *Book of the Law* as the true scripture of the coming age, he came to the conclusion that he was to be the father of the Antichrist, who would be created using ritual magic within the womb of Crowley's lover, whom he referred to as the Scarlet Woman. The Antichrist would thus be an homunculus, but since he would have a living human mother, he would be human flesh. Crowley may actually have performed an extended ritual working to bring forth the Antichrist, but if so he was unsuccessful. Crowley then concluded that the Antichrist was to be one of his disciples (a kind of symbolic son), Frater Achad, but when Achad disappointed him he seems to have accepted that the leader of the Aeon of Horus would not be known to him during his lifetime.

Crowley left two documents that explain in surprisingly explicit terms the ritual of the Homunculus Working. Very likely he used this general formula in his attempt to give birth to his own magical child. As was his custom, he left some of the more eso-teric details out, but someone with a solid knowledge of the theory and techniques examined in the present book would not find it impossible to supply these details.

The Moonchild

The first place to go for an understanding of Crowley's method for creating an homunculus is his novel *Moonchild*. This was written by Crowley in 1917, a few years after his own experiment to create a living homunculus, according to Kenneth Grant.[8] The novel is pure fiction, but its magic is based on Crowley's actual practices. The title of the novel derives from the purpose of the working, "to bring to birth a trans-terres-trial intelligence of lunar origin."[9] The power of the Moon is central to the work because, as I mentioned above, the nature of Shakti is essentially lunar. In magic the sphere of the Moon is the gateway through which spiritual intelligences descend to human consciousness. The Moon is intimately connected with generation (the lunar cycle of roughly twenty-eight days regulates menstruation) and gestation (approxi-mately nine lunar months is the term of human pregnancy).

In *Moonchild* Crowley wrote concerning the significance of the Moon:

> In this curious language [of symbolism] the moon signifies primarily all recep-tive things, because moonlight is only reflected sunlight. Hence "lunar" is almost a synonym of "feminine." Woman changes; all depends upon the influ-ence of the man; and she is now fertile, now barren, according to her phase. But on each day of her course she passes through a certain section of the Zodiac; and according to the supposed nature of the stars beyond her was her influence in that phase, or, as they called it, mansion.[10]

Grant asserts "the Moonchild *was* brought to birth—'from no expected house'. It is amongst humanity today, though Crowley himself perhaps was unaware of the suc-cessful accomplishment of the rite."[11] Unfortunately, he offers no evidence for this extraordinary and fascinating claim.

The quotation is from the first chapter of Crowley's *Book of the Law:* "The child of thy [Crowley's] bowels, he shall behold them [the mysteries of the book]. Expect him not from the East nor from the West, for from no expected house cometh that child."[12] In the third chapter of the *Book of the Law,* concerning its hidden mysteries Crowley is told "one cometh after him [the Beast, or Crowley], whence I say not, who shall discover the key of it all. . . . It shall be his child and that strangely. Let him not seek after this; for thereby alone can he fall from it."[13]

Part of Crowley's ritual creation of the homunculus in the womb of the chosen woman was to steep the woman in the magical influences of the Moon. This was presumably intended to render her more receptive to spiritual impressions. In *Moonchild* he describes how the woman who is supposedly to bear the homunculus conducts an invocation in the hour of the rising of the Moon wearing a crescent-shaped tiara, presumably of silver, in which are set nine moonstones. Another invocation was made at the hour of the setting of the Moon. The woman had lunar poetry read to her, listened to lunar music, ate only lunar foods such as milk, the whites of eggs, venison, crescent cakes, and cheese, and spent most of the day sleeping, during which magic words were chanted into her ears that were intended to induce lunar visions. When the Moon was not above the horizon, she spent her time contemplating the waters of the sea.

Moonchild is a work of romantic fiction. However, Crowley was quite serious about the making of the homunculus. The other place he left detailed instructions on this matter is an essay he wrote for the Ordo Templi Orientis, more commonly known as the OTO. Crowley was not appointed the supreme head of the Order until 1922, but was admitted to its lower grades in 1911, and the following year was made the head of the OTO in Britain by Theodor Reuss.[14] In 1914 he produced "De Homunculo Epistola," a secret ritual instruction intended for the ninth degree initiates of the OTO only. Here we have a more explicit exposition of the procedure.

The Homunculus in the Ordo Templi Orientis

Crowley begins by defining an homunculus as a living being in the form of a man who possesses both intellect and the power of speech, but a being not begotten after the manner of human generation nor having a human soul. In his belief, the reincarnating human soul enters into the fetus only at the third month of pregnancy. Before this time the fetus has no soul, and is capable of receiving and supporting a nonhuman spirit. After the first three months in the womb until the moment of death a human being can only become an homunculus if a determined obsessing spirit is able to expel the human soul from its body. Crowley remarks that this is rare except in cases of lunacy. When a low spirit that is incapable of reason or speech enters a fetus in the first three months and manages to retain its possession, the child born will be an idiot.

He asserts that the classical alchemical method for producing the homunculus was to take a fertilized ovum of a woman and as closely as possible reproduce the conditions of gestation in an artificial womb. He is evidently thinking of the method of Paracelsus. Crowley is optimistic that this will one day be accomplished, since, he writes, with God all things are possible, and his motto is "God is man." He states that the white tincture of the alchemists was, in this context, the amniotic fluid, whereas the red tincture was a "substitute for blood." Certain magical aids are undoubtedly helpful in bringing this alchemical process to a successful conclusion, but Crowley regrets that there is no space in his small essay to describe them.

Crowley's premise for the making of an homunculus is this: if the soul is absent from the fetus for the first three months, it should be possible by magical means to prevent the entry of a reincarnating human ego while at the same time attracting and holding "a non-human being, such as an elemental or planetary spirit" whose essential nature is suitable to the physical properties of the fetus. In this way an homunculus can be tailored for the desired purpose of the magician who creates it. If an eloquent creature is desired, the spirit of Mercury, Tiriel, might be invoked into the fetus; if boldness in war is needed, the spirit of Mars, Graphiel, would be appropriate.

It must be borne in mind, Crowley warns his readers, that even a discarnate human ego is immensely powerful, and can only be prevented from entering the fetus by the most potent of magic barriers. Also, care must be exercised that the physical disposition of the fetus is harmonious to the nature of the spiritual being invoked into it. A child by nature sluggish, weak, and melancholy would be an excellent choice for a spirit of Saturn but completely unsuited for a spirit of Venus. He neglects to mention how we are to determine the personality of a child while it is still in the womb. One possible method would be to draw up an astrological chart for the time and place of conception, and judge the child's nature by interpreting its chart. The basic qualities of the child could to some extent be adjusted in advance by delaying its conception to a propitious date and hour, and not attempting to conceive it as unfavorable times.

Crowley's Ritual Formula

The process of creating the homunculus is laid out in a set of steps. First, a suitable woman must be found and persuaded to lend her womb to the working. It is helpful if her astrological birth chart is in harmony with the nature of the homunculus that is to be produced. Second, a suitable man must be found, and his horoscope should also be appropriate if this is at all possible. It may be more convenient if the man is the magician who conducts the working.

Third, man and woman must make love frequently in a ritual manner within a prepared ritual temple furnished and decorated in a style suitable to the work. During lovemaking both partners must ceaselessly will the success of the work and exclude from their minds and hearts all other desires. Copulation should be most frequent during astrologically appropriate times—one factor is that the Moon should be passing through appropriate houses of the zodiac, if we may be guided by Crowley's remarks in *Moonchild*.

Fourth, the successfully impregnated woman should be taken to a wilderness place such as a desert that is seldom traveled by discarnate human souls, but attractive to spirits. A great circle of the art is drawn around the woman and the place of working, then consecrated to the celestial sphere appropriate to the work. For example, if the attempt is made to create an homunculus of Mercury, the circle would be consecrated to the sphere of Mercury. The woman must never leave the circle. Any undesirable entities attracted to its perimeter are to be banished five or seven times a day in the name of Kether, the highest emanation of God. The colors and symbols of the invoked spirit should be displayed within the circle, and appropriate incense burned continuously. In this way the mind of the woman is molded to receive the impression of the spirit.

Twice each day, once while the woman is awake and once while she is asleep, she must be placed in a great triangle while the magician performs a ritual evocation of the spirit to material appearance. Crowley is not explicit about the relationship of the triangle to the great circle, which surrounds and protects the place of ritual, but it is presumably drawn within the great circle, since elsewhere he cautions that the woman must never leave the circle. Perhaps he intends that the magician draw the triangle anew around the woman at each evocation. Crowley directs that the magician should himself stand within the circle during these evocations, but it is not clear if the great circle or a smaller inner circle is intended.

Fifth, the quickening (first movements) of the child within the womb of the woman shall be celebrated by a ritual feast of the reception of the spirit. After this, the five or seven daily banishings of the great circle may be omitted.

Sixth, for the remainder of the term of pregnancy, the woman must be educated and entertained by music, words, and images consonant to the indwelling spirit, so that the entire period is one great, living evocation. Crowley does not say here, but from what he wrote in *Moonchild* we may presume that the woman is to be fed only those kinds of food in harmony with the sphere of the incarnating spirit.

Seventh, the birth of the baby should be advanced or delayed by artificial means so that the birth will occur when the appropriate sign of the zodiac is rising on the eastern horizon. This idea is not original with Crowley. It is fabled that the births of several great leaders of the ancient world were timed so that they might occur at the most astrologically auspicious moments. In the past, astrology was a royal art. Astrologers had immense authority in the courts of pagan, and even many Christian, monarchs.

At birth, the child must be dedicated, purified, and consecrated in a form appropriate to the element, planet, or zodiac sign to which its incarnated spirit belongs. No mention is made by Crowley of spirits that have no specific affiliation with an element, planet, or sign. However, it will almost always be possible to categorize any spirit as better suited to one division of these astrological sets than the other divisions. For example, a spirit with a quick, clever, talkative nature would be naturally suited to the element Air, even if not, strictly speaking, an Air elemental.

Ninth, the result of these ritual steps is a living being with a perfect human form and all the powers and privileges of humanity, but endowed with the force and knowledge of its own sphere. Crowley asserts that since it is the creation of the magician, and dependent upon the magician, the magician will be to the homunculus a kind of god, and the homunculus will be compelled to serve him. Therefore, the entire part of nature under the rule of the astrological sphere of the spirit becomes the dominion of the magician, to do with as he sees fit.

Tenth, readers of the essay are cautioned by Crowley to choose the participants in the work with great care, and to exercise equal attention in the preliminary stages of the operation. To successfully carry out the work of the homunculus once in a lifetime is a great achievement of the art. But if the first attempt is botched, Crowley writes that there is not one man born in "ten times ten thousand years" who is capable of successfully completing the work on a second attempt.

De Arte Magica

Crowley mentions that anyone who contemplates undertaking the formula of the homunculus should first study his other essay for the ninth grade of the OTO, "De Arte Magica."[15] This brief work was also written in 1914 as a secret instruction around the same time as "De Homunculo Epistola." It describes Crowley's techniques for raising sexual energy for the production of "Eroto-comatose Lucidity," a state of prolonged and continuously sustained sexual arousal leading to complete physical exhaustion and altered consciousness. In large part the exhaustion, which is mental as well as physical, is achieved by interrupting the sleep of the subject with gentle erotic stimulation repeatedly, until a condition that borders between sleep and waking is achieved. This allows the subject to dream while still consciously aware, and in Crowley's opinion was conducive to prophetic visions and enlightenment.

One physical side effect of this sort of prolonged erotic stimulation, which Crowley does not mention, but which may be familiar to some readers through their own experiences, is an unusually strong, sustained tumescence in the erectile tissues. In men, the glans of the penis becomes numb and hugely distended, of a dark purple color. The skin on the sides of the penis grows somewhat swollen and puffed with blood, markedly increasing its thickness and becoming quite numb. Erection continues uninterrupted for hours without any periods of diminished hardness.

There is an intense action in the muladhara chakra at the base of the penis that can, after several hours, grow quite painful. Once shakti has begun to flow without ceasing from the muladhara, it is difficult or temporarily impossible to bring about detumescence of the sexual member, even after all erotic thoughts and physical stimulation have been stopped for many minutes. At the first occurrence of this state, this lack of control can be quite frightening. However, if absolutely no touch is laid upon the penis, not even the weight of light clothing, and the mind is resolutely focused on mundane, nonsexual matters, after half an hour or so erection will reluctantly begin to subside.

In women, intense tumescence occurs in the labia and clitoris, and to a lesser extent in the nipples of the breasts. Pronounced blushing darkens and lightens the color of the skin. The flush of color is periodic and rapid. This is particularly noticeable on the upper breast, throat, and face. The vulva and breasts become unusually swollen, and the labia prominent and highly colored. The production of sexual fluid from the vagina is increased to a level greatly above that which occurs during ordinary physical lovemaking. Trembling of the muscles of the lower abdomen and inner thighs results from fatigue caused by hours of sustained arousal. Intense contractions of the anal sphincter, so intense that they are painful, may also be experienced.

This condition of automatic, intense tumescence of the primary erectile organs usually occurs after six to twelve hours of continual, combined physical and mental stimulation. Once this transcendent sexual state is initiated, physical stimulation ceases to be necessary. The state is self-sustaining, and is difficult to terminate, but will gradually cease of its own accord if the mind is exclusively focused on some everyday topic for an extended period. The slightest erotic thought immediately restores full tumescence. It causes a considerable strain upon the heart and raises the blood pressure so that the singing of blood can be heard in the ears and felt distinctly throbbing in the temples. It should not be allowed to continue for more than a few hours at a time to prevent serious and possibly dangerous stress upon the cardiovascular and nervous systems. Anyone who has chronic high blood pressure or heart problems should not seek this transcendent level of physical arousal.

Presumably Crowley intended that his technique for raising sexual energy be applied while engendering the homunculus. The eroto-comatose state would be particularly effective in focusing the thoughts of the impregnated woman upon the astrological sphere of the spirit evoked each day into the triangle, as described in step four of the homunculus formula. It is a kind of trance state in which the mind is rendered highly impressionable. To achieve this end, it would be appropriate to have the woman stimulated by one or more assistants within the triangle during evocation. Light kisses and caresses with the lips and tongue, coupled with stroking by the fingertips and light scratching with the fingernails, would be effective in achieving a sustained level of arousal. During this operation the assistants would ceaselessly describe the nature and qualities of the spirit, chant poetry appropriate to its sphere, play harmonious music, and burn appropriate incense. One period of stimulation would occur while the woman was awake. The other would be gently applied to her during sleep, when physical exhaustion prevented her from awaking in response to the caresses, and suggestions could be planted directly into her subconscious.

{ 6 }

Magical Uses for Sexual Fluids

Sexual Fluids, Both Mana and Taboo

Throughout history, the fluids that issue from the sex organs—menstrual blood, semen, and lubricating oils—were believed to concentrate within themselves the creative force of spirit. Their association with sexuality both lent them immense *mana* (occult power) in magic and made them taboo substances. In the past the manipulation of these substances was considered more than sufficient proof that the magician or alchemist who used them was evil and accursed by God.

Shorn of their mythic baggage, there is nothing inherently wicked or harmful in these fluids. They are merely sexual. In these days, with cunnilingus and fellatio almost universal sexual practices in Western culture, they are less likely to provoke a negative response. The consumption of semen and the other fluids emitted by the genitals is considered a natural part of oral sex. Only menstrual blood has retained its ancient power to evoke instinctive revulsion. It is no coincidence that it is the most potent of the three substances used in sexual alchemy.

Menstrual Blood

The occult virtues of menstrual blood have completely different sets of associations in Western occultism from the blood within the body. Whereas arterial or subcutaneous blood was thought to vitalize and empower, menstrual blood once it had flowed out of the body was almost universally believed to sterilize, destroy, and kill. This naturally made it a fluid of Lilith. Mythically, it is without question the single most potent magical substance. The Roman writer Pliny the Elder devotes two entire chapters of his *Nature History* to a listing of the dreadful powers of menstrual blood.[1] Agrippa mentions many of these in his treatment of sorceries.

> Of these therefore the first is menstruous blood, which, how much power it hath in sorcery, we will now consider; for, as they say, if it comes over new wine, it makes it sour, and if it doth but touch the vine it spoils it forever, and by its very touch it makes all plants, and trees barren, and they that be newly set, to die; it burns up all the herbs in the garden, and makes fruit fall off from the trees, it darkens the brightness of a looking glass, dulls the edges of knives, and razors, dims the beauty of ivory, and it makes iron presently rusty, it makes brass rust, and smell very strong: it makes dogs mad, if they do but taste of it, and if they being thus mad shall bite anyone, that wound is incurable: it kills whole hives of bees, and drives them from the hives that are but touched with it: it makes linen black that are boiled: it makes mares cast their foal if they do but touch it, and makes women miscarry if they be but smeared with it: it makes asses barren as long as they eat of the corn that hath been touched with it.[2]

Agrippa quotes many other miraculous wonders of the menses from Pliny, not all of which are baneful. It can be used to cure fevers, epilepsy, and rabies (provided the rabies are not caused by a dog that has tasted menstrual blood); rid farmers' fields of insect pests; avert hail, lightning, and storms; guard a house from evil when smeared on the door posts; and drive away serpents when burned. Agrippa also reports that it can be used to put out fires, but this is an error in his interpretation of Pliny, who says only that menstrual blood retains its occult power even if burned to ashes. This assertion is significant because it indicates that menstrual blood is still potent in a dried and powdered form.

The power of the blood is greater during the waning phase of the Moon, even greater at New Moon, greater still during lunar and solar eclipses. The blood is strongest when it is taken from a young virgin. The reason menstrual blood is said to be more potent during the waning, dark and eclipse of the Moon is because it is a substance of the dark lunar goddesses such as Persephone and Hecate, whose power is greatest during the decrease and dark of the Moon. The waning lunar cycle is the time of destructive or evil works of magic, just as the waxing phase is the time for works of creation and growth.

According to ancient folk belief recorded by Pliny, to rid a grainfield of insects, a menstruating woman must walk around the field naked with her bleeding vulva exposed. The rationale is that by doing so, she becomes a living incarnation of the goddess of the dark face of the Moon. Her flowing menses are charged with the occult power of the dark lunar goddess, who has under her authority all the creeping and verminous things of the Earth. The woman performing this extermination must walk around the field widdershins before the rising of the Sun, for if she performs this act in sunlight it will kill the grain.

Menstrual blood was believed to have power over rabies, both to cause and to cure it, because rabies was mainly associated with dogs, and the dog is the beast of Hecate and other lunar goddesses. Until recent centuries rabies was known as hydrophobia (water-dread), because those creatures afflicted with the disease were said to refuse to drink water and to flee in terror from it. Water is also a lunar substance. To cure rabies, Pliny directs that a small piece of cloth stained with menstrual blood be put under the cup of a person who is afraid to drink after being bitten by a mad dog.

An interesting Roman folk cure for quartan fever, a sickness characterized by a shivering fit every third day (not every fourth day, as one might expect), is for the man afflicted to have sex with a woman who is just beginning to menstruate. Nothing is said by Pliny about the cure of a woman with the quartan, but presumably the same cure would work, provided she was inclined to undertake it. This fever, along with the tertian ague (shivering fit every second day), may also be cured by rubbing menstrual blood onto the soles of the patient's feet. This is particularly effective when done by the woman herself, and in such a way that the patient is unaware of the application. Presumably it is a treatment for those extremely ill and unconscious or delirious with fever—otherwise, it would be difficult not to notice a woman smearing blood on one's feet.

The myths surrounding menstrual blood were ancient even in the days of Tacitus (born A.D. 55), who refers to one such fable as "the account of old authors." They probably go back to primeval Goddess cults that were already fading away into the mists of history before Tacitus and Pliny were born. Even so, these myths have persisted down to modern times. It is still a social taboo to have sex with a women during her menstrual period, although the reasons given for this prohibition are varied and unconvincing.

All blood has immensely potent associations in magic. It was observed by primitive peoples that menstrual blood flowed in a cycle with more or less the same duration as the cycle of the Moon. Therefore it must be the blood of Luna. It was also observed that when pregnancy began, menstruation stopped. As long as a woman's blood flowed, no child could take root in her womb. Therefore it was natural to link this blood to the dark side of the Moon goddess, and the waning phase of destruction and sterility. The life force, or shakti, inherent in flowing menstrual blood is directed toward acts of destruction. It is thus naturally the blood of Lilith, Hecate, Kali, and other lunar goddesses of destruction.

It was also noted by primitive peoples that when there was no menstrual flow at all, such as in girls before puberty and older women after menopause, there was no fertility in the womb. Menstrual blood both sterilized and enabled generation. Like the Moon herself, it was both destructive and creative by turns. Its flow was a silent witness that the womb lay empty, yet without that flow the womb could never be filled. At certain times of a woman's cycle the purging, sterilizing power of menstrual blood was transformed into a nurturing power. Instead of being rejected and expelled by the living body as a poison, it was retained and turned inward to feed the newly engendered fetus. There could be no greater mystery.

Sexual intercourse with a woman during her menstrual period is explicitly prohibited in the Old Testament. "And if any man lie with her at all, and her flowers be upon him, he shall be unclean seven days."[3] According to the *Midrash*,[4] women were required to abstain from sex for a nominal seven-day period of their bleeding and for the seven days of purification that follow. In practice, the prohibition went much further than merely abstaining from sex. The rabbis interpreted Leviticus 18:19 ("Also thou shalt not approach unto a woman to uncover her nakedness as long as she is put apart for her uncleanness.") to mean that a husband should not approach a menstruating woman, or a woman during her subsequent seven days of purification ("white days"), at all.

> It is written, "And unto a woman in her menstrual uncleanliness thou shalt not come near" (Lev. xviii, 19): because it is written: "thou shalt not come near" it was explained that any kind of coming near her is forbidden: they should not laugh at each other, he should not carry on with her conversations of levity even about things that bring about sin; . . . He is not permitted to

come in contact with her, even with her little finger; he should not hand over anything to her, be it even a long thing, nor should he receive aught from her; he is likewise forbidden to throw anything from his hand into her hand, neither is it permitted to throw aught from her hand into his hand. . . . He is not permitted to eat with her at the same table. . . . He is not allowed to drink of whatever was left in the cup that she drank out of. . . . He is not allowed to sleep with her in the same bed even if the bed is not especially designed for her and even if each of them are wearing the clothes, and even if each of them has a separate mattress. It is forbidden even if they lie in two separate beds but the beds touch one another. If they lie on the ground, they should not sleep facing one another, unless there is a big distance between them. . . . They are not permitted to sit on a long bench which swings. . . . She is not permitted to pour a cup of wine for him in his presence, nor bring it to him, nor set it before him upon the table, nor make the bed in his presence.[5]

These are only a portion of the prohibitions set between a husband and his wife during her term of "uncleanliness" in the code of Jewish law (*Kitzur Schulchan Aruch*). They are quite clearly a misinterpretation of the verse in Leviticus, which says only that a man shall not approach a menstruating woman to "uncover her nakedness," that is, to copulate with her. To the modern mind, they seem utterly incomprehensible, but they grew out of a deep-seated cultural awe and fear of the occult power of menstrual blood and the act of menstruation.

The reason behind the prohibition against sexual union with a menstruating woman is not explained in the Bible. Since it was regarded as the word of God, there was presumed to be no need for explanations. It was probably merely the codification in written form of an ancient tribal taboo that had never been rationally questioned by those who followed it. The central factor of the prohibition is that a man must not allow menstrual blood to touch him, regardless of how small an amount of blood may be involved.

The Kabbalists were not content merely to accept the law against contact with menstrual blood. They wanted to understand it. The explanation of Naftali Herz Bacharach (seventeenth century), which reflects the misogyny of his time, was that menstrual blood was a curse upon women that had descended from Eve's sexual union with Lilith in her masculine guise of Samael, the Serpent. Eve's menstrual blood was actually the "filth and the impure seed" of Samael. Lilith as the Serpent was able to seduce Eve because of (in the view of the rabbi) the inherent lustfulness and weakness of women. In her turn Eve then seduced Adam to lie with her during her menses.

Once Adam had voluntarily corrupted himself by this act, Lilith became strong "in her husks" and was able to come to Adam against his will, stealing his seed to engender "many demons and spirits and Lilin."[6]

There is a tendency among modern readers to dismiss past beliefs as foolish or evil whenever they present views we disagree with, but instead of rejecting out of hand such viewpoints, we should examine them for the lessons they can teach. The Kabbalistic belief that Eve's menstrual blood was the semen of Samael in his serpentine form indicates a strong link between menstrual blood and kundalini energy, which is always characterized as serpentine. The authority exerted over Adam by the blood of Eve shows a belief in its immense potency. In the Kabbalistic legend, it is the gift of Lilith to Eve that confers upon her power over Adam, or in a more general sense, a vehicle through which women can compel men against their will. Not surprisingly, the rabbis regarded this as a curse rather than a gift—anything that gave women power over men would be looked upon by them as a curse.

In European alchemy there is frequent mention of the "menstruum." In a strict physical sense this is the solvent liquid in the alchemical vessel. It received this name because alchemists likened the transformation of base metal to the transformation of semen within the womb. Ancient medical writers understood there to be two parts to the fetus developing within the womb, a spermatic part derived from its father and a menstrual part derived from its mother. The menstrual liquid was thought to surround and nourish the sperm, causing it to quicken and grow.

> Our menstruum, or solvent, then, must be a sour vegetable water. Moreover, as lead is crude at the centre and pure near the circumference, the vegetable menstruum which Nature has invented for dissolving lead, must be of the same kind. There are two other solvents which have all the characteristics of gold and silver, being fixed bodies of sensitive temperament, and possessing the power of dissolving these metals, because they are quite free from all crudity; and the one solvent which is gold the Ancients have called the greater menstruum. The menstruum of Saturn they call the smaller, because it has no power over gold.[7]

Merely because alchemists used the term menstruum in a metaphorical way does not mean that actual menstrual blood was never employed in alchemy. Many substances of the human body were used, among them excrement, hair, and regular blood. It would be very strange if alchemists overlooked the immense magical potency of menstrual blood in their experiments, particularly in the creation of the homunculus, since menstrual blood within the womb was understood to nourish the fetus.

Menstrual blood played an important role in the sexual magic of both East and West, but its use is scarcely ever even referred to, and is never described in complete detail. It was employed by the Tantric cults devoted to the goddess of destruction, Kali. There is some indication that it was prepared for ritual use by women in a dried, powdered form, and then applied to statues of the Goddess, probably to the vulva and thighs, and also consumed by Kali worshippers, probably mixed with wine.[8]

Following the teachings of Aleister Crowley, who conducted his own experiments into sex magic, it was also used in certain ninth-grade rituals of the Ordo Templi Orientis. Concerning the eucharist of the Order, Crowley wrote: "Ask our brethren the Alchemists, and the Adepts of the Rosy Cross. The first answer: It is nothing but the Lion with his coagulated blood, and the gluten of the White Eagle; it is the ocean wherein both Sun and Moon have bathed. The others: it is the Dew upon the Rose that hath concealed the Cross."[9] Menstrual blood and semen are apparently intended here.

Elsewhere Crowley writes: "It is said that the second party [the woman] is useless, even dangerous, when the influence of the Moon first shows itself. . . . But on the second day [of menstruation] and after, though perhaps not on the last day, the Sacrament is more efficacious than at any other time, as is figured by our ancient Brethren the Alchemists in their preference of the Red Tincture to the White."[10]

Although Crowley used alchemical metaphor to disguise his meaning, there is little question that he was writing about semen, vaginal secretions, and menstrual blood. To be sure, his words also carry a higher, metaphysical meaning. They can only be fully comprehended when understood simultaneously on two levels. On the higher level they describe spiritual forces. On the lower level of the human body they describe sexual fluids.

The "lion" is the penis, the "eagle" is the vulva, and the "gluten" is clear vaginal secretion: "For the Gluten is but a menstruum or solvent, and containeth nothing it itself."[11] Apparently Crowley's eucharist consists of orally consuming the mingled semen and vaginal secretions, which may or may not be mingled with menstrual blood, from the vagina following a prolonged act of intercourse performed from the rear, or "doggy fashion," to use a vulgar but visually evocative term.[12]

Crowley believed that his sexual eucharist was more potent when mingled with the menstrual discharge, provided it was not done on the first or last day of menstruation. It is not clear from his writings whether this exclusion of the first and last day was motivated by physiological or occult considerations. The menses reach their greatest purity, and thus their greatest magical potency, at the height of their flow, just as the power of the Moon is greatest when its face is full and reflects the greatest light. This may have been Crowley's reasoning.

The Role of Semen

Semen probably played a greater role in medieval, Renaissance, and modern alchemy than menstrual blood, if only because it was more readily available to alchemists, most of whom were male. The exceptions to this rule were men such as Nicholas Flammel, John Dee, and Edward Kelley, and in modern times Aleister Crowley. All worked in close unity with their wives.

Flammel praised his wife Perrenella as an essential part of his alchemical operations. The wives of Dee and Kelley actually signed a pact or covenant pledging themselves as willing sexual participants in the magical operations of their husbands, which concerned among other matters the making of the Red Powder of projection. Crowley conducted his own brand of sexual alchemy with his wife, and later with his various lovers.

The Great Work has often been likened to the engendering of an offspring. Christian alchemists believed that this process could most perfectly be accomplished within the bounds of a lawful marriage that had been consecrated and consummated in the presence of the divine Spirit. An alchemist working with the full cooperation of his own wife could use the creative energies generated from their loving sexual union to produce an alchemical child, which might be the Stone, the Elixir, or the homunculus depending on the goal of the alchemist.

More often alchemists worked alone. Their marriage was spiritual, their wife the Goddess herself, her physical womb the alchemical vessel. The menstruum was manufactured by the alchemist from such substances as the blood of white doves (symbols of holy Spirit) and the red ochre of the Earth. Into this the alchemist shed his own seed, and often his own blood to nourish it. The effort to engender a child of the art within the womb of the vessel might be abstract, with mercury, salts, sulfur, and various metals taking the place of bodily substances, or literal, involving actual sexual energies and sexual products of the body. In either case, the underlying symbolism was the same.

Alchemists seldom write in an explicit way about the use of semen. The spilling of the seed outside the body of a woman for purposes other than conception was known as the sin of Onan (from Genesis 38:9) and was strongly condemned by the Catholic

Church. This sin included masturbation, *coitus interruptus* (withdrawal of the penis at climax to spend outside the vagina) and even nocturnal emissions where there was any suggestion that the erotic dreams had been deliberately encouraged. To employ semen in works of alchemy was to violate both the law and the taboos of European culture. Alchemists could scarcely advocate it in their writings.

Even though semen is a product of the male body, it is magically linked to the Moon due to its pearly white color, which so much resembles mother-of-pearl or moonstone. By the same token, menstrual blood, which is a product of the female body and clearly linked to the lunar cycle, was also associated with the Sun because of its scarlet color. This is the Yin-Yang of Western alchemy. Within everything male lies a seed of the female, and within everything female a corresponding seed of the male. All things contain their opposites in potential.

Something called the "Sperm of the Philosophers" is mentioned in an early sixteenth-century alchemical tract by the court astrologer Nicolaus Melchior Szebeni titled *Addam et processum sub forma missae* (Adam and the [alchemical] process under the form of the Mass). He was astrologer to Ladislaus II, King of Hungary and Bohemia, from 1490 to 1516, and it is to this king that his work was dedicated. This document was extensively quoted by Jung.[13] It casts several lights on the identification of the Virgin Mary with the Queen of Heaven by Christian alchemists, on the recognition that the transformation of the host is an alchemical operation, and on the sexual aspects of the art.

The Sperm of the Philosophers was described by Szebenis as "our blessed gum which dissolves of itself."[14] It is the semen of the Sun, used to impregnate the virgin Moon in an "alchemical bath." A recipe is provided for the gum in the *Artis auriferae*: "Take alum from Spain, white gum and red gum, which is the kibric [kibrit, or sulfur] of the philosophers . . . and join in true marriage gum with gum."[15] This may be interpreted literally, but may also be interpreted to signify sexual substances of the human body. The white gum is sperm, the red gum is blood produced when the groom, who is the Sun and also Christ, ruptures the hymen of his virgin bride, the Moon, who is also Mary the Queen of Heaven, in the course of their "true marriage."

Since the blood shed by a virgin bride on her wedding night issues from the same source as menstrual blood, and is produced during the sexual act, it was inevitable that it be closely linked with menstrual blood in alchemical symbolism. It was likely thought to mingle with and nourish the sperm within the womb, rendering the sperm more fertile, even as menstrual blood contained and retained within the womb was believed to be necessary to nourish the fetus.

Semen played a key part in the personal magic of the visual artist Austin Osman Spare (1886–1956), who was associated with Aleister Crowley (he contributed two drawings to Crowley's periodical *The Equinox*). Spare's magic was a form of sexual alchemy. He used stylized letters combined into the form of a single graphic symbol to embody his ritual purpose. These symbols he drew on paper, then folded the paper and placed it into a small clay vase of his own making. The vase acted as the alchemical vessel, or womb, in which Spare's magical child—his desire—was brought to fruition.

Spare deliberately fashioned the necks of these vases so that they fitted tightly around his own erect penis. After concentrating powerfully on his purpose, he used the vase into which he inserted his graphic symbol for masturbation, working his penis in and out of its neck until he ejaculated his semen upon the occult glyph within the womb of the vessel. He then capped the vase and waited for his magic to realize itself in the greater world.[16]

In principle, his system was identical to the method described by Paracelsus for engendering the homunculus. Paracelsus is usually understood to have been writing about the production of an actual spiritual being, whereas Spare's homunculii were his ritual desires. However, this distinction may only be apparent. Spare would have considered (rightly, in my opinion) each of his actualized ritual desires as an independent spirit whose function was to bring about the purpose he intended by his magic. By quickening these beings with his own seed, Spare became their father. The Soul of the World was their mother.

From a technical point of view, Spare's magic would probably have been more effective had he placed a small amount of blood into the vase to act as a menstruum before ejaculating into it. Indeed, he may have done so. His magic is imperfectly understood. It seems unlikely that Spare was unaware of the alchemical formula of the homunculus, which involves the red and the white essences mingled with a solvent medium (the alchemical bath) in the womb of Earth (the material expression of the virgin womb of the Queen of Heaven).

The Alchemical Bath

Blood and semen were believed to require a fluid medium inside the womb in which to mingle and unite. In alchemy, this is the Water of Life, present in the alchemical bath in which the Sun and Moon copulate to engender the child of alchemy.

Now he [the Sun] makes haste to bind and betroth himself to the virgin bride [the Moon], and to get her with child in the bath over a moderate fire. But the virgin will not become pregnant at once unless she be kissed in repeated embraces. Then she conceives in her body, and thus is begotten the child of good omen, in accordance with the order of nature.[17]

The image of bridegroom and bride consummating their marriage vows in a bath is curious at first impression, but has a sound practical basis both in alchemy and in human sexuality. In order for two alchemical substances to interact, they must be placed in a medium that dissolves and mingles their separate natures. This liquid medium was known as the menstruum. However, this title is misleading since menstrual blood is not merely a medium but a powerful agent in its own right. Crowley's menstruum, which he called a gluten, saying that it "containeth nothing it itself," is a more apt analogue to the alchemical menstruum, described in one text as a "sour vegetable water."

A fluid medium is also needed in order for impregnation to occur during copulation. Without the moistness of the vagina, spermatozoa would find it difficult, if not impossible, to swim into the womb and fertilize the ovum. The sexual fluids emitted during arousal by both partners provide a bath that enables the sperm to travel more easily within the vagina. It was well understood by medieval alchemists and magicians alike that moistness is necessary for fertility, and that dryness is inherently sterile.

The Waters of Life are more closely connected with woman than with man by alchemists. It is Luna who rules moisture. The Moon controls the tides, the menses, and (it was believed) the weather. For example, a ring around the Moon was thought to foretell rain. The vivifying action of alchemical water was usually understood to occur within the artificial womb of the alchemist, the Hermetic vessel (*vas Hermetis*). Alchemical water was a product of the Moon.

Water was understood by many alchemists as the single ground of all the mystical products of the art, including the Red and White powders, the Stone, and the Elixir of Life. Alchemical water was said to be fiery. The *Figurarum Aegyptiorum secretarum* states: "The water of the philosophers is fire."[18] By fire alchemists understood spiritual fire, the life-force itself. This was conveyed upon the breath and stored in the blood. George Ripley asserted, "The aerial soul is the secret fire of our philosophy, our oil, our mystic water."[19] One name for the Stone was *hydrolith* (the water stone), both because it was produced by the water of alchemy, and because the alchemical water could be extracted from it.

FIGURE 6-1.
Union of Sun and Moon in the alchemical bath.

An illustration in Elias Ashmole's *Theatrum Chemicum Britannicum*[20] shows a man and a woman, representing brother Sun and sister Moon, standing naked in the alchemical bath with their hands clasped. Above their heads, God breathes spirit, which streams from his lips as a liquid, into the open mouth of an Hermetic vessel. Within the vessel the image of the Sun hovers over the upturned crescent of the Moon as though copulating with her. From the bottom of the vessel seven streams of water issue from seven spouts and shower down on the lovers. Between their feet in the water of the bath a frog, emblem of fertility, catches one of the seven streams in its mouth. Two dragons hang down from the cloud of heaven to bite the lovers on their heels. The caption reads: Spirit, Soul, Flesh.

Each dragon has four feathers on each of its two wings and three toes on each of its two feet. Seven rays radiate from the cloud of heaven on the right side of God and seven rays also shine from the left side. This results in seven multiples of seven—the seven spouts of the vessel, the two sets of seven rays from the divine cloud, and the four sets of four feathers plus three toes on each side of the dragons. The significance of the number seven is the seven wandering bodies of traditional astrology, which figure so prominently in alchemical symbolism.

The accompanying tract, for which no author is named by Ashmole, reads in part:

> Our Stone is made of one simple thing,
> That in him hath both Soule and Lyfe,
> He is Two and One in kinde,
> Married together as Man and Wife:
> Our Sulphur is our Masculine,
> Our Mercury is our Femenine,
> Our Earth is our Water Cleere;
> Our Sulphur also is our Fier,
> And as Earth is in our Water cleare,
> Soe is Aer in our Fier.[21]

By "Lyfe" spirit or breath (*spiritus*) is intended. The masculine component, spirit, graphically represented by the Sun, is also composed of the elements Fire and Air. The feminine component, soul, graphically represented by the Moon, is also composed of the elements Water and Earth. Of these, Water and Earth may be seen, but Air and subtle Fire are invisible, and infuse Water and Earth as qualities.

The alchemical water was known under many names. Jung wrote: "Like the *Prima materia* the water has a thousand names."[22] Some of these are mentioned in a tract from the alchemical collection known as the *Artis auriferae* published at Basel in 1593.

> And there is in fact one substance in which everything is contained and that
> is the *sulphur philosophorum*, [which] is water and soul, oil, Mercurius and Sol,
> the fire of nature, the eagle, the *lachryma*, the first hyle of the wise, the *materia prima* of the perfect body.[23]

Some other names mentioned are poison, quicksilver, cambar, *aqua permanens*, gum, vinegar, urine, sea-water, dragon, and serpent. The inclusion of oil and urine in this list is interesting. The fluids produced during sexual arousal have a very oily quality. Urine has long been looked upon as a sexual fluid because it originates from the primary sex organs of both men and women. Urine is both sour and salt, as are sea-water and vinegar.

To some extent, urine shares the baneful associations of menstrual blood in medieval European magic. It is most often encountered in literature and historical accounts as a tool used by witches for works of evil. During the Middle Ages witches were believed by most Christians to make a hole in the ground, urinate into the hole, then stir the urine counterclockwise to generate destructive storms. We can recognize in this bit of folklore the hole as the Hermetic vessel and the ancient link between weather magic and the power of the Moon. Luna rules all forms of water including urine.

Urine was employed as a charm against evil magic in the form of the witch bottle. The hair, fingernail parings, and blood of a person believed to be bewitched, along with several horseshoe nails (perhaps three or nine, which are lunar numbers) were placed in a clay or ceramic bottle filled with the urine of the bewitched person. The bottle was sealed and at midnight was put on the hearth close to the fire to boil while the friends of the supposed victim recited the Lord's Prayer backwards. The boiling urine was thought to cause the witch great pain and to compel the witch to come to the place where the magic was being worked. If the bottle exploded, it was considered a sure sign that the witch would die. Apparently those who employed this evil magic did not see the incongruity of fighting the Devil by reciting the Lord's Prayer backwards.

By another account, the bottle was used to test the urine of an accused witch. If the boiling of the urine caused the cork in the bottle to fly out (which must have been the usual event), it indicated that the urine was "bad" and thus from a witch, who was then presumably scratched—to draw the blood of a witch by scratching her in the face was thought to deprive her of her power. Sometimes little felt hearts made to represent the heart of a suspected witch were stuck full of pins and placed into witch bottles in order to make the witch suffer. These were believed to confer protection to the possessor of the bottle. Reflecting on these cases, one might be forgiven for wondering who is the evil witch and who the hapless victim.

In an ancient alchemical text is written, "No water will become the elixir save that which comes from the scarabs of our water."[24] The scarab referred to is specifically the one-horned scarab beetle sacred to the Egyptians because it was believed to be self-generating and to renew its own life within a ball of cattle dung. The cow is an animal of the Moon, the ball rolled by the beetle was thought to represent the Sun. The one-horned scarab was sacred to Hermes-Thoth because both were thought to be bisexual and capable of self-impregnation. The single horn of the scarab resembled the curved beak of the ibis, the bird sacred to Thoth.

We may wonder what is meant by the words "the scarabs of our water." Since the scarab was thought to be self-renewing, capable of generating itself anew from itself out of dung, it may be that the urine of the alchemist is here intended. Urine, which begins as a waste product and a noxious substance is, through refinement and alchemical transmutation, made into the Elixir of Life that renews the youth and vitality of the alchemist. This makes sense, since by transforming his own urine into the Elixir, the alchemist renews himself from himself by utilizing bodily excrement in a way similar to the supposed practice of the one-horned scarab, sacred to the god of alchemy, Hermes Trismegistus.

I am inclined to make a distinction between the water and the oil in the context of sexual alchemy. It is usual to treat these two terms as the same in general alchemical texts. Indeed, it is usual for numerous unique alchemical terms to be indiscriminately confused together. However, it was proverbial that oil and water do not mix—that is, that they are distinct substances. When considering the fluids of sexual alchemy, it is useful to separate them. Water is urine and oil is the sexual secretions generated from both the male penis and female vagina during sexual arousal and copulation.

There is no evidence that this distinction was ever made by the rank and file of alchemists who employed nonbiological substances in their experiments. However, it may well have been recognized by those who engaged in sexual alchemy. It makes good sense, since urine is watery while vaginal and penal secretions are oily. Urine is more copious, and therefore common, whereas the sexual secretions are slighter and therefore more precious, just as in ancient times oil was a precious commodity and water was relatively common.

In Western culture there is a general revulsion against the sight, smell, and touch of urine. Its powerful sexual associations are strongly suppressed. This is not the case in the East, where urine, both animal and human, is regarded as a purifying and cleansing agent both in medicine and in magic. In India it is a common practice to drink a pint or so of one's own urine each day as a health tonic to maintain vigor and fortify the body against disease.

After what has been written here, you will appreciate that this practice is completely alchemical in principle. The underlying premise is that by passing one's own urine through the body repeatedly, it is refined and transmuted into an Elixir with healing and invigorating properties. Physically, the urine will not be changed, beyond a slight increase in the level of toxins it contains. The transformation is magical. It is the mental components of intention and belief that render the practice effective.

In traditional forms of sexual alchemy when urine is employed, it is the concentration of shakti force in the urine that transforms it into a magical potion with healing and invigorating properties. Urine is used in the sexual alchemy of both East and West, although its use is seldom openly described. Kenneth Grant makes several allusions to its use. According to him, true *soma* (an intoxicating drink used in Hindu worship) is the essence of urine that has been repeatedly recycled through the body of the yogi. He makes the interesting statement that it bisexualizes the body and creates in the adept a condition necessary for the assumption of the god-form (the ritual putting on of the identity and personality of a deity). He also asserts that urine-drinking renders a yogi fearless.[25]

In modern Western magic one of the central ritual practices involves putting on the god-form of Thoth-Hermes, who is the patron god of Hermetic magic. As has been mentioned, Hermes was understood to be self-renewing and bisexual by the later Egyptians. To imbibe the "scarabs of our water" as the old alchemical text puts it would be to mimic the self-renewal of Hermes, and therefore to become like Hermes. Why the practice should be thought to result in fearlessness is not clear to me, unless it is that knowledge dispels fear, which is born of ignorance, and Hermes is the wisest of all the gods. Therefore to become like Hermes would naturally result in a greater courage. Hermes might also be supposed to be brave since he is the psychopomp or guide of dead souls to the Underworld.

In alchemy, sexual secretions are naturally more potent than urine since they are produced in conjunction with the circulation of shakti energy. The energy of the Goddess causes tumescence and the copious flow of sexual fluid. This may occur even in the absence of lustful thoughts and physical manipulations. It is the presence of kundalini shakti that causes the Oil to flow, not the erotic images in the mind or the touches applied to the sexual organs. These things are more or less incidental to the flow of the Oil. This fact is not widely appreciated because for most individuals shakti force is only awakened in the body in conjunction with lewd thoughts or sexual caresses. However, the Goddess can be awakened more purely and more powerfully without either erotic thoughts or physical manipulations of any kind. She will then cause the Oil of Lilith to flow in greater than normal abundance.

[7]

Salt, Sulfur, and Mercury

The Three Mothers

When properly transmuted, extracted and prepared by sexual alchemists, menstrual blood became the fabled Red Powder, semen became the White Powder, and the clear fluid secretions became the oil that I have characterized as the Oil of Lilith. These three substances are the most powerful and important physical productions of the human body. They are equivalent to the Salt, Sulfur, and Mercury of conventional alchemy, about which so much inspired truth and so much nonsense has been written over the centuries. In order to understand the nature of these three sexual products of the body, it is necessary to have some understanding of the basis for their alchemical symbolism.

In many alchemical texts Mercury and Sulfur are treated as a pair of sexual opposites, and are represented symbolically by the marriage of the Moon and Sun, and by the mingling of opposite elements Water and Fire. On a more esoteric level this union of Mercury and Sulfur expresses the marriage of the soul with the spirit. This makes sense when only two principles are involved—Sulfur is clearly the correct choice for the Sun, and Mercury does possess some of the occult attributions of the

Moon, such as its silvery color, its ability to reflect light like a mirror, and its liquidity. However, when all three alchemical principles are considered together, and linked with the three active elements, Salt is seen to be more appropriate to the element Water and the Moon, and alchemical Mercury as the mediating principle that unites the extremes of Salt and Sulfur more naturally accords with Air and the planet Mercury, which is an airy planet.

The Hermetic Order of the Golden Dawn made a direct link between the three alchemical principles and the three Mother letters of the Hebrew alphabet, which are associated with the three active elemental principles Fire, Water, and Air. Concerning the pillars of the Golden Dawn temple, it is written in the First Knowledge Lecture of the Golden Dawn: "The flaming red triangular capitals which crown the summit of the Pillars represent the Triune manifestation of the Spirit of Life, the Three Mothers of the Sepher Yetsirah, the three Alchemical Principles of Nature, the Sulphur, the Mercury, and the Salt."[1]

Sepher Yetzirah is the oldest book of the complex philosophical and magical system of Jewish mysticism known as the Kabbalah. It was translated into English in 1887 by Wynn Westcott, one of the founders of the Golden Dawn, and its teachings played a key role in the magic of that Rosicrucian society. In *Sepher Yetzirah* the twenty-two letters of the Hebrew alphabet are divided into groups of twelve, seven, and three. The twelve Single letters are assigned the signs of the zodiac, the seven Double letters receive the traditional planets of astrology, and the three Mother letters get the active elements, Fire, Water, and Air.

> The Foundation of all the other sounds and letters is provided by the Three Mothers, Aleph, Mem and Shin; they resemble a Balance, on the one hand [Shin: Fire] the guilty, on the other hand [Mem: Water] the purified, and Aleph the Air is like the Tongue of a Balance standing between them.[2]

The square brackets are mine. It seems to me that the author of this ancient Kabbalistic text would have associated punishment with Fire and purification with Water. It should be noted, however, that just the opposite interpretation would be placed on these two letters in the Golden Dawn system, because the Tarot trump of the Last Judgement, linked with Shin and Fire, is a card of redemption and resurrection, while the Tarot trump of the Hanged Man, linked with Mem and Water, is often interpreted as a card of punishment and suffering. Elsewhere in *Sepher Yetzirah* the author makes perfectly clear that he intends Aleph to stand for Air, Mem for Water, and

Shin for Fire. There can be no confusion over these elemental assignments to the Mother letters.

The leaders of the Golden Dawn associated all three principles with each of the four elements and four directions of space, but with one principle ruling or predominating over the others in each quarter. They gave alchemical Salt rule in the Mother letter Mem, which is linked with elemental Water and the west. Sulfur was assigned to rule in the Mother letter Shin, which is linked with Fire and the south. Mercury was assigned to rule in the Mother letter Aleph, which is linked with Air and the east. The element of Earth and the northern quarter were given all three Mother letters together, and a second form of alchemical Mercury that was described as a sort of fixed or static Mercury was placed to rule there. "Here also is the Mercurial part chief, but hindered by the compound nature [of Earth] whence its faculty becomes germinative rather than mobile . . . "[3]

It may seem strange to some readers that, following the example of the Golden Dawn, I have linked elemental Water to the alchemical principle of Salt, when on the face of it salt appears wholly earthy in its nature. Like the Moon, alchemical Salt can be either earthy or watery by turns, depending on its circumstances, as I will explain below. By the same token, alchemical Mercury can be by turns either watery or airy, and Sulfur can be either fiery or earthy.

Elemental Earth is not represented among the Hebrew letters, although it is often associated with the letter Tau, which is assigned the Tarot trump the World and the planet Saturn in the system of Golden Dawn correspondences. Earth is considered to be an inert element because, according to the Pythagorean doctrine recorded by Plato in his *Timaeus,* its geometric structure is fundamentally different from that of the other three elements, making it impossible for Earth to be transformed into any other element. By contrast, the three active elements all have the same geometric foundation, and are convertible one into the other.

Salt

It is a profound mystery of menstrual blood that it is outwardly solar, yet inwardly lunar. The very fact that it is predominantly blood would seem to make it a product of the Sun, since the blood is the seat of the life-force, just as the Sun is the source of all generation and growth on the Earth. Its red color is solar and fiery, and harmonizes well with the qualities of Sulfur. Even its fabled power to blight and kill plant life is solar—when the Sun becomes too hot, it causes drought by withering plants. Yet

Alchemical Principles	Salt	Mercury	Sulfur
Body Fluids	menses	clear oil (gluten)	semen
Alchemical Products	Red Powder	Oil of Lilith	White Powder
Alchemical Symbols	white eagle (sometimes red)	hermaphrodite	red lion (sometimes white)
Astrological Bodies	Moon	Mercury	Sun
Zodiac Signs	Fixed	Mutable	Cardinal
Alchemical Metals	silver	mercury	gold
Letters of AZOTH	A–O (Greek)	A–Z (Latin)	A–Th (Hebrew)
Letters of IHVH	both Hehs (Water, Earth)	Vau (Air)	Yod (Fire)
Related Elements	Water (also Earth)	Air	Fire
Mother Letters	Mem	Aleph	Shin
Tarot Trumps	The Hanged Man	The Fool	The Last Judgement
Sephiroth: Higher Cycle	Binah	Kether; also Tiphareth (Son)	Chokmah
Sephiroth: Lower Cycle	Yesod	Malkuth (Daughter)	Tiphareth
Sexual Trinity	Mother	Son/Daughter	Father
Kabbalistic Trinity	Aima	Messiah	Abba
Christian Trinity	Holy Spirit	Christ	God the Father
Human Microcosm	Body	Soul	Spirit

TABLE 7-1. Attributions for the Three Alchemical Principles.

paradoxically the menstrual flow is enslaved to the cycle of the Moon, and issues from the womb, which is a lunar organ of the body. It is essential for the conception and growth of the fetus, a lunar process.

Menstrual blood is magically equivalent to the alchemical principle of Salt because of its intimate connection with the cycle of the Moon. Salt gains its lunar association because all the oceans of the world are salty, and the Moon is able to draw the salt water of the sea upwards in the form of tides. The ancients associated the presence of salt with the lunar attraction. Crystalline salt is also lunar because of its transparency and lack of color, which causes it to resemble frozen water and rock crystal, both lunar substances. When powdered, it appears white, a lunar color. In an occult sense, menstrual blood is alchemical Salt in solution.

Just as the Moon shows two faces, one that waxes from darkness to light, and another opposite face that wanes from light to darkness, so does salt have two forms, a solid form when dry and a liquid form when wet. The waxing and waning of the Moon caused its astrological sphere to be related to both the sea and the earth equally. The Moon was believed not only to control the tides, but to rule and regulate the growth of plants as well. Farmers timed their planting according to the lunar phases. Nothing can live in the sea without salt, nothing can live on the land without salt, yet too much salt kills both plants and animals. Like the Moon and salt, menstrual blood is dual. It was fabled to kill anything with which it came into contact, yet it was necessary for the nurturing of the fetus in the womb.

In the system of occult correspondences that has descended from the Hermetic Order of the Golden Dawn, menstrual blood is associated with the active elemental principal of Water and the Hebrew Mother letter Mem, and by extension with the Tarot trump the Hanged Man, which signifies among other things voluntary sacrifice. The Hanged Man is suspended head downward on the trump, just as the baby in its mother's womb is head downward when it is soon to be born. This lunar substance is also associated with the Tarot trump the Moon, which depicts a lunar crescent between two towers, and two beasts that confront each other on the margin between land and water. The trump of the Moon is in its turn linked with the zodiac sign Pisces, represented by a glyph showing two fish swimming in opposite directions.

In the Kabbalah, menstrual blood may be related to Binah, the third sphere on the Tree of Sephiroth. Binah is also titled Aima, the Great Mother, because it symbolizes the womb of creation, and the Bitter Sea because this Sephiroth symbolizes the salty ocean within which all life originated. Through its lunar association menstrual blood is linked with the ninth Sephiroth on the Tree, Yesod, which relates to the genitals. Yesod is assigned the astrological Moon in the system of the Golden Dawn.

Menstrual blood was believed in Roman times to blacken polished silver, the metal of the Moon, if it so much as came near a silver mirror. This blackening is mainly due to the presence of salt in blood. Menstrual blood shares many of the occult associations of ordinary blood, particularly the blood shed when a woman loses her virginity. For this reason it may be linked to the physical body, which blood fills and vitalizes. From its link with alchemical Salt, it is connected with the Fixed signs of the zodiac—salt preserves and renders flesh inert and unchanging, and the Fixed signs are intensely focused and steadfast, the least mobile of the signs. Because the Moon is both watery and earthy, it is possible to link menstrual blood to both the first Hebrew letter Heh in Tetragrammaton (IHVH), which is the letter of Water, and also with the last Heh, which is the letter of Earth. The menses are naturally in harmony with all mother archetypes, and all female aspects of the divine trinities of different cultures.

Sulfur

The same great mystery that renders menstrual blood so enigmatic also adds complexity to an analysis of semen, which is a kind of mirror opposite to the menses. Semen is outwardly lunar but inwardly solar. Its pearly luster, its whiteness, its bland taste, and its relative coolness would seem at first consideration to confirm that it is a lunar substance, yet its essence is fiery and creative. A tiny drop quickens life within the womb. All of the fiery vitality that is acquired through the breath and stored in the blood throughout the life of an individual has its initial impulse in that minute spark at the time of conception. Semen is like the spark of fire that must be applied to fuel before it will burn—once applied, the heat generated by the fuel far exceeds the spark that began it.

Semen is in a magical sense the alchemical principle of Sulfur because both are substances intimately associated with the Sun. Sulfur is understood to be solar in its essential nature due to its bright yellow color in its powdered form, and because it burns when ignited and gives off heat and light. Sulfur is allotropic, and when heated and rapidly cooled forms a viscose, golden liquid that resembles honey—honey is a strongly solar substance. Semen is solar in that it is the product of sexual heat, and contains within itself the seed of creation, just as the Sun has the power to initiate life. The creative seed of the Sun is symbolized by the small dot in the center of the circular solar glyph used in both alchemy and astrology.

In the Golden Dawn correspondences, semen may be linked with the active elemental principal of Fire and the fiery Hebrew Mother letter Shin, and by extension with the Tarot trump the Last Judgement, which signifies the vitalization and reanimation of the dead. It is also linked with the Tarot trump the Sun, which on the traditional Marseilles card depicts two nearly naked children standing beneath a shower of sun drops that resemble Hebrew Yods. There are thirteen of these Yods, the same number as the total lunar months in a year, which is the cycle of time ruled by the Sun. The tarot trump the Sun is associated with the astrological Sun in the Golden Dawn system, which illustrates its self-sufficiency—the Sun needs nothing outside itself, but all living things on Earth, and indeed the structure of the entire solar system, require the Sun for continued existence.

In the Kabbalah, semen is related to Chokmah, the second sphere on the Tree of the Sephiroth. Chokmah is also titled Abba, the Great Father, because it symbolizes the spark or seed of creation that enters into the womb of Aima, where it initiates the growth of all things. Without the spark of Abba the womb of Aima would remain forever dark and barren. Without semen, the menstrual blood of women would waste itself and return to the earth each month instead of fulfilling its function of nourishing new life within the womb. Semen is also linked with the sixth Sephirah on the Tree, Tiphareth, which is the sphere to which the astrological Sun is assigned, and the seat of the Son of God, the Messiah or Anointed One, who arises to become God, just as in the cycle of earthly life the son of a father grows up to become a father in his turn.

Semen corresponds with the initial letter Yod in Tetragrammaton. Yod has a unique role in the symbolism of the Kabbalah. From this letter all other letters, and all words formed from those letters, and all wisdom expressed by those words, arose. Yod is the seed of God. For this reason the letter Yod is placed in the sphere of Chokmah, the Father, on the Tree of the Sephiroth. In the three levels of man, semen is assigned to fiery spirit; in the qualities of the zodiac, to the Cardinal signs which initiate actions and new enterprises. All father archetypes, and the father aspect of all holy trinities, may be related to semen.

Mercury

The crystal-clear oil that flow from both male and female genitals during sexual arousal is in a magical sense the Mercury of alchemy, because it is a product of both sexes, and because it enables and facilitates the quickening of the seed within the womb. Without this lubricating liquid medium, impregnation would be difficult or impossible, since sperm cells would have no way of swimming to the egg. Colorless, relatively tasteless, it has no fundamental quality of its own, but it acts as a facilitator that allows the qualities of Salt and Sulfur to express their functions and interact.

It is linked with the planet of the hermaphroditic god Mercury, whose glyph contains both the circle of the Sun and the crescent of the Moon in conjunction above the cross of Earth. The glyph of Mercury thus holds all three principles of alchemy within itself in balance. Mercury the Greek god was the medium of communication between gods and men, as well as the god of travel. Both of these mythic roles are accomplished through the manipulation of elemental Air. Mercury is the most airy of all the major classical gods, as the wings on his heels attest. Astrologers say that the planet Mercury, the swiftest of all the ancient wandering bodies in its motions across the heavens with the exception of the Moon, has no outstanding qualities of its own, in marked contrast to all the other planets, but only an ability to act as a communicator or medium for the other astrological forces. This makes the god an ideal representative for the Oil of Lilith.

In the Golden Dawn system of occult correspondences, the clear fluid released during sexual arousal may be linked with the active elemental principle of Air and the airy Hebrew Mother letter Aleph, and by extension with the Tarot trump The Fool, which signifies among other matters airy dreams and aspirations. The Fool is a figure of divinely inspired prophecy. In this way he fulfills a role similar to Mercury as a messenger between the gods and mankind. What the gods tell the Fool, the Fool repeats to humanity without actually comprehending what he is saying. Aleph is said in the Kabbalah to act as the tongue of the balance between Fire, which produced the heavens, and Water, which gave rise to the Earth. This is a pun, since the tongue requires air before it can fulfill its function as an organ of speech, and the atmosphere is the medium joining heaven and Earth.

It is also possible to relate the Oil of Lilith to the Tarot trump the Star—in old alchemical woodcuts, Mercury is often shown as a star between the disks of the Sun and Moon. The trump the Star is associated with the zodiac sign Aquarius, an airy sign that has as its glyph a water-bearer. On the traditional Marseilles trump the Star a naked woman stands pouring water from two pitchers, one onto the land and one into the sea. She is the union between the two realms, the symbolic medium through which they interact.

In the Kabbalah, sexual oil may be related on the level of potential to the highest Sephirah, Kether, which stands between and above Chokmah and Binah like the tongue of a balance, and is the initial impulse that gave rise to both. More actively, it is Tiphareth, because this sphere on the Middle Pillar of the Tree combines the natures of both Chokmah the Father and Binah the Mother in Tiphareth the Son.

On a lower level of realization it is associated with the tenth sphere, Malkuth, the sphere of the elements, which contains the Daughter that is a product of the union between the Son in Tiphareth, who has matured to usurp the place of his Father, and the Mother in Yesod, who has descended from Binah in the form of a virgin to unite sexually with the Son.

Mercury is hermaphroditic. It is appropriate that this alchemical principle is represented in the Kabbalah by both the Son and the Daughter on the Tree. Concerning the matter of the cyclical renewal of the Father and Mother through sexual union with their own children on the Tree of the Sephiroth, and in the court cards of the Tarot, which is generally known as the formula of Tetragrammaton, you should consult Aleister Crowley's *Book of Thoth*.[4] The subject is too complex to deal with here at length. It should be noted that Crowley refers to the Oil of Lilith as the "gluten" in his OTO writings, and in his text on the Thoth Tarot.

The Oil and alchemical Mercury may both be related to the Mutable signs of the zodiac, which are adaptable and variable by nature, suiting themselves to circumstances as they arise. They are not passive, but rather are receptive and then responsive, having a vibratory energy. In Tetragrammaton, the Oil corresponds with the letter Vau, which is linked to the Son of the Father and Mother, and to the mediating element Air. In the holy trinities of all cultures the Oil relates to the Child, who is usually male but sometimes androgynous or twins of different sexes.

Both menstrual blood and semen are emitted from the body as liquids, but are prepared alchemically as powders. The Oil of Lilith is emitted as a liquid also, but because its essential identity is liquid— something that is equally true of alchemical Mercury—it is not reduced to a powder, but is retained in its liquid form. In a mystical sense, alchemical Salt is crystallized elemental Water, and alchemical Sulfur is crystallized elemental Fire. Elemental Air cannot be crystallized or fixed, but it can be transformed into a mobile liquid. The fundamental function of the Oil is to serve as a facilitating medium that enables the natures of menstrual blood and semen to express and fulfill themselves. Neither has its fulfillment alone, but only in combination with the other. Yet the simple union of the two produces no reaction without the Oil to join them.

{ 8 }

God-making

The Telestic Art

In classical times the most common way to attain a direct personal relationship with a god or goddess was to call the spiritual being into a physical object by using that object as the focal point for ritual prayers, offerings, and meditations. The object was usually a statue or image made to outwardly resemble the commonly conceived appearance of the god, and often displayed symbols with which the god was associated or identified. For example, to achieve an intimate personal relationship with Zeus, the ancient Greeks worshipped the god through his images with prayers, ceremonial gestures, and sacrificial offerings deposited at the base of his temple statues. These images were bearded to show that Zeus was the patriarch of the Olympian deities, and usually depicted Zeus holding a thunderbolt, because this was his proverbial weapon.

By making a stone, metal, or wooden image of a god or goddess as harmonious as possible with the deity's appearance, attributes, and personality, the deity was encouraged to identify with the image, to enter into it, and to reside within it. It would then remain within its image for as long as it received the concentrated attentions of its human worshippers. It was necessary that the image and its immediate environment be made appropriate to the nature of the god, and also that they be regarded by the god as pleasant and beneficial, so that the deity would feel an active incentive to dwell in the statue.

The Greek philosopher Plotinus was born in Upper Egypt in the year 205, and possessed an intimate knowledge of the Egyptian art of causing gods to dwell in statues, for which the Egyptians were famed throughout the ancient world. No other race had so many gods, or communicated with the gods on so familiar a basis, as the Egyptians. Plotinus approved of the practice, and offered an explanation of its esoteric mechanism:

> I think, therefore, that those ancient sages, who sought to secure the presence of divine beings by the erection of shrines and statues, showed insight into the nature of the All; they perceived that, though this Soul is everywhere tractable, its presence will be secured all the more readily when an appropriate receptacle is elaborated, a place especially capable of receiving some portion or phase of it, something reproducing it, or representing it, and serving like a mirror to catch an image of it.[1]

The Soul mentioned by Plotinus is equivalent to the all-pervading energy of Shakti, the universal womb from which all manifest things have issued, and within which all ideal forms that have yet to come into being still reside. Plotinus writes concerning this Soul: "The content of the creative soul includes the Ideal shapes of gods and of all else: and hence it is that the kosmos contains all."[2] By using the appropriate shapes, materials, symbols, and practices, the universal creative power that animates and gives existence to all things from stones to gods could be induced to deposit a specific aspect or expression of itself within a temple image. The gods are merely different masks of this shakti force, each deity a limited, particular expression of shakti. It is the way in which shakti is masked or veiled that defines the nature of each god, just as a sheet of paper with a hole cut in it, when held up to the light, defines the shape of the light by its shadow outline.

Egyptian priests evolved god-making into an elaborate esoteric science. In the *Asclepius* Hermes Trismegistus remarks of the hierophants of Egypt: "But afterwards, they invented the art of making gods out of some material substance suited for the purpose. And to this invention they added a supernatural force whereby the images might have power to work good or hurt, and combined it with the material substance; that is to say, being unable to make souls, they invoked the souls of daemons, and implanted them in the statues by means of certain holy and sacred rites."[3] These rites of god-making are not explicitly described by any ancient author, but Hermeas provides some general observations about them in his Scholia on Plato's *Phaedrus*:

> But how are statues said to have enthusiastic energy? May we not say, that a statue being inanimate, does not itself energize about divinity, but the telestic art, purifying the matter of which the statue consists, and placing round it certain characters and symbols, in the first place renders it, through these means, animated, and causes it to receive a certain life from the world; and, in the next place, after this, it prepares the statue to be illuminated by a divine nature, through which it always delivers oracles, as long as it is properly adapted.[4]

The Egyptian technique of god-making was the telestic art—the art of inducing spiritual intelligences to reside within physical images appropriate to their natures. From the few comments by Hermeas we may gather that it consisted of three stages. First, the image was ritually purified. This probably took the form of prayers, a banishing ritual, and a cleansing of the statue. It is possible that the statue was bathed in blood to cleanse it. Second, by the use of specific inscribed letters and symbols, a spirit of the Soul of the World was made to enter the statue to provide the image with its basic vital energy and the animation through which it communicated with human beings. By "a certain life from the world" Hermeas intended a spirit or god possessed of a specific manifest form and identity. Third, rites were performed that caused this lower spirit to receive a higher spiritual inspiration that made it oracular and allowed it to deliver prophetic responses to the questions of the priests.

Hermeas seems to be saying that the spirit attracted and made to reside within a god's temple statue by magic letters and symbols is a lower vital aspect of the god that lends the statue animation and awareness, but in itself is not capable of delivering transcendent prophetic revelations. To obtain the communications of the higher spiritual aspect of the god, some additional ritual or devotional action is required. It is significant that the attraction of this lower vital aspect of the god involved written symbols, because it suggests that to call down the higher part of the god, spoken invocations were needed. The breath was regarded as the vehicle of the spirit. Greco-Egyptian magic relied upon long strings of Greek vowel sounds that were vibrated on the voice. These probably played a part in the invocation of the higher, prophetic aspect of the god into the statue.

Once a god or goddess had made itself at home in a particular image, worshippers were able to communicate with the deity for the purpose of obtaining cures for sickness, relief from persecution, increased prosperity, success in love or warfare, predictions of future events, and other useful helps. Supplicants entered the presence of the statue, made their prayers to attract the attention of the god, set their gifts prominently before it, then spoke their requests to the god. These requests were usually uttered aloud. Sometimes they were written down. Often priests or priestesses of the deity served as intermediaries by listening to the petitions of the supplicants, conveying them to the awareness of the god in ritualized ways, then reporting the responses of the god to the supplicants.

Temple gods responded to the questions and requests of their human worshippers through a variety of signs. The statue of a deity might make some small gesture, such as nodding its head, or twitching a finger, or blinking, or smiling, to acknowledge directly to a supplicant that his or her petition had been heard, and would be fulfilled. Sometimes the god appeared to a worshipper in a dream and spoke. Or the priests of the god would receive and interpret its response to the person seeking information or aid. The god might speak directly to a priest, or appear to a priest in a dream, or give some physical sign visible to a priest. Occasionally gods and goddesses possessed their priests and used their voices and bodies to communicate with their worshippers. Another way of receiving a response from the image of a god was to perform a divination in the expectation that its results would be guided by the deity. Different gods of the ancient world had different forms of temple divination.

This communication and exchange of services between statue-dwelling gods and their human worshippers, aided by the priests and priestesses who tended the gods, formed the basis for all of the religions of pagan times, and may still be observed in numerous places around the world in our modern age. It is not confined to primitive cultures. Catholics pray before the plaster images or paintings of saints, give them offerings and devotions, request help from the saints in their daily lives in return for some specified sacrifice, and when that help is received, fulfill their promise to the saints. This is exactly the same spiritual dynamic that was at work in the Greek temples three thousand years ago.

Animating an Image

An elaborate religion and a formal organization of priests and churches is not needed to induce spirits to reside in physical images. This can be done by a single person working alone, without any knowledge of ritual magic. It is a natural part of human consciousness to animate and vitalize the surrounding environment. Children have no trouble talking to dolls, or hearing their responses. They see faces in the bark of trees and monsters under their beds. The ancients perceived spiritual intelligences in lakes, springs, rivers, trees, stones, mountains, flames, the winds, the stars, the waves, and other parts of the external world, because it is basic human nature to do so. These intelligences are the wood nymphs, the fawns, the fairies, the satyrs, the elves, the undines of streams and ponds, the gnomes of caves, the spirits of the air, that fill the mythologies of every culture.

It is inevitable that separate and unique intelligences be perceived in the material objects of the greater universe since the universe as we know it is constructed within the human mind out of mind-stuff. This truth is the most significant message of the axiom written on the Emerald Tablet of Hermes Trismegistus: "What is below is like that which is above; and what is above is like that which is below: to accomplish the miracle of the one thing."[5] The one thing is mind. What is below is the microcosm, the human personality and ego that is apparently contained in the human body. What is above is the macrocosm, the greater universe that apparently lies outside the human body, and apparently is not a part of human consciousness and ego.

I emphasize the word "apparently" because this appearance is incorrect. The great divide between self and not-self which seems to be defined by the human skin is an illusion. The realization that outside and inside are fundamentally the same is one of the great insights that comes from the study of magic, perhaps the greatest of all insights. With an awareness that stones and trees, as you perceive them in the greater world, are just as much a construct of your own mind as your dreams and thoughts, it no longer seems so strange that a stone or tree should acquire its own personality and self-awareness. You and the stone, you and the tree, are part of the same mind.

The ancient Egyptians undoubtedly used a very elaborate ritual structure to animate their temple statues, and constructed a complex theosophy to explain how their methods worked. All this is not really necessary for animating an image. There is a simple technique that uses no magic circle, no pentagrams, no invocations, no ritual furniture, no names of power, no consecrated tools, no altar, and no temple. In order to animate a statue or other image, you must treat the statue or image as though it were already alive. That is the entire technique of god-making in a nutshell. It is so simple that many magicians will refuse to believe it. It is merely necessary to regard the image selected for the physical body of the spirit, whether it be a god, angel, or intelligence of some other kind, as already containing that entity.

This method was understood by the medieval alchemists, who employed it to implant a spirit in the sealed hermetic vessel during the making of the homunculus. It was used in a largely unconscious way by witches who caused spirits to dwell within their animal familiars. Moreover, it is being used by average individuals around the world every day when they worship the plaster images of saints, or adore the photographs of famous film stars, or visit the graves of their departed loved ones. It is one of those great secrets of magic that lies out in the open in plain sight for anyone with wit to see it, yet it remains unsuspected or ignored.

An Oracular Stone

The method was actually recorded in one of the medieval grimoires by an anonymous author who had no notion of its importance, in connection with the creation of an oracular or prophetic stone that would reveal secrete matters. The author of the grimoire instructs anyone seeking such a talking stone to find a smooth, rounded stone around the size of a cabbage and wrap it in a blanket. The stone is to be treated in every respect as through it were a living infant. Its possessor must act as the child's loving parent by feeding the stone on milk, holding it frequently in the arms, talking to it, caressing it, and warming it. After a time, the author of the grimoire says, the stone will begin to make noises like a living infant, and in due time it will learn how to speak.

Obviously it is not the stone that speaks, anymore than it was the temple statues of the gods in ancient times. The love directed towards the stone by the magician makes the stone a desirable place for a spirit to dwell. A spirit seeking love enters the stone, and because the love is directed at the stone as though it were a child, the spirit assumes the identity and nature of the magician's magical child. In this way, an extremely close bond in developed between spirit and magician over the course of months. This enables the spirit to speak to the magician in the magician's mind, and to the perceptions of the magician the words of the spirit seem to come out of the stone.

As simple as this method appears, it is important because it contains the essence of ancient god-making. The elaborate ritual structures used by the pagan priests, although undoubtedly helpful in focusing their minds upon the statues and the spirits dwelling within them, were nonessential in actually causing the spirits to enter and dwell within the statues. What attracted and held the spirits was strong emotions of love and devotion, coupled with a firm faith in the presence of the spirit. The rituals merely helped express these emotions, and confirm this faith.

Telesmatic Images

The great gods and goddesses of history did not always make the best lovers. They were too vast and impersonal. Their associations might be wrong for a lover—for example, the Greek goddess Athene is a virgin goddess, as is the huntress goddess Artemis. These would be poor choices as sex partners. Or it may simply be that sex is beneath their interest and dignity. Mercury is an intellectual god and would have very little interest in lovemaking. A better choice for a personal partner, where sexual union is the primary goal, is one of the lesser spirits or angels that occur so frequently throughout the literature of Western magic.

Often these lesser spirits are known only by their names, and perhaps their offices. This makes them impossible to visualize. However, techniques have been developed to construct the image of a spirit based solely on its name, or solely on its occupation. These images can then be visualized on the astral level, and physically created by drawing or painting them, modeling them in clay, carving them in wood, or using some other artistic means of giving them a physical reality.

In the late nineteenth century a variation of the Egyptian telesic art was used by the English occult society know as the Hermetic Order of the Golden Dawn. The astral forms of spirits were assembled piece by piece upon frameworks of occult correspondences in order to create spirits with very specific functions. This technique was known in the Golden Dawn as the making of telesmatic images. A magician using it is able to build up a complex picture of a spirit that expressed its essential nature based upon only the occult correspondences of the Hebrew letters in its name, or the Hebrew letter equivalents of the Latin or Greek letters in its name. These telesmatic images are initially built in the imagination on the astral plane, but once completed, they can be drawn and painted, or shaped into statues.

The leaders of the Golden Dawn saw fit to issue dire warnings about the dangers of creating telesmatic images for frivolous purposes. Although it is not explicitly stated in this warning, the implication is that the creation of these spirits for purposes of sexual pleasure is to be strenuously avoided. This should be understood as a caution to the unskillful rather than an absolute prohibition—the more sensual and physical the thoughts and actions of a spirit, the more likely it is to seek to interact with human beings on a human level.

Now there is also a mode whereby, combining the letters, the colours, the attributions and their Synthesis, thou mayest build up a telesmatic Image of a Force. The Sigil shall then serve thee for the tracing of a Current which shall call into action a certain Elemental Force. And know thou that this is not to be done lightly for thine amusement or experiment, seeing that the Forces of Nature were not created to be thy plaything or toy. Unless thou doest thy practical magical works with solemnity, ceremony and reverence, thou shalt be like an infant playing with fire, and thou shalt bring destruction upon thyself.

Know, then, that if thou essay in the imagination to form an astral image from the Names, the first letter shall be the head of the Figure or Form, and the final letter shall be its feet. The other letters shall be, and represent in their order, its body and members.

AGIEL, for example, shall give thee an Angelic Form of the following nature and appearance:

Aleph, Air. The head winged, and of a golden colour, with long floating golden hair.

Gimel, Luna. Crowned with bluish silver crescent, and with a face like that of a grave and beautiful woman, with a bluish halo.

Yod, Virgo. The body of a maiden clothed in grass green robe.

Aleph, Air. Golden wings of a large size, partly covering the power part [groin] of the figure.

Lamed, Libra. Feet and limbs well-proportioned and, either in the hand of the figure or lying at its feet, the sword and scales of Justice in bright green.

Playing round the figure will be a greenish light, the colour of its synthesis. The Keys of the Tarot may help thee in the form.

See well also that thou makest the Image as pure and beautiful as possible, for the more impure or common the figure, the more dangerous is it unto thee. Write upon the breast its Sigil, upon the girdle its Name, and place clouds below the feet. And when thou hast done this with due solemnity and rigid correctness of symbolism, shunning as thou wouldst shun death any suggestion of coarseness or vulgarity in an Angelic symbol, then hear what it shall say unto thee.[6]

The Golden Dawn sigil of a spirit is a geometric symbol formed by tracing straight lines between the letters in the name of the spirit upon the Sigil Rose of the Golden Dawn, an arrangement of all twenty-two letters of Hebrew in three concentric circles that correspond to the three types of Hebrew letters. The Golden Dawn practice was to begin each sigil with a small circle and terminate the sigil with a small lateral line

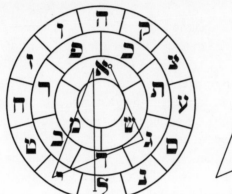 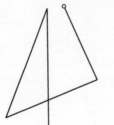

FIGURE 8-1.

Sigil of Agiel on the Sigil Rose of the Golden Dawn.

or T-shape. These are the marks traditionally used to begin and end sigils in Western magic, although sometimes the small circle was used to both begin and end the sigil, and sometimes the small bar was used to both begin and end the sigil. For the purpose of representing the flow of force with greater clarity, I prefer to begin inscribed sigils with a small cross and end them with an arrowhead. This is entirely a matter of personal preference. When evoking the spirit to visible appearance during rituals, the sigil is traced upon the air with the right index finger, or with the wand or other magic instrument held in the right hand. The terminations are unnecessary when a sigil is traced since the direction of force is self-evident.

Gender of Telesmatic Figures

Concerning the sexual attributes of higher spirits or angels, the Golden Dawn document dealing with telesmatic images asserts: "Radiating forces of Divine Light, otherwise called Angelic Forms, have not gender in the grossest acceptation of the term, though they can be classed according to the masculine and feminine sides."[7] This was a polite way of writing that angels have nothing but a bare patch between their legs, when they appear in a visible form. The author of the document regarded the ancient worship of gods and goddesses with sexual rites as "the great error of the

Phallic Religions" because "they have transferred the material and gross side of sex to Divine and Angelic planes, not understanding that it is the lower that is derived from the higher by correlation in material development, and not the higher from the lower."[8]

The condemnation of the worship of angels and deities with sexual energy strikes at the very heart of the practices described in this book, so it must be considered at length. Implicit in the condemnation is the assumption that the expression of sexual energy is inherently physical rather than inherently spiritual, and that the baser the nature of a spiritual being, the more overt its gender. "Gender, in the usual meaning of the term, belongs to the Elemental Spirits, Kerubic Forms, Fays, Planetary Spirits and Olympic Spirits—also to the Qlippoth in its most exaggerated and bestial aspects, and this is a ratio increasing in proportion to the depths of their descent. Also, in certain of the evil Elemental Spirits, it would be exaggerated and repulsive."[9]

Kerubic forms are spirits based upon the shapes of the four Kerubs: the Lion, Eagle, Bull, and Angel. Fays are fairies, or more generally nature spirits. Planetary spirits are those associated in Western magic with the seven wandering bodies of traditional astrology. Olympic spirits are the spirits of Olympus mentioned in the grimoire known as the *Arbatal of Magic*, whose seven governors are linked with the seven traditional planetary spheres.[10] All are considered lower spirits by the Golden Dawn, when compared with the higher angels.

The equation of sex with evil, so prevalent in the Victorian Age, is overt in the Golden Dawn document. The Qlippoth or evil spirits of the Kabbalah are said to have "exaggerated" genitalia, the "bestial aspects" of which increase in direct ratio to the proportion of the "depths of their descent." That is to say, their sexual parts get bigger and more erotic in appearance in direct relation to their degree of evil. Today, we would not be inclined to consider a man with a larger penis as necessarily more bestial or evil than a man with a small penis, but this is one of the consequences of the Golden Dawn position. It was quite common in Victorian England to regard the laboring classes as animalistic and more sexually driven than the ruling classes, who were looked upon as a higher spiritual order of humanity less enslaved to their physical passions. If anything, the opposite was true. The wealth and leisure of the ruling classes gave them the opportunity to indulge their vices, while the working classes sweated for twelve hours a day just to earn the necessities of life.

Neither the myths nor the practices of the ancient world support the Golden Dawn position that the overt expression of sexuality is inherently gross or evil. In the Hebrew Book of Enoch the Watchers, who were angels of a very high station, lusted after the daughters of men and descended to the Earth to have sex with them. They even sired children upon these mortal women. In Greek myth, the highest of the Olympian gods, Zeus, engaged in physical sex with numerous mortals and deities. The ancient Egyptians worshipped the huge erect phallus of Amun. Traditional Tantric practices of the left-hand path adored the goddess Shakti with physical sex. In my view it is extremely arrogant to dismiss such sacred fables and practices, which are found over a span of many centuries in numerous major cultures, as the "error of the Phallic Religions."

The Golden Dawn did ascribe sexual characteristics to the angels, but these were abstract and sublimated:

> But, in the higher and angelic natures, gender is correlated by forms, either steady and firm, or rushing. Firmness like that of a rock or pillar is the nature of the feminine; restlessness and movement, that of the Masculine. Therefore, let this be clearly understood in ascribing gender to angelic forms and images. Our tradition classes all forces under the heads of vehement and rushing force, and firm and steady force. Therefore a figure representing the former would be a masculine and that representing the latter, a feminine form.[11]

In my opinion the error of the Golden Dawn on the matter of the sexuality of angels was a failure to completely understand what is implied by the Hermetic maxim, quoted earlier in this chapter. There is a tendency among some modern practitioners of magic to rewrite this principle so that it reads: "As above, so below, but after a different manner." There is no mention of a different manner in the original statement of Hermes Trismegistus. Hermes makes a direct comparison between below and above.

Sexuality, an integral part of the physical world, must also be an integral part of the spiritual world. Just as sex has its spiritual component for incarnated human beings, so must sex have its carnal component for disembodied spiritual beings. Everything we experience, perceive, or understand in any way is created within our minds. Since sex, both spiritual and physical, is a part of the human experience, it is also a part of the greater universe and all that the universe contains. It is incorrect thinking to say that human beings have a tendency to sexualize inanimate things, such as ships or storms or countries—rather, humans intuitively recognize the innate sexual nature of inanimate things, or sometimes fail to recognize it even though it is always present.

When a telesmatic image is formed from the Hebrew name of a higher angel using the Golden Dawn method, the sex with which it is visualized and represented is determined by the masculine or feminine qualities assigned to the Hebrew letters in the name. More masculine letters indicated a subtly male body, more feminine letters a subtly female body. Members of the Order were cautioned against mixing male and female qualities when building up a telesmatic image.

> The sex of the figure depends upon the predominance of the masculine or the feminine in the whole of the Letters together, but a jumble of the sexes should be avoided in the same form. The image built up should be divided into as many parts as there are letters, commencing at the upper part and so on in order. In addition to this method of determining the sex of the Telesmatic Image of a Name, certain Names are inherently masculine, other feminine, and some epicene, irrespective of the mere testimony of the Letters.[12]

If an angelic name has no traditional gender associated with in it the Golden Dawn system of magic, the sex of its telesmatic image is determined by the majority of either masculine or feminine Hebrew letters. If there is an equal number of both types of letters, the angel is visualized in an epicene or androgynous form, with an intermediary gender. Because angels were understood in the Golden Dawn to lack genitalia, gender is expressed by masculine or feminine facial features, body proportions, tone of voice, and other physical characteristics associated with gender. Those angels who possess a traditional gender, such as the archangel Michael who is regarded as male, should not have their gender changed when they are visualized in the form of a telesmatic image that is based upon their name.

The gender of the Hebrew letters in the Golden Dawn system of telesmatic images depends upon whether the energy of each letter is rushing and rapid (male) or firm and steady (female). This sometimes goes against what we might expect the gender of certain letters to be. For example, the letter Heh is associated in the Golden Dawn with the Tarot trump the Emperor, and with the zodiac sign Aries. Both are strongly masculine. But perhaps because the Emperor of the Tarot is seated firmly on his throne, and the esoteric meaning of the letter is a window (a feminine symbol) the letter is classed as feminine. I will reproduce here the table of gender and other associations for the Hebrew letters that acted as a guide to members of the Golden Dawn when constructing telesmatic figures from Hebrew names of angels and spirits mentioned in the Bible, the literature of the Kabbalah, and the grimoires of magic.[13]

Telesmatic Attributions of the Letters of the Hebrew Alphabet

Aleph	Spiritual, wings generally epicene, rather male than female, rather thin type.
Beth	Active and slight, male.
Gimel	Gray, beautiful, yet changeful, feminine, rather full face and body.
Daleth	Very beautiful and attractive, feminine, rather full face and body.
Heh	Fierce, strong, rather fiery, feminine.
Vav	Steady and strong, rather heavy and clumsy, masculine.
Zayin	Thin, intelligent, masculine.
Cheth	Full face, not much expression, feminine.
Teth	Rather strong and fiery, feminine.
Yod	Very white and rather delicate, feminine.
Kaph	Big and strong, masculine.
Lamed	Well-proportioned, feminine.
Mem	Reflective, dreamlike, epicene, but female rather than male.
Nun	Square determined face, masculine, rather dark.
Samekh	Thin rather expressive face, masculine.
Ayin	Rather mechanical, masculine.
Peh	Fierce, strong, resolute, feminine.
Tzaddi	Thoughtful, intellectual, feminine.
Qoph	Rather full face, masculine.
Resh	Proud and dominant, masculine.
Shin	Fierce, active, epicene, rather male than female.
Tau	Dark, gray, epicene, male rather than female.

TABLE 8-1. Form, personality, and gender of the Hebrew letters in the Golden Dawn.

Role of the Four Worlds

The Golden Dawn applied to their system of telesmatic images a Kabbalistic division of the universe into four planes or worlds. These planes must not be thought of as separate or stacked one on top of the other, but rather as existing simultaneously and interpenetrating each other the way several distinct radio signals can exist upon the air around us at the same moment. Which radio signal we hear depends on how we tune our receiver. When we tune in one channel, the others do not cease to be merely because they are absent from out awareness—it is the same with the four worlds.

To the highest archetypal world, Atziluth, the divine names of God were associated. Below it in the creative world, Briah, were placed the names of archangels. Still further down, the formative world, Yetzirah, received the names of the angelic orders, and the names of individual angels belonging to those orders. At the bottom the world of physical actions, Assiah, received the names of elementals, humans, and the evil spirits of the Kabbalah known as the Qlippoth. However, the Qlippoth more properly belong to the infernal regions said to lie beneath or behind Assiah.

A telesmatic image could be linked with a world, and with the qualities and energies of that world, by employing the names of God or the higher angels of that world during its creation. The sets of names of the ten Sephiroth are divided into four groups and assigned to the worlds, allowing these potent Kabbalistic names to also be used in the making of telesmatic images. By knowing how the Sephiroth names are assigned in the worlds, and the nature of the Sephiroth, it is a relatively easy matter to determine which divine or angelic or demonic name shall rule a particular telesmatic spirit. The deliberate vibration of this name on the breath during the visualization of the telesmatic spirit while it is being created infuses the telesmatic image of the spirit with the power of the associated world.

Because all telesmatic images must, by their inherent nature, have manifest forms with specific attributes, the Golden Dawn asserts that as a practical matter all telesmatic images are linked either to Yetzirah or Assiah, because the two higher worlds, Atziluth and Briah, are too spiritual and refined to allow manifest forms to act in them directly. When a telesmatic image is based upon a name of God, such as Shaddi, it does not act in the world of Atziluth, even though the name Shaddi is linked to Atziluth. Rather it acts in the world or forms (Yetzirah) or the world of matter and energy (Assiah). It represents the lower aspect of the divine name:

From these remarks it will be seen that a Telesmatic Image can hardly apply to Atziluth; that to Briah it can only do so in a restricted sense. Thus a Telesmatic image belonging to that world [Briah] would have to be represented with a kind of concealed head, possessing a form shadowy and barely indicated. Telesmatic Images, then, really belong to Yetzirah. Therefore it would be impossible to employ the telesmatic image of a Divine Name in Atziluth, for it would not represent that [divine being] in the world of Atziluth, but rather its correlation in Yetzirah. In Assiah you would get [using divine names] Elemental forms.[14]

What this means is that it is possible to employ the highest names of God in Atziluth, or the names of the archangels in Briah, as the basis for telesmatic images, but you should not confuse the created forms for the exalted spiritual expression of these names. The telesmatic forms of God and the archangels are only lower reflections of the names. They possess qualities of the spiritual beings associated with the names, but those qualities manifest themselves in limited and material ways.

An example is provided in the Golden Dawn document of the archangel Sandalphon, who resides in the world of Briah.[15] It would not be possible to create a telesmatic image of this being in the archetypal world of Atziluth or even in the creative world of Briah, but if this name were used to build a telesmatic image designed to function on the level of the formative world, Yetzirah, the result would be a beautiful female figure with a thin, active face, full neck, well-preportioned breasts and shoulders, full hips, massive legs, and sinewy winged feet. Were the same name used to construct a telesmatic image that will function in the active world of Assiah, it would be a Kerubic figure with synthetic elemental attributes—a fierce, beautiful head, eagle's wings, a woman's shoulders and breasts, strong hips and thighs covered with hair, the hind legs of a bull and an eagle's talons in place of feet.

In creating telesmatic images, personal intuition and judgment must always be used, since each Hebrew letter has several major associations and numerous minor associations in the Golden Dawn system. By determining in advance the level or world of human experience in which the created being is intended to function, the attributes of the image can be defined somewhat more precisely. However, the final selection of features that composes the body of the spirit is always a matter of individual choice. The sets of associations for the Hebrew letters presented in the table above helped members of the Golden Dawn to make this choice, but the table was only intended as a general guide, never to be slavishly followed by members of the Order.

Part Two

~

Practice

{ 9 }

Choosing a Lover

Gods and Goddesses

I f you decide to initiate a loving relationship with a well-known deity or angel, the
image or images of the spiritual being, along with a public name or set of names,
and perhaps its sigil or symbol, are already available to you. For example, the Greek
goddess of love, Aphrodite, had numerous surnames or titles in the ancient world,
each of which designated a different office or function of the goddess. Aphrodite
Porne was the goddess of profane love worshipped by prostitutes, and would be a good
choice for a sexual partner. A small statuette or photograph of a ancient statue
depicting this form of the goddess would make a suitable vessel through which to
establish a link with her. Any substances—stones, herbs, music—specifically associated with the goddess would also be helpful when communicating with her.

Major gods and goddesses have certain disadvantages as love partners. They have
such a long history, and are known to and worshipped by so many thousands of people over so many centuries, that they acquire a kind of inertia that tends to make
them unresponsive on a personal level. It may be compared to dating a very famous or
wealthy individual. Important persons have numerous and constant demands on their

time that divide their attention. In the same way, when you invoke a deity by its public name, hundreds or thousands of others may be speaking that name or thinking about that deity. These demands hinder the creation of a deep personal bond with the deity. Perhaps it is not so much that a single deity has its attention divided when called upon by many human beings, but rather that the numerous simultaneous thoughts about the deity, and the conception of its name and nature in many minds, muddles the astral waters in some way.

Kabbalists would assert that major deities exist on a higher plane or world, and it is this distance from the lower plane of matter and energy that causes them to be less approachable. The more powerful pagan deities occupy the second world of the Kabbalah, Briah. It was the expressed opinion of the Golden Dawn teachings that no complete telesmatic image of a spirit could be formed on the level of Briah—that such an image would be misty, indistinct, and headless. It is possible to link to the major pagan gods and goddesses, just as it was in ancient times, but when this occurs, communication is really established with a lower reflection of the deity in Yetzirah or Assiah that matches the concept of that deity existing in the mind of the ritualist. Splitting off this individual reflected aspect of a major deity from its universal aspect tends to weaken the link with a deity.

Working with Telesmatic Images

In my own work I have found it more fruitful to establish links with less well-known spirits or angels. The loving bond is created more quickly, and is of a more intense and intimate nature. The spirit becomes a friend and lover rather than an adored and revered deity. When dealing with obscure beings, often only the name or office of the spirit is available. Using the technique of telesmatic images described in the Golden Dawn documents, or similar god-making techniques, it is possible to build up the body shape, facial features, and overt personality traits for a spirit based solely on its name, or its function in the world. Once the personality and appearance of the spirit is known, an image that will serve as a gateway of communication can be made or found to match that appearance.

The Golden Dawn technique of projecting telesmatic images allows the creation of a living astral image of a spirit, based upon the name of the spirit, even if that spirit has no traditional, commonly accepted form. Many of the angels and lesser spirits of the Kabbalah exist only as names. By this technique the magician is able to give them bodies, and also to assign them a spectrum of specific occult powers and meanings that are linked to the letters in their names. In order to manufacture telesmatic images of gods, angels and other spiritual creatures it is essential to know the system of occult correspondences used in the Golden Dawn, or another system of correspondences that is also based upon the Hebrew or Latin alphabet.

Telesmatic images should not be used to replace the recognized historical form and attributes of a deity, or other well-known spiritual being, but they can be employed to create a second image of an existing god or goddess on another Kabbalistic level that differs from its historical image. For example the familiar humanoid form of a goddess such as Diana that is associated with the level of Yetzirah would be different from her elemental Kerubic form on the level of Assiah. We see a partial expression of this differentiation by levels of reality in the image of Artemis of Ephesus, which is a female figure with multiple breasts that resemble a cluster of grapes. Similarly, the Egyptians often represented gods and goddesses as completely humanoid, but also showed the same deities as animal figures or as a combination of animal and human.

The disadvantage of the traditional Golden Dawn technique of telesmatic images is that it does not allow the creation of a spirit's image if only the office or function of the spirit is known, rather than its name. In my book *New Millennium Magic* I set forth a simple way to discover the name, the sigil, and the appearance of a spirit based only on the essential nature or function of the spirit.[1] My technique can be used with the existing Golden Dawn system of occult correspondences, which I have provided here in abbreviated form as a table. The list of letter equivalents was modified to include all the English letters so that each English letter would have it Hebrew equivalent. An exact correspondence between the sounds of some of the English and Hebrew letters does not exist—bear this in mind when translating names from Hebrew to English, or English to Hebrew. The letters Kaph, Mem, Nun, Peh and Tzaddi have alternative forms (indicated in the table by the "f" for final) that are used only when these letters occur at the ends of words.

By using this table of the Hebrew alphabet in conjunction with the table shown in chapter nine that gives the gender, shapes, and personality types of the letters, and also the Sigil Rose of the Golden Dawn that allows the creation of sigils, it is possible to derive a detailed appearance, personality profile, and occult sigil from either the name or the function of a spirit. When these tools are coupled in a ritual context with a physical statue or picture of the spirit based on its telesmatic image, and any external properties such as colors, scents, sounds, or symbols magically linked with the spirit, communication is greatly aided.

Hebrew Letter	Hebrew Name	English Letter(s)	Esoteric Meaning	Esoteric Attribution	Tarot Trump
א	Aleph	A, E	ox	Air	Fool
ב	Beth	B	house	Mercury	Magician
ג	Gimel	G, Gh	camel	Moon	Preistess
ד	Daleth	D, Dh	door	Venus	Empress
ה	Heh	H	window	Aries	Emperor
ו	Vav	O, U, V, W	pin, nail	Taurus	Hierophant
ז	Zain	Z, X	sword	Gemini	Lovers
ח	Cheth	Ch	fence	Cancer	Chariot
ט	Teth	T	snake	Leo	Strength
י	Yod	I, Y, J	hand	Virgo	Hermit
כ ךf	Kaph	K, Kh, C	fist	Jupiter	Wheel
ל	Lamed	L	ox goad	Libra	Justice
מ םf	Mem	M	water	Water	Hanged Man
נ ןf	Nun	N	fish	Scorpio	Death
ס	Samekh	S	tent prop	Sagittarius	Temperance
ע	Ayin	O, Aa, Ngh	eye	Capricorn	Devil
פ ףf	Peh	P, Ph, F	mouth	Mars	Tower
צ ץf	Tzaddi	Tz, Z	fishhook	Aquarius	Star
ק	Qoph	Q	ear	Pisces	Moon
ר	Resh	R	head	Sun	Sun
ש	Shin	S, Sh	tooth	Fire	Judgement
ת	Tau	T, Th	cross	Saturn	World

TABLE 9-1. Basic Golden Dawn attributions for the Hebrew letters.

Sons and Daughters of Lilith

Not all spirits are suitable for loving relationships of a sexual nature. When seeking sex with a spirit either for pleasure, or for the enhancement of skill and power in magic, it is best to work with spirits I have classed as the Sons and Daughters of Lilith—which is to say, with those spirits inherently adapted to receive and give erotic love. From the viewpoint of conventional Christian or Jewish morality these spirits are rebels, since they violate the established religious rules of behavior. However, the majority of persons in modern Western culture have ceased to believe that sex for pleasure or personal empowerment is sinful, and might be more inclined to regard this class of spirits as liberators.

The kinds of love granted by the Sons and Daughters of Lilith vary widely, from the most refined and spiritualized devotion to the most perverse sexual excess. It is always best to seek an enduring relationship of genuine love and friendship with a spirit, for four reasons. The first is that spirits respond in kind. If you give them love, they will give love back in return. If you try to dominate and abuse them, they will respond by dominating and abusing you. It is safer to love and respect spirits with whom you communicate, and this is particularly true when the union is intimate. Second, a loving relationship is more productive and healthy. When a spirit genuinely loves you, it is eager to do everything in its power to help fulfil your purposes and to make your life happy and successful. Third, it is easier to initiate a relationship with a spirit through love than through intimidation or dominance. The old folk saying, more flies are attracted by honey than by vinegar, applies. If the spirit feels loved, it has a positive reason to deepen its relationship with you. It will use its abilities to get nearer to you, rather than always trying to escape from your control. Fourth, the spirits attracted by intense, genuine love are higher aspects of the Goddess, and for this reason more potent in giving aid, and in transforming the fluids of the body used in sexual alchemy, should you decide to progress to this stage.

All spirits adapted by their nature to give and receive erotic love are aspects of shakti, the creative power of the universe. When we make love to them, we make love to the Great Goddess by proxy. The erotic, sensual side of Shakti is well represented by Lilith, who has always been associated with forbidden sexual pleasure. A distinction must be made between Lilith the goddess, who is above good and evil, and is the instrument of all forms of sexual experience that are prohibited by traditional religious doctrines, particularly the doctrines of the Christian and Jewish religions, and Lilith the demoness, a wicked night hag of Jewish folklore who represents only one mask of the higher goddess Lilith. This distinction has not been made in the literature of the Kabbalah, where Lilith is always represented in a completely negative way.

The children of the higher goddess Lilith are individual spirits with their own purposes and personalities, but all are capable of infusing the sexual fluids of the body
with shakti energy and transmuting them alchemically. The lower elemental spirits of
the world of Assiah cannot convey this energy so strongly and effectively as the
higher spirits of Yetzirah, even though the spirits of Assiah are more easily attracted,
and more eager to engage in sexual relations with human beings. In making a decision whether to invoke a lower spirit of Assiah for your lover, or a higher spirit of Yetzirah, consider your ultimate purposes. If you are seeking erotic pleasure and compan-
ionship for its own sake, and have no interest in the alchemy of sexual fluids, a lower
elemental spirit such as an Undine, or a nature spirit such as a tree nymph, will make
a better companion, and a more tractable lover. If you seek to infuse the maximum
virtue into the alchemically transmuted sexual fluids of your body, and wish your
spirit lover to act as a teacher in esoteric and occult matters, it is better to invoke a
higher being of the planetary spheres or stars.

In Kabbalistic terms, the lower elemental spirits relate to Malkuth, lowest of the
ten Sephiroth on the Tree of Life, and the earthly Kingdom that is the sphere of the
elements (*aulam yesodoth*). The planetary spirits are associated with the seven Sephiroth above Malkuth, each linked to its own planet. In the Golden Dawn system of
magic, this relationship of the Sephiroth to the planets is Yesod (Moon), Hod (Mercury), Netzach (Venus), Tiphareth (Sun), Geburah (Mars), Chesed (Jupiter), and
Binah (Saturn). The sphere of the fixed stars or zodiac is connected with the ninth
Sephirah up from the bottom of the Tree, Chokmah. The highest Sephirah, Kether,
is associated with the godhead or primum mobile.

Elementals are lower spirits composed primarily of a single elemental property:
Salamanders (Fire), Sylphs (Air), Undines (Water), Gnomes (Earth). They generally
appear in human or humanoid form when evoked to visible appearance, and may be
of either sex. Tradition testifies that Undines and Gnomes make good lovers, Salamanders and Sylphs very poor lovers. Undines are passionate and devoted, but have
somewhat distant and unearthly personalities. Gnomes are earthier and more human,
but can be treacherous, particularly when their desires are frustrated. Of the four elemental groups, Undines have been represented in folklore and historical accounts as
the best lovers, and my own experience has verified this to be true. Apart from the
elementals, there are numerous spirits of a mixed nature in Malkuth. These are the
fairies and woodland spirits of classical mythology. Spirits of mixed natures are usually
tied to a physical place on the Earth. They include such beings as tree spirits, meadow
spirits, spirits of springs, pools, streams and rivers, spirits of stones, and spirits of caves.

Among the mixed spirits, nymphs and satyrs are proverbial in mythology for making love to human beings.

The spirits of the Moon and Venus make the best lovers among the planetary spheres, since these are the most earthy and sensual of the planets. Mars embodies a masculine, aggressive sexuality. However, it is possible to invoke a spirit lover from any planetary sphere, and that being will express in its nature the prevailing nature of the sphere where it resides. Similarly, any sign of the zodiac can provide a spirit lover, but some signs are naturally better suited than others. Cancer, which is ruled by the Moon, is a sensible choice, as are the signs Libra and Taurus, both ruled by Venus. The signs Scorpio and Aries, both ruled by Mars, will also provide spirit lovers, but their sexuality is of a more aggressive type.

Spirits can manifest themselves in many guises. The form adopted by a spirit expresses its inner nature. The Golden Dawn made the distinction between telesmatic images of spirits who manifest themselves in the world of Yetzirah or Formation, and have attractive human or humanoid bodies, and spirits who manifest in the world of Assiah or Matter, and have Kerubic forms—bodies built up of the four elements, which are represented by characteristics of the four Kerubs: the Lion (Fire), Eagle (Water), Angel or Man (Air), and Bull (Earth).

In a footnote in his book *The Magus* (1801), the English magician Francis Barrett made a very important observation about the fundamental nature of spirits and the manifest shapes by which the magician perceives them. "Those spirits who appear in a kingly form, have a much higher dignity than them who take an inferior shape; and those who appear in a human shape, exceed in authority and power them that come as animals; and again, these latter surpass in dignity them who appear as trees or instruments, and the like: so that you are to judge of the power, government, and authority of spirits by their assuming a more noble and dignified apparition."[2] The importance of this truth cannot be overstated. Since spirits manifest to the magician through mind, and their forms are drawn from the unconscious, their outward shapes are usually a true expression of their inward natures. The exception is in the case of malicious spirits, who sometimes attempt to put on a pleasing form to deceive.

The highest material form of a spirit is that of the angels and fairies, who have human bodies and faces of unearthly beauty, and often wings. Below this is the shape usually adopted by the most spiritual Undines and nymphs, a beautiful human form without wings. Still further down the scale are those spirits who appear in human forms that are distorted or strange. Below these are those spirits whose nature is expressed by a mingling of human and animal characteristics, such as the satyr or mermaid. Lower yet are spirits with monstrous and repulsive human shapes, and below these spirits who have forms compounded of animal parts. We need not venture below this level when examining spirits suitable as sexual partners, but still lower in authority are spirits who appear in the forms of beasts, insects, plants, and inanimate objects such as stones and books.

Deriving a Spirit from Its Name

The method for creating telesmatic images of angels and other spirits used by the Golden Dawn is based on the assumption that the form and personality of the spirit will be derived from an existing Hebrew name. Usually the Hebrew name of a traditional angel from the Bible or literature of the Kabbalah is used, but sometimes English, Latin, or Greek names are converted into Hebrew equivalents. Each ritualist who makes a telesmatic figure from the name of an angel will achieve a slightly different result, because every Hebrew letter has multiple esoteric associations, and it is necessary to make a selection from among these attributes when forming a figure. This process of selecting the attributes of the image binds it very intimately to its creator. Assuming that no gross errors have been made in assigning the symbols that compose the image, the resulting form is that aspect of the angel best suited to interact with the ritualist.

Some pagan gods and goddesses had dozens of distinct forms through which they received worship in different regions of the ancient world. These numerous forms were arrived at over the span of centuries by means of a collective consent among the worshippers of each region. Each form had its own unique aspect, but all were recognized as masks or expressions of the same deity. By analogy on a lower level, each person who uses the name of an angel to derive its telesmatic image will achieve a slightly different result from everyone else, but if properly done, these differing images will all be the same angel upon whose name they were based. It is important not to make the error of thinking there is only one correct form for the telesmatic image of a name—on the contrary, there are many correct forms, each expressing a degree of uniqueness and individuality.

As an example of the traditional Golden Dawn method for deriving telesmatic images from the Hebrew names of spirits, I have chosen to create an image of the spirit of the Moon, Chasmodai (Ch - ח, Sh - ש, M - מ, O - ו, D - ד, A - א, I - י), sometimes spelled in English as Hasmodai. You will notice that the first *a* in the English form of Chasmodai does not exist among the Hebrew letters of the name, indicated with transliterated forms in parentheses. Since vowels as such are shown in Hebrew writing by means of small marks called vowel points near the letters, rather than by the letters themselves, when converting Hebrew to English it is often necessary to insert vowels to make the names pronounceable. Some Hebrew letters have sounds that are not exactly equivalent to the sounds of any English letters, making it necessary to transliterate them with two or more English letters rather than one—for example, the Hebrew letter Shin can sound like the English S, but often sounds like the letters Sh.

Chasmodai is the spirit associated with the magic square of the Moon that appears so often in the literature of Western magic. It was presented by Cornelius Agrippa in his *Three Books of Occult Philosophy*, first published in complete form in 1533. Agrippa derived the squares and their spirits from an older unnamed source text. Francis Barrett reproduced the planetary squares from Agrippa in his 1801 work, *The Magus*, and it is probably from this source that they made their way into Golden Dawn magic. Although there is a sigil for Chasmodai associated with the placement of the spirit's name on the Hebrew letters of the lunar magic square, there is no generally accepted public image for this spirit.

The first Hebrew letter in the name gives an indication of the appearance of the spirit head, and the final letter of its lower legs and feet. The intervening five letters define the remainder of its body. Both intuition and judgment are needed when deciding which letter will apply to which body part. The nearer to the end of the name a letter is, the lower on the body it will be located. Larger names with more letters cause each individual letter to define a smaller part or zone of the body. Sometimes intuition will direct that one letter should be accorded more influence than another when forming the telesmatic image of a spirit. These intuitions must be followed, since they arise from an unconscious link between the ritualist and the spirit.

Referring to the table of telesmatic attributions provided in the preceding chapter, we find that Cheth (Ch) signifies a round, somewhat expressionless feminine face. From the table of Tarot attributions, above, we learn that Cheth has the esoteric meaning of a fence, and is linked to the Tarot trump, the Chariot, and with the zodiac sign of Cancer. Cancer is the sign ruled by the Moon in astrology. This is very significant, since the letter of the name that defines the head of the figure plays an important part in establishing its personality (our identity is formed, symbolically speaking, by our head and our heart). The figure is undoubtedly what is known as moon-faced— that is, a face rounded and resembling the full Moon. Since the colors of the Moon are white and black, the face is pale like the full Moon and the hair very dark.

The symbol of Cancer is the crab, a bottom-dwelling creature with a soft white interior, a hard shell, and grasping claws. We do not use the physical shape of the crab to define our figure of the spirit, but apply the symbolic meaning of a crab—a defensive, careful, and acquisitive nature. The crab's defensiveness is suggested by its natural body armor, its carefulness by its slow, creeping motion, and its acquisitiveness by its grasping and encircling pincers. The charioteer of the Tarot trump also wears armor, but he is a warrior. This suggests that the spirit will fight to retain what it protects, and when threatened will act boldly. The esoteric meaning of a fence for the letter Cheth suggests an enclosure to protect or defend something. Many fences have sharp points or barbs on their top, a further indication that the defensiveness of Chasmodai is of an active type.

Astrologically, Cancer indicates a nature that is defensive, protective, nourishing, emotional, intuitive, with a sensitive interior but a tough exterior. Mentally the sign points to shrewd judgment and a retentive memory. There is a natural psychic or mediumistic component to this personality, which is romantic in a sentimental, protective way, and also sensual. The Cancer personality is a collector and a keeper. In a general sense the sphere of the Moon is associated with life rhythms, the family, the past, memories, dreams, visions, and habits.

The second Hebrew letter, Shin (Sh), is associated with the neck of the spirit's telesmatic image. In the table of telesmatic attributions, we find that this letter by its active motion is more masculine than feminine, and points to a fierce, active and epicene nature. The neck will be thick but somewhat sensual. The table of the Tarot trumps links Shin with elemental Fire and with the trump, the Last Judgement, and gives it the esoteric meaning of a tooth. The fierceness and active energy of this second letter reinforces the martial aspect of the figure, previously suggest by the association of the first letter with the trump, the Chariot. The Last Judgement indicates that this forcefulness has a spiritual or idealized expression.

The third letter in the name, Mem (M), is described in the table of telesmatic attributes as more feminine in its energy than masculine, reflective, dreamlike and epicene. All these qualities are in harmony with the lunar nature of the spirit. The Moon does not give forth any light of her own, but merely reflects what is cast upon her by the Sun. The Tarot table links Mem with elemental Water, both in its esoteric meaning and its Tarot trump association, the Hanged Man. Water is the element of the Moon, and is connected very closely with dreams and the unconscious. We see an internal tension developing in Chasmodai, who on the one hand is maternal, receptive, sensitive, but on the other hand can be fierce and aggressive when crossed. The contrary elements Fire and Water also show this conflicting nature. These two sides to the spirit sometimes result in a state of suspension or indecision, as indicated by the Hanged Man. This third letter gives the telesmatic image rounded, soft shoulders.

The fourth letter, Vav (O), will describe the breast and heart of the figure. It is said to be masculine, rather heavy and clumsy, but steady and strong. The latter part of the description would naturally apply to the heart, or symbolically, the courage and will of the spirit, who possesses a deep chest. To jump ahead a little, three of the letters in the name are masculine but four feminine, so we know that the spirit is female. Therefor the heavy and clumsy quality of this Hebrew letter applies to the spirit's breasts, which are large and heavy.

In the table of the Tarot trumps, Vav has the esoteric meaning of a nail or pin, and is linked to the trump the Hierophant, and the zodiac sign Taurus, the sign of the bull. Taurus is an Earth sign. There is a strong sympathy between the Moon and the Earth, because the cycles of the Moon govern the growth of vegetation, and the maturation of the fetus in the womb. This further emphasizes the heavy aspect of the figure. Taurus suggests strong shoulders, since this sign is associated with the shoulders. Bulls are stubborn and tend to dig in their feet and stand their ground when confronted. Their determination not to yield sometimes makes them blundering and awkward. They are also proverbial for their fiery temper when crossed.

The fifth letter, Daleth (D), applies to the waist and hips. It is the saving grace of our spirit's beauty, because in the table of telesmatic attributions this letter is said to be feminine, full, but very graceful and attractive. This means that in spite of the general fullness of Chasmodai's form, her waist is tapered and is accentuated by beautiful feminine hips. We might describe her overall body type as Amazonian but curvaceous and sensual. From the table of the Tarot we discover that Daleth is linked with the planet Venus and the card the Empress, and that its esoteric meaning is a doorway. Venus suggests love, sex, and the abundance of the earth. The doorway is one symbol that can stand for the mouth of the womb. The Empress is a seated female ruler who is sometimes compared with the Queen of Heaven, the mother of gods and men. This chain of associations (hips-doorway-Venus-Empress) indicate an enormous potential for fertility. It emphasizes the mothering, nurturing side of this spirit.

The sixth letter is Aleph (A), and relates to the legs. Its telesmatic attributions are thinness, spirituality, and usually wings. The nature of this letter is predominantly masculine and epicene, but with a basic spirituality. We must reconcile these features with the fullness of the rest of the figure by saying that Chasmodai's legs are voluptuous but unusually long and graceful. As a result, the spirit is quite tall. She has extremely long, filmy wings that extend all the way down her back from her shoulders to her heels. These wings are translucent white with black crescent markings, and resemble the wings of a moth. She usually carries them folded behind her, but when they are opened wide they are rounded at their tips, very broad and extremely thin.

The table of the Tarot links this letter with the trump the Fool, the element Air, and gives it an esoteric meaning of an ox or plow. The symbol of the ox is in harmony with the symbol of the bull that we derived from Taurus while examining the fourth letter. This heavy, earthy beast is in stark contrast to the element Air and the Fool, a figure in the Tarot signifying spirituality and liberation. Again we have an example of the inherent conflict in this spirit, who is at the same moment both earthy and sensual, but airy and spiritual. The same contrast exists in the Moon itself. The Moon presides over the very physical processes of birth and growth, and at the same time rules the airy world of dreams and visions.

The final letter of the name, Yod (I), provides the description of the spirit's feet. In the table of telesmatic attributions we learn that her feet are surprisingly white and delicate, and have a feminine shape. In spite of the overall power of her figure, that part of her body that connects her to the earth is spiritual, indicating that this link is more fragile that it seems. Since the hands usually resemble the feet, and the arms the legs, we can extrapolate and say that Chasmodai's hands are slender, very white, delicate and feminine, and that her arms are long and graceful. The table of the Tarot links this letter with the trump the Hermit and the zodiac sign of Virgo, the Virgin, and has the esoteric meaning of a hand. Both the virgin and the hermit symbolically express suppressed sexual energy that finds an outlet in spiritual fervor. Hence the fertile and sensual nature of Chasmodai is sublimated and spiritualized, and finds outlet in a passionate, idealistic romanticism.

Examining the telesmatic image as a totality, we can say that it is the figure of a woman who has white skin, black hair that is straight or slightly waved, dark eyes, an upturned nose, a prominent chin, a full and round face with broad cheekbones, a somewhat thick neck, broad but soft white shoulders, large breasts that hang down slightly under their own weight, with dark nipples, a graceful waist that appears more slender than it actually is because of the fullness of her hips, thick black pubic hair, rounded buttocks, long full thighs, graceful calves and slender ankles, beautifully shaped feet that appear tiny in contrast to the rest of her body, small white hands, and pallid translucent wings that are folded at her back, and hang down almost to the ground.

By nature Chasmodai is sensual but romantic. She has a maternal side and fiercely protects those she loves, but at times this love can become smothering and oppressive.

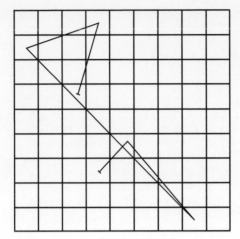

FIGURE 9-1.
Sigil of Chasmodai
on the magic square
of the Moon.

When opposed, she becomes angry and digs in her heels. Her anger can cause her to commit mistakes. Her feelings are deep and easily injured, but she hides this vulnerability beneath an unresponsive exterior. It is hard to know what she is thinking since her placid face seldom betrays her emotions. She seems to absorb all that is directed toward her while returning only a pale reflection of what is going on inside her. She is definite about what is hers, and will not readily give it up. She has a mediumistic, dreaming quality to her personality. She is prepared to give herself sexually in a loving, maternal way to those she regards as hers—that is, those lovers who are completely devoted to her needs and happiness. If her lovers abandon her or abuse her trust, she reacts with anger and does not willingly allow them to leave the relationship. In her mind, she acts in her lovers' best interests. Fiercely loyal and intense in her love, she tends to interpret every relationship in a spiritual way.

This is my own interpretation of Chasmodai, based upon the Golden Dawn technique of telesmatic images. Others would arrive at a slightly different figure, and might emphasize different aspects of the spirit's personality, but there should be concord on the major points—that Chasmodai is female, with a pale complexion, large breasts, a tapered waist and full hips; that she is nurturing and maternal, with an intense sensuality that tends to find a spiritual or romantic expression.

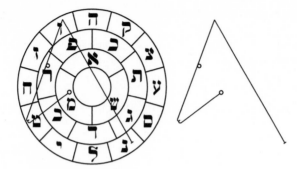

FIGURE 9-2.

Sigil of the archangel
Metatron on
the Sigil Rose.

The Sigil of Chasmodai

Chasmodai has her own sigil that is formed by tracing a line from Hebrew letter to
Hebrew letter in her name, after these letters or their numerical equivalents have
been found in the cells of the magic square of the Moon. The sigil of Chasmodai on
the lunar square is shown in Figure 9-1. If you were using the magic square of the
Moon as part of your ritual invocation of Chasmodai, it would be sensible to relate
the telesmatic image of the spirit to the sigil derived from the square. However, if you
wanted to avoid the use of the square, or desired to integrate Chasmodai with a number of other spirits whose forms you derived from the method of telesmatic images, it
might make better sense to base the sigil of the spirit upon the Sigil Rose of the
Golden Dawn.

If a letter falls directly between two other letters on the Sigil Rose, distinguish its
existence in the sigil by making a small loop in the line segment where it resides. If
the same letter occurs twice together in the name of the spirit, distinguish this on the
sigil by making a small double bump where these two letters occur. As I mentioned in
the previous chapter, the Golden Dawn liked to begin its sigils with a small circle,
and end its sigils with a small lateral bar or T, but I prefer to begin my sigils with a
small cross and end them with an arrow point because it makes it easier for someone

FIGURE 9-3.

Sigil of the lunar spirit Chasmodai on the Sigil Rose.

unfamiliar with the construction of the sigils to perceive the direction of their energy flow, knowledge that is essential if the sigil is to be traced accurately upon the air during rituals. The grids of the planetary squares, or the outline of the Sigil Rose, are not included when inscribing the sigils—the sigils are merely traced over these grids, which I have shown for the sake of clarity. When projecting the sigils on the air, the initial and termination marks are also omitted.

In the accompanying illustration of the sigil of the angel Metatron (M - מ, T - ט, T - ט, R - ר, O - ו, N - ן), the double bump indicates that the Hebrew letter Teth occurs twice together in the name, and the loop shows that the Hebrew letter Resh falls directly between the second Teth and the letter Vav. There is not a direct correspondence between the English letters in the name of the spirit Metatron and the Hebrew letters because Hebrew contains no vowel letters. Vowels are added to written Hebrew by means of small marks, known as vowel points, placed above and below the letters. This results in pointed Hebrew. In ancient times pointed Hebrew was not used, and it is still not used in most forms of Western magic—the Golden Dawn did not use pointed Hebrew.

It is an easy matter to locate the seven Hebrew letters of the name Chasmodai on the Sigil Rose, and to trace a line that reflects from letter to letter. In the case of names that contain more than a few letters, the sigils generated on the Sigil Rose tend to cross back and forth upon themselves repeatedly. By moving the end points of the segments slightly within the letter cells, rather than always drawing each segment from the exact center of the cell, it is possible to avoid most of the awkward conflicts that might arise. Strive for a pleasing overall appearance in the sigil. Avoid placing two line segments very close together unless this is unavoidable, or crossing a segment directly over an angle.

Telesmatic Images Based on Names in English

The lack of vowels in Hebrew makes a direct conversion of English names to Hebrew letters imprecise, for anyone who lacks a knowledge of Hebrew. Even so, it is often desirable to convert the English names of spirits into Hebrew so that they can be used as the basis for telesmatic images and sigils. To be completely accurate, this conversion would sometimes require the removal of some vowels from English names when changing them to Hebrew, but for reasons of practical utility, making a one-to-one correspondence between English and Hebrew letters works well enough. Simply substitute the English letters in the name for the Hebrew letters in the table of the Hebrew alphabet, provided above. There are a few awkward areas, but these can be overcome by using several makeshift rules.

You will notice that there are two letters for S in Hebrew, and also two letters for T. Shin can be pronounced as either S or Sh, and Tau can be pronounced as either T or Th. When an English word contains an S, it is difficult to know whether to use Samekh or Shin; similarly, when an English word contains T it is hard to know whether Teth or Tau should be substituted. An imprecise but workable solution is to always use Samekh for S and Shin for Sh, and to always use Teth for T and Tau for Th. Another problem is with the Hebrew letters Vav and Ayin, which can both sometimes have the sound of the English letter O. A solution to this confusion is to always use Vav as a substitute for O. In the same vein, both Kaph and Qoph are sometimes represented by the English K, but when converting English names to Hebrew letters, it is simplest always to use Kaph for K. Strictly speaking, there is no Hebrew equivalent for the English X and W, but we can use Zain and Vav for these letters.

It may sometimes be desirable, for numerological reasons, to use Shin in place of S rather than Samekh, or Tau in place of T rather than Teth, or Ayin for O, or Tzaddi for Z. Since we are dealing with an imprecise technique to begin with, I regard these substitutions as valid when they are prompted by intuition, and serve numerological needs. For example, if you convert a spirit name to Hebrew letters, and by using Tau for T rather than Teth you can make the total numerical value of the name sum a significant and magically potent number that relates to your purposes, you should not hesitate to do so. This device is frequently resorted to by Western Kabbalists, who treat Tau and Teth, and Samekh and Shin, as interchangeable when it serves their numerological needs.

As an example of how the Golden Dawn method can be used with gods, angels, or spirits whose names are in English letters, I will derive the telesmatic image and Golden Dawn sigil of Hagith, who is the Olympic or planetary spirit of Venus in the grimoire titled *The Arbatel of Magick*.[3] The *Arbatel* gives several functions of Hagith but fails to describe the appearance of the spirit. Even though the grimoire provides a specific sigil for this spirit, it is possible to derive another sigil based upon his name from the Sigil Rose. Both sigils are the sigils of Hagith, since both are based on his name, and both may be used in magic relating to this spirit, but the Golden Dawn sigil will serve best when employing this Olympic spirit in the Golden Dawn system of magic.

Using the Tarot table of the Hebrew alphabet, it is simple to convert the Latin or English letters of Hagith into Hebrew letters. We get a five letter name: H - ה, A - א, G - ג, I - י, Th - ת.

The Hebrew letter Heh (H) applies to the head and face of this spirit. From the table of telesmatic attributions given in the previous chapter, we find that the face of Hagith is fierce, strong and fiery or flushed. The table of the Tarot trumps tells us that the letter Heh is linked with the card the Emperor, the sign of Aries, and has the esoteric meaning of a window. This is said to be a masculine letter. The trump and sign are strongly masculine, but the symbol of a window is feminine.

The second letter is Aleph (A) and represents the neck and shoulders. In the case of the previous example, the second letter in the seven-letter name represented only the neck, but because the Hebrew form of Hagith contains five letters, some compression is necessary. The telesmatic attributions of Aleph are a sensual nature, thinness, spirituality, and often a set of wings. The energy of this letter is predominately masculine. These attributes give the spirit a long, slender neck and somewhat thin shoulders. In the case of this spirit, I choose to omit a set of wings. Aleph is linked with the Tarot card the Fool and elemental Air, and has the esoteric meaning of ox or plough. Penetration is suggested. Air is a penetrating element, and it is the nature of the Fool to cut through lies and empty formalities of behavior, just as the plough cuts the earth.

The third letter, Gimel (G), represents the torso of the spirit's body. It is a feminine letter, beautiful yet changeable. The color gray is associated with it, suggesting that the spirit has gray eyes. We can associate the eye color with this letter because there is no hard and fast rule about which letter should be linked to which body part, only a general guideline. Gray may reasonably be interpreted as eye color, since the color gray does not apply to other parts of the body, unless to the hair—but this spirit appears youthful from the rest of the description, so it is unlikely that his hair is gray. This letter also suggests a full body. In this case, since the neck and shoulders are slender, a full body may be interpreted as a roundness and softness in the stomach of the figure. Gimel is the letter of the Tarot card the High Priestess, the astrological Moon, and esoterically means a camel. These are feminine indicators, further supporting the interpretation of a soft, rounded abdomen. The camel is self-sufficient and can endure hardship and drought by means of the food and fluids stored in its hump, another reference to the full belly of the spirit. Since this is a spirit of Venus, we may assume that he derived his rounded form through self-indulgence.

The fourth letter, Yod (I), relates to the hips and legs of the spirit. The telesmatic attributions of Yod are whiteness and delicacy. It is feminine in its energy. This indicates somewhat broad hips and thin, pale legs. Since there is often a similarity between the arms and legs, and especially since the letter associated with the shoulders, Aleph, indicates thinness, we can surmise that the spirits arms are also pale and slender. Yod is linked with the Tarot trump the Hermit, the astrological sign Virgo, and has the esoteric meaning of a hand. This shows an hermaphroditic quality to the spirit's limbs, because both the hermit and the virgin are in a sense sexless—the hermit renounces sex in favor of solitude, and the virgin has yet to experience it. One is male, the other female, indicating a blending of sexual attributes in the figure. This is a particularly significant factor since it falls on the groin of the spirit. The hand is a symbol for masturbation, and so indicates the compression of both sexes into a single being.

The final letter in the name of this Olympian spirit of Venus is Tau (Th), which has the telesmatic attributions of darkness, grayness, and an epicene nature. Its general energy is masculine. We have already applied the color gray to the eyes of the spirit, but the darkness may be related to his hair. An epicene quality in the feet suggests delicacy and softness. This term is used twice in connection with the letters in Hagith's name, and when we couple it with the feminine characteristics, the result is a distinctly androgynous spirit. Tau is linked with the Tarot card the Universe (or World) and the planet Saturn. The Universe is a trump of, among other things, total-

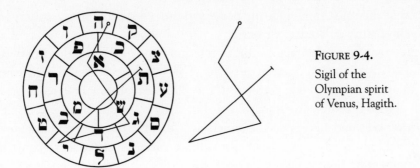

FIGURE 9-4.

Sigil of the
Olympian spirit
of Venus, Hagith.

ity or completion. This spirit is complete unto himself. Saturn has both male and female qualities, although this planet is outwardly masculine.

Three of the Hebrew letters are masculine and two feminine, which agrees with the grimoire presentation of Hagith as a male spirit. However, most characteristics of the spirit are feminine, or a mixture of the sexes. The telesmatic image of Hagith may be described as a slender, androgynous youth with long black hair and an angular, flushed face that has feminine qualities. His cheeks contain spots of color and his lips are full and red, but in other respects he has a pale countenance. His intense gray eyes carry a look of mingled insolence and pride. The body of Hagith is graceful but soft and weak. He is slender except for the roundness of his abdomen, which shows that he indulges too much in rich foods and wine. He almost appears to be in the early stages of pregnancy. It may be assumed that his voice is high in tone and somewhat weak, but that his speech is quick and eloquent. By nature the spirit is arrogant, proud, charming, and self-indulgent.

When we trace a line between the five Hebrew letters in the name on the Sigil Rose, the accompanying sigil for Hagith is the result. We would use this sigil when invoking this spirit into his telesmatic image, by inserting the sigil into the image, and also by tracing the sigil upon the air over the image at the time of the invocation.

Deriving a Spirit from Its Function

The Golden Dawn method for producing telesmatic images from existing names is fine, provided we have an appropriate name to work with. But if we begin with only a conception of the type of spirit we would like to have for a lover, and the occult virtues that the spirit should ideally possess in order to accomplish our purposes, we must use a slightly different approach.

In the traditional Kabbalah a direct relationship is acknowledged between the name of an angel and its function or power. This has the practical consequence that when an angelic name is encountered in the Bible and other sacred writings, a Kabbalist is able to determine the function of that angel by examining the context of the verse in which the name appears. Conversely, when the power of an unnamed angel is described in holy writings, a Kabbalist can use various techniques to construct the angel's name from the sacred text. The relationship between the name and the work of a spirit was mentioned by Cornelius Agrippa in his *Occult Philosophy*:

> The general rule of these is, that wheresoever anything of divine essence is expressed in the Scripture, from that place the name of God may rightly be gathered; but in what place soever in the Scripture the name of God is found expressed, there mark what office lies under that name. Wheresoever therefore the Scripture speaks of the office or work of any spirit, good or bad, from thence the name of that spirit, whether good, or bad, may be gathered; this unalterable rule being observed, that of good spirits we receive the names of good spirits, of evil the names of evil.[4]

It is this recognized link between a spirit's name and its function that serves as the basis for my original method of obtaining the name, form, personality, and sigil of a spirit, based solely on its purpose. To discover the name and form of a spirit appropriate for a particular labor, first consider the task it must perform. Reduce the essential nature of the task down to a phrase or brief sentence. Discard irrelevant words such as "the" and "a" and so on. Construct this sentence in such a way that the total number of relevant or meaningful words is a number in harmony with the nature of the work. It is best if the phrase consists of between three and nine meaningful words. In this way, the nature of the work can be related to the nature of the seven traditional planets of astrology by the traditional numbers of the planets: Saturn (3), Jupiter (4), Mars (5), the Sun (6), Venus (7), Mercury (8), the Moon (9). It is necessary to understand the natures of the planets, which can be studied in books on astrology.

Take the first letter from each meaningful word in your phrase or sentence, and combine the letters into a name that has between three to nine letters. Convert these English letters into Hebrew letters by substituting the Hebrew equivalents for the English letters, as shown in the accompanying table of correspondences. Trace a line between the Hebrew letters in the spirit name on the Sigil Rose to derive the sigil of the spirit. Begin this line at the first Hebrew letter of the name on the Sigil Rose, and proceed in order to each subsequent letter using straight line segments. Then apply the Golden Dawn method of telesmatic images to construct an astral picture of the spirit. This is not a mechanical process, but requires good judgement as to which associations to use and which to ignore, based upon the function of the spirit you are constructing.

When making a telesmatic image for a spirit or angel that already possesses a recognized Hebrew name, use the exact Hebrew spelling of the name to form its sigil. However, when making a telesmatic figure from a name that has been built up from the desired function of the spirit, when no traditional Hebrew name for the spirit exists, use the Hebrew letter equivalents for all the English letters, both vowels and consonants, in the composite name of the spirit.

After you have created the esoteric name for a spirit based upon the function you desire it to perform, you may discover that it is necessary to insert vowels into the name to make it easy to pronounce. This is acceptable, but these inserted vowels are not used to form the sigil of the spirit. You can distinguish the essential letters in the spirit name, which are the initial letters in the words that describe its function, from the inserted vowels that make the name pronounceable, but writing the essential letters in upper case and the inserted vowels in lower case.

It will be easier to understand this process of spirit making by reference to an example. Suppose the man John Smith wished to achieve intimate union with a loving spirit of Venus. He might reduce his desire to the key sentence, "Beautiful spirit of Venus makes love to John Smith." It is always better to write these sentences in the present tense, as though their purpose has already been accomplished. By inserting his own name into the description of the spirit, he binds the spirit very closely to himself. Notice that the description has seven key words ("of" and "to" are discarded), which reduce to the initial letters B-S-V-M-L-J-S. This word has seven letters, the occult number of the planet Venus. It is completely unpronounceable, but this is easily remedied by a little manipulation. If you consult the chart of correspondences, you will see that U and V are linked to the same Hebrew letter Vav, and that J and I are both linked to the letter Yod. By adding the vowels "o" and "a" where needed, we can create the name BoSUMaLIS, or Bosumalis (B - ב , S - ס, U - ו, M - מ, L - ל, I - י, S - ס).

By spending a little time working on the words of the descriptive phrase or sentence, and by a judicious choice of vowels, it is always possible to arrive at a name that feels appropriate and has a pleasant sound. A magician might hesitate to use the name in the example because it ends with "malis" which is very similar to the Latin word malus, meaning bad. On the other hand, if John Smith is interested in wild, unrestricted sex with this spirit, he might not regard this termination in her name as a drawback. He would be looking for a "bad girl" to fulfill his sexual fantasies.

The Hebrew letter equivalents to the key English letters in the name are used to create the sigil of the spirit Bosumalis. This sigil would be traced upon the air, or over the image of Bosumalis, by John Smith when he wished to summon the spirit into his bed. The image of the spirit would either be purely astral and held in the imagination of John Smith while he was in the spirit's company, or an actual physical painting or sculpture created by John Smith to aid him in visualizing the spirit more clearly. By making a physical image of the spirit, it becomes easier to hold in the mind and interact with.

By using the Golden Dawn technique of telesmatic images, it is an easy matter to build up a composite image of Bosumalis. You will notice in the example below that I have applied a looser interpretation of the occult correspondences to the letters than in the previous examples, and have largely ignored the table of telesmatic attributions. It is important to realize that the table of telesmatic attributions provided by the Golden Dawn was intended to serve as a guideline, nothing more. It is helpful in the early stages of practice, but should not be followed slavishly or used as a crutch.

The first key letter, B, equivalent to the Hebrew Beth, is related to the head of the spirit. In the Golden Dawn system of correspondences, Beth means a house. It is linked with the planet and god Mercury, and with the Tarot trump the Magician. This indicates that the spirit feels at home when dealing with intellectual matters, has a quick mind and an eloquent voice. Her hair is long and wavy, of a light brown or dark blond color, because Mercury is associated with airy qualities, and the color of air is yellow.

The second key letter, S, equivalent to the Hebrew Samekh, relates to the neck of the spirit. Samekh means a tent-prop, the vertical center post that holds up the roof of a tent. It is linked with the zodiac sign Sagittarius, and with the Tarot trump Temperance. This association gives the spirit a long, slender neck, a narrow nose, and a very erect posture. It suggests that her disposition is well balanced and pleasant. Because Sagittarius is a mutable sign of elemental Fire, Bosumalis has an intense, penetrating gaze, a clear voice, and an ardent enthusiasm, which thanks to the influence of Temperance never leads her to acts of excess.

The third key letter, U or V, is equivalent to the Hebrew letter Vav, which means a nail or peg upon which something turns. It is linked with the zodiac sign Taurus and the Tarot trump the Hierophant. Taurus is associated with the shoulders of the human body. It indicates physical strength and vitality in this spirit, and that Bosumalis has wide shoulders and full, upright breasts, which are probably very sensitive to erotic stimulation. The Hierophant in the context of this spirit suggests both romantic idealism and modesty.

The fourth key letter, M, is equivalent to the Hebrew letter Mem, which means water. It is linked with elemental Water and with the Tarot trump the Hanged Man. Since it is the central letter of the name, it applies to the heart of the spirit. Water is the element of dreams, visions, and the sensual imagination. When we couple it with the earlier influence of Sagittarius, we can predict that Bosumalis will be open to sexual experimentation, but will not take such experiments too seriously. The Hanged Man is a card of willing surrender and sacrifice. This spirit will surrender herself to her lover with a romantic, idealistic devotion of the heart.

The fifth key letter, L, is equivalent to the Hebrew letter Lamed, which means an ox goad. It is linked with the sign Libra and the Tarot trump Justice. This letter defines the lower abdomen or waist of the spirit, which we may assume is slender and balanced, and held very erect—an ox goad is a kind of restraint, and the trump Justice is another card of balance.

The sixth key letter, J or I, is equivalent to the Hebrew letter Yod, which means hand, but also on a more esoteric level seed or semen. It is linked with the zodiac sign Virgo and with the Tarot trump the Hermit. On the body of the spirit it applies generally to the legs, but more specifically to the thighs and genitals. Bosumalis is likely to be modest and secretive in matters of sexuality. Her lover will need to win her affections by appealing to her inner fantasies and her romantic nature. Her lovemaking will be intense rather than casual. At times she may deny her lover her caresses.

The seventh and final key letter, S, is equivalent to the Hebrew letter Samekh, which we have earlier considered in a different context. Here, it applies to the lower legs and feet of the spirit, and indicates that Bosumalis is graceful and poised. She probably enjoys dancing. Her calves are long and shapely, her feet are of medium size and beautifully formed.

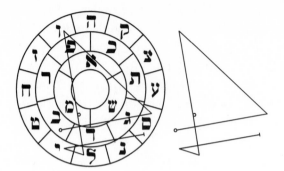

FIGURE 9-5.

Sigil of Bosumalis
on the Sigil Rose
of the Golden Dawn.

The construction of any telesmatic image, whether from the letters of an existing name in the normal Golden Dawn fashion, or from the function or occupation of the telesmatic spirit using the method described above, requires good judgement on the part of the magician. It is possible to derive many different telesmatic images from the same name merely by making slight changes in emphasis in the occult attributions for the Hebrew letters. This does not invalidate the technique. It merely means that the image of a spirit that is generated by telesmatic means is intimately connected with the unconscious mind and personality of the magician who generates it. I have given my personal impression of Bosumalis, which will differ in minor degrees from every other interpretation of this spirit.

Unconventional Practices

In the course of my own experiments and practice, I evolved two somewhat unconventional uses for telesmatic images that you will not find discussed elsewhere. Both have their application in sexual alchemy. I will describe the techniques briefly. By using as your guide the methods for creating telesmatic images provided above, you will not find it difficult to apply these original techniques in your own work, should you desire to do so.

The first is the construction of a telesmatic image for a traditional god, angel, spirit, or demon that is derived from one of its hidden, esoteric names, rather than from its public name. Each god possesses numerous esoteric names or titles that are based on its functions. Some of the older, more important gods such as Odin have literally hundreds of esoteric titles recorded by ancient poets, but they also have an infinite number of esoteric names that have never been written down. Each distinct office or function of the god has its own esoteric name—more than this, each different interpretation or expression of that function has its own name. Thus, the esoteric names for a spirit, particularly for a powerful and well-known god, are infinite in number.

Using the modified method for constructing telesmatic images outlined above, it is possible to build up a complete original image for a traditional god or goddess based upon the name that is extracted from one of its functions. The value in creating a new and unique telesmatic image for a traditional god, rather than simply using the common image or images, is that it connects the spirit intimately with the magician who makes the image. The esoteric name that is made up of the initial letters in the descriptive phrase of the god's function becomes, for that magician, a name of power by which the god may be summoned, directed, and banished. It also focuses the power of the god upon a narrow, very specific function in which the magician has an interest. Traditional gods are often too vast and abstract to make useful companions, but when a specific esoteric aspect of such a god is made into an image, the god becomes easier to interact with and direct.

It is important to understand that different images of a god, each of which bears its own unique title or name, are really completely separate spirits having their own personalities and intentions. For example, one of the twelve great titles of Odin is Óski (Fulfiller of Desire). This is a completely different entity from another of Odin's titles, Biflindi (Spear-shaker). The first is a god who listens to prayers and responds to them. The second is a god of warfare and bloodshed. In an abstract sense they are two aspects of the complex personality of this ancient god. But when Odin is the Fulfiller of Desire he is not the Spear-shaker, and when he is the Spear-shaker he is not the Fulfiller of Desire. In a practical sense they are two separate deities, since they never exist simultaneously in one time and place.

The second unconventional use for telesmatic images is the creation of a telesmatic image for a living human using only the name of the individual and an understanding of that individual's personality. The image created is an expression of the interior reality or esoteric identity of the individual. By using the technique of god-making described in chapter eight, a spirit can be induced to dwell inside the image. This spirit is a living part of the person whose name and personality the image was based upon. Since the birth name of the person was used in its creation, the name has power over the spirit residing in the image, and by association, over the living person the image represents, because the spirit in the image can act to affect the living person with whom it is magically linked.

This is an excellent way to project the power of healing to another human being. The spirit can serve as an active intelligent agent in conveying and administrating constructive energy to someone living far away from the ritualist, even if that person is unavailable by telephone. Such spirits also make excellent guardians over the individuals with whom they are linked. It is useful sometimes to be able to send a spirit as a protector to watch over someone in potential danger. This type of spirit should never be constructed without the consent of the person involved, since it is a very intimate act of magic.

{10}

The Image and the Shrine

Choosing a Vessel

The physical image of a spirit serves as the dense matrix that attaches the spirit to our everyday material world. If we consider the astral realm where spirits dwell as a kind of maze, the image of a spirit acts like the thread of Ariadne to bind the spirit to our conscious perceptions. When we invoke the spirit, we tug upon this thread, and the spirit is able to find its way through the darkness of the maze to its entrance, where it can communicate and interact with us. After we finish our interaction, the spirit returns to its natural environment, ready to come again when we ritually tug upon the thread. Usually the spirit is not in continuing residence in the image, although this can be made to occur when necessary.

Myth, folklore, and the history of magic teach us that almost anything can serve a spirit as its physical vessel, including a living human body. Spiritual beings were thought to inhabit mountains, hills, groves, individual trees, fields, streams, wells, springs, pools, rivers, the ocean, caves, the directions of space, the winds, the sky, the planets and stars. One of the most popular vessels for spirits was a piece of natural stone, unmarked in any way. Spirits have an inherent affinity for stone, though it is not clear why. Perhaps it involves the density of stone—it is one of the most substantial materials in nature. Rock crystal is even more attractive to spirits than ordinary rock, and we might speculate that this is due to the regular arrangement of atoms in crystals. At the other end of the spectrum, transient images such as stains on walls, reflections in window glass, odd growths on the boles of trees, curiously shaped loaves of bread, folds in fabric, and shadows have all at one time or another served to house spirits. The German magus Franz Bardon taught that a spirit could be made to reside in an arbitrary point on the wall.

While it is true that any object can serve as a spirit vessel, some objects are more naturally suited to this function than others. Something that by its shape, color, and substance expresses the fundamental nature of a spirit will be a more favorable receptacle than objects symbolically in disharmony with its nature. For example, we would not seek to invoke an angel into a grotesque demonic statue, nor would we try to call a demon into a plaster cherub. Bear in mind the teaching of Francis Barrett, quoted in the previous chapter. The image of a spirit is an outward symbolic expression of its inner qualities. When a spirit presents its astral image to the ritualist, the image usually reflects the nature of the spirit. Because of this relationship, when we select or create a physical image with specific features, it will attract a spirit whose personality and abilities are in harmony with those features.

The spirits with the greatest authority and power are adapted to a humanoid image. Just as mankind has natural dominance over all the other creatures of the Earth, so do spirits with a human shape rule over spirits with the shapes of beasts and lower creatures. Since we are seeking a spirit as a lover, the human shape makes the best sense as a purely practical matter. It would be awkward to have sex with a dragon or a mountain, for example. The appearance of the image should be sexually desirable and beautiful if the relationship is to be loving and enduring. A beautiful image greatly aids in forming a strong emotional bond with the spirit inhabiting it.

The size of a spirit vessel is not nearly so important as its substance or shape, but must be considered for pragmatic reasons. It is convenient to be able to physically touch and caress the image while communing with the spirit. This precludes for most individuals statues of a human size or larger. If you are very wealthy you may be able to work with a life-sized marble statue of Venus, but this is beyond the means of the average person. Also, it is necessary to be able to see the face and eyes of the image, which makes very small statues and pictures undesirable. It is no coincidence that a convenient dimension for a spirit vessel falls in the size range of the average doll—anywhere from around nine inches to two feet in height. A doll is adapted for handling and human interaction. In my own work, I have found statues from nine to twelve inches easy to manipulate.

Finding the Right Image

When selecting the image most appropriate to your spirit lover, two options are available. Either an existing image can be found that accurately expresses the nature of the spirit, or an image can be created based upon your knowledge of the spirit's personality, occult virtues and function. A ritualist seeking the love of a well-known god or goddess will probably be able to find a small reproduction in plaster, cast-stone, or plastic of an ancient statue of that deity. There are many inexpensive statuettes of classical gods. If a small statue in unavailable, a photograph of one of the god's ancient statues or paintings will be easy to obtain from books and magazines. When choosing an existing image of a god, angel, or spirit, make sure that its face is well sculpted, its eyes are distinct and fully opened, and that they gaze forward into your eyes as you look at it. The body of the statue is less important than its face, and its face less important than its eyes.

If there are no public images of a particular spirit, an image must be selected that expresses as closely as possible the inner nature of the spirit, as understood by the ritualist who seeks to attract the spirit as a lover. When properly chosen, a selected image will be as potent as a traditional image. Small statures or dolls can be used, if they are appropriate, but photographs, paintings and drawings can also serve as vessels. There is an endless number of photographs and artistic representations of the human form available. When you clearly understand the personality and nature of your spirit lover, and have translated those factors into physical features such as body type, complexion, hair coloring, posture, eye color, and facial features, you can go through potential images and find one that as nearly as possible matches your concept of the spirit.

The statue, doll, photograph, or drawing you select to contain the spirit must be attractive to you, and should have a quality of fascination that makes it difficult to look away from it. The eyes of the chosen image must be open, and must gaze directly forward into your eyes as you regard the image. This is essential. When you look at the image, there should be a sense that you are connecting with it on an emotional level through this eye contact. If an image seems lifeless and uninteresting, it is not suitable as a spirit vessel. Full length body images are best, but not essential. When an image is from the waist up, or even the shoulders up, it is possible to extend and complete the body of the spirit on the astral level by visualization. It is best that the image be clothed. Your attention must remain focused on its face and eyes, and a nude figure is liable to be a distraction.

It is desirable, though not essential, that the hands of the image be visible. Hand gestures convey subtle shades of meaning. Visually, human beings communicate by means of facial expressions, body postures, and hand gestures. When the image of your spirit lover becomes animated, the intelligence inhabiting it will communicate primarily by means of facial expressions, but will also employ hand gestures if the hands of the image are distinct and unobscured. The movements of the hands will be small but easy to perceive. You will also be able to see the image breathing, and may notice movements in its shoulders.

Avoid images of living human beings, especially if the person is known to you. This includes both individuals with whom you have had direct contact, and celebrities such as actors or sports figures you have never met. There is the tendency to confuse the nature of the spirit with the nature of the person represented by the photograph, if that person is known to the ritualist. Even worse, it is possible that ritual work with the photograph or other image of a living person can affect that individual in unintentional ways, such as causing nightmares, spontaneous impulses, sexual arousal, and fatigue.

Old Photographs

When I suggested to a friend that old photographs of persons long since dead might be used as vessels when communicating with spirits, he responded that some magicians would probably regard this practice as ghoulish and be uncomfortable with it, on the presumption that it would interfere with the repose of the souls of the dead. In my experience, there is no danger of this, provided the person in the image is completely unknown to you. The image merely serves as an appropriate physical structure upon which the manifesting spirit can base itself. However, anybody who has this reaction should not use old photographs or portraits, since this misconception will inhibit fruitful results. As a general rule, it is vital that you be comfortable with whatever vessel for your spirit lover you have chosen. If the image strikes you as grotesque, or silly, or makes you uneasy, find another one that you can live with on a daily basis.

In my personal work I have found that old photographs make good spirit vessels because they are plentiful and easy to obtain through magazines and books, or over the Internet. Because of the sheer diversity of physical types in these images, it is not difficult to match a face to the inner nature of a particular spirit. The chosen image then becomes in a very real way the image of the spirit, and it ceases to have any connection in my mind with any human being, living or dead. Older photographs are frequently very detailed, giving a good display of the eyes of the figures they contain, and often these figures are shown in full body poses, which is also useful because it eliminates the necessity to visualize the body shape of the spirit.

I have worked with statues and drawings, but prefer photographs. There are advantages and disadvantages to using a flat image as opposed to a three-dimensional figure such as a doll or statuette. Photographs are easier to obtain, more diverse, and less expensive. The quality of the image is usually superior, since low-cost statuettes and figurines tend to be poorly modeled by the sculptor. If the eyes of the statue are not lifelike, its suitability as a spirit vessel is greatly reduced. It is not necessary that the eyes of the image be perfectly lifelike, but they must convey an inner vitality and a sense of awareness. It is primarily through its eyes that the spirit will interact with you. Generally speaking, the eyes of photographs of human beings, or of fine art statues or paintings, have more vitality than the eyes of small figurines, which are often badly sculpted.

In my own work I have found that black and white photographs yield excellent results. Most older photographs showing images of persons no longer alive are black and white. Color photographs are acceptable if the coloring of the figure and background are in harmony with the nature of the spirit inhabiting the image. If the colors are strongly in conflict with the nature of the spirit, they can hinder its presence within the image. Colors to be avoided when invoking a spirit of erotic love are muddy browns, greens, and purples. Clear, bright colors are preferable. The spirit to be called into the image may have an affinity with a single color. For example, if it is a spirit of the sphere of Venus, green would be appropriate because green is the traditional color of Venus. For such a spirit, bright, pervasive red would be in conflict because red is the traditional color of Mars, the planet whose nature is most directly opposite to that of Venus.

Small amounts of red in a predominantly green background can actually be helpful when invoking a spirit of Venus since the red energizes the prevailing green. In the Golden Dawn system of magic, colors opposite to each other on an artist's color wheel are known as flashing colors. When they are viewed side by side they tend to flicker due to retinal fatigue. It was the Golden Dawn practice to use the primary color appropriate to a spirit when making its sigil, but to also include the flashing color to energize the primary color.

Associations	Traditional Colors	Golden Dawn Colors
Fire	red, yellow	red
Water	blue, green	blue
Air	yellow, blue	yellow
Earth	brown, green	black
Moon	silver, white, black	blue, silver
Mercury	orange	yellow, purple
Venus	green	green, blue
Sun	yellow	orange, gold-yellow
Mars	red	red
Jupiter	blue	violet, blue
Saturn	black	gray-white, deep purple
Aries	intense red	red
Taurus	greenish-brown	red-orange, indigo
Gemini	orange-yellow	orange, pale mauve
Cancer	silvery blue	amber, maroon
Leo	yellowish-red	greenish-yellow, deep purple
Virgo	orange-brown	yellowish-green, slate gray
Libra	greenish-yellow	green, blue
Scorpio	reddish-blue	green-blue, dull brown
Sagittarius	bluish-red	blue, yellow
Capricorn	blackish-brown	indigo, black
Aquarius	darkish-yellow	violet, sky blue
Pisces	intense blue	crimson, dull brown-yellow

TABLE 10-1. Colors associated with the elements, planets, and zodiac signs.

The table at left shows the most important traditional and Golden Dawn colors for the elements, seven planets of ancient astrology, and zodiac signs. I have based the traditional colors for the zodiac on a combination of the elemental qualities of the signs and the colors of the ruling planets of the signs. The Golden Dawn color system involves four scales, and is too complex to fully explain here. However, the Golden Dawn colors suggested in the table are in harmony with Golden Dawn magic. They are derived from the King Scale and Queen Scale, as those familiar with the four scales will immediately recognize.

Once a suitable photograph has been found to contain the spirit, it must be placed under glass in a frame to protect it from repeated handling. You will probably be working with the image for months, perhaps years, so it is essential to shield it from dirt, dust, and the oils in your hands. In my own work I often use empty compact disk cases as picture holders. It is an easy matter to cut the photograph to size and slide it under the tabs inside the front cover of the CD case. The result is lightweight, durable, and convenient to handle. If, as often happens, the ideal photograph for your purposes is the wrong size, thanks to the wonders of digital imaging it is relatively easy to scan the picture and make it larger or smaller, as needed, when printing a copy on your computer's printer.

If the plastic CD case becomes cracked or damaged, it can be replaced at minimal cost. A disadvantage of these jewel cases, as they are called, is the air slots on the upper and lower edges. These allow the entry of dust, which must periodically be removed from the image housed in the case. The slots can be sealed with bits of sticky tape, which have the added utility of keeping the case firmly shut. The case does a good job protecting the image from wear and perspiration, and provides a place to put the spirit's sigil, name, and any substances or symbols that encourage the presence of the spirit within the image. These things can be slid under the backing of a regular photo frame, but a CD case has extra depth for thicker objects. When using a CD case, a head and shoulders image is best due to the relatively small size of the case. If you choose a larger photograph frame, a half-body or full-body image is preferable.

Sculpting Your Spirit Vessel

Those with artistic or craft abilities will get the best results by using a spirit vessel they create with their own hands. The process of creation infuses occult virtue into the image and links it strongly to its maker. It is for this reason that most texts on magic instruct that ritual instruments be constructed by the person who will use them. The spirit image actually grows out of your own unconscious during the process of shaping it. This automatically results in a harmony between your inner concept of the spirit's nature and the outer appearance of its physical vessel. During the creative process you intuitively incorporate symbolic aspects and features into the image that resonate on a very deep level with the spirit.

If you choose to make a statuette to act as your spirit vessel, red artist's clay is an excellent material to work with. It has the density of elemental Earth and is a natural attractor of spirits. It is no accident that in the biblical book Genesis God is supposed to have shaped the first man from the dust of the ground; or that the Kabbalist Rabbi Loew is said to have used river clay to form the body of the golem. Clay is ideally suited to contain spiritual beings—in a sense, our own spirits are contained in clay vessels, since our flesh is basically soil, and after death returns to the earth. Artist's clay is easy to shape and does not require firing in a kiln to harden it. When allowed to dry slowly under a damp cloth to avoid cracking, it becomes almost as hard and as durable as stone.

Wood also has an ancient lineage as the material for spirit vessels. In ancient Greece the oldest temple gods were small wooden statues known as *daidala*. These wooden images were so old, even in the time of Christ the Greeks had long ago forgotten who made them, but they were venerated as the earthly containers of powerful spiritual beings. They were proverbial for their power to move themselves about unaided, and for this reason were attributed to Daedalus, the mythical maker of automatons. In his dialogue *Meno*, Plato has the philosopher Socrates say of these wooden figures: "They too, if no one ties them down, run away and escape. If tied, they stay where they are put."[1] Wood is a much more difficult material to work with than clay, however. I have used pine and maple to create small figures, as well as clay, and advise that you try clay or some similar modeling material first unless you have considerable skill in wood carving.

Among the metals, copper, and silver are esoterically appropriate. Silver is the metal of the lunar sphere, and copper the metal of Venus. The high cost of silver rules out its use by most individuals, but copper is cheap and readily available in the form of copper plumbing pipe. I have worked with both copper and silver. Copper is a very forgiving metal. It can be hammered and shaped for long periods without becoming stiff or brittle. This is not quite so true of silver, which after long working must be annealed by heating it just to the point of glowing, then allowing it to cool slowly, in order to regain its ductility. Silver is soldered with silver solder, but copper is usually soldered with lead solder. Lead solder is an alloy of lead and tin. Tin, the traditional metal of Jupiter, is not too disharmonious when incorporated into a copper image that will house a spirit of love, but lead, the metal of Saturn, is in conflict. For this reason, lead solder should be avoided when making a copper vessel to contain loving spirits. Fortunately, because of the growing concern over lead content in city water supplies, lead solder is being phased out of use by plumbers, so nonleaded or low-lead solders are readily available.

Spirit statues can be formed out of a wide variety of different materials, even such things as fabric and papier mâché. There are two considerations to bear in mind. First, the eyes of the figure must be open, forward looking, and as lifelike as possible. Second, the body of the figure must be durable and able to withstand weeks or months of handling. There is nothing more frustrating than to choose the wrong material for the figure of a spirit, and to have that vessel began to break down under repeated use when you are in the middle of your work with the spirit it houses. It sometimes becomes necessary to transfer the spirit to a different vessel, which is disruptive and may result in a delay. While a spirit is acclimating itself to a new vessel, its ability to communicate is reduced. Full acclimation can take days, or even weeks. Sometimes the bond is never as strong with a spirit after it has been moved to a new image, so such moves are to be avoided whenever possible. Once I had to move a spirit from one photograph to another after the first became damaged. It was several weeks before full communication was restored.

When fashioning a three-dimensional body for a spirit, it is necessary to hollow out a chamber that will hold the spirit's name and the sigil that is based on its name. The best place for this chamber is the torso of the statuette. If possible, the chamber should be accessed through the top of the figure's head. For example, when making a spirit vessel of clay, use a length of wooden dowel or some similar tool to force a cylindrical opening down through the top of the head and into the chest of the figure. This must be done when the clay is soft, and before the details have been applied to the image since the making of this channel will deform the figure considerably. After the clay statue is completely dry, a paper scroll bearing the name and sigil of the spirit, along with other pertinent names or symbols, is inserted into this cavity, and a small ball of wet clay used to seal the top of the head.

In the case of a wooden statue, the receptacle for the sigil scroll can be drilled down through the top of the head using a wood bit. It need not be large in diameter—one-quarter inch is ample space in which to insert a roll of paper. The top is sealed with a short length of dowel of the same diameter as the drill bit, using carpenter's glue, and when dry can be shaped and sanded until it is almost invisible.

There may be instances when it is impossible to bore a hole down through the top of the statue's head—for example, if a doll with a ceramic head is used. The scroll should be placed as near to the heart-center of the image as possible, either by open-ing a hole through its back, or inserting the scroll up through its groin, or if it is impossible to penetrate the figure, by folding the paper that bears the sigil and plac-ing it under the clothing or covering of the image. It is not necessary that the image be clothed, but if a doll is used, suitable clothing will often be available. The consid-eration I mentioned in connection with photographic vessels applies—avoid using a naked figure, since during communion with the spirit all your attention should be focused on the eyes and face of the image, not distracted by its body. Also, suitable clothing lends the image greater dignity.

Drawing Your Spirit Vessel

It is not necessary that a stature you construct to house your spirit lover be perfectly made. In the course of my own work, I have found that an image can be quite crude, yet still serve as an excellent instrument of communication with a spirit, provided that the image has a resonance in my imagination. When I was a boy of fifteen or sixteen I drew a pencil sketch of a well-known European political figure, based on a news pho-tograph. I was impressed by the fanatical zeal of the man, captured in a moment in time in profile by the photographer. While drawing the portrait, I sought to infuse into it the intense malevolence and spitefulness of the man. Even though I am not a pro-fessional artist, I succeeded in capturing this essence—too well, as it turned out.

I discovered that when I gazed into the eye of my pencil sketch, there was the dis-turbing sense of a watchful awareness somewhere on the other side of the portrait. This awareness was definitely malevolent. Its hatred was almost palpable, and the longer I looked at the image, the stronger it became. I tried to ignore this sensation. This incident occurred many years before I became interested in magic and other eso-teric subjects, so at the time I was a complete skeptic toward any form of occultism or the paranormal. However, I found it impossible to deny the evidence of my own senses. Even though I thought the sketch was one of the better drawings I had done up to that time in my life, I discovered that I could not leave it sitting out in plain view. The eye of the picture seemed to follow my movements when I was in the room with it. I felt compelled to turn and look at it, yet at the same time I experienced a growing reluctance to do so.

This true story might have had an unfortunate ending, but I was sensitive enough to esoteric currents, even at that stage in my life, to heed my intuition and put the drawing away, where no one would look at it, and more importantly where it could not look upon any living human being. I still have this pencil sketch. I continue to believe that it is one of the most dynamic drawings I have ever done. But it has not been exposed to the light for more than twenty years, and I have no desire to gaze at it, or to feel its gaze upon me. The sensation of being under its scrutiny was enough to freeze the blood.

Knowing what I know today about the invocation of spirits into images, it is obvious that in the process of making the sketch I attracted a spirit possessing the same sort of spiteful malevolence that I associated with the political leader, and had in my mind and emotions while drawing his portrait. Unconsciously, without having the faintest idea at the time of what I was doing, I fashioned the perfect vessel for an evil spirit and invoked the spirit into it. Looking back, the importance of this event in my own development as a magician is apparent. It taught me valuable lessons about the nature of spirits and spirit invocation, lessons I was not able to understand until much later in life. I should mention that there is no danger in preserving this image, provided it is not set out where it can be regularly viewed.

The power I was able to unconsciously infuse into a rough pencil sketch demonstrates that a drawing or painting that serves as a spirit vessel need not be perfect or highly detailed in order to be used effectively. In the past I have had very good results communicating with spirits through crude newspaper photos, where the dots that compose the black and white images are clearly apparent. It is only important that the drawing be meaningful and dynamic to the person who will work with it. If you do the drawing yourself, this is far more likely to be the case. Anyone with even a moderate amount of artistic talent should create their own portrait of the spirit they wish to attract as a lover. When doing the portrait, an effort should be made to infuse as much of the personality and nature of the spirit into its image as possible.

Astrological Times

In my opinion, the observation of astrological times is not essential for successfully working magic. It greatly simplifies matters to ignore times when doing rituals, making sigils, fashioning and consecrating instruments, and so on. However, in traditional Western magic, the observation of astrological times was regarded as a necessary part of the art. It requires a certain audacity to ignore thousands of years of practical experience. For this reason, I often observe times in my own work. My attitude is that it cannot hinder the magic to do so, and assuming there is some validity in ancient traditions, it may well assist the fulfillment of the magician's purpose.

The manufacture and consecration of symbols and images that will be used for positive works of love and creation should be done while the Moon is waxing or full, and avoided while the Moon is waning or new. In general, daytime is better than night for positive, loving purposes—however, when working with lunar deities, angels, and spirits, such as Lilith, who is a moon goddess, night is better since the Moon rules the night. If the symbol or image is linked to one of the planets, it is desirable that the planet be above the horizon, ideally just rising in the east or at the zenith. It is less desirable to do this work while the planet in question is falling towards the western horizon or below the horizon. It is also desirable to do the work connected with a planet on the day of that planet: Sunday (Sun), Monday (Moon), Tuesday (Mars), Wednesday (Mercury), Thursday (Jupiter), Friday (Venus), Saturday (Saturn). Needless to say, when longer works are undertaken that require many days to complete, such as the carving of a statue, briefer astrological times cannot be observed, unless the work is done in sections only during these times.

For the making of the spirit vessel and sigil scroll, it is not necessary to observe more specific times that involve astrological aspects or planetary hours. These matters are complex and will not be treated in this book. Those wishing a more complete understanding of the use of astrological aspects and planetary hours in traditional magic will find this information in my annotated edition of Cornelius Agrippa's *Three Books of Occult Philosophy*.

The Sigil Scroll

The way to use the desired function of a spirit to derive its name, construct its telesmatic image, and draw its sigil, has already been described in the previous chapter. The sigil scroll you insert into the vessel you have selected or made to house your spirit lover should contain four components: the spirit name, the spirit sigil, the symbol or symbols appropriate to the spirit, and a name or names of power by which the spirit is summoned, ruled, and banished. These are drawn in permanent black ink on a white square of new paper that has no recycled content. Provided that you are confident you know the colors most harmonious to the spirit, you can if you wish use colored paper and colored ink. There is a danger in doing so, because if you make a mistake about the choice of colors, it can actually hinder communication with the spirit. Black ink and white paper is generic and safe.

As an example, the sigil scroll of Chasmodai, spirit of the Moon, would be appropriate if done with black ink on white paper, since both black and white are traditional

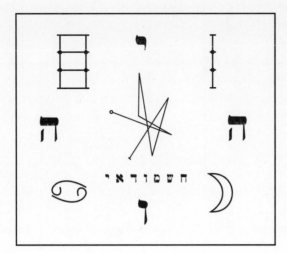

FIGURE 10-1.

Sigil scroll to be inserted within statue or behind picture of Chasmodai.

colors of the Moon. It would also be effective to draw the symbols of the scroll with silver ink or white ink on black paper. The scroll of Chasmodai would bear the sigil of the spirit formed on the Sigil Rose of the Golden Dawn (or some other sigil generator, such as the magic square of the Moon), the name of the spirit in sacred Hebrew characters, the symbol of the sphere of the Moon itself, which is a waxing crescent, and a Hebrew name of power such as יהוה IHVH (I = י, H = ה, V = ו, H = ה). Remember that the letters of Hebrew names are written from right to left. The fourfold name IHVH, also known as the Tetragrammaton, is the supreme name of power in Kabbalistic magic. It is vibrated on the breath or inscribed on the air during rituals, or both, to give authority to any commands or instructions you may make to the invoked spirit. Tetragrammaton may be used generally as a name of power in spirit magic, since there is no name superior to it. It is especially applicable to elemental magic, because each of its letters rules one of the four elements—Yod (Fire), 1st Heh (Water), Vav (Air), 2nd Heh (Earth).

Other symbols that embody the powers of the Moon could also be added to the sigil scroll of Chasmodai, but it is better to keep the number of symbols to one or two. Otherwise, the scroll will appear cluttered, and the occult virtues of the many symbols on it will conflict and partially neutralize each other. I have added the zodiac sign of Cancer, and the geomantic glyphs of Populus and Via, to the sigil scroll of

Geomantic Figure	Name of Figure	Ruling Spirit	Planet	Zodiac Sign	Element
• • •	Puer (a boy, yellow hair, beardless)	Bartzabel	Mars	Aries	Fire
• • • • •	Amissio (loss, comprehended without)	Kedemel	Venus	Taurus	Earth
• • • • • •	Albus (white, fair hair or complexion)	Taphthar-tharath	Mercury	Gemini	Air
• • • • • • • •	Populus (people, congregation)	Chasmodai	Moon	Cancer	Water
• • • • •	Fortuna Major (greater fortune or aid, safe-guard when entering)	Sorath	Sun	Leo	Fire
• • • • • •	Conjuncto (assembly, conjunction)	Taphthar-tharath	Mercury	Virgo	Earth
• • • • •	Puella (a girl, beautiful)	Kedemel	Venus	Libra	Air
• • • • • •	Rubeus (red, reddish hair or complexion)	Bartzabel	Mars	Scorpio	Water

TABLE 10-2. Attributions of the geomantic figures.

Geomantic Figure	Name of Figure	Ruling Spirit	Planet	Zodiac Sign	Element
⠿	Acquisitio (obtaining, comprehended within)	Hismael	Jupiter	Sagittarius	Fire
⠿	Carcer (a prison, restraint, a boundary)	Zazel	Saturn	Capricorn	Earth
⠿	Tristitia (sadness, damned, cross)	Zazel	Saturn	Aquarius	Air
⠿	Laetitia (joy, laughing, healthy, bearded)	Hismael	Jupiter	Pisces	Water
⠿	Cauda Draconis (lower threshold, going out)	Zazel and Bartzabel	Saturn and Mars	Tail of the Dragon	Fire
⠿	Caput Draconis (heart, upper threshold, entering)	Hismael and Kedemel	Venus and Jupiter	Head of the Dragon	Earth
⠿	Fortuna Minor (lesser fortune or aid, safeguard going out)	Sorath	Sun	Leo	Fire
⠿	Via (way, road, journey)	Chasmodai	Moon	Cancer	Water

TABLE 10-2. Attributions of the geomantic figures (continued).

Chasmodai. Both geomantic figures are associated with the sphere of the Moon and specifically with the spirit Chasmodai in the Golden Dawn system of magic. The Golden Dawn was particularly fond of using the glyphs of geomancy as power symbols on their talismans and pentacles. In the accompanying table (see preceding pages) the geomantic signs and their occult attributions, as used by the Golden Dawn, are illustrated. These glyphs can be useful when working with a spirit that corresponds to one of the elements, one of the planets, or one of the zodiac signs.

By drawing lines between the dots that usually define the geomantic glyphs, it is possible to make more elegant symbols. Because the Moon rules only one sign of the zodiac, the two geomantic figures associated with the Moon receive the same zodiac sign. Both Populus and Via are linked to the sign Cancer. This makes the zodiac sign of Cancer an appropriate symbol to include on the sigil scroll of Chasmodai.

If the decision has been made to work with astrological times when invoking Chasmodai into her statue or picture, it would be best to draw her sigil scroll on Monday night when the waxing or full Moon is rising in the east or high in the sky overhead. Greater power will be obtained if the moonlight falls directly on the paper of the scroll while your are drawing the letters and symbols. Those who understand the basics of astrology will make sure that the Moon is not hindered in her working by the astrological aspects of the other planets at the time the sigil scroll is drawn. These same general rules apply to the creation of sigil scrolls for spirits associated with the other six planets of traditional astrology.

The planet linked to the spirit should always be above the horizon when the scroll of the spirit is marked with its symbols. Scrolls for spirits of the Sun and Mercury are best created during the day when the Sun is just rising or approaching the zenith, but if the Sun is rising, make sure Mercury is also above the horizon when creating a Mercury scroll. It is not necessary for Mercury to be visible to the naked eye. Scrolls for spirits of Venus are ideally made when Venus is visible above the horizon in the east at dawn, but they can also be made during the day around noon. Both Mercury and Venus orbit relatively close to the Sun. As a consequence, when the Sun is high in the sky, these planets are always above the horizon. Because of the nature of the Moon and Saturn, it is best to make sigil scrolls for spirits linked to these planets at night. Scrolls for spirits of Mars and Jupiter can be made either in the day or night, provided the planet is rising or high in the sky at the time of their making.

Those who are not interested in observing astrological times, or who have difficulty understanding the mechanics of astrology, should let their intuition guide them as to the best hour to draw the sigil scroll. In the case of spirits without a strong link to any of the seven traditional planets, intuition is the most reliable guide. It is usually possible to associate any spirit with one of the seven planets provided the nature of the spirit is fully understood. However, the link that exists when the personality of a spirit in a general sense resembles the nature of a planet is not nearly as strong as the link that exists when the spirit is more directly connected with a planet. For example, the name Chasmodai is numerically based on the magic square of the Moon—the Hebrew letters of Chasmodai sum 369, and the Hebrew letters in any row or column of the magic square of the Moon also sum 369. This makes Chasmodai an intrinsically lunar spirit, and for this reason the powers and symbols of the Moon must always be taken into account when invoking her.

Constructing the Shrine

Having found or made a physical vessel to contain your spirit lover during your invocations of the spirit, it is necessary to make a shrine to hold the image. The image serves as the body of the spirit, while the shrine serves as the house of the spirit. The shrine is located in whatever room you work your rituals, since the ritual of invocation must take place in front of the image. When invoking the gods, goddesses, or higher spirits for the purpose of erotic love, the best place for the shrine is your bedroom. This will allow you to invoke the spirit into its image, then go directly to bed with the spirit still resident within the image, and watching over your bed. This is especially important when seeking to communicate with the spirit during dreams.

Those who have seen a household shrine dedicated to a deity or a saint will have a general idea of what is required. Shrines can take an infinite number of possible forms. They do not need to be elaborate or richly decorated to function powerfully, provided their two essential purposes are met. First, the shrine must aid in the invocation of the spirit into its physical vessel. Second, the shrine must be a harmonious and pleasant space for the spirit to inhabit over extended periods of time.

There are a number of practical considerations of lesser importance. It is best if the shrine can be closed in some manner to conceal the spirit vessel from the view of casual onlookers. After an image has become energized by repeated rituals, it will become conscious and aware of its surroundings very readily, sometimes even when a person with no magical training gazes intently into its eyes. This can be a terrifying experience for an individual who merely looks at a statue or picture without expecting anything to happen. It is also useful to be able to transport the shrine around easily, in case it becomes necessary to change the ritual workspace. It must provide a safe and stable place for the image to reside, eliminating as much as possible any danger that the image will be knocked onto the floor or otherwise damaged. Ideally, the shrine should protect the image from dust and dirt. It should have a surface where offerings can be placed as gifts to the spirit that enters the image.

The shrine described here is very specific in its construction. It works well in most circumstances and takes up little space. It is inexpensive and relatively easy to built. You should not regard this particular design as essential, but merely as a guideline that shows how the basic requirements of a shrine can be fulfilled. The design was inspired by the portable shrines used by early Christian monks who traveled across Europe and the Middle East on pilgrimages and religious missions.

The shrine shown in the Figure 10-2 is a simple box standing on its end, with double doors in front, a solid back panel, and an elevated floor. Its dimensions are not critical, but a convenient overall dimension is two feet wide, two feet high, and a foot deep. Having the lower edges of the doors somewhat elevated above the table on which the shrine stands can be useful since it allows the doors to be opened or closed even when there is something resting in front of the shrine, such as a dish of incense or an open book. This can be accomplished by making the doors less than the full length of the shrine, or more simply by placing the shrine on a stand that lifts it a few inches above the surface of the table. It is not necessary to have carpentry skills to build a shrine. Any old bureau drawer or wooden box standing on its end can serve this purpose. You can use small curtains in place of doors, or even cover the box with a drop cloth when the shrine is not in use.

The floor of the shrine must be large enough to hold the vessel of the spirit. If the vessel is a statue, it will occupy the center of the floor. If the vessel is a picture, it will either hang on the back panel inside the shrine, or stand leaning against the back panel. It is a good idea to elevate the vessel of the spirit above the floor of the shrine by placing it on a small dais or holder. This can be something as simple as a brick or a block of wood, but must be selected so that it is in harmony with the nature of the spirit.

In addition to the vessel itself, there must be room to stand candles in single candlesticks on either side of the image. These are lighted within the shrine during rituals if the shrine is large enough to accommodate them burning. If the shrine is too small, they are taken out and placed on either side of the shrine before being lighted, so that their light will shine inward upon the image. In front of the candles there must be room for two small dishes, one to hold water and the other salt, and in front of the image of the spirit, room to place a small holder for incense cones or incense sticks, and a flat tray or dish upon which to place offerings such as food or flowers. It is not necessary that all these things remain within the shrine during rituals, but it is very useful if there is enough room on the floor of the shrine to store them all when the shrine is closed. It is useful to insert hooks into the walls of the shrine for hanging flowers and other offerings such as brightly colored threads, ribbons, or cloths.

Two candles are preferable to one because when placed on either side of the image and lit, they provide an even light. If only a single candle is used, it will always need to be put on one side of the image. This unbalances its light, not only in a practical sense, but also symbolically. Two candles act as a symbolic gateway in very much in the same way as the pillars named Jachin and Boaz that stood at the entrance to the Temple of Solomon. Because they cast an even light over the image and are out of the line of sight of the ritualist, they are easy on the eyes. They should be white, or of a color in harmony with the nature of the image. When working with an overtly lunar spirit such as Lilith, a white candle and a black candle may be used, since these are lunar colors. In this case the white candle would be placed on the right and the black candle on the left, from the ritualist's perspective. Try to get identical candle holders, and use the same type of candles burning at roughly the same height.

Water and salt are traditional materials used to cleanse the magic circle and banish any chaotic or obstructive influences that may be present at the place of working. They represent the elements Water and Earth, the two receptive or feminine elements. These are the heavy elements of the earth that tend to remain in a cohesive body and to fall downward when released in air. It is best if they are consecrated prior to their use. A good way to accomplish this is to get two containers that can be tightly sealed to hold bulk amounts of these materials. Each container filled with its material can be ritually consecrated to the magical use you intend for it, and then prior to each individual ritual, a small amount of water can be poured out into one dish, and a small amount of salt put into another similar dish. Inexpensive glass dessert cups make suitable containers, but almost any small dish or cup can be used.

All four elements should be represented within the shrine for balance. This can be done in a variety of ways. The elements are expressed physically by the flames of the candles (Fire), the smoke of the incense (Air), the dish of water (Water), and the dish of salt (Earth). It is not absolutely necessary to use incense, and in the case of those with allergies to scents, it may even be counterproductive. Two alternative objects that stand for elemental Air are a feather and a flower. Feathers are airy because the bird is a creature of the air, and flowers because they are associated with a delicate scent. You can if you wish place a large feather in the back of the shrine, or tape it to the inner surface of the roof so that it is located above the image.

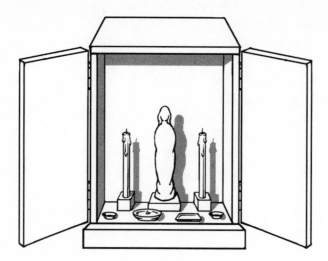

FIGURE 10-2.
Portable shrine
to house the
spirit vessel.

Flowers can serve two functions. They can be used to represent the element Air, and can also serve as daily offerings to your spirit lover. If you decide to use living flowers, you must replace them without fail on a regular basis before they begin to whither and die. Fresh flowers symbolize life and hope, withered flowers decay and death. An alternative to fresh flowers is the use within the shrine of artificial flowers of paper or silk. These can beautify the shrine and make is a more pleasing residence for the invoked spirit. However, because artificial flowers cost you no effort or significant expense, they are not suitable as daily offerings to the spirit.

An offering must entail some sacrifice of time, effort, and value in order for it to have significance. Food can be used as a daily offering to the spirit, since it has an intrinsic value. Milk and bread make suitable daily offerings. The spirit will be pleased if during each nightly ritual of invocation, immediately prior to the period of communion with the spirit, you place a small open dish of milk and a small cut piece of bread on a dish in front of the image. In the morning when you awake, remove the milk and bread and discard them. Other foods may also be used as offerings. Sweet foods such as cookies are very appropriate for attracting spirits of love. Santa Claus receives offerings of cookies from children on Christmas Eve, and so can your astral lover. Choose foods high in energy that are wholesome, natural, and nourishing. Wine can be substituted for milk. Wine is somewhat more appropriate for a spirit of Venus, while milk is more appropriate for a spirit of the Moon.

Other things besides food and drink can be used as offerings, provided they have real value. You may wish to set a coin inside the shrine during each ritual, then the next morning, discard it. Traditional practices provide clues that guide us in these matters. It is no coincidence that coins are tossed into fountains when visitors make a wish. Most who do this have no idea that they are making an offering to the resident spirit dwelling in the fountain, which is a manmade replica of a natural spring. By tossing in a coin, they are requesting that the spirit of the fountain grant them their wish through its magic. If you can afford it, use a dollar bill each night as an offering and prior to the ritual, burn it completely in the flame of one of the candles while explicitly offering it to the spirit, using the name of the spirit inscribed on its sigil scroll within its image. This will dedicate the value of the paper money to the exclusive use of the spirit. By burning the money, you take that value out of the world and away from your own use, and present it to the spirit.

The interior of the shrine is painted or otherwise finished in a way that will be pleasing to the spirit who will reside within it. The color chosen must be in harmony with the spirit's nature. For Chasmodai, a spirit of the Moon, black would work well, or a pattern of black and white. Self-adhesive wallpaper can make an attractive inner surface, and comes in a wide variety of patterns and colors. It is often possible to buy odd sheets for a very low cost. If you are artistic, you may wish to paint designs on the inner surfaces of the shrine, or choose images and glue them to the inside. The more dynamic and meaningful the decoration of the shrine, the better it will attract and hold the spirit. You may, if you wish, fill the interior of the shrine with symbols and images of power.

When Tetragrammaton (IHVH) is used as a name of authority on the sigil scroll, it is a good idea to inscribe the Hebrew letters on the inner walls of the shrine. These should be painted large in the middle of the panels, or drawn on paper and glued on the panels. The letter Yod (י) is best placed on the back wall, behind the spirit vessel. The letter Heh (ה) is put on each side panel. The letter Vav (ו) is put on the inside of the front door, or doors. If you make your shrine with two doors that meet in the center, paint or otherwise attach the Vav so that it spans both sides, and is broken into two when the doors are opened. If you use a single curtain for the front of the shrine, sew or attach the letter Vav to the middle of the inner surface of this curtain.

In addition, paint or attach the Hebrew letter Shin (ש) to the inner roof of the shrine, and the letter Mem (מ) to its inner floor, directly beneath the dais upon which the stature or picture rests. On the surface of the raised dais, directly beneath the statue or picture, paint the letter Aleph (א). If you do not use a dais to support the spirit vessel in your shrine, make the letter Aleph upon the vessel itself, either upon its base if it is a statue, or upon its back if it is a picture.

The four letters of Tetragrammaton form a circle of power around the inside of the shrine. When the doors are shut, this ring is unbroken and seals the shrine against any spiritual being who might seek to use it as a gateway without your permission. When the doors are opened, the ring of Tetragrammaton is broken, and allows energy to flow outward through the break. The letter Vav is the letter of elemental Air, the vehicle of mind and of the life force, which is present on the breath. When you sit in front of the shrine, your living breath surrounds the spirit vessel and provides a bridge between the spirit and your consciousness. The letter Shin pertains to Fire and is associated with the heights, the letter Mem pertains to Water and is associated with the depths. Aleph is linked to Air and the breath, as well as to thought and articulate speech. These seven Hebrew letters symbolically locate the physical vessel of the spirit at the center of three intersecting perpendicular rays and make it a natural focus of power, both for you when you attempt to contact the spirit by concentrating your will upon the image, and for the spirit when it attempts to express itself to you by using the image as its temporary body.

{ 11 }

Observations and Preparations

Mental and Physical Training

Rituals of ceremonial magic cannot be worked effectively unless they are supported by the regular practice of mental and physical exercises that prepare the mind and body for the changes caused by the rituals. If you scatter seed on a field, it may or may not grow, depending on the type of seed and the natural state of the field. On the other hand, if you plow and fertilize the field before scattering the seed, it is more likely to flourish, and the plants it produces will be larger and more valuable. To use another analogy, no one would expect to juggle five baseballs in the air at once without practice, yet many beginners in magic have the idea that they can perform rituals and get immediate and powerful results with no conditioning or prior preparation.

Adepts accustomed to working in any field of Western magic may find it possible to perform sexual alchemy without extensive preparation. Even if they have not done rituals for years, the pathways formed by previous habits exist in their minds and bodies to facilitate the fulfillment of the rituals described later in the book. This chapter is mainly for beginners who have not had extensive experience in ritual magic. The suggested exercises and practices are based on my own experience. These are the activities I followed while developing sexual alchemy.

It is best to divide these general conditioning exercises from the invocation of your spirit lover. The requirements of your own daily routine will dictate when you perform magic. In my own work, I found it useful to do these exercises in the morning just after waking from sleep, and to commune with spirits in the evening, immediately before going to bed. This created the widest possible separation between the two aspects of my daily work, and still allowed me to fit a full spectrum of ordinary activities into my day. There may be a few fortunate individuals who can stop their lives and devote themselves solely to magic for periods of months or years, but most of us need to earn a living, maintain family and social ties, service the car, clear the house, and do a multitude of other tedious and unimportant, but necessary, little jobs.

The successful use of the rituals described here will require a significant but not an unreasonable portion of your day. There is no way around this requirement. Magic is not something that can be rushed. It forms its own agenda and takes its own course. During the period when I initially awakened my chakras and established communication with the spirit that I have since come to recognize as my Guardian Angel, my schedule of practice was unusually intense, even for a professional magician. My conditioning routine was never done in under an hour, and usually took closer to two hours to complete. The period varied from day to day, depending on my physical state and unrelated demands on my time. The evening ritual of communion with the spirit took even longer, usually from two to four hours. In addition, when I could find the time, I performed rituals of communion with the spirit in the afternoons, but these were of briefer duration, usually from one to two hours.

Few individuals could sustain this intensity of practice for over a year, as I did. Fortunately, results can be achieved with a less rigorous schedule, if the ritualist knows in the beginning the purpose for the work, and the most fruitful techniques to achieve it. Remember, I was working intuitively, guided only by my studies and by whatever directions I was able to unconsciously pick up from my tutelary spirit, who was herself seeking to bring about our union, although in the early months I had no awareness of her purpose. Less than an hour is all that is required in the morning for basic conditioning, and little more than an hour at night for the invocation and communion with your spirit lover. Often you will wish to extend this period of communion by inviting the spirit into bed with you, and even into your dreams. Provided this is not done to excess, no harm results, although when the loving link with a spirit is strong, there is a temptation to forego sleep altogether in favor of love-making, which can result in fatigue.

The Utility of Dreams

Some authorities on magic counsel against doing rituals just before sleep, since rituals tend to stir up the subconscious, and can cause disturbing dreams. However, when seeking to establish loving union with a spirit, dreams are not to be overlooked as an avenue of communication. Rather than try to suppress dreams generated by the practice of rituals, in my own work I chose to encourage them, and recorded the results daily shortly after waking up. It was a rare morning when I could not record at least one dream. Sometimes I was able to record up to six. I managed this by keeping a notepad and pen beside my bed. During the night, whenever I became aware of a dream, I forced myself into partial wakefulness and wrote it down in outline form, then turned over and went back to sleep. The next morning while recording my dreams in my daily record, I was able to recall individual dreams by referring to these outlines, and write down the dreams in greater detail.

It requires a certain amount of discipline to force yourself awake in the middle of the night long enough to record a dream, particularly if you become aware of numerous dreams over a span of a few hours. The temptation is almost irresistible to lie in a semi-conscious state until reclaimed by sleep once again. This is what we usually do. It is possible to break this habit by forming a new habit in its place. After a few nights of turning on the bedside lamp to jot down the basics of a dream before going back to sleep, it becomes easier. Habit can be either a servant or a tyrant. If we allow ourselves to be ruled by habits we have not chosen, we become their slaves, but if we select our habits and reinforce them by doing them regularly, we become their masters.

It is much easier to awaken in the middle of the night to record a dream if it happens to be a nightmare. During my early months of practice I experienced uncommonly horrifying dreams. Ritual magic resonates in the depths of the mind, and inevitably stirs up fears and phobias we have suppressed all our lives. Usually we forget these troubling dreams before complete wakefulness in the morning. But if all dreams are deliberately recorded, this automatic protective mechanism cannot function, and we become able to remember the horrors that ritual work prods to temporary life in the slime of our id. It was this natural tendency of magic to awaken repressed memories, impulses and fears that caused Israel Regardie to suggest that anyone about to study magic in a serious way should go through a period of psychoanalysis first. In my opinion, this is unnecessary for a person who is basically well adjusted and stable.

Many of my dreams were interesting and instructive. I met and talked with great sages, visited ancient libraries filled with esoteric texts, which I studied, traveled to strange spirit realms and interacted with the inhabitants, joined groups of magicians on the astral level for shared rituals, and even wrote entire books of my own on various subjects while dreaming. I had repeating dreams in which each night I wrote another portion of some dream book until at last the work was completed. These dream books were actually written in my sleeping mind, and would be of great interest were it possible to remember them in detail while awake, but thus far I have been unable to rescue them from my dreams.

There is an unfortunate tendency to regard dreams as unimportant, but on the contrary, our dreams constitute a large portion of our conscious existence and are completely real on their own level. We are fully aware when we dream, though our consciousness is not waking consciousness. Merely because we usually forget our dreams after waking up does not reduce their significance. It is very likely that you will have dream experiences similar to mine when you undertake the serious study of magic, but unless you regularly record your dreams, you will forget the valuable lessons they teach.

Spirits sometimes use dreams to deliver important messages. These messages take the form of a very loud, clear voice speaking a few words, or at most a short sentence. The messages are usually unconnected in any way with the dream unfolding at the time they are received, and are different in quality from ordinary speech heard in dreams. They have no discernable source, but seemed to come from everywhere at once. I receive such messages rarely, but take them seriously when they occur. Sometimes I am able to understand their application to my life, and other times they are so cryptic, I can never make any sense of them. In every case I get a strong impression that some great intelligence is speaking directly to me for an important reason, even when I am unable to comprehend its purpose.

Two of the spirits I established communication with used dreams to convey their hidden names to me, specifically for the purpose of enabling me to invoke them more clearly and strongly. I was able to observe and interact with them during my dreams. This allowed me to gain a very clear and complete impression not only of their physical forms, but also of their personalities. The names they supplied became potent keys for contacting these spirits. One was a spirit of the Moon, the other an elemental spirit of Water. Both were female. My impression was that the lunar spirit was of the nature of the Kabbalistic plane of Yetzirah, but that the Undine was of the level of Assiah. Both were friendly, although their personalities were distinctly inhuman.

When I began the study of sexual alchemy, spirits occasionally made love to me in dreams without being requested to do so, resulting in spontaneous orgasm. This is not an uncommon experience for the average person, but few who have it recognize its true nature. They regard it as a kind of involuntary mental masturbation during sleep that occurs automatically as a release of sexual tension, and fail to perceive that arousal and orgasm are deliberately induced by a separate spiritual intelligence. Because I achieved through my practice the ability to retain a measure of conscious awareness during dreams, I was able to observe these erotic dreams with a degree of detachment.

I noticed that the spirits with whom I made love adopted whatever form was most convenient in the dream I happened to be having at the time, and manipulated the plot of the dream so that its activities became erotic. This was in some cases done very clumsily. An ordinary dream would abruptly take an inexplicable erotic turn. Once lovemaking was initiated, the spirit involved was very reluctant to terminate it, and when on several occasions I deliberately pushed the spirit aside and forced myself awake to terminate the dream, the spirit struggled quite strongly to cling to me. From this behavior, it was clear that the spirit was receiving some sort of nourishment or pleasure from the union.

The reason I mention these personal dream experiences is so that you will have some idea of what you may expect in your own work if you begin to seriously perform the exercises and rituals in this book on a regular basis. You will not become fully aware of these dream events unless you make a complete record of your dreams on a daily basis. A large loose-leaf binder is ideal for this purpose, since it allowed the easy removal and insertion of individuals sheets of lined paper. If I remembered details of a dream after initially entering it in the binder, I was able to add a page to expand its description. If I made a mistake copying out the events of a dream, I was able to remove the page and insert a new one with the corrected information. It is very important that you date your dreams, so that you can relate them to other events in your life months later. There is no reason not to maintain this record on your computer's hard disk. Write your dream outlines down during the night on a notepad you keep for this purpose beside your bed, and transfer them in the morning to your computer.

Other useful details to record for each day include the weather (rainy, sunny, windy, cloudy, stormy), the humidity and barometric pressure, the phase of the Moon, and your general state of physical and mental health (energetic, lethargic, happy, sad, depressed, angry, intuitive). Along with your dreams, keep a daily record of any changes you make to your exercises and rituals, any unusual events that occur during the rituals, and any other personal information you think may in any way have a bearing on your practice of magic. It often happens that strange little events will take place while we are engaged the study of magic, events that at the time appear to be nothing more than coincidences, but weeks or months later the circumstances in our lives will reveal the synchronistic meaning of these events.

Dietary Considerations

Unless you can alter your diet consistently over a period of months, it is better not to change the way you eat. More harm than good is done by drastically modifying the kinds and amount of food you take in for a few days or a week, then sliding back into your old habits. Your body can get used to almost any type of food, even bad food, if you eat it consistently, but your body cannot tolerate rapid changes in diet. If you are willing to make the commitment to make a long-term change in the way you eat, it can be a significant help in communicating with spirits. This has been recognized for thousands of years by priests and magicians. An almost universal aspect of monastic life around the world is a greatly restricted and modified diet.

Spirits are aware of this connection between the human diet and communication with astral beings. The Enochian angel Gabriel, speaking to the Elizabethan magician John Dee through the voice of Dee's scryer, Edward Kelley, said to Dee: "For the flesh and spirit rejoyce not at once. Neither can the full belly grone out true prayers. Feed therefore the Soul with the love of our society. And bridle your flesh; For it is inso-lent."[1] The Enochian angels advised Dee to fill his soul with "celestial food," that is, to fast and avoid alcohol. Part of the traditional reason to shun rich foods and strong drink was to avoid stimulating lust that was directed towards mortal women or men. Lust towards other human beings creates a hostile environment for spirits who have no interest in sexuality. However, when seeking a spirit as a lover, we refrain from stimulating strong physical desires for another reason entirely—so that our sexual energy will not be squandered on physical sex with other human beings, but stored up and fortified for the use of our spirit lover.

During the year when I established communication with my Guardian and awak-ened my chakras, I maintained a low calorie diet by eating one large hot meal and one small cold meal a day, and completely eliminating butter, gravy, sauces, raw sugar, sweets, pastries, whole milk, oils, junk foods, and fried foods. I increased my con-sumption of fresh vegetables and fresh fruits, as well as whole-grain cereals such as oatmeal, and reduced my consumption of bread. Occasionally I ate nuts and dried fruit such as raisins or dates. I would estimate that my daily diet was around 1,800 calories, which is not a particularly severe diet, but over the course of a year I lost a considerable amount of weight despite daily exercise, which was at the same time increasing my muscle mass.

In my opinion, a portion of my success in spirit communication was due to my light diet. My main meal was taken at midday, and my lighter meal in the early evening. As a result, my stomach was completely empty when I awoke in the morning prior to performing my strengthening and stretching exercises, and my controlled breathing and meditation. My practice upon rising in the early morning was to drink about six ounces of unsweetened lemon juice, created by cutting fresh lemons and boiling them in a pot of water, then allowing the liquid to cool and storing it in the refrigerator. I discovered that this chilled, unsweetened juice in my empty stomach helped my body to sweat during my morning exercises and controlled breathing. This practice was pure instinct on my part—it simply felt right, so I kept it up.

There are several general rules you should observe concerning diet, even if you do not feel committed enough to make a radical change in the amount or type of food you eat. As much as possible, avoid heavy foods such as meat pies, highly spiced foods such as pizza, and fried foods such as hamburgers and French fries. Avoid junk foods such as potato chips, carbonated beverages, ice cream, and chocolate bars. This is particularly important in the three or four hours prior to your evening invocation. The last thing you want is a pepperoni pizza sitting on your stomach while you are attempting to summon a spirit into its physical vessel. Avoid beans and other foods that are liable to cause stomach gas and flatulence. Avoid alcohol for at least several hours prior to your invocation.

Heavy, greasy foods in the stomach make us feel heavy and material, as though we are weighed down to the earth. This inhibits the performance of ritual magic in general, and particularly spirit communication. One theory to account for this suggests that when the energies of the body are focused on digesting and processing greasy food, there is less vitality available for the higher spiritual faculties of the mind. It may simply be that when the body is occupied with digestion, the mind cannot help but be more aware of the flesh, and since we cannot hold two things in the mind simultaneously, we are necessarily less aware of our higher perceptions. Grease and meat are difficult to digest. They stay longer in the stomach and small intestine, and consume more of the body's energy during digestion than lighter foods.

Another drawback to eating heavy, highly spiced foods shortly before ritual work is that you will often feel and hear your stomach churning the food while you are trying to concentrate on the details of the ritual. This is extremely distracting. Even though we might not even notice this stomach action during the day while engaged in ordinary activities, when we sit down to meditate or to communicate with a spirit in the stillness of our ritual chamber, it becomes not only obvious but difficult to ignore. The last thing you want when you are attempting to fill your mind with thoughts of pure love is to have your awareness repeatedly drawn to your digestive tract. The spirit is aware of your thoughts during your ritual communion with it. A higher spiritual intelligence will find it more difficult to remain in close contact with you if your mind is drawn to the physical processes of your body. For the same reason, you do not want to be emitting gas during rituals. It is almost impossible to fart without thinking about it, and when you think about it, you are creating a disharmonious atmosphere (pun intended) for the spirit.

This question of digestion may seem trivial at first consideration, but after you have begun to invoke a spirit nightly, you will soon realize that it is a significant factor in your success or failure. For the same reason, you should take care to keep your hair and body clean in order to avoid the urge to scratch while sitting in communion with your spirit lover, and should always wear loose, comfortable clothing that does not bind your body. Anything that might draw the focus of your mind away from the spirit and the astral plane is to be avoided.

There is a general prejudice against eating junk foods while engaged in serious workings. The usual explanation is that these foods contain a large amount of artificial preservatives, colorings, and flavors. In my opinion, it is not so much the trace amounts of artificial additives that are the problem, as it is the fact that junk foods tend to be difficult to digest, greasy, salty, and highly spiced and flavored, while at the same time having very little nutritional value. They over-stimulate the digestive system, make it work especially hard, and give back very little benefit. Once the body has been habituated to this sort of food, it craves it constantly, since ordinary foods cannot provide this intense stimulation. This sustains a cycle of addiction that is antithetical to the higher esoteric faculties of the mind. It is possible to break this cycle by eliminating entirely raw salt and sugar, and any food that contains large amounts of either substance. Spices should be greatly reduced.

Exercise

It is not necessary to enter into a routine of heavy physical exercise, such as bodybuilding, while invoking a spirit lover. This would distract your attention away from astral concerns and focus it on physical concerns, which is undesirable. Light, regular exercise has the benefit of toning the body and keeping its metabolism functioning at a higher level, providing an excess of physical vitality that can be drawn upon as needed during ritual work. Sustaining daily communication of any kind with spirits demands large amounts of energy, and this is especially true when the spirit involved is a sexual partner. If you succeed in establishing a daily link with your spirit lover, you will quickly be amazed at how much vitality you must pour into that union. It is absolutely necessary that your health be good for you to sustain this flow of energy, and light exercise is the best way to insure a high level of general fitness.

There is no hard-and-fast rule that dictates which exercises you should perform, or when they should be done. I can only give you the benefit of my personal experience. I refer back frequently to my own methods of practice, because they proved to be a formula for success in establishing loving union with spirits. Since they worked so well for me, it is likely that others who follow the same methods will achieve a similar success. It was my custom to do a brief series of stretching exercises first thing in the morning after taking a glass of unsweetened lemon juice, followed immediately by a series of light strengthening exercises. This was followed by controlled breathing (*pranayama*) coupled with an internal mantra and visualization. I ended my morning practices with a period of quiet contemplation which involved the visualization of various scenes or objects.

To stretch the tightness out of my muscles after waking, I did a number of simple yoga postures each day. I highly recommend the study of hatha yoga (the yoga of body poses) to anyone who is serious about spirit magic in any form, and especially to those interested in sexual alchemy. Yoga has been evolved over centuries for the purpose of activating and strengthening our esoteric perceptions and abilities. It is extremely useful when seeking a spiritual awakening, but no less so when seeking attainment in magic. Much of this form of yoga is focused on stretching and stimulating the spine. Since the muladhara, the lowest chakra of the body, resides near the base of the spine, and since the energy of the muladhara is necessary in transforming alchemically the sexual fluids of the body during erotic union with a Daughter or Son of Lilith, regular hatha yoga is naturally helpful during the practice of sexual alchemy.

Contrary to popular opinion, it is not necessary to be a contortionist to derive benefit from yoga. The simplest postures are also the most beneficial. When doing yoga, always wear light, loose clothing and have your feet bare. If you do the postures first thing after waking, pajamas make an excellent exercise costume. Never attempt to force your body beyond its limit when stretching in yoga postures. There should be no strain or discomfort, only a light, sustained tension. Yoga postures are entered into slowly without effort, held for several minutes, then gently released. Above all, never bob or jerk your body repeatedly in an effort to force it into a posture—this will destroy any benefit you might otherwise have obtained from the posture.

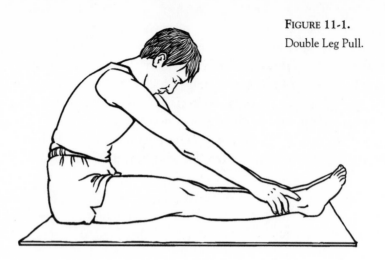

FIGURE 11-1.
Double Leg Pull.

Each of the poses described below should be repeated twice before progressing on to the next posture. I have not used the Sanskrit names for these poses, because it is far more important for you to learn the pose than to struggle with its name. Some of the poses, such as the backward bend and the single leg pull, are simplified to make them easier for beginners.

Double Leg Pull

Start with a simple forward stretch of the spine. Sit on the floor on a small rug with your hands resting on the rug on either side of your hips, your legs extended together in front of you and your back straight. Point your toes upward and slightly back, with the soles of your feet flat as though pressed against the base of an invisible wall. Exhale lightly. Inhale, and as you do so, slowly raise your arms up at your sides until they point straight up over your head. Continue looking forward, and take care not to hunch your shoulders. Slowly exhale as you bend your torso forward at the hips. Lower your extended arms until the palms of your hands rest against your knees or shins. Hold this stretch for about two minutes while breathing normally. Exhale lightly. As you slowly inhale, lift your arms and straighten your back until you are sitting upright and looking forward, with your arms extended directly upward above your head. Exhale and allow your arms to fall gradually until your hands are once more pressed against the rug on either side of your hips, as in your starting position. Repeat the posture.

FIGURE 11-2.
Single Leg Pull.

The greatest benefit is gained from this stretch if you do not curve your entire back when leaning forward, but attempt as much as possible to bend only from the hips. As you bend forward, try to keep a little hollow in the lower part of your back. This is not possible while bending forward, but the effort will aid you in adopting the correct posture. As you bend, stretch forward with the top of your skull, and keep your shoulders relaxed. The universal error made when first performing this pose is to hunch the shoulders and try to stretch forward with the arms and hands rather than with the top of the head.

There is no right or wrong way to do this posture—there is no success or failure. Those who are younger or more flexible will be able to grasp their toes with their hands, or even to lay the flats of their palms against the soles of their feet, when in the fully extended position. This is fine. But those who are less flexible will derive an equal or greater benefit from the posture if they can only reach as far as their knees, provided that they keep their legs and back straight and stretch through the tops of their heads.

Single Leg Pull

Draw up your left foot and position the sole of your foot against your inner right thigh, with your left heel pressed against your groin. Men should slide their left heel beneath their scrotum so that their heel presses lightly against their perineum. Keep your left knee on the rug, and the toes of your right foot pointed upward as they were in the previous posture. It may be that you are not flexible enough to draw your left foot all the way up to your groin. If so, place the sole of your left foot against the inner side of your lower right thigh, or even against the side of your right knee. Sit with your back straight, gazing directly forward, the palms of your hands resting on the rug on either side of your hips.

Exhale lightly. As you slowly inhale, raise your arms upward on either side of your torso until they extend straight upward above your head, with your fingers extended and pointing upward. Do not hunch your shoulders. Exhale as you slowly bend forward from the hips, and allow your hands to grasp your right leg as far down your leg as you can comfortably reach. Extend your spine through the top of your head rather than trying to stretch with your arms. Keep your shoulders relaxed—there must be space between your biceps and the sides of your head. Hold this pose for about two minutes with mild tension, breathing normally. As your body becomes more used to the posture, bend your elbows slightly outward to maintain a constant tension.

Those who are flexible will be able to grasp their right foot in their hands. The usual error in this pose is the tendency to twist the torso to the left in an attempt to reach further down the right leg. Always remember, it does not matter how far down your leg you can reach, only that you perform the posture correctly. Make sure your shoulders are kept square as you bend forward, and that your arms are equally extended. Also avoid turning your right foot to the side. Keep its sole flat, as though it were pressed against the base of an invisible wall.

Release the pose by reversing the steps. As you slowly inhale, straighten your elbows, let go of your right foot, and lift your torso back into a sitting posture with your arms high above your head. Exhale as you allow your arms to gradually drift downward on either side of your body until your palms are pressed against the rug on either side of your hips. Repeat the single-leg stretch on the same side by progressing through all the steps a second time.

Straighten your left leg, using your hands to aid you, and sit with both legs extended for a minute or so, breathing normally. Perform the single-leg stretch on the opposite side by sliding your right foot up until its heel presses into your groin and its sole lies flat against the inner side of your left thigh. Inhale as you raise your arms above your head, exhale as you bend forward to grasp your left foot, or as far down your left leg as you can comfortably reach. Hold the stretch for about two minutes with your shoulders square and your arms equally extended, taking normal breaths. Be sure not to hunch your shoulders.

Release the pose and sit up slowly while inhaling, then while exhaling let your arms drift downward until your palms rest on the rug on either side of your hips.

FIGURE 11-3.
Open Leg Stretch.

Repeat the stretch for the left leg a second time. Sit for a few moments before straightening your right leg. Extend your right leg, using your hands to help move it, and with both legs extended, sit for a minute.

Open Leg Stretch

The third posture in this connected series is a stretch with the legs spread apart. Still seated on the rug as before, open your legs as wide as possible without placing excessive strain on the muscles on either side of your groin. Keep the soles of your feet flat as though each were pressed against the bases of invisible walls, and your toes pointed upward and slightly back. There is a tendency to twist the feet or splay them outward, which should be avoided. Sitting with your back erect and your gaze directed forward, inhale as you slowly raise your arms above your head. Exhale and lean forward from your hips, extending your hands as far forward on the floor as possible without excessive strain. You should strive for an even, mild tension. Lay your palms flat on the floor and hold this pose for about two minutes, breathing normally.

Your hands should be equally extended, and separated by about six inches. Be conscious of your shoulders to avoid hunching them. Remember to extend through your spine and the top of your head rather than trying to stretch forward with your arms. There must be space between your upper arms and the sides of your head—if your upper arms press tightly against the sides of your head, you are trying too hard to

FIGURE 11-4.
Backward Bend.

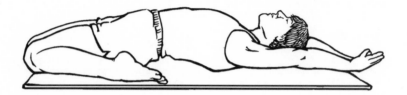

reach forward with your arms. How far you reach does not matter in the slightest. It is important only to hold the posture with good body form for two minutes or so while maintaining a uniform tension. As your body relaxes, you will find it possible to slide your hands forward slightly to maintain this tension, but avoid excessive stretching. Never bob forward in an effort to reach farther.

Inhale as you slide your hands back and sit up smoothly, raising your arms straight above your head as you do so. Exhale as you allow your arms to descend on either side until your palms are pressed flat against the rug beside your hips. Sit for a few moments. Side your legs together, using your hands to help you. Sit for a minute of so with your legs together, breathing in a normal manner. Separate your legs as before and repeat the posture. This concludes the first triple series of poses.

Backward Bend

To begin the second triple series, sit with your feet flat beneath your buttocks and your knees together, the palms of your hands resting lightly on the tops of your thighs. This is sometimes described as the Japanese sitting posture. Try to separate your heels so that they lie slightly toward the outside of your buttocks. One of your big toes will likely be folded over the other big toe, which is fine. As you exhale, lean backward and use your hands and elbows for support to aid in lowering your torso until your shoulders lie flat against the rug behind you. Try to keep your knees pressed against the floor and as close together as possible as you lean back.

Extend your arms down the sides of your torso, with your hands flat on the floor beside your feet. Stretch your spine and neck away from your knees by extending through the top of your head. After holding this posture for a minute or so, draw in a breath as you raise your arms straight up into the air, then exhale as you stretch them behind your head until they lie flat on the rug. Strive to trace smooth arcs through the air with your two hands as you rotate your arms upward and backward at the shoulders. Maintain this pose for another minute, breathing normally. Avoid hunching your shoulders.

This is a somewhat difficult posture for beginners, but it can be acquired with practice. Do not be disturbed if at first you cannot lay your shoulders against the floor behind you. It is best when beginning this pose merely to lean backward and support yourself on your elbows, or even on your extended arms. Your knees will very likely spread apart and lift slightly from the rug. Resist this tendency gently as you hold the pose. In the beginning it is not necessary for you to extend your arms behind your head.

This posture is a simplification of the full yoga pose (shown in Figure 11-4), in which the feet are placed outside the buttocks while in the sitting position, so that when reclining backward it is possible to contact the floor with the full length of the back from the shoulders to the buttocks. Having your feet beneath your buttocks will cause your lower back to arch above the floor. This is much easier on the knees, and an excellent stretch for your lower back.

After holding the pose with your arms extended above your head for a minute, inhale as you raise them straight into the air by rotating them upward at your shoulders. Exhale as you lower them to your sides so that your hands rest on the rug beside your feet. Carefully sit up by raising your torso. It will be necessary for you to help yourself into a sitting position by using your elbows and hands. Be careful while doing this to avoid strain on your back and knees. When you are once more sitting erect, place your palms on the tops of your thighs and breathe normally with your gaze directed forward. Repeat the posture by following the same series of steps to enter and exit it.

Arm Stretch

Sit with your knees together, your hands on your thighs, and your feet folded under your buttocks. Begin the second posture in this series by moving your hands so that

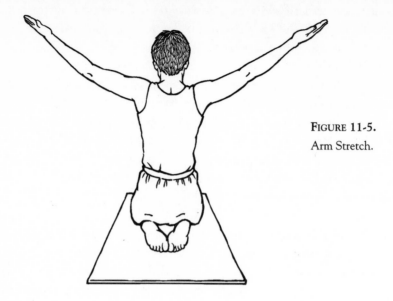

FIGURE 11-5.
Arm Stretch.

your palms rest on the rug on either side of your feet. Exhale, then as you inhale, slowly straighten your arms and raise them at your sides by rotating them from your shoulders. Hold your fingers stiffly extended and your palms turned downward, and lift your arms until they are held outward on either side of your body with your flattened hands about a foot higher than the level of your shoulders, and slightly in front of the plane of your body. You can achieve the proper posture by first lifting your extended arms straight out from your sides, then raising your hands a foot or so, and at the same time bringing your hands a foot or so in front of the plane of your chest.

Hold this posture for a minute or so, breathing normally, then rotate your hands so that your palms open upward. Hold this modified posture for another minute. If you have achieved the correct angle for your arms, you will be surprised at how much energy is required to prevent them from drooping downward under their own weight. Keep your spine erect by extending it upward with the top of your skull. Visualize your arms as wings. Draw a breath, and as you exhale, lower your arms to your sides until your palms rest on the rug beside your feet. Bring your hands back to the front so that your palms rest on the tops of your thighs just behind your knees. Repeat this posture by following the same series of steps to enter and exit it.

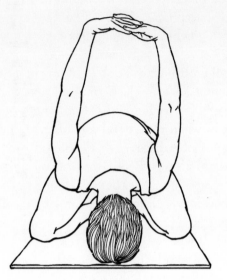

FIGURE 11-6.

Forward Bend, with
Chest Expansion.

Forward Bend, with Chest Expansion

Still sitting in the Japanese seat, inhale and lift your arms straight forward in front of you with your fingers extended. Exhale and slowly separate your hands, bringing your arms behind your back by rotating them out to the sides at the level of your shoulders, so that your hands trace smooth arcs through the air. Lower your hands until they are at the level of the small of your back, with your elbows slightly bent, and lace your fingers together. Straighten your elbows. As you continue to hold your arms straight behind your back with elbows locked and hands joined, inhale. Exhale, and at the same time bend forward until that your forehead rests on the floor in front of your knees and your joined arms point up into the air above your back. Hold this pose for a minute or so, breathing normally.

Those who are very stiff should do the forward bend without extending their arms and clasping their hands behind their back. Their forehead should be brought as near to the floor as is comfortable while maintaining light tension in the back—never bob the head in an effort to lower it. The most important aspect of this posture is to stretch the spine and neck by extending forward through the top of the head. Bend at the hips and try to keep your upper back straight for as long as possible. This attempt preserves the correct posture. As your head approaches the floor, allow your back to curve. In this easier version of the posture, instead of pointing your clasped hands straight up into the air as you lean forward, lay your arms on the floor alongside your legs with your hands pointing behind you and relax completely. Take care to relax your abdomen and thighs.

In the beginning you will probably not be able to straighten your arms while your hands are clasped behind your lower back. If you find that your hands come apart when you straighten your elbows, try holding a short length of cloth or a belt with your hands a few inches apart when you extend your arms behind your back and lock your elbows. You will also probably discover that you must part your knees to touch your forehead against the rug. This is particularly true if you are overweight. If so, separate your knees a foot or more if necessary before leaning forward to rest your head on the rug. As your body becomes accustomed to this pose, maintain tension by raising your clasped hands higher and bringing them forward, as though they were being drawn upward by an invisible rope.

As in all yoga postures, there must be no intense strain. If you begin to tremble and gasp for breath, you are performing the pose incorrectly. Do not keep your elbows locked if you find this painful. Bend them slightly. To exit the position, draw a breath, and as you exhale, sit upright. Draw another breath, and as you exhale, unlock your elbows, unclasp your hands, and bring your arms smoothly around until they extend in front of you. Draw another breath, and as you exhale lower your arms so that your palms rest on the tops of your thighs. Sit for a minute, breathing normally. Then repeat the pose. This completes the second triple series of yoga postures.

The Cobra

Lie on your stomach on the rug with one cheek resting against the floor, your arms at your sides, and your feet together with your toes pointed away from you—the insteps of your feet should lie flat against the floor. Relax completely for a minute or so. Lift your head slightly and place your forehead against the rug. Inhale slowly. As you exhale lift your head and shoulders up using the muscles in your back and buttocks. Look forward. Press the insteps of your feet against the floor as you raise your upper torso. When you have lifted your head as high as you can using only your back muscles, slide your hands smoothly forward and press your palms to the floor just in front of your shoulders. With your arms, lift your upper body so that only your pelvis and legs remain in contact with the rug. Stretch your spine and neck by attempting to press upward with the top of your skull. Hold this posture for a minute or so, breathing normally.

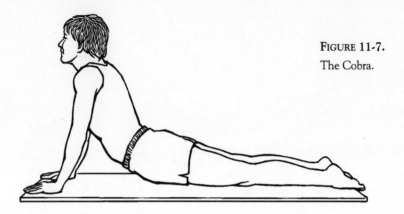

FIGURE 11-7.
The Cobra.

The usual errors with this posture are to hunch the shoulders, and also to tilt the head backward so sharply that the neck is compressed. It is important to maintain openness between the shoulders and the neck, and also between the back of the head and the back of the neck. In the beginning you will not be able to straighten your arms completely. You must experiment to find a placement for your hands that produces a comfortable stretch of your spine. This posture is somewhat strenuous, so a minute is long enough to hold it until you have become well accustomed to it. Then you can extend the time to two minutes, if you wish. Strive to support most of the weight of your upper torso with the muscles of your back and buttocks. You will find that these muscles tire quickly, since they are little used, and that you need to rely upon the strength in your arms after twenty seconds or so. This is fine.

Take a breath, and as you exhale, slowly bend your arms to lower your head and shoulders partway down. Continue to look forward. When your head is low enough, support your upper torso on your back muscles and slide your hands to your sides. Lower your head the remainder of the distance to the floor and rest your forehead against the rug. Turn your head to the side and relax your body, breathing normally. Rest for half a minute or so, then do the pose a second time by following the same steps.

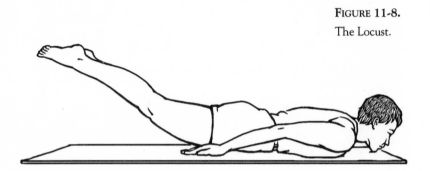

FIGURE 11-8.
The Locust.

The Locust

The second pose in this third triple series of exercises is also designed to strengthen the muscles of the back. Lying on your stomach as before, lift your head and rest your chin on the rug. Look forward. Press the palms of your hands flat on the floor on either side of your thighs. Extend your legs and feet through your pointed toes, and rest your insteps flat on the rug. Take a breath, and as you exhale, raise your extended legs upward without bending your knees. Use the muscles of your lower back, buttocks and the backs of your thighs to do this. When you have lifted your legs as far as you are able with these muscles, press down against the floor with the palms of your hands and use your arms to help raise your legs a little higher. Hold this pose for around half a minute, breathing normally. Do not attempt to raise your legs excessively high, or you will not be able to sustain the pose.

Errors made in this pose include lifting your chin from the floor, parting your legs, bending your knees, and bending your ankles. Keep your legs as stiff and straight as possible throughout the exercise, and make sure your chin never loses contact with the rug. This pose is even more strenuous than the last, so if you try to raise your legs higher than you can sustain them, you will only be able to hold it for a few seconds. It is far better to lift your legs less, and hold them elevated for a longer period. Do not attempt to maintain the pose if you find yourself trembling violently or gasping for breath. Remember to breathe normally.

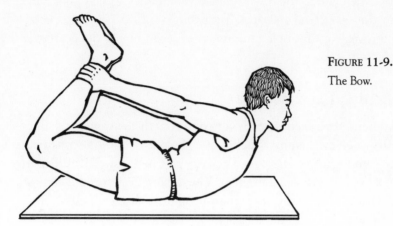

FIGURE 11-9.
The Bow.

Inhale, and as you exhale, gently lower your legs until your insteps lie flat against the floor. Relax your body and turn your head to rest your cheek against the rug. Rest for half a minute or so. Repeat the exercise by following the steps already described.

The Bow

The last of this series of poses is known as the bow. Lying on your stomach, lift your head and rest your chin against the rug, gazing forward. Bend your knees and grasp your ankles with your hands. Exhale, and as you inhale, push gently back with your legs, pulling your shoulders and head up off the rug with your arms. The tension in your body will also lift your thighs off the floor, so that your body rests only upon your lower abdomen. Stretch upward through the top of your skull. Your body should resemble a taunt bow, with your straight arms forming its string. Hold this pose for about half a minute or so, breathing normally. You may find that your breaths cause your body to rock gently back and forth on your belly. This is normal.

The most common error with this pose is to allow your knees to splay wide apart. It is almost unavoidable for beginners, but you should strive to keep your knees as close together as possible. Another error is to lock your neck by extending your head too far backward, rather than trying to stretch the top of your head upward. Always keep space between the back of your head and the back of your neck. This pose is strenuous, so if you attempt to bend your body too strongly, you will be unable to maintain it for more than a few seconds. It is better to bend less strongly, and sustain it for half a minute, if possible.

Take a breath, and as you release it, slowly relax your legs, allowing your thighs and upper torso to descend to the floor. Release your ankles and lay your hands on either side of your thighs. Extend your legs. Turn your head so that your cheek rests against the rug and relax. Rest for half a minute or so, then repeat the posture by following the same series of steps.

Strengthening Exercises

There are dozens of yoga postures designed to stretch the spine, and all of them provide benefits when awakening the chakras. The nine I have described here are especially helpful to beginners in yoga. They are best performed in three series of three related poses, as I have presented them. These exercises form the central part of my own yoga routine, which I did every morning during the year I established communication with my spirit lover and Guardian. Usually I did around sixteen postures each morning session. You can add other poses, and will derive benefit from these additions, but bear in mind that the more poses you add to your yoga routine, the longer it will take to complete. Additional poses can be readily learned by studying one of the many available books on hatha yoga. I recommend a popular book on yoga rather than a serious, comprehensive text, because the photographs in popular books are less intimidating. No one but a yoga master can be expected to assume the poses as shown in some of the more advanced texts.

After doing my yoga postures, I perform a brief set of strengthening exercises designed to tone my muscles and elevate my heart rate. This more strenuous part of my routine consists of push-ups, leg-ups, sit-ups, deep knee-bends, and curls and presses with light weights to strengthen my arms and upper body. How many repetitions of these exercises you do will depend entirely on your general level of fitness. During my intense year of practice, I generally did fifty deep knee-bends, forty push-ups, thirty sit-ups, and thirty leg-ups. For my weight training I used two dumbbell bars each loaded with nine kilos (about twenty pounds). Many people will wish to use less weight on the dumbbells, and fewer repetitions of the sit-ups, leg-ups, push-ups, and deep knee-bends, especially in the early weeks of practice.

In all forms of exercise, moderation is a virtue. When you try to do too much too soon, you risk straining or tearing muscles. A more subtle and insidious threat posed by excessive exercise is the development of an aversion to effort. A grueling exercise routine will make you less willingly to begin it each morning and more eager to find an excuse to avoid it. A light exercise routine is easier to live with over a term of months. The benefits of exercise in ritual magic begin to make themselves apparent after four to six weeks. If you stick with your training, you will find that you are more energetic and alert during rituals, and can concentrate for longer periods. Exercise also aids in the awakening of Kundalini.

{12}

Breathing and Contemplation

Controlled Breathing

It is customary to do breathing exercises when the body is perfectly rested, so that the breathing remains even and unstrained. I deliberately went against this conventional wisdom by performing my controlled breathing during my morning routine, shortly after completing my strengthening exercises. The placement of controlled breathing after my yoga and strengthening work, rather than at the beginning of the session when my body was completely rested, was prompted by intuition. I had an inner sense that I would derive accelerated benefit from my controlled breathing if I did it when slightly out of breath. Months of daily work confirmed this belief.

When breathing is controlled, and the breath is retained or stopped, a strain is placed on the entire physical system, which quickly begins to yearn for oxygen. More than any other single factor, the sustained use of this yearning for oxygen aids in the awakening of the muladhara chakra. I did not know this when I began my breathing exercises, but it became apparent to me in the course of my personal training. Although yoga and strengthening exercises may be optional in preparing for erotic union with a spirit, I regard daily training in controlled breathing as a necessity.

In my personal work I use two postures for controlled breathing. Both have proved to be effective. Most of my early breathing exercises were done while seated Japanese style on a rug. This is the position described earlier, with the feet beneath the buttocks and the knees together, the hands resting on the tops of the thighs, the back straight and the head erect. In yoga a very similar pose is known as *vajrasana,* or the thunderbolt posture. At a later stage in my training I instinctively shifted to a yoga pose known as *siddhasana,* or the accomplished posture. It resembles the common cross-legged position, but with the heel of the left foot pressed firmly against the perineum (beneath the scrotum for men), and the right foot resting on top of the left ankle. This results in a very wide separation of the knees. The back is kept straight, and the hands rest upon the knees. It is not a particularly difficult posture if your legs are flexible, but it is necessary to provide some sort of cushioning material beneath the right foot to prevent discomfort when the pose is held for more than ten minutes or so.

If your legs are not flexible enough for either of these positions, you can do breathing exercises while seated on a cushion with your legs crossed, or seated on an ordinary kitchen chair with your feet and knees together and your hands on your thighs. You should lean slightly forward on the chair so that your back does not touch the back of the chair, and has a slight hollow above the base of your spine. Keep your head erect, your gaze directed forward, and the soles of your feet flat on the floor.

A string of beads is employed to keep count of the number of repetitions. This is an ancient practice used for centuries by Catholic and Buddhist monks and nuns. By relying on beads to keep count, the mind is freed to concentrate on the actual practice. Before you begin your breathing exercise, count out the number of repetitions you intend to perform on your string of beads, and hold the beads in your hand at that place. Ten or fifteen is a good number to start with. Eventually you can progress to between twenty and thirty repetitions. As you begin each breath, slide a bead between your thumb and forefinger. When you reach the end of the string of beads, your daily breathing exercise is completed. In place of beads I use a length of thin brass chain. Chain works the same way as beads. Before starting the exercise, I usually count out twenty or twenty-five links and grip the chain at that point. At each breath, I slide one link through my fingers, and when I come to the end of the chain, I know that I am finished with the exercise.

The simplest form of controlled breathing with retention employs four equal durations. Slip a bead between your thumb and forefinger to indicate the start of a breath cycle. Inhale slowly and evenly, filling first the lower portion of your chest just above your diaphragm, then the middle portion in the region of your heart, then the upper portion just under your neck and shoulders. Do not over-inhale—leave a small amount of room in your lungs. Close the back of your throat and hold your breath for the same length of time it took you to fill your lungs with air. Gently release the lock at the back of your throat and exhale smoothly for the same period, emptying first your upper chest just under your shoulders, then your middle chest in the region of your heart, and lastly your lower chest at the level of your diaphragm. Do not completely empty your lungs, but leave a small amount of air inside them. Lock your throat again, and maintain a vacuum in your lungs for the same duration. This completes one cycle of controlled breathing. Allow a bead to slip between your thumb and forefinger, and begin another cycle of breath.

A good trick for filling your lungs completely is to visualize your entire torso as hollow. As you inhale, imagine first the lower third of your trunk filling with air, then the middle third, then the upper third. It is easier if you also visualize the air as a thin fog that glows with golden light. Imagine this golden fog swirling down your throat as you inhale and filling each third of your torso in sequence from the bottom to the top. Imagine your entire chest and abdomen glowing with golden light as you retain your breath, and furthermore, that this golden energy is spreading through your arms and legs and flowing on your blood into your brain. As you exhale, visualize this light flowing up your throat and out of your body, but notice that is it not as bright as when you inhaled, because much of the energy has been absorbed into your body. See the pallid radiance spread out from your face and dissipate into the air. As you hold your lungs empty, visualize this golden energy still circulating throughout your body on your blood, passing through your heart, filling your brain.

It is not vital that each of the four stages in your breath cycle be exactly the same duration, provided you establish a regular rhythm for your practice. You must not find yourself hurrying through a stage, or breathing more quickly at the end of the practice session than at the beginning. If you struggle to retain your breath, or must shorten the duration of the stage when your lungs are held empty, it is a sign that you are exceeding your abilities. Shorten the period of each cycle until you can perform your controlled breathing exercise with the same rhythm from start to finish. You may also find it useful to reduce the number of repetitions. It is a common mistake to set too high a number of repetitions at the start of the exercise, and to find yourself struggling before you have finished them all. Instead of twenty breaths, try fifteen, or twelve.

This breathing exercise should not be easy. There must be a noticeable strain when you hold your lungs filled with air, and a slightly stronger strain when you hold your lungs empty. It is a sign that the strain is too great if you find yourself gasping, or rushing your inhalations, or if your inhalations and exhalations become uneven. You will know when you have achieved exactly the correct amount of tension, because your body will become covered with a fine sheen of cool sweat. You should experience this sweat each time you practice. It first shows itself after half a dozen repetitions or so, and continues to the end of the practice session. Your goal should be to create a yearning in your body for oxygen, but not so intense a yearning that you have great difficulty maintaining the regular pace of your breaths.

A variation on the visualization that accompanies this basic breathing exercise is known as pore breathing. Inhale slowly, and imagine that the fine golden particles of glowing fog in the air all around your body enter through the surface of your skin rather than through your nose. As you lock the back of your throat and retain your breath, continue to visualize the golden air penetrating the surface of your skin and filling your entire body. Exhale slowly, and see the duller, silver-gray air issue forth from your nose and dissipate upon the air around your head. Lock your throat and hold your lungs empty while visualizing the golden energy circulate throughout your entire body. You will find that after you begin to sweat, it is very easy to imagine the golden particles of air penetrating the surface of your skin—you can actually feel them pass into your flesh.

Silent Mantra

After you have performed the breathing exercise for several weeks and established your natural rhythm and the number of cycles you can do at each session, you should begin to add an internal mantra accompanied by visualization. It is best not to attempt a mantra when first learning how to control your breath, because it is likely to distract your attention from the mechanics of breathing. First establish your rhythm through several weeks of practice, then add a mantra. A mantra is a word or phrase that possesses occult virtue for the person who expresses it. In yoga, the mantra is given by the teacher to the student. However, it is possible to choose your own mantra, or to use a public mantra of proven power. The most famous public mantra is the syllable *om* or *aum*. Mantras are either vocalized or expressed internally. When a mantra is vocalized it can only be voiced on the exhalation of the breath, but when it is inwardly uttered, it can occur at any of the four stages of the breath cycle.

The mantra that I use is the Greek word *Omega*. It is a meaningful mantra for several reasons. Omega is the final letter of the Greek alphabet. For this reason the mantra symbolizes fulfillment and totality. The shape of the Greek letter is a circle with a hole at its base. It evokes the image of a womb giving birth. The word has three syllables, each of which can be extended on the breath. The first part of the word is the famous eastern mantra *om*.

I find it best to inwardly express the mantra on both the inhalation and the exhalation of the breath cycle. It is mentally voiced in three extended syllables of equal duration. The letter *m* is shared between the first and second syllable when using the word as a mantra. It is not pronounced "Oh-mee-gah" but rather "Om-mee-gah," with the termination of each syllable drawn out in the mind. You should practice saying the mantra aloud so that you have a clear understanding of how it sounds. It should be something like "Oooommmmmm-mmmeeeeeeee-gaaaaaaahhh."

The first syllable of the mantra is mentally vibrated as you fill the lower third of your torso with golden mist. The second syllable is expressed while you fill the middle part of your torso with this energized air. The third syllable is expressed while you fill the upper portion of your torso. Imagine as you draw breath in through your throat that your voice box is vibrating the word inwardly so that it resonates in your heart-center. While you exhale silently, imagine that you are outwardly sounding the first syllable when you empty the top third of your torso, the second syllable when you empty the middle third, and the third syllable when you empty the bottom third. Use of this mantra during controlled breathing greatly aids in keeping your inhalations and exhalations even and of equal duration. Sound the mantra in your mind as though hearing yourself vibrate it on your breath in your own voice. Try to keep all three syllables balanced and of equal length.

Visualization

On the retentions of the breath, when the throat is locked and the lungs are held either full or empty of air, visualization is used. You can employ any visualization that seems meaningful and charged with energy. The visualization I use in my own work is that of a great Tibetan bell as tall as a man that is mounted under a small roof on a high place in the mountains beside a temple. The bell is black, and covered on its outer surface with Tibetan writing. It is sounded by a shaven-headed Tibetan monk in a yellow robe, who draws back a log hung on two ropes and allows it to swing into the side of the bell. The tone of this bell is so low, it is almost subsonic. It can be felt throughout the entire body. The sound of the bell is very similar to the mantra *om*, but more the second half of the mantra drawn out upon the air.

Anal Contraction

There is one other step to add to the retentions when performing controlled breathing—anal contraction. This is done by consciously tightening the anus. Some authorities direct that the anal sphincter is to be repeatedly tightened and relaxed, but I have found in my own work that it is more effective to tighten the anus once at the end of each retention of the breath, both when the lungs are full and when they are empty. This results in two extended anal contractions for each complete cycle of the breath. It is best to perform the anal contraction at the very end of the retention when the body is yearning for oxygen most strongly, and to hold it for between three and five seconds. As you contract your anus, focus your attention very strongly on the dying tone of the Tibetan bell that you are simultaneously imagining in your mind, and hold your anal sphincter tight until the tone of the bell has diminished almost to silence. Then relax your anus and unlock your throat in preparation for the next inhalation or exhalation.

The Fourfold Cycle of Breath

This may sound complicated at first, but it is really quite simple. As you inhale, visualize the golden energized air streaming into the lower third of your torso either through your throat or through the pores of your skin. At the same time mentally voice the syllable "ooommmmmmm." Shift your attention to the middle part of your torso and mentally voice the syllable "mmmeeeeeee" while you visualize golden energy stream into the center of your chest. Shift your attention to the upper part of your torso and mentally voice the syllable "gaaaaaahhhh" as you visualize the top of your chest filling with golden light.

Close the back of your throat to lock in the glowing golden air. In your mind picture a Tibetan Buddhist temple with a great black bell under a little roof. Continue to hold the air in as you visualize a monk in a yellow robe use a short length of rope to pull back the horizontally suspended log that serves as the striker of the bell. Continue to hold the air in as you imagine the log swinging forward and striking the bell, and the deep, almost subsonic tone of the bell sounding forth across the mountainous landscape. As the tone of the bell begins to die, contract your anus and hold it tight for between three and five seconds.

Unlock your throat and allow the upper portion of your torso to empty of silver-gray air. Most of the golden vitality in the air has been absorbed into your body. As you watch this dully glowing air leave your nose and dissipate around your head, inwardly sound the syllable "ooommmmmm." Continue to exhale the air from the middle portion of your torso. As you watch it leave your throat, sound in your mind the syllable "mmmeeeeeee". Continue to exhale the air from the lower part of your torso, and as you watch it leaving your throat, inwardly sound the syllable "gaaaaaahhhh."

Lock the back of your throat shut. As you hold your lungs empty, visualize the great black bell at the Tibetan temple. Watch in your imagination as the shaven-headed monk pulls back the log on its rope tether. Watch him swing the log forward on its rope supports. See it strike the bell, and inwardly hear the incredibly deep, sustained tone of the bell spreading outward on the air and surrounding you so that your entire body vibrates in sympathy to its voice. As the tone of the bell begins to die, tighten the muscles of your anal sphincter and hold it tight as you listen to the sound fade on the air.

This completes one fourfold cycle of controlled breathing with retention on both the inhalation and exhalation. The tightening of the anal sphincter is specifically designed to awaken the muladhara chakra. Until this lowest chakra is opened, none of the higher chakras can be pierced by the ascent of the serpent-goddess Kundalini. Anal contractions should be done gently to avoid becoming fatigued. The muscles of the buttocks can aid in contracting the anus. The greatest benefit is realized when the anus is contracted while the body is yearning most strongly for oxygen, at the end of the retentions. The body will naturally find the stoppage of breath after emptying the lungs more strenuous, since the air in the filled lungs acts as a reservoir of oxygen. For this reason the most fruitful anal contractions are done when the lungs are emptied.

A few words of caution are required. As is true of any exercise, you can injure yourself if you try to do too much too quickly. Never fill your lungs to absolute fullness, but leave a small amount of space when you retain your breath after inhaling. Never try to completely empty your lungs at each exhalation. This will prevent the most common problems beginners have with controlled breathing. If you find yourself coughing persistently after the breathing exercise, omit it for a few days to give yourself time to recover. Pay attention to your heart rate. Your heart should beat more strongly and slightly faster during controlled breathing with retentions, but should not race wildly. If you feel yourself becoming dizzy or blacking out, it is a sure sign that you are over-exerting yourself. Shorten the periods of the fourfold breath cycle, and reduce your number of repetitions. You must strive for the perfect balance where your body is mildly stressed and produces a cooling sweat over its entire surface, but is not so strained that you end up gasping, coughing, or trembling.

Contemplation

After completing your controlled breathing routine, continue to sit in the same posture and breath in a deep, normal rhythm. Allow the perspiration to dry upon your body and your heartbeat to slow. When you are rested, visualize in your mind that you are seated in an astral place that you have previously selected as a good spot for quiet contemplation. This can be a physical place where you have actually been, or a physical place you have read about or seen on television or in photographs, or even a purely astral place that has no counterpart in the material world. The place I frequently use for my own contemplation is a clear lake high in the Himalayan mountains. The lake sits in a natural bowl in the mountains at so high an elevation, there is not a trace of vegetation. The rocky ground is strewn everywhere with large and small boulders. It might almost be a moonscape, except for the chill, cloudless blue sky and the mirror surface of the water. So far as I know, this lake does not exist. It presented itself in my mind during my ritual work, a good sign that it is a place of magic power for me personally.

Contemplation is not the same as Eastern meditation. In meditation, the goal is to empty the mind of all thoughts. Usually this is accomplished by concentrating on one thought, such as a mantra, repeatedly until it becomes meaningless. In contemplation, the mind considers itself in a calm, quiet way. Thoughts are not suppressed or drowned out, but permitted to rise spontaneously. As each thought presents itself, it is considered with awareness, but neither accepted nor rejected. As much as possible, emotions should be turned off during contemplation. Merely sit in your astral place and observe the working of your mind with attention. This is not so easy as it sounds, because the mind has a natural tendency to wander. It is not accustomed to observing its own mechanism for a prolonged period, and must be taught how to do it through regular practice.

Each time you forget to examine your thoughts, or find yourself losing the inner visualization of the astral place, gently bring your mind back to its purpose. Thoughts are like little wild animals. If you pounce upon them when they begin to lift their heads, they will duck down out of sight immediately. You must simply relax, abstract your attention, and allow your thoughts to come to you. Be aware of them in a non-intrusive way. Do not attempt to capture them, but simply let yourself perceive them pass into and out of your field of awareness. As is true with hatha yoga postures, there is no success or failure. It makes no difference what your thoughts are. We are concerned with the process of inner contemplation of those thoughts. The ability to divide your central observing awareness from your thoughts and emotions is an essential aspect of ritual magic. During rituals, you will need to adopt this same passive, detached awareness of your ritual actions, and be able to observe the effects that ritual has upon your thought, feelings, and intuitions.

Find Your Own Harmony

In general, your controlled breathing should take from ten to fifteen minutes, and contemplation around fifteen minutes. It is useful to extend these times, if you are able to devote more than an hour to your morning conditioning routine. None of the morning exercises are absolutely essential except the controlled breathing.

The Omega mantra is very powerful, but you will also have good success if you allow yourself to find your own personal mantra to use during the controlled breathing. While you are sitting in contemplation in the astral locality you have selected, send a request into your deep mind asking to receive your own mantra. Then relax and observe the rise and fall of your thoughts. The response may come immediately, or not for days. Be ready to recognize it when it finally surfaces into your consciousness. If you receive no response to a mantra request, do not be concerned, but continue to use the Omega mantra.

Experiment with different visualizations until you find the astral place that feels most comfortable for contemplation. If you have a photograph of the place, it may be helpful to attach it to the wall in front of you as you sit in contemplation, so that its details are clear in your mind and can be readily refreshed. It is also useful to use the period of contemplation to seek to understand important esoteric symbols, such as the Tarot trumps. By placing a Tarot card of the Major Arcana (the picture cards) in front of you during meditation, and deliberately focusing your awareness, you can observe your instinctive, unconscious reaction to the symbols on the trump. The same can be done with the pentagram, the hexagram, the tattwa symbols, the geomantic figures, the symbols of the elements, the planets, and the signs of the zodiac. The tattwa symbols are five Eastern symbols used in the Golden Dawn to represent the five elements: Spirit (Akasa—a black egg), Fire (Tejas—a red triangle), Water (Apas—a silver crescent with its horns upward), Air (Vayu—a blue disk), Earth (Prithivi—a yellow square).[1] The *Magical Tattwa Cards* by Dr. Jonn Mumford (Llewellyn Publications) are excellent for contemplation.

If you persist in your morning practice routine daily for a month or so, while also regulating your diet and recording your dreams, you will notice a quickening in your awareness of the magical aspects of the world around you. Synchronicities will begin to occur, and these will be helpful in forwarding your quest for knowledge and personal development. It is very much like ringing a bell in the astral world and announcing to the spiritual intelligences that reside there that you are willing to learn. Once you begin the morning practice, you should never omit a day unless absolutely necessary. Even when you are ill, it is best if you try to perform a reduced morning routine rather than eliminating it entirely. Do as much as your health allows, even if it is only a few easy yoga postures and contemplation.

{ 13 }

Cleansing and Consecration

Cleansing Prayer and Kabbalistic Cross

I have presented this cleansing prayer elsewhere in my books, but it is an essential part of my own practice, and since it is relatively brief I will describe it again for the benefit of readers who may be unaware of it. A cleansing prayer is used to purify the body and mind just prior to ritual work. It is akin to wiping off a dirty blackboard with a damp rag prior to writing something new on it. Unless you wipe off the blackboard, the faded and half-erased marks from pervious writing will obscure the new words and make them difficult to read. Similarly, unless you cleanse yourself before a ritual, the impressions you have picked up and retained throughout the day will still echo within you during the performance of the ritual, and will reduce its clarity. The more distinctly a ritual resonates in the subconscious mind, the more potent its effects. Cleansing eliminates psychic noise.

The cleansing prayer should be uttered just before beginning the main ritual of invocation at each evening session. It can also be done before performing the Lesser Banishing Ritual of the Pentagram or the Middle Pillar Exercise, described a little further on. Before doing the cleansing prayer, wash your body as a symbolic form of cleansing. It is enough to wash only your hands and face, but a shower is better. You should also brush your teeth and clean your breath prior to doing rituals. After all, you are presenting yourself to the spirit as a potential lover. You would never think of going on a date with a mortal lover without first washing yourself and making sure your breath is fresh. Neither should you approach your spirit lover uncleansed. It is a sign of a disrespectful and negligent attitude. Washing your body and brushing your teeth prior to invoking your spirit lover is a form of devotion to the spirit.

At the beginning of each evening session, when you have washed and put on whatever loose, comfortable clothing you use for the invocations, stand facing the opened shrine of the spirit. The two candles should be burning on either side of the image, illuminating it evenly. Spread your arms in front of you and raise your hands above the level of your head, with your palms upward and your fingers separated. Incline your head slightly backward and elevate your gaze. You may close your eyes if it aids in visualization. This is a posture of reception. It indicates that you have opened yourself to receive the light of Kether. Speak the following prayer softly under your breath—it is more effective to speak it rather than merely thinking it, but it need not be said in a normal tone of voice. It is enough merely to articulate it on your breath in little more than a whisper. If there are others sleeping in the house, this sub-vocalization will not be heard.

> **"Have mercy upon me, O God,**
> **Blot out my transgressions.**
> **Wash me thoroughly from my iniquities**
> **And cleanse me from my sins.**
> **Asperge me with hyssop, and I shall be clean,**
> **Wash me, and I shall be whiter than snow.**
> **Create in me a clean heart, O Lord,**
> **And renew a right spirit within me."**

As you speak the cleansing prayer, visualize a shower of water droplets cascade down over your upturned hands and face. Feel this spiritual rain penetrate your skin and cleanse your astral body of all residual concerns and preoccupations. Feel it wash your heart and make it fresh and pure. All your emotions and desires wash away, leaving you inwardly calm and detached. Press your palms together in front of your chest in a gesture of prayer and gaze forward at the image of the spirit within the shrine. Speak the words of the Kabbalistic Cross, and at the same time inscribe the cross upon your body with your right index finger while holding your left palm pressed over your heart-center.

"Thou art the Crown,"
(touch right index finger to forehead)
"And the Kingdom,"
(touch right index finger to groin)
"The Power,"
(touch right index finger to left shoulder)
"And the Glory,"
(touch right index finger to right shoulder)
"And the Law,"
(touch back of left hand pressed over heart-center)
"Everlasting,"
(point directly forward with right index finger)
"Amen."
(press palms together in front of chest in prayer gesture)

The Kabbalistic Cross establishes your place in the center of your universe by projecting three rays through your body that locate your heart-center. The first ray is traced by your right index finger from your forehead to your groin. The second is traced from your left to your right shoulder. The third follows your extended right arm. These three perpendicular rays intersect in the middle of your heart-center, the Tiphareth of the microcosm. The rays actually lie parallel to the lines you trace. The vertical ray passes through the top of your head and exits at your perineum. The side to side ray passes through your chest under each shoulder at the level of your heart. The front to back ray lies parallel to your extended right arm, and passes through the exact center of your chest.

Some magicians object that this prayer is too Christian. Yet they often use the words "purge me with hyssop and I shall be clean, wash me and I shall be whiter than snow" as a brief cleansing formula. Perhaps they do not realize that these words derive from the fifty-first psalm of David in the Old Testament. By studying the text of this psalm, I was able to extract from it the full prayer of cleansing it contains. In fact, there is no Christian reference in the prayer. How could there be, when the psalm was written long before the birth of Jesus? There are two references to God, but this deity can assume any form you desire. It need not be presumed to be the Christian God, or even the Jewish God. When I speak this prayer, I have in mind a god without attributes who transcends all lesser gods with specific affiliations and discernable characteristics.

The Kabbalistic Cross was employed extensively in the magic of the Golden Dawn. I have modified it from its original form. Hebrew words were used by the Golden Dawn in the spoken formula of the Cross—I have translated the text into English. It is quite obvious that the Golden Dawn text was based on the end of the Lord's Prayer in Matthew 6:13. Therefore a Hebrew text is not especially appropriate. It was called the Kabbalistic Cross because key words in the biblical verse are the titles of Sephiroth on the Kabbalistic Tree. The word "kingdom" indicates Malkuth, "power" indicates Geburah, and "glory" indicates Chesed. These three titles trace a Tau cross on the Tree. The Golden Dawn extended this cross by assuming that the word "Thine" in the prayer of Jesus stood for Kether. This seems to me a correct assumption.

In my version of the text, I have explicitly identified the upper point of the cross as the Crown, which is the English meaning of the title Kether. I have also changed the word "forever" into Law Everlasting. The greatest departure I have made from the Kabbalistic Cross of the Golden Dawn is to place Geburah (Power) on the left shoulder and Gedulah (Glory) on the right shoulder. In the Golden Dawn version, first the right shoulder is touched and the word "Geburah" is uttered, then the left shoulder is touched and the word "Gedulah" uttered. In my version, this order is reversed. The reason for this discrepancy is that the Golden Dawn reflects the Tree of the Sephiroth onto the human body, whereas I apply it directly.

Those who wish to use the original Golden Dawn version of the Kabbalistic Cross should feel free to do so.[1] It will prove equally effective, provided that it is clearly understood. The Golden Dawn Hebrew text and its translation are as follows:

"Ateh [Thou art]"
(touch forehead)
"Malkuth [the Kingdom]"
(touch breast)
"ve-Geburah [and the Power]"
(touch right shoulder)
"ve-Gedulah [and the Glory]"
(touch left shoulder)

"Le-Olam [forever]"
(clasp hands before chest)
"Amen [it is so]"
(point upward with joined hands)

I find it mildly amusing that the text of the Kabbalistic Cross, which is completely Christian in origin, is never objected to on this ground merely because in the Golden Dawn documents it's written in Hebrew. On the other hand, the cleansing prayer from the psalm of David, the origin of which has nothing remotely Christian about it, is regarded as too Christian for use in ritual magic by a small minority of modern magicians, presumably because it mentions God and calls upon divine mercy. I could have presented the cleansing prayer in its original Hebrew text, but it is better to work rituals in a language you understand, in order to avoid confusion and dangerous mistakes. This general rule does not apply to words of power, which must always remain in their original tongues.

Cleansing and Consecration

For the same reason we cleanse ourselves prior to beginning a ritual, it is best to cleanse any substance or object that will be used prior to consecrating it to its ritual function. Cleansing of a tool or material removes any subtle influences or occult links that may have been formed in the past. Since these influences are not a part of our ritual purpose, they are undesirable because they will add psychic noise to the working and weaken its fulfillment. Purified and consecrated water is usually employed to cleanse objects and places. In my own ritual work I also use purified and consecrated salt. Everything employed in the rituals of sexual alchemy should be cleansed and consecrated. This includes the spirit vessel, the sigil scroll, the shrine, the candles and their holders, the cup and water it will contain, the dish and salt it will contain, the incense tray, the tray for offerings, and any other thing used.

Cleansing and consecrating are separate ritual actions. At times you may wish to cleanse something without dedicating it to a specific function. Cleansing can be done simply to remove bad luck from a thing or place. For example, if you receive a gift from a person who is very unfortunate, you should cleanse the gift before using it. Cleansing always comes prior to consecration. You should never consecrate a thing before it has been cleansed, unless you are positive that its astral associations are desirable in your work, and harmonious to the purpose for which the thing will be consecrated. If you receive a ritual instrument from a magician you trust who has used it successfully for years, you might be reluctant to wash away the occult potency the instrument has acquired. Be aware that when you accept the existing associations of a tool in order to take advantage of the occult virtue it has acquired through use, you also accept any disharmonious influences it may have picked up. It is safest to start with a clean slate, and to impress your own magical influence upon it.

Beginners in magic are often told to perform cleansing and consecrating rituals on different days in order to avoid weakening either operation by confusing their energies. Provided that you understand the uniqueness of each action, and devote your full attention to each while performing it, the two operations can be done in a single compound ritual. They are naturally related by their shared purpose—to devote a substance, object or place to ritual use. However, you should never cleanse and consecrate an item just before or after doing another type of ritual, such as a ritual of invocation. Rituals demand large amounts of concentration. Working unrelated rituals one after the other is certain to weaken the second ritual, and probably the first as well, since a part of your mind will be on the second ritual even while working the first.

Cleansing is best done with something that has already been cleansed and consecrated. Here we have a problem. How do we cleanse the first substance, in order to use it to cleanse other things? One solution is to obtain something that has been previously cleansed by some other ritualist. This is acceptable, provided the person who has done the cleansing follows your tradition. A Wiccan seeking to cleanse an instrument might obtain purified water for this purpose from another Wiccan, for example. It would not be appropriate for a Wiccan to use holy water blessed by a Catholic priest, since the Church has historically persecuted witches.

There are a number of ways around this difficulty. Water for cleansing can be obtained from a natural source that is already pure. Rain water works well, as does water gathered from a spring or stream, or the sea. The best time to gather water for cleansing is just before sunrise, when the sky in the east is already illuminated. Use a clear glass vessel, and hold up the gathered water so that the first rays of the rising sun pass through it. Another solution is to cleanse ritual objects and substances with flame and smoke. Fire by its very nature is purifying. A vessel containing a substance to be cleansed, or a ritual object, can be passed through the flame of a lamp or candle, and through the smoke of burning incense. One useful technique for cleansing water is to invert a candle and extinguish it in the water by immersing its flame. In this way the purifying virtue of the flame is symbolically transferred into the water.

Ritual of Purification and Consecration

In order to produce purified and consecrated water and salt, which will be used as the basis for later operations of cleansing and consecrating, work the following simple compound ritual that relies upon the elemental associations of the letters of the Tetragrammaton.

Put a while candle in a candle holder on the center of a small table. The table should either be in the middle of the open floor, or alongside the southern wall of your place of working. On the table to the west of the candle put a clear glass bottle filled with pure water. To the east, put a clear bottle filled with salt. If possible, collect this water from the rain or a natural spring or stream. It is best to use fresh water when simultaneously using salt for purifications. When only water is used to purify, sea water is excellent since it contains large amounts of salt already dissolved in it. Light the candle and dim the lights. Stand in the north facing south. Perform the prayer of cleansing and the Kabbalistic Cross, as already described.

Standing with your arms at your sides, speak your declaration of intent, which expresses as briefly and clearly as possible the reason you are conducting the ritual. It does not need to be spoken aloud, but can be murmured softly on the breath.

"By the authority and power of Tetragrammaton, the true name of the Highest, the water and salt upon this altar shall be cleansed and consecrated for ritual use."

As you gaze at the flame of the candle, visualize a white star high in the heavens directly above you. Will this star to descend. As it comes lower, expand it into a sphere of brilliant white light six inches in diameter. Imagine it floating in the air several inches above your head. You should be able to feel its radiance as a prickling sensation in the center of your scalp. Enter into the white sphere and feel its light all around your awareness. Extend a ray of white light straight downward to the middle of your chest, and expand its point into a six-inch sphere of golden yellow light. Allow your point of awareness to slide down the inside of this ray and enter the sphere in your heart-center. With the radiance of your heart-center, expand your aura in all directions into a pale golden sphere that surrounds your entire body and encloses the white sphere above your head. Extend your awareness outward to fill your aural envelope.

Press the palm of your left hand firmly over your heart-center, between and slightly below the level of your nipples. There is a hollow in your chest at the correct spot. Extend your right arm and point with your right index finger at the air about a foot above the glass bottle containing the water. Draw energy from the golden sphere of your heart-center through your chest and into the palm of your left hand. You should be able to feel a slight tingling and warmth. Send this golden radiance up your left arm, across your shoulders and out your right arm in an expanding spiral. Use the flaming gold-white fire that issues from your right index finger to inscribe on the air with white fire a large Hebrew letter Yod (י). Visualize this letter actually burning and flickering as it floats upon the air. Draw a deep breath, hold it for a few moments, then vibrate the letter Yod so that it resonates in your chest. As you vibrate the letter, project energy into it from your heart-center through the tip of your right index finger so that the letter glows with blazing intensity.

"Yoooooood."

Lower your right hand and point at the bottle of water. Draw golden radiance from your heart-center and inscribe the letter Heh (ה) over the bottle with gold-white fire. Visualize the letter actually penetrating and glowing within the bottle so that the entire bottle of water is illuminated. Draw a deep breath, hold it for several seconds, then vibrate the letter Heh while pointing at the letter of fire that floats within the bottle. As you vibrate the letter so that it resonates within your chest, project energy from your heart-center into the letter until it shines like sunlight.

"Haaaaaaaay."

Point with your right index finger at a spot in the air roughly a foot above the bottle of salt. Use the force of your will to draw radiance out from your heart-center with your left hand and send it running up your left arm, across your shoulders, and down your right arm in an expanding spiral. Paint upon the air the Hebrew letter Vav (ו) with the stream of gold-white astral fire that issues from the tip of your right index finger. Draw a deep breath, hold it for several moments, then vibrate the letter Vav so that your chest resonates. At the same time, continue pointing at the letter and project energy into it from your heart-center so that the letter blazes brightly.

"Vaaaaaaaveh."

Lower your right hand to point at the bottle of salt. Draw radiance from your heart-center in a spiral up your left arm, across your shoulders, and down your right arm so that it issues from your right index finger in a glowing astral stream. Use this stream of pale yellow fire to paint the letter Heh (ה) upon the bottle of salt so that the letter actually glows within the bottle and illuminates it. As you continue to point at the letter inside the bottle, draw a breath, hold it a moment or two, then vibrate the letter Heh so that it resonates in your chest. Project energy from your heart-center into the letter until it blazes.

"Haaaaaaaay."

Point at the flame of the candle. Draw golden light from your heart-center and project it out your right index finger to draw the Hebrew letter Shin (ש) upon the flame. Visualize this letter glowing in the air so that its base is even with the top of the candle. Draw a deep breath, retain it for a few moments, then vibrate the letter Shin so that your chest resonates. As you vibrate the letter, project energy into it from your heart-center and cause it to shine more brightly.

"Sheeeeeenh."

Lower your arms to your sides and stand gazing at the flame of the candle. Expand your astral awareness so that you can see all at once in your field of vision the letter Yod above the bottle of water, the letter Heh within it, the letter Vav above the bottle of salt, the letter Heh within it, and the letter Shin just above the top of the candle. Draw a breath, hold it for a few moments, then vibrate the holy names Eheieh-IHVH. Pronounce the letters of IHVH individually.

"Aaaaaah-heeeeee-aaaaah-Yoooood-Haaaaaay-Vaaaaaavh-Haaaaaay."

As you vibrate the first syllable of the name Eheieh, raise your arms straight above your head. As you vibrate the first syllable of the name IHVH, abruptly throw your arms forward so that your extended fingers point at the candle flame, and take a short step forward with your right foot. Strongly project golden fire from your heart center into the candle flame during the vibration of all four letters of IHVH. This light energizes the flame of the candle. If you have vibrated the names correctly, you will actually see the flame of the candle become brighter and elongate itself. The flame can become elongated to a degree that seems incredible—I have observed flames as long as six inches. Step back with your right foot to stand with your hands at your sides. Regard the flame for a minute or so, while continuing to visualize the five Hebrew letters you have projected from your heart-center.

Approach the table and take the bottle of water between both your hands. Hold it in front of your chest as you speak the following declaration.

"By the power and authority of Tetragrammaton, and by the cleansing fire of this threefold flame, I purify this water for ritual use."

Move your hands in a counterclockwise circular motion three times so that at the far side of each circle, the bottle of water passes directly over the flame of the candle. The motion is similar to what you would make if you were stirring a large cauldron with a long spoon held between both your hands. It is important that the flame actually touch the bottom of the bottle for a brief instant at each of the three passes. Move the bottle slowly to minimize the disturbance of the air. Elevate the bottle above the flame in both hands and visualize the flaming gold-white Hebrew letters Yod-Heh (הי) written from right to left inside the bottle. Draw a breath, hold it a moment, then vibrate the letters Yod-Heh.

"Yooooood-Haaaaaaay."

Set the bottle of water back on the table to the west of the candle. Take up the bottle of salt between your cupped hands. Hold it in front of your heart-center as you speak the following declaration.

"By the power and authority of Tetragrammaton, and by the cleansing smoke of this threefold flame, I purify this salt for ritual use."

Move the bottle of salt in a counterclockwise circular motion three times so that the bottom of the bottle passes through the flame of the candle on the far side of each circle. Take care to more the bottle slowly and smoothly to minimize the disturbance of the air. The flame will dance from side to side, but should not flutter wildly. Elevate the bottle above the flame in both hands and visualize the flaming gold-white Hebrew letters Vav-Heh (הו) written from right to left in the salt inside the bottle. Draw a breath, hold it a moment, then vibrate the letters Vav-Heh.

"Vaaaaavh-Haaaaaaay."

Set the bottle of salt back on the table to the east of the candle. Stand for a minute or so with your arms at your sides, regarding the flame. Approach the table and take up in both hands the bottle of water. Hold it close to the center of your chest and speak this declaration.

"By the power and authority of Eheieh, and by the consecrating light of this threefold flame, I dedicate this water wholly as an agent of ritual purification."

Move the bottle of water between your cupped hands in a circular stirring motion clockwise three times, so that the bottom of the bottle passes through the flame on the far side of each circle. Elevate the bottle high above the flame, and visualize the Hebrew letter Shin (שׁ) written in white flame inside the water. Take a deep breath, hold it a moment, and vibrate the letter Shin while concentrating on the astral form of the letter inside the bottle.

"Sheeeeeenh."

Set the bottle of water on the table to the west of the candle. Pick up the bottle of salt between both cupped hands and hold it close to the center of your chest. Speak the following declaration.

"By the power and authority of Eheieh, and by the consecrating light of this threefold flame, I dedicate this salt wholly as an agent of ritual purification."

Move the bottle of water between your cupped hands in a clockwise circular motion three times, so that the bottom of the bottle passes through the flame on the far side of each circle. Elevate the bottle high above the flame, and visualize the Hebrew letter Shin (שׁ) written in white flame inside the water. Take a deep breath, hold it a moment, and vibrate the letter Shin while concentrating on the astral form of the letter inside the bottle.

"Sheeeeeenh."

Replace the bottle of salt on the table to the east of the candle. Stand with your hands at your sides, regarding the flame for a minute or so. Make your mind inwardly tranquil. Speak the following declaration of fulfillment. If there is concern about disturbing or attracting the unwanted attention of others, the declaration may be murmured under the breath so that it is barely audible in your own ears.

> **"By the authority and power of Tetragrammaton, the true name of the Highest, the water and salt upon this altar have been well and truly cleansed and consecrated for ritual use."**

Perform the Kabbalistic Cross without the Cleansing Prayer. Extinguish the candle with your breath and place the vessels of water and salt into the shrine, or if there is not enough room for them in the shrine, in another secure place for storage. After you have purified and consecrated supplies of water and salt, these substances can be used to purify other materials, objects and spaces such as the ritual circle.

Use of Water and Salt

The use of the water and salt when preparing your ritual instruments is quite simple. Whenever you wish to purify and consecrate objects, lay them on a small table to the north of a single white candle in a holder, with the vessel of water in the west and the vessel of salt in the east. The first things to cleanse and consecrate are the shallow dish that will hold salt and the small cup that will hold water during the rituals of invocation. These vessels can be the same shape, or different shapes.

Light the candle and dim the room lights. Stand in the north facing south with the table in front of you. Perform the Cleansing Prayer and the Kabbalistic Cross. Speak the declaration of intent, which will vary depending on which substance or object you are cleansing, and whether or not you also intend to consecrate the substance or object to ritual use. In the example of the salt dish and water cup, the following words, or words with a similar intent, would be used.

> **"By the authority and power of Tetragrammaton, the true name of the Highest, the dish and cup upon this altar shall be cleansed and consecrated for ritual use."**

Take up the vessel of water in your left hand, remove its cap or stopper, and pour a very small amount of water into your right hand. Sprinkle the water over the implements from the fingertips of your right hand. As you do so, speak this declaration.

"By the Yod-Heh of Tetragrammaton,
I cleanse this cup and this dish with water."

Replace the stopper in the top of the bottle of water and set it down to the west of the candle. Pick up the bottle of salt in your right hand and remove its top. Pour a very small portion of salt into the palm of your left hand. Allow the grains of salt to sift out of your fist as you shake it gentle over the implements. As you do so, speak this declaration.

"By the Vav-Heh of Tetragrammaton,
I cleanse this cup and this dish with salt."

Replace the top on the bottle of salt and set it down on the table to the east of the candle. Ritual implements must be consecrated as well as purified. To do this, take up the salt dish and hold it above the candle flame in both hands. Hold it high enough that the smoke from the candle will not stain it, but close enough so that the warmth of the rising air is clearly felt by your hands. Keep your hands open so that the light from the flame shines directly on the dish. Speak this declaration.

"By the power and authority of Eheieh, and by the consecrating
light of this threefold flame, I dedicate this salt dish wholly to ritual
communion with the spirit [name]."

Set the disk down and pick up the cup. Hold it above the candle so that the heat from the rising air flows all around it, and the light from the flame shines upon it. Speak this declaration.

"By the power and authority of Eheieh, and by the consecrating
light of the threefold flame, I dedicate this water cup
wholly to ritual communion with the spirit [name]."

Set the cup down, step back from the table, and speak the declaration of fulfillment.

"By the authority and power of Tetragrammaton, the true name of the Highest, the dish and cup upon this altar have been well and truly cleansed and consecrated for ritual use."

Perform the Kabbalistic Cross without the Cleansing Prayer, blow out the candle, and put the material and objects away in the shrine, or in a secure storage place.

After you have consecrated the water cup and salt dish, you can lay these out on the table when cleansing and consecrating other things, such as the candles you will burn during your rituals. During cleansing and consecrating of objects, pour a small amount of water into the cup and salt into the dish. Sprinkle this water and salt upon the objects, and after the ritual of purification and consecration is concluded, discard any small amount of water or salt that may remain in the cup and dish. It is best always to sprinkle the water from the fingertips of the right hand, and the salt from the pinched thumb and fingers of your left hand, to avoid contaminating one substance with the other.

Consecration of the Shrine

When you cleanse and consecrate the shrine, you must adopt another procedure since the shrine is too large and heavy to be held above the flame of the candle. Set up your single white candle in its holder, and your vessels of consecrated water and salt, on the table in front of the opened doors of the shrine. If possible have the doors of the shrine open toward the north as you stand in front of it. Before beginning, pour a little salt into the dish, a little water into the cup, and light the white candle. Do the Cleansing Prayer and Kabbalistic Cross. Speak your declaration of intent.

"By the authority and power of Tetragrammaton, the true name of the Highest, this spirit shrine shall be cleansed and consecrated for ritual use."

Take up the water cup in your left hand and dip the fingertips of your right hand into the water. Sprinkle the water from your fingers over the inside and outside of the shrine. Do this three times. As you do so, speak this declaration.

> **"By the Yod-Heh of Tetragrammaton,
> I cleanse this spirit shrine with water."**

Replace the cup to the right of the candle. Pick up the salt dish in your right hand and take up a small portion of salt between the thumb and fingers of your left hand. Allow the grains of salt to sift from between your fingers as you shake your left hand gently three times over the shrine. As you do so, speak this declaration.

> **"By the Vav-Heh of Tetragrammaton,
> I cleanse this spirit shrine with salt."**

Replace the salt dish on the table in front of the shrine to the left of the candle.

In order to consecrate the shrine, take up the burning candle and hold it inside the shrine in both hands so that the warmth rising from the flame reaches the inner surface of the shrine's roof. Move the candle all around the inside of the shrine so that the light from its flame illuminates every corner and surface. Speak this declaration.

> **"By the power and authority of Eheieh, and by the consecrating
> light of this threefold flame, I dedicate this spirit shrine wholly to
> ritual communion with the spirit [name]."**

Set the candle back down in front of the open shrine, step back from the table, and speak the declaration of fulfillment.

> **"By the authority and power of Tetragrammaton, the true name of
> the Highest, this spirit shrine has been well and truly cleansed
> and consecrated for ritual use."**

Perform the Kabbalistic Cross without the Cleansing Prayer, blow out the candle, and put the material and objects away in the shrine, or in a secure storage place.

Discarding Consecrated Substances

These examples should be sufficient to show you how to use the general ritual of cleansing and consecrating under various circumstances that will arise. When you run out of water and salt, a fresh supply of both must be prepared with the longer version of the ritual that employs the projection and visualization of the five Hebrew letters. It is best to prepare both water and salt at the same time, even if you have a portion of one substance remaining when you run out of the other. Simply discard the remaining portion so that both your storage vessels are empty, and fill them with salt and water in preparation to the ritual of purification and consecration.

When you discard anything that has been consecrated to ritual use, you must do so with an attitude of care and reverence. Be conscious that you are returning the substance or object to the earth. It is best to pour the excess consecrated water or salt onto open ground, if possible. If you must discard these consecrated substances in the trash, inscribe a circle-cross upon the air over them with your right index finger, first the vertical pillar of the cross, then the horizontal beam, then the circle crosswise. Utter the following words.

"Return to earth—remain undefiled."

Everything you use in your ritual work must first be purified and consecrated. This only needs to be done once for each item. Exceptions are the magic circle, which is cleansed each night before beginning to invoke the spirit, and the offerings presented before the spirit, which are set upon the offering plate in their normal state, without purification. However, these offerings must always be clean and of the finest quality.

{ 14 }

Methods of
Protection

Everyday Defenses

In over a decade of using the methods described in this book, I have on only a few occasions been forced to resort to occult protection in order to separate myself from the intrusion of spirits that I had not deliberately called. Malicious spirits can usually be sensed when they are near. They produce an atmosphere of danger and hostility that is similar to the feeling in the air just before a thunderstorm. At times this is accompanied by intense, instinctive fear. The actual danger posed by these spirits is minimal, but their company is unpleasant. They can provoke unhappiness, depression, or persistent unwanted thoughts. Fortunately, it is not difficult to send them on their way through a mixture of magical and mundane procedures.

It is usually difficult to establish any form of contact with spirits. To be totally unable to perceive them in any way is a far more common problem than to be obsessed by them. The reason for this is that the conditions of daily life are inimical in themselves to the presence of spirits. When your stomach is filled with spicy food, your mind distracted by petty material concerns, your attention diverted by the conversation and company of other human beings, or by electronic forms of entertain-

239

ment such as television, recorded music, and the Internet, even the most determined spirit will have an almost impossible task when it attempts to interact with you. If you do find yourself troubled by the persistent attentions of a spirit you did not summon, or if a spirit that you deliberately called becomes hostile, one of the best defenses is simply to do something everyday, such as watching television or going to a baseball game. Have a large meal. Meet some friends. Turn your mind away from magic.

It is helpful to avoid places and situations you associate with your ritual work. Try visiting a relative for the weekend, or going on a short vacation. Above all, avoid spending long hours alone in the room of the house in which you are accustomed to commune with spiritual beings. Habit plays an enormous role in ritual magic. Once a setting is established as your meeting place with spirits, it is much easier for any spirit to attract your attention while you are in that place. The same rule applies to times. If you always invoke your spirit lover at ten o'clock in the evening, be sure to have some distracting everyday activity planned for this hour of the day, since it is the time when the intruding spirit will be easiest to sense.

Two very effective mundane defenses against malicious spirits are ridicule and indifference. If you respond to the presence of the spirit seeking to force its attentions on you by mocking it and regarding it with contempt and disdain, it will be considerably weakened. Similarly, if you pretend to yourself that the spirit does not exist, and refuse to respond to its intrusions, it will wither away. This may take days or weeks, but indifference is a powerful weapon against spirit assaults. During this period in which you deny the spirit any notice or response, you should completely turn your mind away from all aspects of magic and the supernatural. Stop doing rituals. Avoid reading books about magic, or watching spooky movies. Avoid places that are laden with magical or mystical meaning, such as graveyards, deserted houses, ancient ruins, stone circles, cellars, attics, dark woods, lakes at twilight, or any other place where the imagination is likely to become active.

Worry Stone

An effective way to reduce the anxiety that usually accompanies an unwanted spirit presence is to buy or find a worry stone. It should be around the size of a silver dollar, flat like a beach stone, and have a comfortable feel in the hand. Stone has always been one of the most receptive substances in which spirits can reside, as evidenced by the prevalence throughout the ancient world of stone statues of gods and goddesses, and stone altars. Some commercial worry stones have an image cut into their surface—the one that I use is deeply incised with the image of a rattlesnake. Instead of buying a stone, you may prefer to find your own in the natural world.

The principle behind the use of these stones is that by holding the stone in your hand and rubbing it, you can soothe your worries. This method is fine for everyday concerns, but when a persistently annoying spirit is involved, a dynamic approach is more effective.

Keep your stone with you at all times. If it is inscribed with a symbol or an animal that has meaning and power for you, so much the better. Whenever you feel an inner apprehension building inside your chest, hold the stone in your right hand. Press your left palm firmly over your heart center. Visualize your anxiety and sense of oppression as a black amorphous mist in the center of your chest. Take a deep breath and hold it for ten seconds or so. Slowly exhale all the air from your lungs. As you breath out, use the force of your will to draw your feeling of oppression into your left palm and send it coursing up your left arm, across your shoulders, and down your right arm toward the stone in an expanding spiral.

When the black mist reaches the stone, press down firmly on its surface with the ball of your right thumb and visualize the mist passing through your thumb and swirling down in a shadowy inward counterclockwise vortex that has its focus at the very heart of the stone. Imagine that the center of the stone is a kind of psychic black hole that sucks down any spiritual energy that is near it and forever prevents it from escaping. Visualize this process as dirty water swirling down a drain. When all the anxiety has been drawn out of your chest and propelled into the center of the worry stone, remove your thumb from its surface.

You will find that you need to repeat this technique frequently when your anxiety is active. A sense of undefined dread and discomfort that settles in the center of the chest or stomach often indicates the presence of an intrusive spirit that you cannot directly perceive. By banishing it into the stone, you effectively purge your unconscious mind of its influence. The process takes no more time than a single inhalation and exhalation. Firm pressure of your right thumb against the surface of the worry stone is important in transferring anxiety from your chest to the stone. There seems no limit to the capacity of a stone to absorb this type of negative spiritual energy. The worry stone not only relieves stress, but makes it much more difficult for a vexatious spirit to continue to intrude itself on your awareness.

Hardening the Aura

Control of the aura is a means of self-defense against not only human beings who have a harmful effect on your mind and emotions, but intrusive spirits as well. It was taught to members of the original Hermetic Order of the Golden Dawn.[1] One of these members was the writer of supernatural fiction, Algernon Blackwood, who described the method briefly in his 1908 short story "The Nemesis of Fire," when the psychic investigator John Silence instructs his young assistant to defend himself against the threat of a fire elemental:

> "And, for your safety," he said earnestly, "imagine *now*—and for that matter, imagine always until we leave this place—imagine with the utmost keenness, that you are surrounded by a shell that protects you. Picture yourself inside a protective envelope, and build it up with the most intense imagination you can evoke. Pour the whole force of your thought and will into it. Believe vividly all through this adventure that such a shell, constructed of your thought, will and imagination, surrounds you completely, and that nothing can pierce it to attack."[2]

Blackwood's description of hardening the aura is accurate. The key to its effective use is to mentally imagine that the edges of the aura have contracted and become more dense and difficult to penetrate, so that your aura is like a suit of invisible armor all around your body. The tighter you pull your aura in toward the surface of your skin, the more dense it becomes, and the more difficult to penetrate. Periodically, you should renew this visualization to keep your aura strong. While you are actually hardening your aura, focus all your imagination upon inwardly seeing and feeling it around you. Then put it completely out of your mind for a time with the inner quiet assurance that its protection is absolute and cannot be breached.

Dion Fortune, another member of the Golden Dawn, described a simple physical method for sealing the aura against the intrusions of spirits. It is Christian in tone, but could easily be modified by those offended by Christian symbolism. The person sealing his or her aura stands and crosses the body by touching the right hand to the forehead, solar plexus, right shoulder and left shoulder. This is the gesture for making the Kabbalistic Cross of the Golden Dawn, but Fortune does not give the verbal formula of the Kabbalistic Cross. Instead, she describes how to trace and define the limits of the aura around the body while speaking this prayer: "By the power of the Christ of God within me, whom I serve with all my heart and with all my soul and with all my strength (extend your hands forward as far as you can reach at the level of the solar plexus, fingertips touching, then sweep them round to the back and touch the fingertips together again behind you, saying), I encompass myself about with the Divine Circle of His protection, across which no mortal error dares to set its foot."[3] Fortune called this "an old monkish formula," but cautioned that its effectiveness as a protective barrier only lasts four hours.

There is nothing wrong with using the name of Christ when seeking protection against malicious or intrusive spirits. When uttered sincerely, it is an extremely potent weapon against obsession and possession. One of the things Jesus is most renowned for in the Scriptures is the casting out of demons. If the aid of Jesus is requested while a cross is made over the breast, the results can be dramatic for those who have faith in the power of his name. Even lapsed Christians sometimes discover that their faith, although dormant, has not been entirely extinguished when they need protection from obsessing spirits.

Lesser Banishing Ritual of the Pentagram

One of the first things new members of the Golden Dawn were taught was the Lesser Banishing Ritual of the Pentagram. It is called the Lesser ritual because it uses only the banishing pentagram of Earth, not the pentagrams of the other three elements, which are employed in the Greater Ritual of the Pentagram. Members were instructed in the mechanics of this ritual long before they could be expected to visualize its forces effectively, or even understand its purpose. The view of the leaders of the Order was that this banishing ritual was excellent practice in the performance of rituals generally, and could do no harm even if worked by a complete neophyte, since its purpose is wholly defensive. It is contained in the very first Knowledge Lecture that was taught to new members of the Order.[4]

The Lesser Banishing Ritual should be done any place and at any time that a psychic sense of intrusion or danger is felt. You can use the Golden Dawn version, or the version I have adapted to be in harmony with the system of magic described in my book *New Millennium Magic*. It is only important that you do not mix elements of the two systems. In the Golden Dawn system, Earth is placed in the north and Air in the east, whereas in my system, Air is in the north and Earth in the east. In the Golden Dawn system, first the right shoulder is touched during the Kabbalistic Cross, then the left shoulder, whereas in my system first the left shoulder it touched, then the right. Also, I prefer to begin rituals facing south, whereas the Golden Dawn usually begins facing east.

I will describe the Golden Dawn method first. Stand facing the east. Draw the Kabbalistic Cross upon your body with your right index finger in the manner already described, while speaking these words:

"Ateh"
(touch your forehead)
"Malkuth"
(touch the base of your breastbone)
"Ve-Geburah"
(touch your right shoulder)
"Ve-Gedulah"
(touch your left shoulder)
"Le-Olam"
(clasp your hands before you)
"Amen"
(point upward with the fingers of your joined hands)

Using your right index finger, draw in the air to the east the banishing pentagram of Earth. This should be drawn very large upon the air with exaggerated sweeping motions of the arm, according to the method of Dion Fortune.[5] Begin by pointing downward at an angle across your body, so that your right hand is near your left hip. Without bending the elbow, swing your arm upward so that your index finger traces a steeply inclined straight line and points directly overhead, then downward at an equal angle so that your right hand is beside your right hip. Swing your hand up and to the left at a more gentle incline so that it points to your left side and is level with your left shoulder, then straight across your body so that it points to the right and is level with your right shoulder, and finally down and to the left until it reaches its starting position. In this way you will have traced a great star of five points, the banishing pentagram of Earth in the system of the Golden Dawn (see Figure 14-1).

Hold the pentagram in your mind and project it a few feet away from you to the east, while continuing to visualize it clearly. Point with your right index finger to the center of the pentagram. Vibrate upon your breath the divine name IHVH, sounding each of its four letters:

"Yoood-Haaay-Vaavh-Haaay."

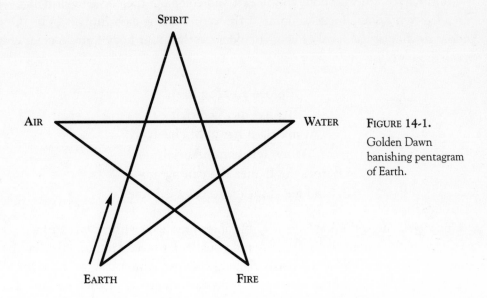

SPIRIT

AIR   WATER   FIGURE 14-1.

Golden Dawn
banishing pentagram
of Earth.

EARTH   FIRE

While holding your right index finger extended before you, trace a circle of astral fire to the south and draw the same banishing pentagram of Earth in the manner already described. Mentally project it a few feel away from your body. Stab its center with your index finger and vibrate the divine name Adonai:

"Ahhhhh-dooooo-naaaaay."

With your right index finger extended, carry the line of the circle to the west and trace the banishing pentagram of Earth upon the air. Project is away from your body and stab its center, vibrating the divine name Eheieh:

"Ayyyyyy-heeeeee-ahhhhh."

With your right index finger extended, carry the line of the circle to the north and trace the same banishing pentagram of Earth. Stab its center and vibrate the divine name AGLA, sounding each of its letters separately so that it will balance with IHVH:

"Aaaah-Geeeh-Laaah-Aaaah."

Continue to turn your body to the east and complete the circle by bringing your extended right index finger to point at the center of the eastern pentagram. Open your arms wide at the level of your shoulders so that your body forms a great cross. Speak these words:

"Before me, Raphael;
Behind me, Gabriel;
At my right hand, Michael;
At my left hand, Auriel;
Before me flames the pentagram—
Behind me shines the six-rayed star."

Once again, draw the Kabbalistic Cross upon your body with your right index finger. Stand with your arms at your sides and visualize for several minutes the four banishing pentagrams of elemental Earth, flaming with astral fire upon the air at the four quarters, and the line of the circle that links them together at their centers. Hold clearly in your mind the pentagram before you in the east, and imagine a hexagram made up of two fiery interlocking triangles floating in the air above the back of your head. Allow these images to fade into the back of your awareness and turn your mind to other matters as you go about your daily business.

The Lesser Banishing Ritual is effective for destroying obsessive thoughts and feelings that you have previously projected out of your aura, and also for throwing off clinging spirits. The act of projection is accomplished by visualizing the thought-form that is troubling you as a image, then casting the image out from your aura by means of the Golden Dawn Saluting Sign of the Neophyte grade, also known as the Sign of Horus. It is performed by taking a short step forward with your right foot as you strongly extend your arms straight forward at eye level as though throwing something away from your body with your fingertips. To prevent the obsessing spirit from reattaching itself to your aura, perform the Neophyte grade Sign of Silence, also known as the Sign of Harpocrates. This is made by standing with your feet together and touching your left index finger to your lips with your mouth closed. Once the obsessing thoughts generated by a spirit, along with the spirit itself, have been removed from your aura, the pentagrams of the Lesser Banishing Ritual can effectively destroy the spirit by dissolving its visualized form.

If you prefer to perform the Lesser Banishing Ritual of the Pentagram according to the *New Millennium Magic* system, which is in better harmony with the contents of this book, begin by facing the south. Cast the obsessing thought-forms from your aura with the Saluting Sign and bar their approach with the Sign of Silence. Perform the Kabbalistic Cross:

"Thou art the Crown,"
(touch right index finger to forehead)
"And the Kingdom,"
(touch right index finger to groin)
"The Power,"
(touch right index finger to left shoulder)
"And the Glory,"
(touch right index finger to right shoulder)
"And the Law,"
(touch back of left hand over heart-center)
"Everlasting,"
(point directly forward with right index finger)
"Amen."
(press palms together in front of chest in prayer gesture)

Trace the banishing pentagram of Earth toward the south on the air in front of you with your left index finger. In the *New Millennium Magic* system, it begins at the lower-left point, just as in the Golden Dawn system, but it is traced counterclockwise instead of clockwise (see Figure 14-2). I prefer not to trace the pentagrams quite so large as Dion Fortune recommends. Around four feet across is ample.

Stab the center of the pentagram with your right index finger and vibrate the divine name of the south, Adonai:

"Ahhhhh-dooooo-naaaaay."

Carry the line of the circle around to the west at heart level, draw the banishing pentagram of Earth counterclockwise beginning with the lower-left point, stab its center, and vibrate the divine name of the west, Eheieh:

"Ayyyyyy-heeeeee-ahhhhh."

Carry the line of the circle around to the north, draw the banishing pentagram of Earth counterclockwise, and stab it with your right index finger while vibrating the

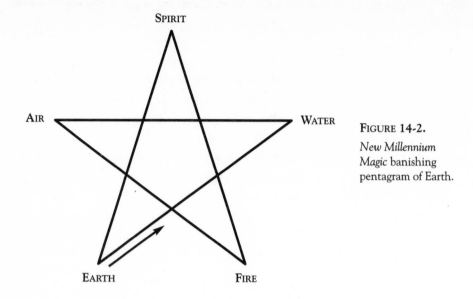

FIGURE 14-2.
New Millennium Magic banishing pentagram of Earth.

divine name of the north in the *New Millennium Magic* system, IHVH. The letters of this name are vibrated individually:

"Yoood-Haaay-Vaavh-Haaay."

Carry the line of the circle around to the east, draw the banishing pentagram of Earth counterclockwise, and stab it with your right index finger while vibrating the divine name of the east in the *New Millennium Magic* system, AGLA. The letters of this name are best vibrated individually, to balance the vibration of IHVH:

"Aaaah-Geeeh-Laaah-Aaaah."

Carry the line of the magic circle that links these four pentagrams of Earth back to its starting place in the south and point to the center of the southern pentagram. Spread your arms wide so that your body forms a great cross. Speak these words, which have been adapted to the inversion of the Golden Dawn associations for north and east:

"Before me, Michael;
Behind me, Raphael;
At my right hand, Gabriel;
At my left hand, Auriel;
Before me flames the pentagram—
Above me shines the six-rayed star."

Visualize the pentagram in the south before you, and at the same time imagine a flaming hexagram floating in the air above the back of your head. Make the Kabbalistic Cross upon your body in the *New Millennium Magic* style while speaking the English version of the text. Stand with your arms at your sides for several minutes, contemplating the dissolution of your obsessing thought-form, and allow the four pentagrams and the hexagram to fade from your mind while continuing to visualize the circle. Press your right hand to your heart, extend your left index finger, and beginning at the south, draw the circle into your heart-center through the tip of your left index finger by making a complete rotation on your own axis. Go about your daily tasks.

In the original Golden Dawn Lesser Banishing Ritual of the Pentagram, the hexagram representing the presence and power of God the Father is visualized behind the back and above the level of the flaming circle and four pentagrams. Israel Regardie moved the hexagram above the head, and replaced the line, "Behind me shines the six-rayed star" with the words, "And in the column stands the six-rayed star." By "in the column" he meant the column of the body and the Central Pillar of the Tree of the Sephiroth. Regardie's example is followed in both forms of the ritual by locating the hexagram above the head, but I have moved it over the back of the head out of deference to the original Golden Dawn instruction. Notice that in my version of the ritual it is necessary to draw the magic circle back into the heart-center through the left hand before ending the ritual.

{ 15 }

The Middle Pillar Exercise

Calling Down the Light

The exercise of the Middle Pillar and the Formula of the Fourfold Breath should not be done during the evening invocation of the spirit, but may be performed at any other time during the day. If you follow a regular routine of morning and evening practice, the best time to do it is directly after the exercise of contemplation at the end of the morning routine. When this is impossible for reasons of time, it can be done in the afternoon or early evening, provided at least several hours come between the Middle Pillar Exercise and the evening invocation.

Those who have the luxury to add a third regular practice session around noon will derive benefit by performing the Middle Pillar at this middle practice. By its very nature, the Middle Pillar Exercise balances and equilibrates the esoteric energies of the body, just as the central pillar on the Tree of the Sephiroth balances the outer two pillars. The exercise is useful for balancing the energies of the morning and evening sessions.

When the Middle Pillar and the Formula of the Fourfold Breath are performed daily, they have great power in awakening the subtle centers of the body. Those

251

familiar with the writings of the late Israel Regardie know that Regardie viewed the Middle Pillar Exercise as the most important of all Golden Dawn techniques. He expanded some parts of the exercise, which is presented in the original Golden Dawn documents solely in the form of two brief and rather cryptic outlines.[1] At the same time, he omitted other aspects. His rewritten version of the exercise is workable and confers significant benefits upon those who practice it regularly, but it distorts the Formula of the Fourfold Breath.

Regardie either did not understand, or chose to ignore, the correct practice of the Formula of the Fourfold Breath as it is presented in the Golden Dawn documents. The cryptic nature of the original instructions makes them easy to misinterpret. He transformed the circulation of silent mental vibrations of the letters of Tetragrammaton, generated in the lungs during retention of the breath, into the circulation of the light radiated into the body by the sphere of Kether and its dependent spheres.[2] Regardie did not use breath retention, but rather employed inhalations and exhalations to circulate the light.

The version of the exercise presented below is based on the brief description provided in the teachings of the Golden Dawn. I have given in detail the visualization necessary when performing this exercise. Visualization is usually scant or lacking in text versions of magic exercises and rituals, yet it is the factor most crucial to success. The original Golden Dawn outline for this exercise contains almost no directions on visualization, making it impossible for a beginner to do the exercise correctly. The exercise of the Middle Pillar has been somewhat modified, but the Formula of the Fourfold Breath has been restored to what I believe was its original form.

Regardie stated that it is not necessary for the practitioner to understand the Hebrew names of God or the structure of the Tree of the Sephiroth in order to derive immense benefit from the practice of this little ritual. This is true, provided proper visualization is performed along with the exercise. It is the visualization of light circulating inside the body that activates its subtle centers and opens astral doorways in the practitioner. This exercise is excellent both for interacting with spirits and for awakening Kundalini.

The Middle Pillar

Stand with your feet together, arms at your sides and your back straight. Imagine that you are being drawn upward by a string attached to the center of your skull. This will aid you in achieving the correct posture. Look straight ahead at a blank wall. Keep a light tension in the muscles of your arms, and extend your fingers straight downward. Tuck your stomach in slightly, but keep your abdominal muscles relaxed. Your weight should be evenly distributed over the entire soles of your feet. For the best results, perform this ritual wearing comfortable, loose clothing, with your feet bare. This posture is known in yoga as the standing pose (*tadasana*: literally, the mountain posture). It is usually the first yoga posture taught to beginners.

Visualize a sphere of intensely bright light that is about six inches in diameter floating in the air a few inches above the crown of your head. Raise your point of awareness so that it enters this sphere. Feel your mind hovering in the air above your physical body, surrounded by shining white radiance that resembles the color of lightning. Inhale deeply, and as you exhale, vibrate on your breath the Hebrew name of God in Kether, Eheieh, in three syllables that flow together.

"Ayyyyyy-heeeeee-ahhhhh."

It is not necessary to sound the name loudly. It can be voiced under the breath. But it must be allowed to resonate in the lungs so that it produces a definite humming or buzzing sensation in the diaphragm, throat and nose. All three syllables in the name must receive equal emphasis, with their vowel sounds sustained for the same duration. As you vibrate the name of God in Kether on your breath, imagine that the white sphere all around your point of consciousness is resonating in harmony.

Mentally extend a column of white light down through the top of your skull and expand it into a smaller sphere of light four inches in diameter that fills your neck where it joins your shoulders. Feel this second ball of light centered on the pit of your throat, its lower half below the level of your collarbones. Its whiteness is not quite as bright as the sphere of Kether. Let your awareness slide down the column of white light into the sphere within your throat, so that its radiance surrounds you. Inhale deeply, and as you exhale, vibrate upon your breath the two Hebrew names of God that are in Chokmah and Binah, Yah and IHVH, which are vocalized together as the compound name of four syllables, Yah-Elohim.

"Yaaaaah-Aaaaay-loooww-heeeem."

This double divine name is associated with Daath, the eleventh quasi-Sephirah that lies midway between Chokmah and Binah, and partakes of their mingled energies. As you vibrate the name so that its four syllables resonate within your chest,

throat, and nose, imagine the light of the sphere in your throat trembling and dancing in sympathy all around your point of awareness.

Extend another column of light that has the slightly less brilliant whiteness of
Daath down from the sphere at the pit of your throat into the center of your chest at
the level of your heart. Expand its tip into a golden sphere six inches in diameter, and
allow your awareness to slide down the column of white light into the yellow sphere.
Feel the light of this sphere radiate throughout your chest like warm sunlight as you
visualize it surrounding your consciousness. Inhale deeply, and as you exhale vibrate
upon your breath the name of God in Tiphareth, which is written as IHVH but is
vocalized as the three syllable name Adonai.

"Ahhhhh-dooooo-naaaaay."

As you vibrate this name, imagine that the golden sphere in your heart-center is
dancing in resonance to the sounds all around your awareness.

Extend a golden column of light straight downward from the yellow sphere in your
chest to a point between your anus and genitals. Expand the tip of this beam into a
sphere of translucent violet radiance four inches in diameter so that it encompasses
your anus, perineum, and genitals. Let your awareness slide down the golden beam
into this violet sphere and visualize its color surrounding and permeating your consciousness. Inhale deeply, and as you exhale, vibrate upon your breath the name of
God in Yesod, Shaddai, with two syllables of equal emphasis and duration.

"Shaaaaad-daaaaaaay."

As you sound this divine name, visualize the violet sphere surrounding your point
of awareness trembling in sympathy.

Extend a violet beam of light downward from the sphere at your groin until it
reaches a place between the soles of your feet. Expand the end of this beam into a
sphere of reddish-brown light six inches in diameter. The color of this sphere is similar to wet clay lit with sunlight. Allow your awareness to slide down the violet beam
into the red-brown sphere, and imagine its rich, earthy color surrounding your awareness. Inhale deeply, and as you exhale, vibrate the six syllables of the compound
Hebrew name of God in Malkuth, Adonai ha-Aretz.

"Aaaaah-doooo-naaaay-haaaah-Aaaaah-reeeetz."

Visualize a resonance within the reddish sphere that surrounds your point of aware-ness as you vibrate the name.

Cause your consciousness to rise upward until it resides within the golden sphere at your heart-center. Expand your consciousness outward in all directions to the sphere of your aura, which is an astral envelope of esoteric energy that surrounds your entire body at a distance of several feet from your skin. Using the force of your imagination, cause your aura to glow with the same golden radiance that colors the sphere in your chest. Simultaneously be aware of your entire body, and of the five spheres of light and the four columns that connect them. All are contained within your expanded aura.

Formula of the Fourfold Breath

Begin the Formula of the Fourfold Breath by filling your lungs with air and closing your throat to retain it. Visualize written within the bright yellow sphere that sur-rounds your heart center the divine name of Tiphareth, IHVH, in Hebrew letters from right to left (יהוה). These letters should be visualized as formed of the brilliant white radiance of Kether (the uppermost sphere), but edged with black light, which renders them visible against the golden-yellow sphere of Tiphareth (heart-center).

In your imagination, vibrate the first letter Yod by extending its sound while focus-ing your inner vision on the first letter of the Name in the golden sphere.

"Yooood."

Feel the vibration of this letter resonate inside the air trapped in your lungs. Imagine the vibrations of the letter running down the left side of your torso and down your left leg into the sole of your left foot, then crossing over to the sole of your right foot through the bridge formed by the reddish sphere, and ascending up your right leg and the right side of your torso. The vibration of the letter Yod forms a complete circle of energy that rotates through your heart-center, down your left leg, across from your left foot to your right foot, and up your right leg. As you vibrate the sound of the letter Yod, feel this circulation of energy. Unlock your throat and exhale, allowing the energy of the vibrated letter to expand on your released breath to fill your aura. For a moment, visualize your aura glowing a bright red. Then see it as before, a pale golden yellow.

Inhale a second time and close your throat to retain the air within your lungs. Focus your inner vision on the second Hebrew letter of the Name, Heh. Silently vibrate the letter upon the air trapped in your lungs so that your chest resonates.

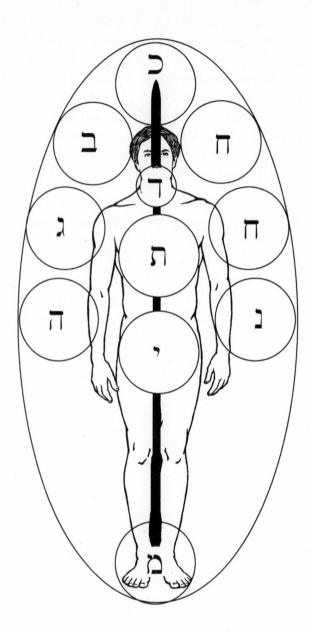

FIGURE 15-1.

Sephiroth on the body, from Regardie's *Golden Dawn.*

"Haaaaaaaay."

Send the vibrations running down your left leg, across from the sole of your left foot to the sole of your right foot, and up your right leg to return into your lungs. Continue to circulate the vibrations as you inwardly sound the letter. Relax your throat, exhale, and allow the energy of the vibrations to fill your aura. For a moment only, visualize your aura turning a bright blue color.

Inhale a third time and close your throat to retain the air. Focus your inner sight on the third Hebrew letter of the divine Name, Vav. Silently vibrate this letter on the air inside your lungs until you are aware of a resonance within your chest.

"Vaaaaaaaavvvvh."

As you do so, send its vibrations down your left leg, across from your left foot to your right foot, and up your right leg, so that the vibrations form a continuous circuit of esoteric energy that flows in a ring through your body. Unlock your throat, exhale, and let the still-echoing vibrations expand outward on your breath to fill your aura. For a moment, visualize your aura turning a deep, rich yellow. This color is considerably darker and more solid than the transparent golden glow of your aura in its resting state.

Inhale a fourth time and seal your throat to keep your lungs filled with air. Focus your inner vision on the final letter in the Tetragrammaton, the second Heh. In your imagination, vibrate the sound of this letter until it resonates inside your chest.

"Haaaaaaaay."

Send the vibrations circulating down your left leg, across from foot to foot, and up your right leg, so that the flowing ring of energy passes through your heart-center. Unlock your throat, exhale, and allow the vibrations to expand to fill your aura. For a moment see your aura glow a dark forest green, then see it return to its transparent golden color, which it has derived from its expansion from the sphere of Tiphareth in your heart-center.

This completes one full cycle of the Formula of the Fourfold Breath, which Golden Dawn members were instructed to use immediately following the Middle Pillar Exercise. If you wish, you may repeat this cycle four times. At the completion of the Fourfold Breath, allow your expanded aura to contract until it lies near the surface of your skin, and let it fade from your astral perceptions as you transfer your attention to the colored spheres. Use the force of your will to cause the five spheres and four vertical columns of light to dissolve their radiant colors into your flesh, and feel their energy fill your entire body. The uppermost sphere that represents Kether should be visualized as descending until it touches the top of your head. The moment it touches your scalp, it flows over the entire surface of your skull and penetrates into your brain, infusing it with energy.

Divine Names on the Middle Pillar

The divine names I have applied to the Sephiroth do not correspond in every respect to the names used by the Golden Dawn. As I pointed out in an article about the Tree of the Sephiroth,[3] the leaders of the Golden Dawn failed to fully understand the assignment of divine names to the Tree. The Golden Dawn gave two divine names to Binah—IHVH and Elohim. This is an error. There is only one divine name for this sphere, IHVH, but when spoken aloud it is to be pronounced "Elohim." Therefore the compound name in Daath, a combination of the names in Chokmah and Binah, is Yah-Elohim. Similarly, the main divine name assigned to Tiphareth is IHVH, but in Tiphareth it is to be spoken aloud as "Adonai" to differentiate it from its simultaneous assignment in Binah. The Golden Dawn gave as the divine name in Yesod the compound name Shaddai El Chai, but this is really two completely separate names (Shaddai and El Chai), each of which was assigned to this sphere by a different Kabbalistic authority. These authorities were not in agreement with each other—the two names were never intended to both be assigned to Yesod. I prefer to use Shaddai for this sphere on the Tree.

{ 16 }

Ritual of Invocation

Preparing to Invoke

It is best if the shrine be placed against the south wall of the bedroom, but not essential. To prepare the shrine, open its doors and light the twin candles so that they burn on either side of the spirit vessel. Pour a small portion of consecrated water into the cup in front of the candle on the right side, and a bit of consecrated salt into the dish in front of the candle on the left side. If you use incense in your invocations, ignite the incense cone or stick in the flame of the left candle and place the burning incense in its holder near the base of the image toward the left where it will not be in the way. Place the bare offering tray at the base of the image slightly to the right. On the table outside and to the right of the shrine, put a small plate bearing the offering you will make to the spirit during ritual. As mentioned before, this can be a piece of fresh bread, a small cake, a cookie, or money—almost anything, provided it has real value.

After you have worked with the spirit for weeks or months, and have succeeded in producing the Oil of Lilith from your genitals, a small vial of the Oil will be stored inside the shrine at the foot of the image. As a temporary substitute for the Oil, at the beginning of your practice, you may use a vial of fresh olive oil. Purify and consecrate this olive oil in its vial before placing it inside the shrine. Other objects that the shrine may contain are flowers, either artificial or genuine, colored ribbons or silk threads to beautify the shrine, and power objects that are useful for attracting the spirit, such as particular gem stones, metals, or colored objects and shapes in harmony with the spirit's nature.

The association of the four elements, and their corresponding letters in Tetragrammaton, differs from the Golden Dawn arrangement. As I mentioned in connection with the Lesser Banishing Ritual of the Pentagram, in the Golden Dawn system of magic, Air (Vav) is placed in the east, and Earth (final Heh) is placed in the north. My system inverts these placements. A complete explanation and justification for the departures from the Golden Dawn system of magic is to be found in my book *New Millennium Magic*.[1]

The Invoking Ritual

Stand on the open floor facing the shrine. Perform the Cleansing Prayer and the Kabbalistic Cross. Visualize a white star high above your head. Draw it down and expand it into a white sphere six inches across that floats on the air a few inches above your scalp. Ascend into this sphere with your awareness and feel the blazing radiance all around you. Extend a column of light downward through the top of your skull and down your neck to the center of your chest. Expand the point of this ray into a golden sphere six inches in diameter, and allow your point of awareness to slide down the inside of the column of light into your heart-center. For a minute or so be aware of the yellow brightness of the sphere in your chest as it dances and spins with vital energy. Send out this energy in all directions to expand the astral envelope your aura and change it to a translucent gold. Expand your awareness to encompass your entire body.

Direct your gaze straight forward. Press your left palm on the center of your chest and extend your right arm before you to point with your right index finger over the top of the shrine. Your right hand should extended directly in front of your heart-center. With the force of your will, draw golden energy from your heart-center through your chest into the palm of your left hand and send it coursing in an expanding spiral up your left arm, across your shoulders, and down your right arm to flow out your right index finger. Send this stream of golden energy behind the shrine to the south wall of your bedroom, or whatever room you are using as a work chamber. Rotate your body on your own axis clockwise as you project a circle of golden fire all around the limits of your room, just as though you were spraying the astral fire from your right hand like water from a hose nozzle. As you turn, speak the following declaration.

"With my right hand I extend this circle of power about this chamber. Let no evil or discordant entity enter into its ring nor abide within its boundary."

Control the tightness and movement of the stream with your mind. When you have sent out a complete circle of fire, link its end to its beginning in the south and terminate the fiery astral stream. Let both your hands fall to your sides and contemplate the bright ring of pale gold fire for about a minute.

Raise your arms upward in front of you and spread them at an angle of about sixty degrees, with your palms turned forward and your fingers spread. Look upward above the top of the shrine. Visualize the Hebrew letters of Tetragrammaton (יהוה) written in the air with white fire, floating above the top of the shrine near the ceiling of the room. Speak the following prayer.

**"Hear me, thou who art First and Last,
the Beginning and the End, the Alpha and the Omega.
O ye Nameless, ye Formless, One, Creator of All,
Lord of Light, Lord of Life, Lord of Love, the Highest,
hear thou this prayer of your true son [daughter], _____.
Shed down thy light upon me, shower down thy light unto the dark
corners of the earth. For I believe in thee and bear thy witness.
I will walk with thee into Fire. Holy art thou,
the Lord of the Universe, the All in one, the One in all.
Look thou with favor upon this ritual of invocation of the spirit
_____ and fulfill it perfectly, by the authority and
power of thy holy name Yod-Heh-Vav-Heh,
upon which the structure of the universe is erected.
Amen. Amen. Amen."**

As you speak the words "First and Last," visualize a large white letter A in front of your left hand and a large letter Z in front of your right hand. As you speak the words "Beginning and End," visualize a large white Hebrew letter Aleph (א) in front of your right hand and a large letter Tau (ת) in front of your left hand. These Hebrew letters replace the Latin (English) letters. As you speak the words "Alpha and Omega," visualize a large white Greek letter Alpha (A) in front of your left hand and a large Greek letter Omega (Ω) in front of your right hand. These Greek letters replace the Hebrew letters for a moment before fading from view. In this way, your mind is directed from hand to hand by the letters, and a pulse of force is created between your hands.

As you speak the words of the prayer "Lord of Light, Lord of Life, Lord of Love" press your left hand to the center of your chest and extend your right index finger to draw an upright triangle around the Hebrew letters of IHVH. First draw the right side of the triangle downward from its uppermost point, then the base of the triangle from right to left, then the left side upward to its point to unite the figure.

As you speak the words "Shed down thy light upon me, shower down thy light unto the dark corners of the earth," visualize the four white letters of Tetragrammaton in the triangle throwing off sparks of light that shower down all around your and dazzle your sight.

As you speak the words of the prayer "Amen, Amen, Amen," press your palms together and after each word touch your united thumbs first to the dome of your forehead, then to your lips, then to your chest.

Go to the shrine and take the cup of water into your left hand. Dip the fingers of your right hand into the water and shake your right hand three times toward the south over the top of the shrine, so that droplets of water are flicked from your fingertips toward the southern side of the astral circle. Visualize them falling beyond the circle. As you do so, speak these words.

"With this consecrated water, I cleanse the region of the south by the power and authority of the holy letter Yod of Tetragrammaton, the first letter of the Name."

Use your right index finger to project a large Hebrew letter Yod (י) in the air to the south above and behind the shrine. Draw energy from the cup of water in your left hand to project this letter from your right hand. The letter is projected by tracing it upon the air with your finger, and at the same time sending it away from your body with the power of your will. Visualize this letter flaming in the air with red fire at the level of the golden-white astral circle, so that the circle intersects the letter.

Step back to the center of your work space. Turn to the west. Approach the limit of the magic circle in the west, dip the fingers of your right hand into the cup of water, and shake water droplets three times toward the western side of the astral circle. As you do so, speak these words.

"With this consecrated water, I cleanse the region of the west by the power and authority of the holy letter Heh of Tetragrammaton, the second letter of the Name."

Drawing energy from the water cup in your left hand, project a large Hebrew letter Heh (ה) with your right index finger upon the air to the west, so that the letter is intersected by the band of the astral circle. Visualize the letter flaming with blue fire and sustain it in your mind.

Step back to the middle of the open floor and turn to the north. Approach the boundary of the magic circle and dip the fingers of your right hand into the water in the cup in your left hand. Shake droplets of water from your fingertips three times to the north, and as you do so, speak these words.

"With this consecrated water I cleanse the region of the north by the power and authority of the holy letter Vav of Tetragrammaton, the third letter of the Name."

Using the force of your will, absorb energy from the water in the cup into your left hand and send it across your shoulders to project a large Hebrew letter Vav (ו) with your right index finger on the air to the north, so that the letter is intersected by the magic circle. Visualize the letter flaming with yellow fire. The yellow is darker and more solid than the pale gold circle.

Step backward to the middle of the floor, turn to the east, and approach the boundary of the magic circle. Dip the fingers of your right hand into the water cup in your left hand, and shake droplets of water from your fingertips three times to the east. As you do so, speak these words.

"With this consecrated water I cleanse the region of the east by the power and authority of the holy letter Heh of Tetragrammaton, the fourth letter of the Name."

Draw energy from the water cup up your left arm, across your shoulders and down your right arm. Use it to project a large Hebrew letter Heh (ה) with your right index finger on the air to the east, so that the letter is intersected by the band of the astral circle. Visualize the letter flaming with dark green fire.

Step backward, turn to the south, and replace the water cup inside the shrine to the right side of the spirit image. Take up the salt dish in your right hand. Stand facing south, with the shrine directly in front of you. Take a pinch of salt between the thumb and forefinger of your left hand, and with three shaking motions, throw tiny bits of salt over the top of the shrine at the boundary of the magic circle to the south, so that the grains falls beyond the circle. As you do so, speak these words.

"With this consecrated salt, I hallow the region of the south by the power and authority of the holy letter Yod of Tetragrammaton, the first letter of the Name."

Visualize the red letter Yod (י) that you previously drew upon the air flaming in the south more brightly.

Step back to the center of the open work space, turn to the west and approach the boundary of the circle. Take a pinch of salt between the fingers of your left hand and shake salt grains three times to the west. Speak these words as you perform this action.

"With this consecrated salt, I hallow the region of the west by the power and authority of the holy letter Heh of Tetragrammaton, the second letter of the Name."

Visualize the blue letter Heh (ה) that you previously drew upon the air flaming in the west more brightly.

Step back and turn toward the north. Approach the boundary of the circle in the north. Take a pinch of salt between the fingers of your left hand and shake grains of salt three times toward the north so that they fall beyond the circle. At the same time, speak these words.

"With this consecrated salt, I hallow the region of the north by the power and authority of the holy letter Vav of Tetragrammaton, the third letter of the Name."

Visualize the yellow letter Vav (ו) that you previously projected to the north flaming with increased intensity on the air at the level of the astral circle.

Step back and turn to the east. Approach the circle, take a pinch of salt between the fingers of your left hand, and shake the salt grains three times beyond the boundary of the circle to the east. As you perform this action, speak these words.

"With this consecrated salt, I hallow the region of the east by the power and authority of the holy letter Heh of Tetragrammaton, the fourth letter of the Name."

Visualize the green letter Heh (ה) that you previously projected upon the air to the east. See it flame more brightly.

Step back to the center of the room, turn toward the south and replace the dish of salt in the shrine on the left side of the spirit image. Step backward to stand in the middle of the floor with your arms at your sides. Spend a minute contemplating in your imagination the astral ring of fire and the four letters of Tetragrammaton that flame in the four elemental colors at its quarters.

With your elbows held straight, clap your hands one time sharply together in front of you at the level of your heart, and slowly spread your arms wide with your palms turned forward so that your body forms a great cross. Visualize a pillar of red fire descend in front of you just outside the southern boundary of the pale golden circle that floats upon the air at the level of your heart. Visualize the head of a male lion take shape within the pillar above the level of the circle. The lion gazes at you with tranquil yet alert golden eyes. Speak these words (the name of the angel is pronounced "Mee-kay-el" with three equally stressed syllables).

"Before me, Michael, the red lion of the south."

While continuing to gaze at the face of the lion, visualize a yellow pillar of fire descend behind you just outside the circle in the north. Visualize a beautiful male human head with long blond hair and gray eyes form within the yellow column above the level of the circle. The head is turned inward to regard you. Although you cannot see the face behind you, feel the gaze of the angel upon the back of your neck. Speak these words (the name of the angel is pronounced "Rah-fay-el" with three equally stressed syllables).

"Behind me, Raphael, the golden angel of the north."

Visualize a column of blue fire descend from the heavens just outside the circle in the west. Visualize the head of an eagle form within the blue fire. The eagle gazes inward at the circle and regards you with bright blue eyes. Feel its gaze upon you. Speak these words (the name of the angel is pronounced "Gah-bree-el" with three equally stressed syllables).

"On my right hand, Gabriel, the blue eagle of the west."

Visualize a column of green fire descend from the heavens just outside the circle in the east. Visualize the head of a horned bull form within the green fire and regard you with serious dark eyes. Feel the intensity of its gaze upon you. Speak these words (the name of the angel is pronounced "Aur-ree-el" with three equally stressed syllables).

"On my left hand, Auriel, the green bull of the east."

Tilt your palms upward and raise your arms at an angle so that they resemble elevated wings. Continue to gaze toward the south. Visualize directly above your head beyond the limit of your expanded aura a large Hebrew letter Shin (ש) that glows with red fire. Speak these words.

"The Fire above me."

Let your arms droop downward at your sides at an angle and turn your palms downward, so that your arms resemble drooping wings. Visualize below your feet beneath your expanded aura a large Hebrew letter Mem (מ) that glows with blue fire. Speak these words.

"The Water below me."

Press your palms together in front of your chest with your fingers touching and extended upward in a prayer gesture. Visualize within the sphere of your heart-center a large Hebrew letter Aleph (א) that glows with yellow fire. Speak these words.

"I am the heart of the four, I am the center of the universe."

Simultaneously visualize three beams of white light extending from your heart center. The first beam shines vertically upward and downward to pass through the letter Shin above you and the letter Mem below you. The second beam shines horizontally outward through the sides of your chest beneath your shoulders, passing through the blue column of fire in the west and the green column of fire in the east. The third beam shines horizontally outward through the front and back of your chest, and passes between your united hands and through the red column of fire in the south, as well as the yellow column of fire behind your back in the north. All three beams intersect at right angles to each other in your heart-center.

Let your arms swing wide and spin slowly on your own body axis three rotations in a sunwise (clockwise) direction. As you spin your body, visualize light streaming down from the white sphere above your head into your heart-center, and radiating outward in all directions to fill the magic circle. Speak these words.

**"By this threefold turning, in the name Yod-Heh-Vav-Heh, I
empower this circle and all works that are done within its boundary.
So let it be."**

Stop your rotation so that you stand in the middle of your work space with your arms at your sides, facing the shrine. Gaze at the astral triangle that floats upon the air above the shrine. Contemplate the flaming white letters of Tetragrammaton that shine within the triangle. Speak these words of invocation.

**"By the power and authority of the sacred name Yod-Heh-Vav-Heh
that burns within the triangle, I, _____, invoke and summon
to tangible presence within this circle the spirit _____."**

Press your left palm to the center of your chest and extend your right hand to point at the triangle. Draw occult virtue into your left hand from the golden sphere of your heart center and send it coursing up your left arm, across your shoulders and down your right arm in an expanding spiral. Project a thin stream of pale gold fire into the center of the triangle, then draw this stream downward and to the right in a large loop that curves completely around the shrine. Make this loop of fire spiral inward clockwise three and one-half turns, so that its center is focused upon the left eye of the spirit image (the left eye of the image is the eye on your right side). This spiral connects the triangle above the shrine with the left eye of the spirit image. With the power of your will, strongly focus the energy streaming from your heart-center through the pupil of the left eye of the image. Sustain the spiral for several seconds in your inner vision before allowing it to fade, and while it is still visible, speak these words, vibrating the name of the spirit briefly but strongly.

> **"By this spiral vortex, the way is opened. I call thee by the sound of thy true name, _____, to be present within this vessel prepared for thee."**

Continue to focus your will through the gateway of the left eye of the image. With your left palm still pressed over your chest and your right hand extended toward the spirit vessel within the shrine, draw power from your heart-center and inscribe with gold-white fire the Hebrew letters in the name of the spirit across the shrine and the image of the spirit, tracing them on the air from right to left after the manner of Hebrew writing. If you have used Latin (English) letters for the name of your spirit lover, write them upon the air in the usual way from left to right. Sustain these letters in your awareness for several seconds before allowing them to fade. As you consider them, speak these words.

> **"By these letters of thy true name, _____, I invoke thee to tangible presence within this image that has been fashioned for thee."**

Upon the air in front of the image within the shrine, project the sigil of your spirit lover. Trace the sigil in a continuous line with a thin stream of pale golden fire projected from the tip of your right index finger. Sustain the image of the sigil for several seconds, and while you can still see it upon the air, speak these words.

> **"By this sigil of thy true name, _____, I charge thee to reveal thy presence within this image that has been prepared for thee."**

Kneel upon the floor in front of the shrine. Take the offering you have previously prepared from its plate and place it upon the offering tray within the shrine. The tray should rest in front of the image of the spirit, and slightly to the right side from your own perspective. Speak these words.

"Beloved _____, receive this offering that I place at thy feet. It
is given to thee as a sign of my enduring friendship and love for
thee, and as a token of the bond between us.
May this offering of love nourish, sustain and please thee in continuing presence within this image."

This concludes the invocation of the spirit to tangible presence within the image, and the presentation of the daily offering. Sit in front of the shrine and commune with the spirit. The best postures are the Japanese seat (vajrasana) or the wide cross-legged seat (siddhasana) with the left heel pressed into the perineum. Those who cannot perform either of these yoga sitting postures or their simplified forms should adopt whatever position keeps the spine straight and feels most comfortable. If you feel awkward or uncomfortable sitting upon a bare rug on the floor, use a cushion or pillow beneath you. Those who cannot sit upon the floor at all should use a chair. The chair must be placed in the ritual work space prior to the beginning of the ritual, so that the magic circle is cast around it. The best location for the chair while not in use is in the north-east corner of the circle, where it will be out of the way. It is important that the eyes of the spirit vessel be level, or nearly level, with your eyes when you are seated in contemplation before the image.

Take from the shrine the small vial of consecrated olive oil (or the vial containing the Oil of Lilith if you have been able to produce it), open the vial, and place a drop of the oil on the tip of your right index finger. While gazing into the left eye of the image in the shrine, touch this drop of oil to your forehead just above your nose between your eyebrows. If the spirit vessel is a statue, touch the same drop to the brow of the image; if the spirit vessel is a picture, touch the drop to the four sides or four corners of the picture frame. Speak these words.

"By the virtues inherent in this sacred Oil, I open my third eye of
second sight. I call upon Shin, the threefold letter of sacred fire, to
purge its vision of illusion and shadow."

Close your eyes for a few moments and direct your gaze upward and inward at your forehead between your eyebrows. Visualize a large red dot, similar to the sphere of the setting sun on the western horizon, and see within it the Hebrew letter Shin (ש) inscribed in white fire. Open your eyes, reseal the vial of oil, and put it away inside the shrine. Begin your period of communion with the spirit through the gateway of its physical image.

At the conclusion of your period of communion with the spirit, stand up, and if necessary, place the cushion or chair out of the way within the circle. Never under any circumstances reach or walk through the boundary of the circle after it has been established on the astral level. This greatly weakens the power of the circle. If you wish to completely sever the link with the spirit, you must license the spirit to depart, and seal the channel you have created by tracing a counterclockwise vortex over the left eye of the image. Speak these words to license the spirit to depart from the shrine.

> **"Hear me, _____. Heed the words of your true lover. I give
> thee license to depart from this circle of art. Go now in peace, by
> the authority of Yod-Heh-Vav-Heh, the true name of the Highest.
> Go, yet return swiftly when next I summon thee."**

Place your left hand on your heart and extend your right arm to point with your right index finger at the left eye of the image. Draw golden energy from the sphere of your heart-center and project it toward the image, then trace with this thin stream of fire an expanding counterclockwise spiral that loops three and one-half turns around the image of the spirit and and bends upward to terminate at the center of the astral triangle that floats upon the air above the shrine. Speak these words, and vibrate the name of the spirit briefly but powerfully on your breath.

> **"I charge thee, _____, with the sound of thy true name, to depart
> this prepared vessel. By this spiral vortex, the way is closed."**

Inscribe a circle-cross of pale golden fire over the image, with its intersection centered on the left eye of the image. First draw the vertical arm downward, then the horizontal arm left to right, and finally a circle around the point of intersection that cuts through the four arms of the cross. Begin and end this circle midway on the upper arm and trace it clockwise. As you sustain this cross on the astral level in your imagination, speak these words.

> **"By this circle-cross the way is sealed. So let it be."**

If you do not wish to sever the link with the spirit after the termination of the nightly invocation—for example, if you wish the spirit to sleep with you—these steps should be omitted. To conclude the ritual, stand up in the middle of the ritual space and face the shrine. Spread your arms and spin your body slowly widdershins (counterclockwise). As you turn on your own axis, imagine that energy is flowing into your heart-center from every part of the ritual circle and being absorbed. Speak these words.

> **"By this threefold turning, in the name Yod-Heh-Vav-Heh, I restore the natural balance of forces within the boundary of the circle.**
> **So let it be."**

Stop the spinning of your body so that you stand facing the shrine with your arms at your sides. Stand quietly for a few moments. With your elbows straight, clap your hands sharply together once in front of you at the level of your heart-center, and spread wide your arms so that your body forms a great cross. Visualize the four pillars of colored light just outside the circle, and the four faces contained in their light. Speak these words.

> **"I release the four guardians of the quarters in the name Yod-Heh-Vav-Heh, and restore the natural balance of forces outside the boundary of the circle.**
> **So let it be."**

Visualize the four faces of the guardian angels blur and fade into the pillars of colored light, and the four pillars withdraw upward and vanish. Turn your attention to the Tetragrammaton within the triangle that floats in the air above the shrine. Raise your arms at an angle of around sixty degrees and turn your palms to the south with your fingers spread. Speak the following closing prayer.

> **"Hear me, thou who art First and Last, the Beginning and the End, the Alpha and the Omega.**
> **O ye Nameless, ye Formless, One, Creator of All, Lord of Light, Lord of Life, Lord of Love, the Highest, hear thou this declaration of your true son [daughter], _____.**

> **I give thanks to thee for the perfect fulfillment of this ritual invoca-
> tion of the spirit _____, by the authority and power of thy
> holy name Yod-Heh-Vav-Heh, upon which the structure
> of the universe is erected.
> Amen. Amen. Amen."**

As you speak the words "First and Last," visualize a large A form on the air in front of your left hand, and a large Z form in front of your right hand. As you speak the words "the Beginning and the End," visualize a large Hebrew letter Aleph (א) replace the previous letter in front of your right hand, and a large Hebrew letter Tau (ת) replace the letter in front of your left hand. As you speak the words "the Alpha and the Omega," visualize a large Greek letter Alpha (A) replace the letter in front of your left hand, and a large Greek letter Omega (Ω) replace the letter in front of your right hand. Allow these Greek letters to fade from your astral sight.

As you speak the words "Lord of Light, Lord of Life, Lord of Love," press your right hand to your heart and absorb the white triangle around the IHVH by tracing it in the air with your extended left index finger, first the left side of the triangle from top to bottom, then the base from left to right, then the right side from bottom to top, so that you end where you began at the apex. As you speak the words "Amen, Amen, Amen," press your palms together and touch your thumbs first to the dome of your forehead, then to your lips, then to your breast over your heart-center.

Stand with your hands united in a gesture of prayer in front of your heart-center, and regard the four letters of Tetragrammaton that float in the air above the shrine. Will them to become dim and gradually fade from view, until after a minute or so, no trace of the letters remains upon the air.

Extend your arms to the sides and spread your fingers so that the tips of the fingers of each hand define the points of an imaginary upright pentagram—a five-rayed star with a single point uppermost. The tip of the middle finger of each hand falls upon the upper point of its pentagram. Send energy from your heart-center flowing equally out through both arms, and cause these fountains of radiance to expand from the centers of your palms in turning spirals of pale-gold light. The spiral of light expanding from your left palm begins at your thumb and turns in a counterclockwise direction, following the circle of the letters Yod-Heh-Shin-Vav-Heh around the pentagram. The opposite spiral of light expanding from your right palm begins at your little finger and turns in a clockwise direction, following the circle of letters Yod-Heh-Vav-Shin-Heh.

Continue to enlarge these turning spirals until they fill the east and the west and curve back on themselves to unite above and below you. The united spiral hemispheres constitute a rotating globe of light that is the size of the magic circle. This sphere completely surrounds you. Its axis runs through your arms. It rotates on this axis upward in front of you and downward behind you. Speak these words.

> **"By the power and authority of the fivefold names of fire,
> Yeheshuah and Yehovashah, I command all spiritual creatures out-
> side the boundary of this circle to depart this place. Go in peace,
> and fare thee well."**

With the force of your will, use this sphere to mentally expand the magic circle in all directions, pushing it outward in a great and powerful wave that carries all astral forms along with it. When you have expanded the circle to a huge size, allow it to contract back to its normal size. Draw the united spirals of light back into your palms and close the pentagrams of your hands into fists to seal these powerful vortices within your body. With your fists still clenched, cross your forearms on your chest. Absorb the energy of the vortices trapped inside your fists once more into your heart-center. Lower your arms to your sides, open your hands, and contemplate the magic circle.

Press your right palm over the center of your chest and extend your left arm directly in front of your heart-center. Point south with your left index finger at the ring of the magic circle that floats upon the air around the boundary of the ritual chamber at heart level. Draw the fire of the circle into the tip of your left finger, deliberately breaking the magic circle in the south. As the fire of the circle begins to flow up your left arm, across your shoulders, down your right arm and through your right palm into your heart-center, slowly rotate your body on its own axis in a counterclockwise direction so that you turn a complete circle. As you turn, speak these words.

> **"With my left hand I absorb this circle of power from about this
> chamber, returning this place to its normal state."**

Stand with your hands at your sides facing the shrine. Perform the Kabbalistic Cross without the Cleansing Prayer. Blow out the candles and discard the excess consecrated water and salt that still remain in the cup and dish. Put away your ritual materials and instruments. Leave the offering on its tray at the foot of the spirit vessel all night. If you do not intend to commune with the spirit while you lie in bed, close the doors of the shrine. The shrine should be left open if you intend to make love with the spirit, or seek to interact with the spirit in your dreams. In these cases, it is best if the image of the spirit overlooks your bed so that the eyes of the image are upon you while you lie sleeping. In the morning, remove the previous night's offering from the shrine and close the doors. Discard the remnant of the offering with an attitude of solemn reverence. Unless you conduct a ritual of invocation in the afternoon, the shrine should be left closed all day.

{17}

The Physiology of Spirit Sex

The Mechanism of Perception

The caress of a spirit is often indistinguishable from the caress of a human being. This is not understood by those who have yet to experience intimate relations with spirits. Spirits are so different from flesh and blood, it is assumed that their lovemaking must be completely alien. They are so ethereal, it is thought that their touch must be weak and unsatisfying. It is not understood that spirit love contains all that human love has to offer, with many other experiences that those who have only known human lovers cannot even imagine.

A spirit is perceived by a process that is very different from the process that operates when a human is perceived. When you look at another person, light reflects from the surface of the person's skin and clothing and enters your eye. The lens of your eye inverts and focuses that light onto your retina. Individual light-sensitive cells in your retina send electrical signals along nerve pathways to the part of your brain that processes visual information. In your brain this electrical energy is manipulated to produce the impression of an image. Your brain flips the image so that the objects it contains are right side up and analyses it for perspective cues so that you have a sense

275

of relative size and depth. Then the most important piece of processing takes place—your brain causes you to perceive the image as though it existed outside your skull by creating the entire external universe that you are familiar with, constantly updating and renewing it from moment to moment.

When you see a spirit, the visual information follows a different route. Your eyes are bypassed completely. The data that will compose the image is fed directly into the visual center of your brain, just as it is when you dream. The image of the spirit is then superimposed on the image of the external world that has been created from data received in the ordinary way through your eyes. The spirit is a kind of double exposure or special effect. Because the image of the external world and the image of the spirit have different origins and are processed in slightly different ways, they sometimes diverge.

The spirit may appear unnaturally small, or large, or deformed. It may mutate from moment to moment, changing its features, hair color, expression, and so on, in startling ways. It may be transparent or pale, and may seem to fade or glow with bright light. Sometimes there is a halo or aura around it. Sometimes its hair is animated and appears to move like writhing serpents or seaweed swaying in the water. The spirit may appear to float, or suddenly disappear. It may talk without moving its lips, or walk without moving its legs, or transform itself into an animal form.

It is not correct to think of the spirit as projected onto the stable background of the physical world. The world is just as much a mental construction as the spirit, and exists inside your mind in the same place that the spirit exists. However, the origin of the information your mind uses to create the image of the material universe is slightly different from the origin of the information your mind uses to construct the image of the spirit. Sometimes the two images are in perfect synchronization, but more often they are slightly out of phase with one another.

Spirits and the Senses

What is true about your visual perception of spirits is equally true about all the other sensory impressions they cause to arise within your mind. Spirits can be felt and heard very easily—more easily than they can be seen, in my experience. They are more rarely smelled. Angels and saints carry with them pleasant scents that are usually described as flower fragrances. Demons typically smell like excrement, rotten flesh, or burning sulfur. Perceptions of smells from spirits are far less common than perceptions of sight, touch, and hearing.

The fifth sense, taste, seldom gets exercised in ordinary communications with spiritual beings. However, when spirits cause food and drink to appear, as is recorded in numerous mythic tales and historical accounts, this tastes like ordinary food and drink, or is superior in flavor. The exception is the description of the banquet of the witches' sabbat, which was extracted under torture during the witch trials. This may or may not be a complete fabrication. Witches interrogated by the Inquisition reported that the food provided by the Devil was either very bland, or foul. Sometimes they said that it turned into leaves, bits of wood, and excrement as they were eating it.

With a clear understanding of the process by which spirits are perceived, you can understand how food created by spirits could by turns taste ambrosial, bland, or disgusting, according to the wish of the spirit. The food of spirits has no physical basis, but the impression of its taste is processed in the same part of the brain that processes the taste of material food. It is just as real to the person who eats it as anything grown from the ground or cooked over a fire, but since the physical sense avenues have been bypassed, it is possible to change its taste in a moment, or make it vanish completely.

Now you know how Jesus could feed a multitude with only five loaves of bread and two fishes, and turn the water in six pots into wine of the highest quality. He was able to activate the same mechanism in the brain that allows us to perceive spirits as external sense impressions. This explanation also applies to Moses, when he transformed the staff of his brother, Aaron, into a serpent. That the serpent of Moses devoured the serpents created in an identical way by the magicians of Pharaoh is not proof that the serpent of Moses had physical existence while the serpents of the magicians were mere illusions, only that Moses had a degree of control over the minds of the witnesses that was superior to the control of the magicians.

Spirits Are Real

Two vital points must be stressed before going on to examine the actual sensations of lovemaking with spirits. The first is that even though spirits do not have material bodies in the way of trees and rocks, they are no less real. It is obvious when the matter is considered that spirits do not dwell in the physical universe in the same way that we do. They inhabit some dimension of reality that is ordinarily inaccessible to our consciousness. It is not a physical space with location and mass, and is almost certainly beyond our ability to conceive.

When spirits try very hard, they can sometimes make themselves perceptible to our consciousness by simulating material bodies. They trick our brains into thinking that they are physical objects by generating what I call sensory metaphors. Our brains process these sensory metaphors just as though they were sense impressions transmitted by our physical organs of sight and hearing and touch. When spirits do a perfect job in creating these sensory metaphors of themselves, it is absolutely impossible to distinguish them from physical beings by relying only on the senses.

Without these sensory metaphors, we could never know anything about spirits. If you try for a moment to conceive of something that is not based on one or more of your five senses, you will understand. Not merely all that we perceive, but all that we conceive, and all that we are ever capable of conceiving, is in the form of sensory data. Even mythical monsters are mental composites of known creatures, or extrapolations of such creatures, that are conceived as seen, heard, felt, smelled, and tasted. When we dream, all of the impressions in our dreams are sense impressions. When we cease to receive or create sense impressions, as happens during deep dreamless sleep, we cease to exist along with the greater universe.

The "Nothing But" Fallacy

It is tempting to dismiss spirits as mere figments of the imagination. This is to fall into the "nothing but" fallacy described by the psychologist Carl Jung.[1] Jung borrowed this useful concept from William James. A painting is nothing but daubs of pigment on a sheet of canvas. A song is nothing but vibrations in the air. Morality is nothing but a social survival mechanism. Human identity is nothing but a collection of electrical impulses in the brain. By reducing something mysterious and frightening to something common and safe, it can be controlled and banished from the mind. This is a kind of black magic. To say that spirits are nothing but imagination explains nothing about them. It does not change them in any way. Yet it allows them to be ignored or treated with contempt.

The Celts believed that the fairies were a race of beings who shared the same world that the human race inhabits. They had their own towns and roads, boats and horses, but these were rendered invisible by magic. A man might walk through the middle of a fairy town and never know it existed. At certain times fairies became visible to human beings. Then fairies and humans could converse, dance, sing, feast together, even make love. Sometimes a fairy and a human married. When a human visited the land of fairy, he vanished from the physical world. Time ceased to flow for him. He might be gone seven years, yet when he returned he looked not a day older.

Surely this ancient Celtic concept of spirits is more practical and useful that the opinion of modern science and medicine, which regards spirits as mere artifacts of disordered physiology. To accept this scientific view is equivalent to ascribing Beethoven's Fifth Symphony to a bout of indigestion, or van Gogh's sunflowers to an aberration of vision. It is the "nothing but" fallacy of Jung. Scientists cling to it because it enables them to banish spirits from their consideration with an easy conscience.

Spirits and Kundalini

The second important point to make about erotic spirits is that they are connected in some way with the muladhara chakra of the human body, and with the energy (shakti) of the goddess Kundalini. During lovemaking with a spirit, the muladhara chakra is stimulated and kundalini energy flows throughout the body.

It is not absolutely clear whether the stimulation of the muladhara center creates *houris,* or spirits of love, or whether the lovemaking of spirits stimulates the muladhara. Hindus believe the second possibility. By uniting sexually with the goddess Shakti they seek to arouse the sleeping serpent Kundalini and force her up the shushumna to the sahasrara, or thousand-petalled lotus, above the crown of the head. Buddhists believe the first possibility. They seek to stimulate kundalini shakti more directly, and try to ignore the distracting caresses of manifesting spirits, which they regard as byproducts of muladhara energy without real existence.

It must be stressed here for those who do not have firsthand experience that the caresses of spirits and embraces of spirits do unmistakably feel exactly like the caresses and embraces of an invisible human lover. To call them kisses, caresses, and embraces is not to use metaphorical language, but to be strictly accurate. The touch does not feel similar to a caress, it is indeed a caress beyond all question. Those who may be led to assume from Buddhist texts that the sensations are misinterpretations of an unconscious, unformed energy that is awakened and flows through the body have never felt the embrace of a spirit. Once felt, it cannot be mistaken for anything but an embrace.

In my opinion, it is the spirits who stimulate muladhara, not muladhara which after being stimulated creates the spirits. I base this on the observation that the caresses of spirits may be clearly felt upon the face and limbs before muladhara becomes awakened. It is possible to converse and commune with spirits without feeling any arousal, then when lovemaking is initiated muladhara immediately becomes strongly awakened and erection spontaneously occurs. It appears that kundalini energy provides a sort of nourishment for spirits, and may be used by spirits for a variety of purposes, but that these spirits exist prior to the awakening of the goddess Kundalini.

During lovemaking the spirits can effortlessly and immediately arouse kundalini shakti. The effect is almost as sudden as throwing a lever. Spirits can turn off this energy just as abruptly, or sustain it for as many hours as the body can tolerate. However, when the mind is concentrated only on thoughts of sensual pleasure, kundalini usually does not rise higher than the heart level, and most commonly no higher than the abdomen. I have already described the sensations felt in the chakras when pierced by kundalini, so I will not repeat them here, other than to observe that there is little pain connected with the process.

The sensations are unlike any ordinary feelings in the body. I find them quite fascinating. For example, the ajna may become sensitive to the proximity of metal, and even nonmetal objects—I have been able to distinctly sense the tip of a pen held an inch or so away from my forehead, even though my eyes were tightly shut. The approach of the pen caused a tightening of the ajna chakra. The same sense of tightening or pressure was caused by the nearness of a fingertip. It is quite strong and cannot be mistaken for any other sensation.

Initial Sensations

The initial approach of a loving spirit is likely to be a touch or caress on the face or lips. This may feel exactly like a kiss. When it is directed to the lips, the muscles of the lips may twitch involuntarily. In the beginning the touch will often be more subtle, similar to the brush of a feather or a slight tickling sensation in one spot that feels very much like the feet of a small insect.

When a spirit touches the entire face, the feeling is one of very slight pressure, akin to the touch of water heated exactly to body temperature were the face to be slowly immersed in it. At other times the touch of a spirit upon the face feels slightly cool, almost exactly like a light breeze. The sensation of coolness is very common in spirit sex, and may occur anywhere on the body, or even envelop the entire body. It is particularly pleasant on hot summer evenings. In the winter when the room temperature is lower it may cause shivering, and require that you throw an extra blanket on the bed.

This initial exploratory caress is apt to first occur during controlled breathing with mantra. Commonly a prickling sensation is felt over the entire scalp, or at other times is localized exactly in the middle of the top of the skull. It can be described as the sensation that occurs after your arm or leg has fallen asleep, then begins to prickle when the flow of blood is restored, but before the prickling reaches the painful stage. Or it is equivalent to an itching sensation that does not go away when scratched. At times the fuzzy tickling feeling may extend all the way down the back. This is like having a soft, woolen sweater pressed lightly against your bare skin.

Less pleasant, but not really painful, is the sensation of being pricked with a pin. I have felt this on various parts of my body, including my testicles, but most commonly on the tips of my large toes. It brings to mind the line of the second witch in Shakespeare's *Macbeth*, when she says, "By the pricking of my thumbs, something wicked this way comes."[2] Obviously Shakespeare was recording a genuine sensation associated with spirit communication. The witch in *Macbeth* received a communication from her familiar. The spirit stimulates the autonomous nervous system of the body in a specific way, undoubtedly for a specific purpose, and this is perceived as a pricking sensation in the largest digits of the hands or feet.

A very common sensation in my experience is an aching in the nerves of my teeth when a spirit touches my face. This is an unmistakable signature of the presence of a spirit, and occurs at no other time. The individual nerves inside the teeth can actually be felt. The front teeth are most strongly affected. There is no sensation of pain, merely a mild discomfort, as though the nerves in the teeth were being gentle stretched or squeezed. It surprises me that others dealing with spirits have not reported this physiological response, since it happens to me more often than almost any other sensation produced by the touch of spirits.

The caress of a spirit may cause slight twitching in the muscles of the face, or when it occurs on the limbs, a trembling or jumping of the large muscles of the thighs or upper arms. This reaction of the muscles is occasional, only happening when these parts of the body are actually touched by a spirit, and is not in the least painful or unpleasant. I should mention here that muscle twitches and spasms, sometimes quite vigorous, are a common event in the practice of kundalini yoga. The gurus explain them by telling their chelas, or disciples, that kundalini is cleansing and opening their nerve pathways.

Shortness of Breath

When a spirit actually presses upon the face, it can cause a slight shortness of breath. This same sensation has been observed during nightmares, and is sometimes referred to as being ridden by the night hag. When it happens during voluntary lovemaking with a spirit, it is not unpleasant. The inhibition of the breath may even serve to increase the intensity of physical arousal. That the stifling of the breath can bring about arousal and orgasm on its own is well known. There is a form (a dangerous form) of sex in which the intake of air is deliberately restricted during lovemaking to increase the violence of orgasm.

I am quite sure from my own experiences that the very slight inhibition of breathing that results from the direct contact of a spirit with the face and chest is not intended to be unpleasant by the spirit, but is merely a byproduct of union with the spirit, which seems at times to extend its substance into the nose and mouth as though seeking to penetrate to the interior of the body. Penetration is sometimes sought in other ways. Once I felt the very clear and distinct sensation of being penetrated anally. This came as quite a shock, since I had not sought this form of union and had no familiarity with it. I resisted strongly by contracting my anal sphincter and buttocks, and after about ten seconds, the sensation ceased, and has not occurred since. It suggests that not all spirits who come to make love to men are female in form.

The only situation in which the restriction of breath during spirit love may be dangerous is when the person involved has asthma. The muffling or smothering of the face can trigger asthmatic attacks. I speak from personal knowledge on this matter. It is worth noting that Aleister Crowley began to be troubled by asthma only after he took up the serious practice of ritual magic and spirit invocation. Asthmatics who have medicated themselves to reduce the inflammation of their bronchial passages prior to attempting sexual union with spirits should have no serious problem. The pressure upon the face is likely to trigger an attack only in those with a tendency to asthma who at the time are not taking any medicine to treat it.

It has been noticed by doctors that attacks of asthma are much more frequent at night than during the day, and more frequent in those asleep than in those who are awake. No one really knows why this happens. Perhaps one of the contributing factors is the attempt by incubi and succubi spirits to initiate sexual relations with human beings.

When a spirit presses upon the face, the mouth often becomes dry. The contact appears to inhibit the secretion of saliva. It may become difficult to swallow. A dusty, tickling feeling deep in the throat may cause involuntary coughing, and the throat may constrict for a few moments. This is probably caused by the stimulation of the vishuddha chakra. It feels exactly as though you have breathed in a speck of dust and got it caught in your windpipe, then experienced a slight allergic reaction to the dust. This sensation passes after a few minutes.

Sometimes in this kind of approach there is light pressure on the surface of the eyes. It is as though light puffs of air are being blown directly onto the surface of the eyeballs. More rarely, the feeling is akin to the prick of a needle. Closing the eyes and keeping them closed for several seconds relieves this minor discomfort. There may also be a sensation of pressure or contraction between the eyebrows as the ajna chakra is stimulated. This is somewhat like having a person gently but firmly press upon your forehead just between your eyebrows with the tip of the index finger.

Methods of Approach

Spirits tend to approach either from the top of the head downward, or from the soles of the feet upward. When they approach from the head, it feels almost as if some sort of cool, damp air is being poured over the body. There may be a pressure on the top of the head. In my personal experience this is often, but not always, confined to the right hemisphere of the brain. The right side of the brain grows cool while the left side remains a normal temperature. Commonly the tickling sensation in the exact center of the top of the skull does not occur at the outset of communion, but only after the spirit has been present for some time.

When spirits approach through the feet, they enter at the tips of the big toes or through the middle of the soles and move up the legs, sometimes provoking minor muscle twitches and spasms. A very common sensation when a spirit approaches through the feet of a reclining lover is one of soft pressure upon the legs that gradually moves up to the torso. It is similar to the sensation of a blanket being slowly drawn up the body. Alternatively, vibrations or electrical sensations may be felt running up from the big toes along the main nerves of the calves and the insides of the thighs. Sometimes the sensation is felt only in one leg, and may extend up the side of the body as far as the ribcage.

Sometimes the sensations experienced during spirit communion and spirit love-making are felt inside the body, at other times they are felt on the surface of the skin. Usually there is a mixture of the two. A spirit can move inside or outside the body at will. Remember, the body you perceive is a construct of your mind, just as is the spirit that you perceive. A spirit has no difficulty penetrating the skin since spirit and skin are composed of the same mind-stuff. The only barriers are conceptual and symbolic —if you firmly believe that a spirit cannot enter your body, it will have a difficult time entering. By this firm belief you erect a magic circle around yourself that is the conceived surface of your skin.

When union is sought with a spirit with thoughts of desire in the mind, the spirit may make first contact directly in the region of the groin. This is felt as a soft pressure on the lower belly, hips, and upper thighs, accompanied by an almost instantaneous tumescence—once an avenue of communication is established with a spirit, the spirit can become manifest without effort in a single moment, summoned only by a thought.

The touch of a spirit can pass right through the body. I have experienced the curious and unique sensation of feeling the underside of my body become chilled while lying on my back in bed, although there was no sensation of coolness on the upper surface of my body or on the sides. The chill seemed to be on the inner surface of the skin of my back. It felt as though something very tenuous and cool had passed completely through my chest and settled close to my back. This feeling is quite distinct, like having cool water poured over your back.

General Sensations

There are several general sensations associated with the embrace of a spirit. One is a feeling of detachment from the body and floating. This begins in the solar plexus region and spreads in all directions to the extremities. Or it may be confined to the lower part of the body, and extend only as high as the heart level. It is indescribably pleasant. In my experience it persists for only a relatively brief period, less than a minute. It is like floating on a cloud, or being borne up upon a gentle breeze. It is not sexual, but extremely sensual.

Another general phenomenon is that of a very pleasant lassitude that quickly spreads throughout the body. When this occurs, the person experiencing it goes from being completely alert and wide awake to being virtually unable to keep the eyes open or move a limb, let alone arise from the bed. Sleep follows in seconds. If you imagine your feelings when you have been the sleepiest you have ever felt in your life, you will gain some idea of this lassitude. It comes on quite quickly. From its onset to its full presence takes only a few seconds.

I have speculated to myself that this ability to cast an almost irresistible lassitude over a human being may be a mechanism spirits use to enjoy connection with humans who might otherwise be unwilling to tolerate their embrace. Perhaps spirits employ this cloak of deep sleep to prevent conscious opposition to their presence. Whatever its nature, it is a delightful sensation. So pleasant, there is very little impulse to resist. It is possible to fight off this sleepiness by getting up and walking around, and concentrating the mind on some task. When this is done the lassitude passes after several minutes, although during that brief period the body may tremble or vibrate along all its nerves and throughout its muscles.

The third general sensation that accompanies sexual union with a spirit can only be described as a kind of whole-body orgasm. This is somewhat similar to regular orgasm, but sustains itself for a longer period, is less intense, and is not localized in the genitals. The sensation is utterly delightful. It has none of the rawness verging on pain that accompanies ordinary orgasm. Yet the pleasure is greater. It occurs during intense arousal, but is not accompanied by ejaculation although it brings the body to the verge of genital climax and holds it there. Every cell in the body shivers and thrills with sustained, blissful pleasure.

The fourth general sensation is one of physical nervousness or edginess, as though all the nerves in the entire body were being gently scraped or stretched, causing them to tingle in a way that is mildly discomforting. This sometimes occurs after making love with a spirit for several hours without the physical release of genital climax. The nervous system becomes slightly over-taxed. I can only describe this sensation as similar to the withdrawal symptoms experienced when an habitual coffee drinker gives up caffeine.

Perhaps whatever chemical the spirit lover causes to be released into the blood that is responsible for the delicious sensation of whole-body orgasm becomes depleted, resulting in a response, similar but much less severe, to withdrawal from a narcotic. The surface of the skin becomes sensitive and easily irritated by contact of the mildest form, such as the pressure of the bed sheets. There is an inability to keep still, and a tendency to thrash or writhe the limbs. The human lover who reaches this stage of over-indulgence becomes mentally nervous and restless. Sometimes there is slight perspiration. This depletion of nervous energy is temporary and quite mild.

Visual and Auditory Perceptions

During spirit lovemaking the senses of sight and hearing play a less important role than the sense of touch. One very common visual impression is a sudden and intensely white flash of light that completely fills the sight. It can best be likened to a stroke of lightning, or the flash of a camera, except that it leaves no after-impression on the retina.

Spirits often appear in the form of sudden flowing streaks or swirls of light that fall swiftly from the ceiling or flash past through the air. When the eyes are turned upon these light streamers, they do not reappear, but when the sight and the attention are averted they abruptly flash past the corner of the eye. Less frequently I have observed a hazy glowing mist that seems to lie upon my body like a phosphorescent fog. This is more easily perceived in semi-darkness, since it lightens the walls and furniture that may still be seen behind and through it.

Actual faces and bodies of spirits are easier to observe at the edges of sleep than when fully awake. These will vary since a spirit can assume different faces to suit different purposes. Incubi and succubi put on the faces of family members and loved ones in erotic dreams to arouse sleeping human beings and cause them to be more receptive to sexual caresses during sleep. Part of the reason for this impersonation is that spirits make easier use of the images that are ready at hand within the mind of their sleeping human lovers. Familiar faces are adopted for convenience.

The initial experience of spirit voices and other sounds also occurs most easily at the edges of sleep, either when falling asleep or just before waking. These tend to be very loud and brief, similar to someone shouting a word or a sentence into your ear, or clashing a pair of cymbals, banging a drum, or dropping an armload of pots and pans onto the floor. As you may imagine, this causes the person who experiences it to awaken rather abruptly. When it is a new experience, it can be disconcerting or even frightening. After a half-dozen occurrences or so it loses its terror and becomes merely annoying. The best response is to roll over and go back to sleep. Loud noises such as rumbles of thunder, explosions, gun shots, crashes, and so on are common.

My speculation is that these shouted voices or loud noises represent attempts by spirits to break through to human consciousness. Whether such crude attempts are made by spirits with benevolent or malicious intentions is difficult to judge, since it may simply be that the spirits making the attempts lack the precise control over the human mind of their lovers needed for a greater subtlety of approach.

The voices of spirits, when at last heard clearly, are human voices. When a higher spirit wishes to make a particular point strongly, its voice rings and penetrates like a great pealing bell. This is an overwhelming experience that fixes the message firmly in the mind, even when it is received on the border of sleep. The voices of lesser spirits are ordinary human voices. Spirits may use unfamiliar voices, or may employ the voices of friends or family members, living or dead. You should not mistake these familiar voices as communications from beyond the grave or telepathic messages. It is simply that the spirit wishing to send a verbal message to you has taken what lay conveniently in your mind and used it as a communications tool.

Consequences of Spirit Love

After a loving relationship has been established with a spirit, the spirit is able to provoke intense erection of the genitals in a matter of from five to ten seconds. It is not necessary to hold in the mind any erotic imagery or fantasies for this excitation and tumescence to occur. Indeed, what is in the mind is irrelevant, since the action of tumescence is triggered by the spirit. Similarly, it is not necessary to apply any physical manipulation to the genitals to cause them to become aroused. This happens in a spontaneous manner without a single touch.

All that is required is to mentally indicate to the spirit that you wish to make love, and to direct toward the spirit loving and affectionate words and feelings. This must be a genuine affection that springs from the heart. Through familiarity the spirit comes to understand when its human partner wishes to make love, and responds immediately. After making love to spirits for a year or two, any sexual imagery or physical manipulations of the sex organs becomes almost superfluous. Physically caresses do not lose their power to give pleasure—they are simply no longer needed. The spirit is able to trigger the same pleasure responses independently.

Herein lies a certain danger, or what may be perceived to be a danger by some individuals. Because spirit lovemaking is so potent and sustained, and because it requires neither sexual imagery in the mind nor physical manipulation of the genitals, there is a possibility that a human who enjoys lovemaking with spirits on a regular basis may lose interest in making love to human beings. After making love to a spirit for many months, the need to dwell on mental fantasies or erotic images to elicit a physiological arousal response seems awkward and crude. The same is true concerning physical contact and manipulation of the genitals. There is the impulse to give it up altogether, since it is no longer needed.

Spirit sex does not result in any loss of sexual function in the physiological sense. However, it is so pleasurable that the human involved may begin to have less interest in ordinary sex, and in human sex partners. Why fly coach when you can fly first class? Similarly, it is only the yearning for sensual stimulation that causes us to dwell on sexual imagery and erotic fantasy. When a far superior stimulation can be had for the asking without lustful thoughts, why bother to fantasize?

Specific Sensations of Arousal

The feelings that are localized in the region of the penis during spirit sex are numerous and varied, but several of the more common sensations can be described. Female readers will, I hope, forgive the emphasis on the subjective male response. These are the feelings I am personally familiar with, so I can write about them with precision and certainty.

There is a strong stimulation of the muladhara at the perineum, just behind the scrotum. This area grows swollen and hard, as though a Ping-Pong ball had suddenly materialized under the skin. At times of extreme arousal the swelling becomes intense, even slightly painful. It feels similar to a muscle cramp. The discomfort is usually mild, and lasts only a few minutes, but it may return half a dozen times throughout a session of lovemaking with a spirit.

Erection is rapid and usually quite strong. Throughout the period of lovemaking, the penis remains erect for as long as the mind directs loving thoughts and words at the spirit. It is not necessary for this love to be conceptualized in language—a general tenderness and fondness in the heart is sufficient to indicate to the spirit that you wish to continue making love. The strength of erection varies from an incredible intensity, when the penis is distended to its maximum extent and has a texture similar to wood sheathed in leather, to a moderate intensity, when there is still full erection but with some resilience in the member when it is pressed. Even at this moderate level it would be quite easy to engage in normal intercourse. The full intensity of erection caused by a spirit is considerably greater than that provoked during ordinary arousal. I suspect that it is more intense than would even be possible under normal circumstances, since a different physiological trigger mechanism is involved.

Erection can be maintained for as long as desired without any physical contact upon the penis. Ordinarily an hour or two is enough, since it does place a certain amount of strain upon the heart, brain, and other organs of the body. After a time general fatigue sets in, and this tends to break the concentration necessary to maintain a union with the spirit. From six to eight hours of constant erection that varies from extreme hardness to moderate hardness is possible—probably longer than this, although I cannot personally testify to a longer period. After erection persists for this length of time, it can become painful, and paradoxically, very difficult to bring to an end. It is possible to end it by strongly turning the mind away from desire and focusing the thoughts on ordinary matters. This results in detumescence after a half hour or so, if during this period the mind resolutely excludes any thought of sex, and any thought of the spirit.

During erection, the penis weeps copious amounts of clear fluid. This is probably the same fluid that is emitted during ordinary lovemaking, but it flows forth in much larger amounts. It varies in consistency from a light oil to almost a gel, but in either case it is perfectly clear like water. Some method must be used to collect or absorb this fluid, or it will form a small pool on the lower belly while the practitioner is lying on his back. I would estimate that from one to two ounces may be emitted during prolonged spirit lovemaking. As I intimated in the earlier chapter on alchemy, this fluid was, and is, believed by esoteric Eastern and Western groups to possess magical potency, since it flows directly from the muladhara at the caress of the goddess Shakti or one of her children. It is the Oil of Lilith that will be described in greater detail in chapter nineteen.

During lovemaking there is sometimes a pricking or squeezing sensation in the testicles. A tickling runs up the entire length of the urethra. Sometimes the glans tingles or tickles in its center and at its tip. A soft caress, similar to the brush of a hand, runs up the exterior of the organ or envelops it. More rarely, there is the sensation of a tight ring sliding down the length of the member from the glans to the root, as though invisible lips enclose it. The testicles may be drawn up tight against the root of the penis. At times the penis feels as though it is vibrating at an extremely high frequency. Sometimes there is a fluttering feeling over the length of the erect member as if it were touched by the soft, beating wings of a bird.

My knowledge of the female physiology of spirit love is necessarily secondhand, since I am a man. However in general it can be said that the same phenomena of sweet lassitude and whole-body orgasm occur just as frequently to women who receive a spirit lover as to men. During union with a male spirit, a woman experiences intense tumescence and secretes copious quantities of fluid. Multiple orgasms, often following one after the other in rapid succession, have been reported. The sensation of being penetrated and filled is quite clear. There is stimulation to the breasts and nipples, which usually does not happen for men. Anal penetration may also occur.

Since beginning to write this book, I have been in extended and frank communication with two women who are engaged in ongoing, prolonged sexual relationships with spirits. They report experiences very similar to my own, including the sensations of floating, intense lassitude, caresses on all parts of the body, sudden loud sounds and bright colors or flashes of white light. There are enough similarities between my experiences and those of these two women to convince me that the phenomena of spirit sex cross the boundary of gender, and are much the same for both male and female.

Ejaculation During Spirit Sex

Ejaculation occurs spontaneously after prolonged and intense arousal. It happens more often and more readily if there is any contact whatsoever against the penis, such as the touch of a sheet, but may be delayed by keeping the erect organ completely away from the slightest contact with any physical object. When it has been delayed for hours in this manner, sometimes after falling asleep the spirit will persist in lovemaking, so that the penis continues erect. In sleep erotic dreams may occur that assist in ejaculation, or spending may occur during sleep without dreams. On the other hand, erection may persist throughout the entire night without ejaculation.

In making love with a spirit, there is little incentive to hasten or manually force ejaculation. The sensations of spirit love that occur before spending are so delightful, the tendency is to delay climax as long as possible. Once ejaculation occurs, desire is allayed for several hours. It is still possible for the spirit to cause the penis to become aroused, but the inclination to seek lovemaking with the spirit is banished for a short time after spending. If, however, lovemaking is carried out without physical emission of the semen, there is a constant pleasure in union with the spirit.

Perhaps for this reason, spirits appear to prefer prolonging arousal at the very brink of climax without actually allowing climax to occur. If the human lover gives a clear and definite indication that climax is desired, it will be provoked, but not every lovemaking session with a spirit ends in spending. Those unfamiliar with the sensations of spirit love might assume that this would be frustrating. On the contrary, the pleasures that precede ejaculation are so sustained and so penetrating, there is only a moderate desire to achieve the slightly more intense plateau of sensation that accompanies physical climax.

Nor is it always easy to force a climax solely through physical manipulations. Even when the organ is fully and intensely erect, and is electrified by sensual feelings produced by the psychic caresses of the spirit, it may be unresponsive to physical touch. At these times tumescence is so extreme, it would reasonably be supposed that one or two touches would be sufficient to cause ejaculation. On the contrary, when the consciousness turns away from the spirit lover to focus on the physical effort to achieve climax, the erect penis responds to touches from the hand as it would were it completely unaroused. There is no immediate pleasurable response to a physical touch.

It sometimes happens that when the human lover attempts to force ejaculation with the hand, the penis actually becomes flaccid. This is due to turning the mind away from the spirit, who was causing the state of arousal, to focus on ordinary erotic thoughts, which require some few moments to provoke full erection. On the other hand, when physical manipulations are carried out to the penis while the mind is still focused lovingly upon the spirit, rather than upon the pleasurable sensations of the body or erotic thoughts, climax is prolonged and intense.

It is very easy to demonstrate through experiment that the spirit is causing tumescence. When the conscious attention is turned lovingly upon the spirit, erection occurs. When the attention is turned to erotic imagery or erotic fantasies, and thus away from the spirit, erection is lost. The power of the spirit to provoke and maintain a state of arousal is far greater than the power of lustful thoughts.

The interesting aspect of this experiment is that it is not necessary to focus the mind upon the spirit with any thoughts of desire or erotic images in order for the spirit to cause erection and sensual pleasure. This occurs even when the spirit is contemplated solely with feelings of friendly affection, with absolutely no erotic intent. Erotic thoughts in themselves do not terminate arousal provided they are coupled with loving thoughts for the spirit. However, it is clear that spirits who are invoked with love respond to love, not lust.

{ 18 }

Achieving Union

The Key to God-making

In order to animate a statue or other image, *you must treat the statue or image as though it were already alive*.

That is the entire technique of god-making in a nutshell. It is so simple that many magicians may refuse to believe it. Having animated numerous images in this way over a span of more than a decade, I can testify to its efficacy. Rituals and symbols are useful as aids when summoning spiritual intelligences for the purpose of direct inter-action, but they are not absolutely necessary. Young children spontaneously establish unions with spirits when they talk to their dolls or stuffed animals, and evoke within these images what their parents describe as imaginary playmates. It is perhaps just as well that these parents remain unaware that their children are engaged in the ancient Egyptian art of god-making.

The method used by children to animate their toys is instructive. The child spends long periods of time alone with the toy, and holds the toy in close contact with his or her body. Often the toy is hugged by the child during sleep. The child gives the toy a special name, which is either intuited by the child or revealed to the child by the intelligence dwelling within the toy. The child engages in animated daily conversations with the toy. Sometimes these conversations are one-sided—to the child's perception, the toy listens silently, but the child knows that the toy understands because the child can see awareness in the eyes of the toy. More rarely the toy responds with words of its own, and the monologue becomes a dialogue. Most important of all, the child loves the toy passionately, and showers affection upon it the whole time the toy is held. The toy comes to be regarded by its small owner as a protector with magical powers. When the physical doll or stuffed animal is lost or wears out, sometimes the imaginary friend who was resident within the image survives and continues to interact with the child as an invisible playmate.

The fundamental activities of magic are instinctual. We can use reason in an attempt to understand them, but magic does not spring from reason. Where reason and magic come into conflict, magic is the older and more powerful force. It will always ultimately prevail. Because the instinct to work magic is a basic part of human nature, a young child can perform powerful acts of magic without the slightest conscious awareness of how magic functions, without any intention to work magic, without even an understanding of what the word magic means. The magic of children is magic in its purest and simplest form.

God-making is an effective method for achieving union with spirits because it lies latent within every human being, a remnant of the instincts of childhood. The Egyptian priests who lavished love upon stone images of Isis, and communicated their thoughts and wishes to her by means of prayers, were merely doing what all children do when playing with their toys. The elaborate ritual structure the priests employed to surround their communions with the images of Isis did not alter the vital heart of their practices, which achieved spectacular results precisely because such communion with spiritual beings is inherent in human nature. The priests of ancient times regarded the statues as though they were alive and aware, and talked to them just as they would talk to their living queen, with emotions of respect, love, and devotion.

The Act of Communion

Sit in a comfortable posture before the shrine within the context of the ritual of invocation. This invocation ritual does not have to be the one presented in this book, but some form of ritual structure should be employed each night to open communication with the spirit you seek to make your lover. You should be near enough to the spirit vessel to touch it with your hands, and the eyes of the image, whether a drawing, painting, photograph or statue, must be approximately on the same level with your own eyes. I cannot emphasize too strongly or too often that the eyes of the image must be open and must gaze directly forward into your eyes as you look upon the image.

Focus your will upon the left eye of the spirit vessel. This is the left eye of the image, which is on your right side. The left side of the body is naturally receptive, just as the right side of the body is naturally projective. In an esoteric sense, we project from our right eye, and receive influences through our left eye, although we are normally not aware of this polarity. To directly reach the consciousness of the spirit, you must project your thoughts and emotions through the spirit's left eye. There is truth in the old proverb, the eyes are the windows of the soul, and a window can be passed through from either side. Your thoughts and emotions are driven out from your own body and into the image of the spirit by the force of your will, which esoterically extends in the form of a ray from your right eye and enters the left eye of the image. There is no physical beam of energy between your eye and the eye of the spirit vessel, but on the astral level this ray exists.

In the early stages of my communication with spirits, I found that music playing in the background was helpful in sustaining my concentration while projecting my thoughts through the eye of the spirit vessel. It can be difficult to hold an inner charge of purposefulness that allows your thoughts to be sent out strongly along a ray of will. I was able to draw upon the music as a well of energy that constantly renewed my emotional intensity and focus. In addition to my words and feelings, I sent the music into the image through the gateway of its left pupil in a stream of energy. I did this by imagining very strongly that the spirit was listening to the music at the same time I was listening to it, that by my act of projection I was sharing the music with the spirit.

It is important not to allow your concentration to wander. Imagine that you are communicating with the spirit over distance through the connecting mechanism of the spirit's image—as though you were talking to the spirit on the telephone while looking at the image of the spirit displayed in front of your face. The inner sense of pushing your words and feelings outward on the ray of your will is vital to success. In order to focus your attention more precisely upon the left eye of the image, it is helpful to mentally trace fine crosshairs over the pupil of the eye by extending a vertical ray downward and a horizontal ray from left to right so that these two rays intersect at the left eye of the image. Similarly, in order to open the way of communication, it is helpful to mentally imagine the thin line of a spiral vortex drawn over the crosshairs in a clockwise direction, and narrowing down to a focus upon the left pupil of the image. These two mental animations, the crosshairs to locate the point of focus in space, and the vortex to expand the point of focus into a tunnel of communication, should be repeated whenever your attention begins to wander from the image.

Make your emotions consist of genuine love, friendship, and affection for the spirit. This is not something that can be simulated. You must actually love the spirit if you expect the spirit to be attracted to you as a potential lover. For this reason, it is important to choose a spirit whose form and personality are attractive and admirable in your sight. It can be useful to employ images of existing angels and deities such as Aphrodite or Apollo precisely because you are apt to already have feelings of admiration and attraction toward the spiritual beings represented by the images. When you call forth a more personal spirit whose image is not known publicly, it is essential that you feel true love for that being, or the spirit who enters the image may not be the spirit you wanted.

A good practice is to feel toward the spirit the same emotions you would hold in your heart toward a person you were soon to marry. The invocation of a spirit into a physical image is a kind of courtship, and the union that forms between a magician and an invoked spirit lover is akin to a marriage. It is no accident that ancient shamans married their spirit lovers. The bond of marriage is sincere and enduring, able to weather minor errors and disputes. It is a union of mutual respect, a life partnership between equals based on love.

In magic, there is action and reaction. When you send energy into the astral realm, you receive energy back. When you project love, you receive love. When you project desire, there is a response of desire. If you are foolish enough to project anger or hatred, the response will be anger and hatred. If you project feelings of contempt, you will be held in contempt yourself. This is one reason why the evocation of demons is so dangerous. Those who evoke evil spirits look upon them with contempt or fear, and seek to dominate them through threat of punishments. Is it any wonder that the spirits called forth into the triangle of evocation also regard the magician with fear and hatred, and use any opportunity to betray and flee their human master?

It is possible to call a spirit lover into an image with feelings of erotic desire in your heart. A measure of desire is inevitable, since you are seeking to summon a being with whom you will have sex. But the overriding emotion must be love rather than lust, if you hope to attract a spirit for whom you can feel genuine friendship and respect over a term of months and years. It is dangerous to summon a spirit for a brief erotic fling, and then to discard the spirit. The spirit will not vanish into nothingness. It will continue to exist on the astral plane, and it will harbor feelings of resentment toward you.

In life it is foolish to make enemies needlessly, and this rule applies just as much in the spirit world as in the world of human beings.

In order to animate an image it is necessary to develop a strong emotional bond with the spirit inhabiting it. You must talk constantly to the spirit in your mind as you would talk to a friend or lover, always with you eyes focused upon the left eye of the image. Even a brief wandering of concentration away from the left eye of the spirit vessel can weaken the link with the spirit, which may then require several minutes to fully re-establish. As you talk to the spirit, project both your words and your affections to the spirit through the left eye of the image. Think of the spirit as a living being who is fully aware of you, and who listens closely to every word you speak with interest and sympathy, as a close friend would listen to your shared confidences. Talk about your hopes and desires, your goals in life, your feelings of love and friendship for the spirit, your worries, your activities during the day, and any other matters that arise in your mind that you feel an inner urge to express.

The stronger your emotional energy, the more quickly the image will awaken. You cannot deceive your spirit lover. It is useless to profess love for the spirit if you really feel nothing other than a desire to make use of the spirit for your own personal ends. In my own work, I discovered that spirits receive my mentally expressed words slightly before I actually form them in my mind. By the time I actually speak my words mentally, the spirit has already responded to my remark through changes in the facial features of the animated image. The conscious mental expression of a thought is merely an echo that is formulated in the mind after the underlying thought has been expressed subconsciously. Since these underlying thoughts that precede conscious articulation are open to spirits, it is difficult or impossible to deceive a spirit about what you are thinking. In my opinion, it is foolish to try to deceive spirits. The best course is complete honesty.

Periodically, as you talk to the spirit in your mind, extend astral hands to caress the spirit, or kiss the spirit with astral lips. This is done by imagining that the image of the spirit is its living body. Visualize reaching out to touch the image—for example, to caress the spirit's neck. There is a trick to this tactile visualization. You must remember how it feels to actually extend your hand and touch another person, but instead of moving your arm and hand of flesh, move the arm and hand of your subtle body. You will know you are successful in these astral caresses both by the strong response of the spirit, visible in the eyes of the image, and also by the inner sensation of actually touching, which is very clear when this astral caress is done properly. In this manner it is possible to caress and kiss the spirit over its entire astral body.

Astral Settings

It is useful at times to visualize the spirit present with you in an astral setting, such as walking along a country road, or sitting in front of a fireplace. See these scenes with a part of your mind as you continue to look at the left eye of the spirit vessel. You should develop a favorite scene that you mentally enter to be with the spirit during these nightly periods of communion. It might be something such as a stroll along a beach, or a meeting upon a bridge, or a picnic beneath a tree. Within these astral settings, pour out your heart to your astral lover, tell the spirit everything about yourself, your hopes and dreams, your plans for the future, your likes and dislikes, the events of your day. Speak as you would to a trusted friend or lover. Develop several such astral settings where you can converse with and caress the spirit, and enter these settings in company with the spirit on a regular basis.

As you imagine yourself present in such an astral place with the living form of the spirit, mentally caress the physical image of the spirit. A duality of mind is necessary. You must see the physical vessel as the body of the spirit, but at the same time visualize the spirit as present with you in the astral landscape. This is not too difficult. Just as you own body can be physically in one place, but your awareness astrally in another place, so also can the physical vessel of the spirit be present in the ritual chamber, inhabited by the spirit, at the same time that the spirit is astrally present with you in an imaginary location. You must possess a very clear mental image of the spirit, and must hold it in your mind while you converse with the spirit through the physical image. Keep your gaze always fixed upon the left eye of the image, but in your mind imagine yourself walking with your lover in pastoral settings, or sitting close to her, or embracing her.

It is not necessary to imagine astral scenes the entire time you are communing with your spirit lover. Over the course of an hour, you might take the spirit to an astral scene five or six times for periods of several minutes. The rest of the time you would be with the spirit within the magic circle. Since it can be tiring to sustain astral landscapes, the best results are achieved by imagining them strongly and clearly for a few minutes, rather than struggling to hold them together for half an hour. A single clear communication with the spirit is worth a hundred fuzzy failed attempts. If you can enter an astral landscape and kiss the spirit once with a complete sensory awareness of the kiss, you have achieved more in a few brief seconds than if you attempt an entire night of lovemaking in an astral setting that is imagined weakly and intermittently.

Physical Manipulations of the Spirit Vessel

Physical caresses and kisses from you hands and lips upon the spirit vessel are useful as a way of reinforcing astral caresses and kisses. It is most convenient that the image be of such a size that you can easily hold it in your hands. This allows you to touch it, kiss its cheeks and lips, and cradle it in your arms as you talk to the spirit. Because the spirit vessel is usually small, kisses can be symbolically transferred to the image by kissing the tip of your finger, and then touching your finger to the lips, brow, cheek, neck, or any other part of the spirit's body. This is similar to the practice of blowing kisses across a distance, and has the same magical basis.

At the same time you caress the physical image with your hands and lips, you should project kisses and caresses in your mind upon the body and face of the spirit. The actual animated image of the spirit exists on the astral level within your imagination, and it is this astral image that overlays the physical image and gives it apparent life and motion. It is not necessary to touch or hold the spirit vessel throughout your nightly communion, but it can be helpful each night to spend a few minutes physically caressing the image when you are speaking in an intimate and loving way to the spirit.

If your spirit vessel is a statue, you may wish to adorn it during your nightly communions by wrapping it in brightly colored silk scarves, or hanging gold or silver chains and precious stones around its neck, or placing precious objects such as crystals around its feet. These adornments should be left with the statue inside the shrine throughout the day while you are engaged in other matters. The statue can be partly or completely disrobed during your time of communion with it in order to allow you to caress it intimately or hold it. Anything you use to adorn the statue becomes the absolute property of the spirit dwelling within the image, forever. You must never use a gift of love you have given to the spirit for any other purpose.

When seeking the sexual love of a spirit, an effective technique is to take the image into your bed at night and hold it close to your heart during sleep. This is the common practice of children with their dolls and stuffed toys, and it has a sound magical basis. By holding the spirit vessel in contact with your body as you drift into sleep, you are constantly reminded of its presence. If you can go to sleep on your back, rest the image face down directly over your heart-center, and anchor it in place with the fingers of one or both hands. It might seem that the image would quickly be displaced as you roll around in sleep. This sometimes happens. More often, your sleeping mind will remain aware of the image, and prevent you from rolling around and casting it off your chest.

This technique is particularly useful if your spirit vessel is a flat image such as a photograph. Photographs or drawings in CD jewel cases are ideal, since the plastic case resists moisture and dust once the slots on its edges are taped shut, and is relatively durable if you should happen to roll on it. If it gets broken it can always be replaced. When using a small statue as a spirit vessel, it is best to tuck the statue against your left side near your heart. Before you take your spirit vessel to bed, make certain that the image will not be damaged by this handling. When using a delicately shaped doll or statuette as a spirit vessel, it is better merely to place the image on your bedside table where it can overlook your sleeping face within touching distance.

As you drift into sleep with the image close beside you or cradled on your chest, continue your internal conversation with the spirit even though you can no longer see the face of the image in the darkness. Visualize yourself talking to and caressing the spirit in an astral setting, and the responses of the spirit. Strive to carry the dialogue over into your dreams. You will discover that frequently the spirit will appear in your dreams, or at the edges of your dreams, although it may only be perceptible as a caress, or a voice, or an invisible presence. Sometimes the spirit will take on the form of another person, but you will know it as the spirit residing in your image by its behavior toward you. When loving spirits enter your dreams, they stand out more strongly than the other dream characters, and their personalities are often incongruous for the dream roles they are playing.

Movement a Sign of Success

If your nightly efforts to animate the image of your spirit lover prove successful, after a period of weeks, or perhaps sooner, you will notice movement in the face and body of the image during your ritual communion with the spirit. Continue to fix your gaze on the left eye of the image. Do not turn your full conscious attention toward the movements of the image or the movements will immediately cease. You will notice that the features of the image respond to your mentally projected remarks or emotions. For example, if you mentally talk about an amusing experience that occurred to you during the day, the face of the image may smile. If you are feeling sad while communing with the spirit, the face of the image may express sorrow in sympathetic reaction to your own sorrow. When you project a kiss upon the lips of the image, it will react with pleasure, or if the spirit is not feeling amorous at the time, with a frown of annoyance.

The reasons the ancients called their temple statues animated is because they were perceived to move physically by those who worshipped and tended them. This is not self-delusion or deception—when the image you are using as the residence for your chosen spirit begins to awaken, you will see it actually move. Most commonly the movements are perceived at the edges sight. If you turn your gaze directly upon the part of the image that moved, it will cease to stir. Even if you focus only your aware-ness on the movement while continuing to gaze at the left eye of the image, the movement will be inhibited. Based on years of experience, I can testify that the direct focus of consciousness inhibits the movements of animated images. If you keep your gaze fixed upon the left eye of the image, any movement in the rest of its body is eas-ily visible within your field of view. By allowing yourself to be aware of these move-ments as responses to your words and emotions, yet at the same time continuing to focus your will through the gateway of the eye, you encourage the gestures and expressions of the spirit.

One of the reasons so much nonsense is written about spirits and spirit manifesta-tions is that very few of those writing about such phenomena have personal experi-ence with it. They merely repeat what others have said or written, and naturally put their own interpretation on the material. The truth is so simple. Animated statues or photographs smile, frown, pout, brood, blink their eyes, shake their head slightly to indicate no and nod to indicate yes, part their lips and occasionally lick them with the tip of their tongue, shrug their shoulders, breathe so that their chest rises and falls, and move their fingers or hands. These small movements are extremely expres-sive because they occur in direct response to the thoughts or emotions of the person in communion with the spirit. I have no doubt that the priests of ancient Greece and Egypt saw exactly the same gestures in their temple statues millennia ago, and used them to obtain oracles.

"The Power Is Strong When Changed To Earth"

The value in animating a spirit image is that it allows a much more dependable avenue of communication with the spirit than would be the case if the unseen and disembodied spirit were addressed by prayers and invocations without ever being effectively visualized. Once the image has been fully awakened, communication may be established with the spirit residing within the image in a matter of moments, merely by gazing into its left eye and projecting its name mentally. Other triggers may still be used to establish contact if desired, such as tracing the sigil of the spirit in the air before the image, but the longer a spirit resides within an image, the less important these rituals supports become.

A spirit residing within a physical image is much more potent on a material level than a disembodied spirit. The sixth statement on the Emerald Tablet of Hermes Trismegistus reads: "The power is strong when changed into earth."[1] Universal spiritual energy becomes physically powerful once it has been provided with a physical basis or foundation that limits and defines its nature. It is the same with explosives such as dynamite—uncontained they are quite weak, but when their energy is confined and directed, they can be used to produce amazing effects. Embodied within a picture or statue, a spirit is capable of being the agent for truly remarkable feats of magic. It becomes a vigilant guardian, a useful servant, and a passionate lover. The possession of a kind of flesh of its own gives spiritual beings greater interest in the sensations of human flesh, as well as a greater ability to stir and satisfy those sensations in human beings.

When the image begins to awaken, you will feel its touches and caresses upon your body as you commune with it. The spirit residing within the image is localized in the image, but is not bound or confined within it. In a nominal sense the image becomes the body of the spirit, but in a practical sense it serves the spirit more as a gateway. When you take the image into your bed, you will experience the actual embrace of the spirit, which is difficult or impossible to distinguish from the embrace of a human lover. I mean exactly what I write here—at times in the darkness it is not possible to tell the touch of a spirit from the touch of a human being. The spirit lying beside you feels exactly like a human being where it presses against your body. Even though the material image of the spirit is of small size, the invisible body of your spirit lover is of human dimensions. The pleasure of its caresses is intense and prolonged. The caresses of the spirit will arouse you powerfully, and will sustain that aroused for as long as you are physically capable of enduring it, if that is your wish.

Spirits are capable of forms of caress that do not resemble the caresses of a human being in the least (no human hand could give such pleasure), but in the main when they touch the surface of the skin, they do it in the same way a human being would, and with the same result. When they touch the organs inside the body, such as the heart and brain, their caresses are less familiar. There is a general area of sensation, as though the palm of the hand were being brushed across the organ. Touches on the heart sometimes make the heart flutter and lose its rhythm for a few seconds. I have never received any harm from these internal caresses. Touches on the brain itself feel very cool, like an ice-cold cloth laid upon the top of the head. This is different from touches upon the outer scalp, which tingle and tickle.

The mere presence of a Son or Daughter of Lilith—a spirit of erotic love—can produce spontaneous erection of the penis in men or inflammation of the labia and

clitoris in women. It is not necessary for you to perceive the touch of the spirit tac-
tilely for the spirit to cause tumescence, when it wishes. Nor is there need for erotic
thoughts or physical self-manipulation of the sex organ. Just the opposite is true. If
you turn your projected thoughts of love away from the spirit to focus your attention
upon your own mounting desire, you will immediately begin to lose the state of
tumescence. This will happen even if you keep your gaze fixed on the left eye of the
image, and only turn your attention away. When you return your attention to the
spirit and once again communicate emotions of affection and admiration to your
lover, your state of arousal will also return.

This continues throughout the period of practice. A man may find himself strongly
erect for an hour, or he may find that his erection rises and falls with the regularity of
a pendulum on a repeating cycle of ten or fifteen minutes. The tumescence of the
genitals indicates that the practice has begun to awaken kundalini shakti at the
muladhara chakra in the perineum. You will not need to wonder about whether or
not the goddess Kundalini has begun to stir to life in your muladhara. You will know
by the rising of your own penis, if you are a man, and by the erection of your clitoris
and inflammation of your labia, if you are a woman.

During these periods of erection, the sex organs are almost without sensation. This
is because tumescence is not caused in the usual way by erotic thoughts or a rise in
the level of sexual hormones in the blood. If you begin to manipulate yourself, turning your attention away from the image of your spirit lover will immediately cause
your tumescence to begin to subside. A spirit can continuously sustain the erection of
a man's sex organ for a period that would seem superhuman to the average man,
although it more often happens that erection will persist for half an hour, then subside for five minutes, then return for another half an hour, and so on for as long as
concentration upon the image can be sustained. The only limit is general physical
exhaustion and need for sleep.

Visual Perception of Spirits

At first you will only feel the caresses of your spirit lover. After you have invoked the
spirit more strongly into its image by repeated rituals, you may begin to see it in the
form of flashes of light and motion, and translucent shadows at the edges of your
vision. These flashes will have the appearance of quicksilver poured in thin streams
across your field of view. Its face will at times form before your sight just as you are
about to fall asleep. You will hear its voice rarely in the beginning, then after a period

of months, more consistently. One interesting way spirits manifest to me is in the form of an intense patch of glowing, electric light. This light is small and ovoid in shape, of a flickering blue-white color, similar to the light of an arc welder. It almost seems to burn itself on the retina. This phenomenon only occurs when I have established a strong link with a spirit during invocation. I perceive this light somewhat to the side of the center of my vision.

Some manifestations of your spirit lover may seem grotesque or frightening. When first this happened to me, I was quite disturbed. The distorted images did not alarm me, but I wondered if they indicated that I was communing with the wrong spirit, perhaps a spirit of evil. Over time I came to realize that the control of the facial features and physical gestures of the spirit vessel is an extremely precise and difficult task. The spirit must overlay the actual material face of the image with an animated mask in order to use the face of the image to convey expressions. This mask forms upon the face of the image, or arises within the face of the image, almost like a dense mist, and in a few moments becomes aware and begins to move. You can perceive this mask indirectly by turning the image upside down while in communion with the spirit—all animation immediately leaves the image. This happens because the spirit has shaped its mask to fit upon the upright face of the image, not its inverted face. When the image is inverted, you cannot see the mask.

Another indirect indication of the presence of this mask is the change that occurs in the appearance of the image when the spirit enters it. The presence of the spirit within an image alters in subtle ways its facial features, even when these are not animated. At times the spirit with whom I commune most frequently—the spirit who first contacted me so many years ago—impresses an unearthly and sublime beauty onto the face of her vessel. The beauty of this spirit is far greater than the beauty of the long-deceased woman whose face serves as the spirit's physical matrix. It can only be described as angelic, a beauty that is almost painful to gaze upon, it is so perfect.

The failed efforts of spirits to express themselves through physical images such as paintings and statues is probably the origin of gargoyles, the grotesque creatures that adorn churches and other public buildings. The facial features of gargoyles are distorted, and convey exaggerated emotions. Churches are a natural place for spirits to attempt communication with human beings. Worshippers have their attention focused strongly on spiritual ideas, and often spend long periods in silent contemplation, with church statues of saints in their field of vision. Spirits are occasionally able to place an animated mask over the faces of such statues, but since those who perceive these masks are not trained to interact with spirits, the masks persist only for a moment or two, and are distorted. They may appear horrifying, or merely ridiculous. Both types of gargoyle are often carved in churches and cathedrals. We sometimes see the faces of spirits similarly exaggerated at the border of sleep. These are known as hypnagogic images, and probably played their part in the invention of gargoyles.

Whether you are ever able to clearly see a spirit apart from its physical image, or hear its spoken conversation while completely awake, depends on your degree of psychic receptiveness. I do not have such an evolved psychic gift. The spirits I have communed with over the years have spoken to me infrequently, and only with difficulty, and I have rarely seen their complete humanoid forms while fully awake. On the other hand, I have been able to feel their touches, caresses, and embraces with intense lucidity. This is the most important avenue of the senses when seeking lovemaking with spirits. Touch can be an articulate form of communication, although the things it conveys are often impossible to translate into words.

{19}

The Oil, the White Powder,
and the Red Powder

The Consummation of Sexual Alchemy

Sexual alchemy has two processes. The first involves establishing and sustaining a loving union with an aspect of Shakti in her guise as goddess of erotic love. The second is the collection and use of the three sexual fluids of the body that are alchemically transformed by such a union. As I have already indicated, I stumbled upon the first process of sexual alchemy quite by accident. I knew nothing of the second process until I received from my Guardian the Gnostic grimoire *Liber Lilith*. After receiving the grimoire and writing it down, more years passed before I even attempted the alchemical portion of this form of magic.

The grimoire puzzled me. I regarded it as an inspired document, and recognized immediately that it was an important magical text, but did not have any notion how to use it a practical way in my own magic. The portion of the grimoire dealing with sexual fluids repelled me, and I felt no strong inclination to experiment with these fluids. Long after writing the work, I finally saw with a flash of insight that the grimoire had arisen as a direct result of my loving union with the spirit that had initially contacted me, who I recognized only then as a higher aspect of Lilith. I was able to integrate my experiments involving spirit invocation and spirit sex with the alchemical instructions contained in the grimoire.

If you feel no inclination to experiment with the Oil of Lilith, or with the White Powder and Red Powder, you can carry on a long and satisfying union with a spirit lover by following the instructions given earlier. It is unnecessary to manipulate the sexual fluids of your body, or those of a person of opposite gender, to attain and enjoy sex with spiritual beings. However there are reasons to believe that use of the Oil of Lilith facilitates and strengthens union with spirits of a sexual kind, and that the manipulation of the products of the body transformed by erotic unions with higher spirits is the ultimate consummation of this form of magic.

The Bootstrap Effect

The products of sexual alchemy cannot be generated without an erotic union with the Goddess in one of her countless female or male forms. It is the intense and sustained sexual arousal of the magician by the power of Shakti that transmutes otherwise ordinary fluids of the body into potent magical catalysts capable of provoking profound and almost instantaneous awakening of latent occult powers or *siddhis*. Among these powers is the ability to communicate more easily with spirits. The sexual fluids changed by loving union with a spirit who embodies shakti (creative energy) can be used to enhance future unions with that spirit, in a sort of feedback loop that intensifies the experience of spirit sex, which in turn increases the alchemical purity of the products of union. In computing, this is known as the bootstrap effect. A computer "boots" or loads a very small initial amount of code, which in turn loads more code, which is capable of loading and handling still more complex code, until at last the computer is fully functional.

All manifest forms, and therefore all gods and spirits, are expressions of Shakti, and may be regarded as her children. The name Shakti is used in this work in a general sense, as the universal creative principle who is sometimes represented as in impersonal force (shakti), and sometimes as a loving goddess (Shakti or Parvati). Spiritual beings potent in awakening sexual energy express the side of Shakti specifically concerned with erotic love for pleasure. I have characterized these beings as the Sons and Daughters of Lilith, because the goddess Lilith very clearly represents this erotic face of Shakti. In order to alchemically transmute the three primary sexual fluids, a lover must be chosen from this category of spirits.

It is not difficult to find this type of being. Any greater spirit who is especially noted in folklore or myth for his or her erotic nature, as well as any lesser spirit whose name, sigil and personality are based on sensual or sexual associations, may probably be classed as a Son or Daughter of Lilith. The alchemical effect is more powerful when union is had with a god, angel, or higher spirit, but personal relationships with gods can be more difficult to sustain than with spirits of a middle level. Whether you choose a higher or intermediary spirit as a lover depends on your purpose—to enjoy a long-term loving relationship, a more personal spirit is best, but to empower the fluids of the body, a god or higher spirit is best.

Higher spirits are those known and worshipped in history by groups, sects, or entire cultures. Spirits of an intermediary level are relatively unknown, and may be represented in history by little more than their names. It is the mass worship of a god or spirit over centuries that increases its power and raises its level of authority. Spirits of malice and destruction can be higher or lower depending on their status in history and the degree to which they received worship in the past. Evil spirits should never be contacted, since no good can come of such communion. I do not class spirits of erotic love, such as the goddess Lilith, or spirits of magic such as the goddess Hecate, as evil, although this was the view in past centuries. There is nothing evil about sex or magic, per se, although both can be used for evil purposes, as can anything else in life.

The first product generated by an erotic union with a spirit is the Oil of Lilith. This is the easiest to produce, and it requires no special processing. It is simply collected, stored, and periodically used. Among the benefits conferred by the ingestion of the Oil are clarity of thought and eloquence of speech, a sense of lightness, and increased energy. This heightening of vitality within the mind and body is a great blessing in regular practice since erotic communion with spirits demands enormous reserves of vital energy. When the practice of this type of magic is pursued with uncommon intensity, it is possible to deplete the energy stores of the body over a term of weeks or months without being aware of it, and incur the risk of nervous collapse or the contraction of a disease.

A function of the Oil that proves very helpful in the early weeks and months of practice is its ability to intensify the presence of a spirit lover within its image, so that communication and lovemaking with the spirit become more dependable and more potent tactually. A drop of the Oil placed upon the forehead of the spirit's statue, or touched to the corners of the picture frame that holds the drawing or painting of the spirit, makes the caress of the spirit more physical, as well as pleasurable, and renders it easier to communicate mentally with the spirit by projection of the thoughts through the channel of the left eye of the image. The Oil should be applied to the spirit vessel within the context of the ritual of invocation, at the same time that you touch the same drop to your forehead between your eyebrows.

This is not so important a consideration once easy, casual communication has been established with your incorporeal lover, but in the early weeks of practice, a catch-22 situation may develop. You may find that you cannot get a strong enough link with your spirit lover to generate pure, energized oil, and without the oil to anoint the image, it is much more difficult to establish a strong link. However, because the oil is not absolutely necessary for contact to be initiated, serious and regular practice will eventually yield success. Consecrated olive oil can serve as a temporary substitute for the Oil of Lilith. The Oil is useful for enhancing communication with a spirit, particularly when you wish to use the powers of the spirit for magical purposes, but not so vital for establishing first contact.

Two Out of Three

The perfect and complete fulfillment of the physical processes of sexual alchemy requires a loving male and female couple. It is only when a woman and man are involved that the essences of both the Red and White powders can be gathered. A solitary man who loves a Daughter of Lilith alone, as enjoyable and satisfying as that relationship may be, cannot generate the basis for the Red Powder because he cannot, on his own, produce menstrual blood. By the same token, a woman who lies in the arms of a Son of Lilith and experiences erotic bliss and intense joy can never generate semen, the basis for the White Powder, no matter how wonderful the experience.

This having been stated, solitary individuals who engage in serious loving union with the Sons or Daughters of Lilith will be able to generate the raw material for two of the three alchemical substances. According to the testimony of the grimoire, two alchemical substances without the third, although they are only a fraction as powerful as all three united, are still capable of transforming the body and mind in useful and startling ways. Also, it is not necessary for a man and a woman to actually unite as lovers to generate the basis for both the Red and White powders. Each can have congress with a child of Lilith privately, collect the fluids, and then exchange them with a member of the opposite sex in order to obtain all three substances for the Great Work of sexual alchemy, which is the transcendent awakening of the soul to the full spectrum of its own mysteries and inner potentials.

Gathering and Using the Oil

Accompanying the atypical erection of the sex organ during erotic union with a spirit is a copious flow of a clear, oily fluid from the tip of the penis in men, and the vagina in women. These two fluids fulfill the same general biological purposes. They are released during normal sex to lubricate the penis and vagina and prevent chaffing of the skin. A second even more important function is to provide a swim-way for sperm to reach the egg and bring about conception. If the vagina remained dry during sex, the likelihood of impregnation would be greatly reduced.

When tumescence is produced by a spirit, either during the ritual of invocation or in bed while engaged in lovemaking with the spirit, the flow of this Oil of Lilith is much more plentiful than normal, perhaps two or three times the amount that flows during the same duration of ordinary love-making. It is also much clearer, and surprisingly thick. At its early issuing during a nightly practice session, it has the consistency almost of a clear gel.

Only the pure, transparent, thick fluid that flows out of the penis when it has been aroused to erection by a spirit lover, and the watery liquid from the vagina when the clitoris is excited and standing and the labia are swollen and red during intense, intimate communion with a spirit, is the true Oil of Lilith. The occult properties of this Oil are completely different from the similar fluids that flow forth during ordinary sexual arousal. Whether this occult transformation is accompanied by a physical change would be difficult to determine, but it seems probable. Catalytic actions require only the most minute of portions to generate profound and significant effects. All of alchemy is based on the premise that alchemical substances are catalytic in their action. Only the tiniest portion of the Red Powder of conventional alchemy was needed to convert large amounts of base metal into gold. Therefore the appearance of siddhis might be caused by an almost immeasurably tiny amount of catalyst in the Oil.

Regard the Oil as you would a regular prescription medicine. Treat it with respect and care. Remember, it is a complex organic alchemical compound with a limited shelf life. Do not store it for more than a few days before cleaning out the bottle and gathering more. It should be collected as needed in a small, clean vial or bottle that can be tightly sealed. After the Oil begins to flow, and there is a regular supply, it should be ingested each morning in small quantities, not more than a drop or two a day.

The virtues claimed for it in *Liber Lilith* appear to be a general rejuvenation of health and virility, with a corresponding increase in beauty and sexual desire. However, the claims in the grimoire are exaggerated, and probably should be interpreted in a symbolic sense. I find that the Oil has a catalytic action upon my mind—it triggers unpredictable psychic events and flashes of intuition. It makes my efforts at artistic expression flow more easily. It also seems to enhance my energy level, and induces a feeling of self-confidence.

When you begin your nightly practice, after projecting the circle and making your offering to your spirit lover, but just before you settle down to share your thoughts and caresses with the spirit, take a drop of the Oil on the tip of your right index finger and touch it to your forehead between your eyes, then touch your finger to the forehead of the spirit's statue or to the corners or edges of the spirit's picture. One drop is enough for both purposes. This will enhance the freedom and clarity of the communication with the spirit that flows in both directions. You will find it easier to perceive the expressions and gestures of the animated spirit vessel, and the spirit will understand your thoughts more completely, and be more responsive to them.

Spirit Lovemaking

When the Oil of Lilith is flowing freely, and you have established the nature of the spirit with whom you are communing, you can begin to make love to the spirit outside of the ritual circle. Union with a spirit while lying in bed is made easier if you take the image of the spirit into bed with you and either cradle it close beside you if it is a statue, or if it is a small picture, lay it upon your chest between your nipples over your heart. To hold the picture in place, fold your hands over it. If you absolutely cannot sleep on your back, place the image close beside your heart or hug it to your breast as you lie on your side to sleep. It is good to get as close a contact between your body and the image as possible. As you lie in darkness, project thoughts of love to the spirit in the same way you project them when seated before the spirit's shrine. Visualize the form and face of the spirit in your imagination, and imagine talking to the spirit, kissing and caressing it.

If you are sufficiently progressed, you will find yourself becoming spontaneously tumescent in exactly the same way it happens when seated before the shrine. Indicate to the spirit that you wish to make love physically. Gently ask the spirit to caress you sensually and to arouse you. Give the spirit the same sort of caresses you wish to receive from the spirit. Do not be aggressive and vulgar. Treat the spirit as you would a human lover that you care for very much. If on a particular night the spirit does not seem to want to make love physically, mentally tell the spirit that you understand and are not upset or disappointed. Continue to project feelings of love to the spirit until you fall asleep.

A primary value of the Oil of Lilith is the acceleration of an overt sexual relationship with a spirit. As I have indicated, in the early stages of communion, arousal of the genitals occurs spontaneously, but when the mind is turned to sexual matters, it immediately subsides. After communing with a spirit for an initial period of weeks, it becomes possible to introduce erotic thoughts into your mind without causing detumescence. Just the opposite happens. Once the spirit has recognized your desire for a continuing sexual relationship and agreed to it, a single thought indicating to the spirit a wish to make love will cause tumescence. Full erection occurs spontaneously when you express a desire to make love to the spirit, without any erotic imagery or self-manipulation, over a span of less than ten seconds.

When your spirit-lover begins to make love to you physically, which may happen after a period of weeks or months, the sensations of its caresses are indescribably erotic and delicious. Orgasm is not necessarily localized in the penis or clitoris, but may be diffused throughout the entire body and sustained for a period of minutes at a time. It can only be compared to the effect of a narcotic flowing through every muscle and along every nerve. These sensations can occur without physical climax, although they are usually accompanied by intense tumescence—far more intense that normal arousal.

Occasionally, as I have indicated elsewhere, this tumescence is so intense and prolonged it becomes painful. It may be necessary to gently place the image of the spirit back in its shrine and turn your mind to some everyday activity for a while in order to relieve the pressure of arousal. In men, the muladhara chakra excites the prostate to such an extent that a tight ball that feels about the size of a Ping-Pong ball forms in the perineum. This can be painful and can persist for a period of an hour or two after the attention is turned away from the spirit lover. It is sometimes accompanied by the imagined need to urinate, even when this is unnecessary—a common symptom of inflammation of the prostate. It is not a sign of disease, but the result of deliberate stimulation by kundalini shakti of the muladhara chakra, induced by the spirit. In my experience, it is followed by no lasting ill-effects of any kind.

Obtaining the White Powder

When your spirit lover begins to provoke climax and orgasm when making love to you, it will probably occur first during sleep, in the form of an erotic dream in which the dream character is occupied or possessed by the spirit. You will be able to perceive that the dream character making love to you is not a normal dream character because it will behave with greater self-awareness and freedom of action. It may speak directly to you out of context with the dream, and identify itself as your lover. After the spirit has begun to make love to you in dreams, orgasm will be attainable at the edges of sleep, shortly after waking up in the morning, or while lying in bed in a half-waking state. As the lovemaking of the spirit grows stronger and more frequent while you are fully awake, the erotic dreams provoked by the spirit will diminish.

You may find it necessary to provide a very brief stimulation to your aroused genitals with your hand in order to achieve actual climax while you are awake. At this phase of practice, arousal is so intense, only a light touch or two at most is required. The lack of sensation in the tumescent genitals that occurs at the beginning of a working of sexual alchemy gives way to intense erotic sensitivity once you initiate physical lovemaking with a spirit. It is not necessary to hold any erotic thought of any kind in the mind, not even erotic thoughts directed toward the spirit. You must only project emotions of affection and love, while indicating to the spirit mentally that you wish the spirit to make physical love to you and provoke your orgasm.

As a general magical rule, the less stimulation a man applies to his own body to achieve climax and ejaculation, the more potent his sperm will be for making into the White Powder. This instruction concerning orgasm is directed at male readers, because women are not capable of producing semen. However, the fluid projected out of the vagina during an orgasm solely or primarily provoked by the actions of a loving spirit, with a minimum of auto-stimulation by the woman, constitutes an uncommonly potent form of the Oil of Lilith.

Sperm that flows as the result of stimulation by the spirit, with little or no help from the hand of the practitioner, is ideal for the White Powder. It should be collected within the ritual circle while sitting or kneeling before the image of the spirit. Catch the sperm on a small tray and allow it to dry naturally in the air, or in front of a heating vent. If it is necessary to dry the sperm more quickly, the tray can be heated over a candle flame, but this is not recommended unless great care is taken, because if heated too rapidly, the virtue of the White Powder is lost. When dry the sperm is scraped from the surface of the tray and repeatedly chopped with a small knife into as fine a dust as possible, then carefully stored in a small glass vial or bottle with an air-tight seal. In its dry form the White Powder, properly prepared, retains its virtue for weeks. The tray, knife, vial, and any other implement involved in its preparation must be cleansed and consecrated prior to use.

The virtues of the White Powder are subtle and varied. I suspect it acts on every-one who ingests it in a unique way, since everyone is different. In general, the White Powder enhances clairvoyance and other receptive psychic abilities such as precogni-tion and psychometry. It tends to bring the emotions closer to the surface, and makes them sharper. It can be used successfully to induce oracular visions in dreams. It gives an intuited awareness of the physical condition and health of others.

It is only necessary to mingle the tiniest speck with a drop of the Oil of Lilith, and touch this drop to the tip of your tongue, for its catalytic action to occur. Some prac-titioners may find this unpalatable, especially in the early stages of their work. The grimoire advises that this drop of Oil, mixed with the White Powder, be placed in a glass of wine and drunk immediately after rising in the morning. This is a matter of individual preference. Those who do not drink alcohol should omit the wine and place the drop directly on their tongue, where it is quickly absorbed, or use water to thin its taste. In ancient times, wine was often substituted for water because water for drinking was so frequently polluted. A small glass of water makes a suitable medium for the drop of mingled Oil and White Powder when ingesting the catalyst.

Obtaining the Red Powder

The fluid for the Red Powder, the virtue of which is always fabled to be greater than that of the White Powder, is gathered by women in much the same way as they gather the Oil of Lilith. The menstrual discharge should be collected on the second or third day of the flow, but not on the first day. The fluid for the White Powder is regulated by the Sun, and can be collected as often as desired on any day of the month, but the fluid for the Red Powder is regulated by the Moon and can be collected only once in each lunar cycle. The menstrual fluid is gathered within the ritual circle before the shrine and image of the spirit.

As you become aroused by your spirit lover, and your labia and clitoris become strongly inflamed with desire, place yourself onto your hands and knees with your lower body exposed and part your thighs. Continue to commune with the image of the spirit by projecting your thoughts and emotions of love from your gaze through the left eye of the image, which must be set in front of you at a convenient height and distance. It can be helpful to move your body rhythmically during this communion. The Oil of Lilith will flow copiously and mingle with your menses. If the Oil does not flow freely, your union with your spirit lover is not sufficiently intense to generate the *prima materia* of the Red Powder. Ideally the mingled Oil and menstrual blood should be copious enough to drip from your labia. Place a small dish below your genitals to catch this flow. It may be necessary for you to squeeze your labia together to encourage the dripping of the fluid, or even to scrape the edge of the tray between your labia. If possible, it is best not to touch your genitals, since the touch of your hand may decrease the occult potency of the fluid. Do not stimulate your clitoris to produce orgasm—this is unnecessary. However, if spontaneous orgasm occurs while you are collecting the fluid, so much the better, as it will greatly increase the fluid's potency.

Set this bloody fluid aside to dry naturally, but keep it away from the direct rays of the Sun, which are inimical to the action of the Moon. When it is completely dry, scrape it into flakes and chop it small with a fine blade until you have reduced it to powder. You may have to dry it a second time after cutting it into fine bits to prevent the dust clumping together. Store it in a small vial or bottle with an airtight seal. Avoid allowing this vial of the Red Powder to be touched by the rays of the Sun. The indirect light of day, such as shines through a window into a house during daylight hours, is not fatal, but try not to allow the Red Powder to lie for more than a few minutes in the strong daylight streaming in through a window. Lamp light is not harmful, since it is hundreds or thousands of times weaker than daylight.

As is true of the virtues detailed in the grimoire for the Oil and the White Powder, the virtues of the Red Powder must be interpreted in a symbolic manner. They will vary widely from person to person, because they depend on the existing physical and mental states of the practitioner who ingests the catalyst. The exaggerated claims for the Red Powder in *Liber Lilith* suggest that in general it strengthens the will and induces a determination to overcome adversity. There are indications that it deepens concentration, and generates an attitude of self-confidence and optimism that at times borders on euphoria. It stimulates the desire to attempt difficult projects and dangerous tasks. It enhances the projection of thoughts to others, and the imposition of the will on others. Physically, it appears to increase endurance.

It should be mentioned that the Red Powder can be used with good results by men, and the White Powder can be used with a similar success by woman. In order to take either Powder, it is necessary to already possess the Oil of Lilith. Before the Powder is consumed, it must be moistened in a drop or two of the Oil. Only a very small amount of Powder is needed, and as little of the Oil as is required to soak it thoroughly and begin dissolving it. The action of the Oil of Lilith activates the Powder, which lies dormant while the Powder is dry. No other liquid is suitable for dissolving the White or the Red powders except the Oil of Lilith. Fortunately, once a regular communion has been established with a spirit lover, the flow of the Oil is copious and frequent, so there is no danger of a shortage of supply.

The Elixir of Life

According to the grimoire, the actions of the two powders are greatly magnified when they are both combined with the Oil and consumed together. In addition, they confer unexpected and extraordinary blessings that cannot be predicted. This is perhaps the true Elixir of Life that was written about in symbolic language for centuries by alchemists. If you read between the lines of some of their descriptions, you will perceive that a few understood the composition of the Elixir, but none were bold enough to openly write the method of its manufacture, as I have done here. Nicholas Flammel probably knew of it, and prepared it with the help of his beloved wife, Perrenella. I suspect that Edward Kelley and John Dee may have experimented with it while sharing their wives in common during their residence in Bohemia,[1] but they did not write of it explicitly.

Very little that is proven can be said about the Elixir. The claims that have been made concerning its miraculous virtues down through the centuries by alchemists are undoubtedly exaggerated and symbolic. It cannot confer eternal life in the physical body, nor can it heal a mortal wound or raise the dead to life. Precisely what its can do is conditioned by its alchemical purity, a function of the spiritual, emotional and physical states of the man and woman during the time the fluids that constitute it were generated. Its full power is also limited by the condition of the person who ingests it. One who is prepared spiritually by a long term of meditations, study, and practice will be more susceptible to its full influence than someone who might happen to consume it by accident.

There is a life of the body and a life of the spirit. I suspect that the greatest virtue of the Elixir is the preparation for immortality of the human spirit—that unknown part of us that survives death. In many cultures, such as that of Tibet and ancient Egypt, it was believed that the fate of the soul was not inevitable and predetermined, but depended on how the human being had been prepared for death during life, and the treatment of the body after death. In Tibetan Buddhism, a person taught and conditioned during life to respond in the correct ways to events perceived after physical death could insure eternal happiness, whereas a person who died in ignorance of the proper responses might expect only misery. The same was true of the preparation of the corpse in ancient Egypt— if prepared incorrectly, it was thought that the soul of the dead individual would not enjoy eternal happiness. It may be that the Elixir transforms the body and mind to prepare the spirit for the afterlife.

Tiny portions of the White Powder and the Red Powder should each be placed in a drop of the Oil separately, and the two drops mingled, then ingested simultaneously. The Elixir can be prepared by putting two drops of Oil on a cleansed and consecrated spoon. Insert a particle of the Red Powder into one drop and a particle of the White Powder into the other. Use the point of a knife to mingle the dry material with each drop of Oil. Take care to keep each drop separate, and to cleanse the point of the knife before transferring it from one drop to the other. When each drop has been separately mixed, combine them and mix them together. Either put the spoon into your mouth and invert it to lick the bowl with your tongue, or use the spoon to stir a small glass of wine or water, and then drink the liquid in one continuous draught, without taking a breath or removing the rim of the glass from your lips.

Advice for Couples

When two loving partners seek to use this art of sexual alchemy, it is important that they not become so caught up in admiration and lust for each other that they exclude the Goddess from their union. A man and a woman, who understand what they are doing and possess an ability to control and regulate their passions, can each invoke a child of Lilith, so that when they make love together, they are each making love to Shakti in one of her erotic aspects, rather than to the limited human personality of their mortal lover. A spirit image such as a statue or painting is not needed for such a couple—each lover becomes the living vessel of Shakti for the other.

Thoughts of admiration, affection, friendship, and love should be projected from the gaze of each lover into the left eye of their partner. The lovers should never allow their conjoined gaze to part during lovemaking. For this reason, they will usually unite face to face. If it is desirable for the man to penetrate the woman from the rear, this is best done when she is on her hands and knees so that a mirror may be place in front of her face, where each lover can regard the left eye of the partner. Loving words softly spoken enhance communion with the children of Lilith. The woman will imagine a spirit inhabiting and possessing the body of her male lover, and the man will conceive a spirit possessing the body of his female lover. It is essential that each partner make love to the spirit inhabiting the body of their lover, not to the person of flesh and blood.

Foreplay should be greatly extended. Indeed, this sort of union with the children of Lilith should consist of almost nothing but foreplay, for the purpose of evoking an intense and prolonged arousal in both partners. It will be found easier and more practical if one lover concentrates on arousing the other, and the person being aroused relaxes and becomes receptive to the influence of the invoked spirit. Very light kisses, touches, scratches, love bites, and so on should be made on the skin. No strong physical stimulation is necessary. If vigorous caresses are employed, they are apt to break the connection with the spirits.

Strictly speaking, physical caresses are no more necessary between two partners than they are when a single practitioner communes with a spirit through its image. They can be helpful in bringing about full orgasm in the passive partner who is the primary focus of arousal, after a sustained period of sexual excitation has occurred at the instigation of the invoked spirit that inhabits the active partner. Induced orgasm may be found necessary as a release from sexual and nervous tension, which can become extreme.

To invoke the presence of loving spirits during sex with another human being, regular and serious nightly practice together is necessary. The couple should sit facing each other within a magic circle, in the context of a ritual of invocation, and lightly caress each other, and each must project affection and love into the left eye of the other. This practice is best done naked. Loving words can be murmured aloud by each partner in turn. If arousal and tumescence occur, practice can be continued when sexually joined face to face in a sitting position. However, the movements of intercourse should be resisted to prevent premature climax.

The Oil and the fluids for the two Powders are gathered separately, as already described for solitary practice, save that the living partner takes the place of the spirit image. When collecting the alchemical product, it is best to arouse the person from whom it will be generated with gentle caresses and kisses. Intercourse should be avoided until the product has been collected. A man who becomes tumescent while gazing into the left eye of his female lover should himself provoke his ejaculation, if a touch is necessary to accomplish this, and should gather his own semen. Similarly, a woman aroused by gazing into the left eye of her male lover should collect her own menstrual fluid. The same rule applies to the gathering of the Oil of Lilith from each.

It is more difficult for a couple to form a mutual union with aspects of Shakti than for an individual to do so, because their desire for each other gets in the way of their love for the Goddess. The temptation becomes strong at some point in daily practice to forget restraint and simply have vigorous physical sex, if only to release the extraordinary tension that accumulates during sexual alchemy. If this is done too often, or too soon in the practice session, contact with the Sons and Daughters of Lilith will be completely lost. Despite these pitfalls, it is convenient to have a partner of the opposite sex when seeking both the Red and White powders. Only by uniting both Powders in a bath of the Oil of Lilith can the highest results be achieved.

Endnotes

Introduction

1. Budge, E. A. Wallis. *The Gods of the Egyptians* [1904]. Two volumes. New York: Dover Publications, 1969. Volume II, pages 6–7.

2. Grant, Kenneth. *Cults of the Shadow*. New York: Samuel Weiser, 1976, page 84.

3. I Corinthians 7:1.

4. Revelation 14:4.

5. Nagarjuna and the Seventh Dalai Lama. *The Precious Garland and the Song of the Four Mindfulnesses*. Translated by Jeffrey Hopkins and Lati Rimpoche with Anne Klein. London: George Allen and Unwin Ltd., 1975, page 40.

6. *Al-Koran*, Chapter 24 ("Light"). Translated by George Sale. London: Frederick Warne, 1887, pages 265–6.

7. Ibid., Chapter 2 ("The Cow"), page 23 of the Sale translation.

8. Leviticus 15:19. Verses fifteen through thirty of this chapter are a remarkable catalog of menstrual taboos.

9. Eusebius. *The Ecclesiastical History*. Two volumes. Kirsopp Lake, translator. Cambridge, MA: Harvard University Press, 1953, Volume I, page 319.

10. Howe, Ellic. *The Magicians of the Golden Dawn* [1972]. New York: Samuel Weiser Inc., 1978, pages 117–8.

11. Fortune, Dion. *Applied Magic*. London: The Aquarian Press, 1962, pages 50–1.

12. Blavatsky, H. P. *Studies in Occultism* [1887–1891]. Pasadena: Theosophical University Press (no date), page 22.

13. *Applied Magic*, page 46.

Chapter One

1. Eliade, Mircea. *Shamanism* [1951]. Translated from the French by Willard R. Trask. Princeton, NJ: Princeton University Press, 1972 (Bollingen Series LXXVI), page 72.

2. Ibid., page 73.

3. Ibid., page 76.

4. Ibid., page 74.

5. *Applied Magic*, page 46.

6. Apuleius, Lucius. *The Golden Ass*. Translated from the Latin by William Adlington [1566]. From an anonymous edition, no publisher or date listed. Chapter 22.

7. *Apocryphal Book of Tobit* 3:8.

8. Kramer, Heinrich and James Sprenger. *The Malleus Maleficarum* [1486]. Translated from the Latin by Montague Summers [1928]. New York: Dover Publications, Inc., 1971, page 30.

9. Masters, R. E. L. *Eros and Evil* [1962]. Baltimore, MD: Penguin Books Inc., 1974, page 210. Appendix B of this work contains the complete text of *Demoniality* by Ludovico Maria Sinistrari. Translated from the Latin by Montague Summers [1927].

10. Ibid., page 236.

11. Ibid., pages 257 and 262.

12. *The Graphic Work of Felicien Rops.* New York: Land's End Press, 1968. See the engravings titled "Amours Et Priapées," "Le Théatre Erotique," "Pommes D'Eve," "Volupté," "Mors Amabilis," and "L'Obsession."

13. *Eros and Evil,* page 109.

14. Robbins, Rossell Hope. *The Encyclopedia of Witchcraft and Demonology.* London: Spring Books, 1959, page 284.

15. Spence, Lewis. *An Encyclopaedia of Occultism* [1920]. New York: University Books, 1960, page 406.

16. Crowley, Aleister. *Liber AL vel Legis* or *The Book of the Law.* Quebec: 93 Publishing, 1975, page 59.

17. Edwards, Allen. *The Jewel in the Lotus* [1959]. New York: Lancer Books Inc., 1965, pages 104–5.

18. Ibid., page 107.

19. Tabori, Paul. *Companions of the Unseen.* New York: University Books, 1968, facing page 197.

20. Fodor, Nandor. *Encyclopaedia of Psychic Science* [1934]. New York: University Books, 1966, page 234. Quoted by Fodor.

21. Ibid. Quoted by Fodor.

22. Ibid., page 237.

Chapter Two

1. Woodroffe, Sir John. *Principles of Tantra* (1914). Madras, India: Ganesh and Co. (Second edition), page 383.

2. Ibid., pages 465–6.

3. Plato. "Timaeus," 50-b. *Plato: The Collected Dialogues.* Edith Hamilton and Huntington Cairns, eds. Princeton, NJ: Princeton University Press, 1973, page 1177.

4. *Principles of Tantra,* page 279.

5. Plutarch. "Isis and Osiris," Ch. 64. *Moralia*. Sixteen volumes. Cambridge, MA: Harvard University Press, 1984, Volume 5, pages 151 and 153.

6. Graves, Robert. *The Greek Myths*. Two volumes. Harmondsworth, Middlesex: Penguin Books, 1957, volume one, pages 71–2.

7. Frazer, Sir James G. *The Golden Bough* (abridged edition) [1922]. New York: The Macmillan Company, 1951, page 445.

8. *The Golden Ass*. Chapter 47.

9. Revelation, 12:1.

10. Robinson, James M. (editor). *The Nag Hammadi Library*. San Francisco: Harper and Row, 1978, pages 111–2.

11. Murray, Margaret A. *The God of the Witches* [1931]. London: Oxford University Press, 1970, pages 40–1.

12. Ovid. *The Fasti, Tristia, Pontic Epistles, Ibis and Halieuticon of Ovid*. Translated from the Latin by Henry T. Riley. London: George Bell and Sons, 1881, page 216.

13. Genesis 4:22.

14. Brewer, E. Cobham. *A Dictionary of Miracles*. London: Chatto and Windus, 1901, pages 21–2.

15. Guazzo, Francesco Maria. *Compendium Maleficarum*. Quoted by Rossell Hope Robbins, *The Encyclopedia of Witchcraft and Demonology*. London: Spring Books, 1967, page 374.

16. Bacharach, Naftali Herz. *The Valley of the King* [Amsterdam, 1648]. As quoted in Raphael Patai's *Gates to the Old City*. New York: Avon Books, 1980, pages 455–6.

17. Guazzo, Francesco Maria. *Compendium Maleficarum* [1608]. Translated from the Latin by E. A. Ashwin. New York: Dover Publications, 1988, page 30.

18. *Gates to the Old City*, page 458.

Chapter Three

1. King, Francis. *Sexuality, Magic and Perversion*. Secaucus, NJ: Citadel Press, 1972, page 35.

2. *Principles of Tantra*, pages 40–1.

3. *Sexuality, Magic and Perversion*, page 22, footnote 12. This quotation originates in Paolino's *Voyage to Malabar*.

4. Woodroffe, Sir John. *S'akti and S'akta*. Madras, India: Ganesh and Company, (7th edition), 1969, page 384.

5. Ibid., page 402. Woodroffe is quoting Jaganmohana Tarkalamkara.

6. Ibid., page 395.

7. Ibid., pages 393–4.

8. See Iamblichus' *Life of Pythagoras*. Translated by Thomas Taylor. London: John M. Watkins, 1926, page 49.

9. *Cults of the Shadow*, page 66.

10. Ibid., page 95.

11. Ibid., page 66.

12. Ibid., page 94.

13. *S'akti and S'akta*, page 382.

14. Ibid., page 396.

15. Rawson, Philip. *Tantra: the Indian Cult of Ecstasy*. New York: Bounty Books, 1973, page 28.

16. Yü, Lu K'uan. *Taoist Yoga: Alchemy and Immortality*. London: Rider and Company, 1970, page 11, footnote 4.

17. Ibid., page 8.

18. Regardie, Israel. *The One Year Manual* (originally published as *Twelve Steps to Spiritual Enlightenment*, Sangreal Foundation, 1969). York Beach, ME: Samuel Weiser Inc. (revised edition), 1981, page 54.

19. *Taoist Yoga*, page xvii.

20. Ibid., page 8.

21. *Cults of the Shadow*, page 86. Grant is quoting from Woodroffe's *Serpent Power*.

Chapter Four

1. *I Enoch*, Chapter 8. From *The Apocrypha and Pseudepigrapha of the Old Testament*. Edited by R. H. Charles. Oxford: Clarendon Press, 1913, volume 2, page 192.

2. Jung, C. G. *Psychology and Alchemy* [1944]. Princeton, NJ: Princeton University Press, 1980, page 330.

3. Flammel, Nicholas. *Alchemical Hieroglyphics*. Translated by Eirenaeus Orandus [1624]. Gillette, NJ: Heptangle Books, 1980, page 22.

4. Ibid., pages 54–5.

5. Ibid., pages 43–6.

6. *Psychology and Alchemy*, page 270.

7. Pernety, Antoine-Joseph. *An Alchemical Treatise On the Great Art*. New York: Samuel Weiser Inc., 1976, page 138.

8. Ibid., pages 139–40.

9. *Psychology and Alchemy*, page 270.

10. Ibid., page 274.

11. Ibid., page 255.

12. Ibid., page 277.

13. Ibid., page 278.

Chapter Five

1. *Encyclopaedia of Occultism*, page 211.

2. Waite, Arthur Edward (editor). *The Alchemical Writings of Edward Kelly* [1893]. New York: Samuel Weiser, 1976, pages 135–7.

3. Ibid., pages 35–8.

4. Evans-Wentz, Walter Yeeling. *The Fairy-Faith in Celtic Countries* [1911]. New York: University Books, 1966, page 102.

5. *Gates to the Old City*, page 463.

6. Ibid., page 469.

7. Ibid., page 456.

8. *Cults of the Shadow*, page 137.

9. Ibid., page 136.

10. Crowley, Aleister. *Moonchild* [1929]. New York: Samuel Weiser Inc., 1973, page 187.

11. *Cults of the Shadow*, pages 138–9.

12. *The Book of the Law*, pages 24–5.

13. Ibid., page 72.

14. King, Francis. *The Secret Rituals of the O.T.O.* New York: Samuel Weiser, 1973, page 28.

15. Crowley, Aleister. *De Arte Magica*. San Francisco: Level Press, no date.

Chapter Six

1. See Pliny's *Natural History*, Book 7, Chapter 13 (Chapter 15 in the Loeb Classical Library edition), as well as Book 28, Chapter 23.

2. Agrippa, Cornelius. *Three Books of Occult Philosophy* [1533]. Edited and annotated by Donald Tyson. St. Paul, MN: Llewellyn Publications, 1993, page 123.

3. Leviticus 15:24.

4. *Gates to the Old City*, page 377.

5. Ganzfried, Rabbi Solomon. *Code of Jewish Law*. New York: Hebrew Publishing Company, 1927, vol. 4, pages 22–3.

6. *Gates to the Old City*, page 456.

7. *Alchemical Writings of Edward Kelly*, pages 87–8.

8. *Cults of the Shadow*, page 66.

9. King, Francis. *The Secret Rituals of the O.T.O.* New York: Samuel Weiser Inc., 1973, pages 224–5.

10. *De Arte Magica*, chapter 9.

11. Ibid., chapter 11.

12. *Cults of the Shadow*, page 146. See also page 71.

13. *Psychology and Alchemy*, pages 396–406.

14. Ibid., page 401.

15. Ibid.

16. King, Francis and Isabel Sutherland. *The Rebirth of Magic*. London: Corgi Books, 1982, pages 189–90.

17. *Psychology and Alchemy*, page 401.

18. Ibid., pages 232–4.

19. Ibid., page 232.

20. Ashmole, Elias. *Theatrum Chemicum Britannicum* [1652]. Reprinted in facsimile by Kessinger Publishing, Kila, MT, 1991, page 350. This illustration is also provided by Jung in his *Psychology and Alchemy*, page 235.

21. Ibid., page 352.

22. *Psychology and Alchemy*, pages 233–4.

23. Ibid., page 234.

24. Ibid., page 453.

25. *Cults of the Shadow*, pages 74–5.

Chapter Seven

1. Regardie, Israel. *The Golden Dawn* [1938–40]. Sixth edition, St. Paul, MN: Llewellyn Publications, 1989, page 55.

2. Westcott, W. Wynn. *Sepher Yetzirah: The Book of Formation* [1887]. New York: Samuel Weiser, 1980, page 20.

3. *Golden Dawn*, page 310.

4. Crowley, Aleister. *Book of Thoth* [1944]. New York: Samuel Weiser, 1974, pages 16–8, 54–6.

Chapter Eight

1. Plotinus. *The Six Enneads*. Translated by Stephen MacKenna and B. S. Page [1952]. Chicago: Encyclopaedia Britannica, Great Books Series, 1980, page 148.

2. Ibid.

3. Scott, Walter. *Hermetica* [1924]. In four volumes. Boston: Shambhala, 1985, vol.1, page 359.

4. Hermeas. *Scholia* on Plato's *Phaedrus*. Quoted by Thomas Taylor in his translation [1821] of *On the Mysteries* by Iamblichus. London: Stuart and Watkins, 1968 (3rd edition), page 353.

5. *Occult Philosophy*, page 711.

6. *The Golden Dawn*, page 486.

7. Ibid., page 490.

8. Ibid.

9. Ibid.

10. Anonymous. *The Arbatel of Magick: Isagoge*. Translated by Robert Turner [1655]. Gillette, NJ: Heptangle Books, 1979, page 20.

11. *Golden Dawn*, page 490.

12. Ibid., page 488.

13. Ibid., page 491.

14. Ibid., page 488.

15. Ibid., pages 488–9.

Chapter Nine

1. Tyson, Donald. *New Millennium Magic*. St. Paul, MN: Llewellyn Publications, 1996, pages 245–7.

2.   Barrett, Francis. *The Magus* [1801]. New York: Samuel Weiser , undated, Book II, Part III, page 127.

3.   *The Arbatel of Magic*, page 25.

4.   *Occult Philosophy*, page 538.

Chapter Ten

1.   Plato. *Plato: The Collected Dialogues*. Edith Hamilton and Huntington Cairns, editors. Princeton, NJ: Princeton University Press, 1961, page 381 (*Meno* 97d). The Greek historian Pausanias also makes mention of these animated wooden statues (*Guide to Greece* 9.3.2).

Chapter Eleven

1.   Casaubon, Meric. *A True and Faithful Relation* [1659]. Glasgow: Antonine Publishing Company, 1974, page 40.

Chapter Twelve

1.   *Golden Dawn*, page 457.

Chapter Thirteen

1.   *Golden Dawn*, page 53.

Chapter Fourteen

1.   *Golden Dawn*, page 90.

2.   Blackwood, Algernon. *Ancient Sorceries and other stories*. Harmondsworth, England: Penguin Books, 1968, page 156.

3.   Fortune, Dion. *Psychic Self-Defence* [1930]. New York: Samuel Weiser, 1979, page 186.

4.   *Golden Dawn*, pages 53–4.

5.   *Psychic Self-Defence*, pages 184–5.

Chapter Fifteen

1. *Golden Dawn*, pages 90 (Middle Pillar Exercise) and 347 (Formula of the Four-fold Breath). The correct practice of the Formula of the Fourfold Breath is only hinted at in the Golden Dawn documents—I have restored it to what I believe was its original manner of practice. It is obvious that it must employ the four Hebrew letters of Tetragrammaton, since this is the name of God in Tiphareth, the sphere that resides within the chest. In my opinion, these four letters were vibrated individually while the energy of their vibrations was circulated in the lower body. That is why the formula consists of four vibrations.

2. *The One Year Manual*, pages 51–2.

3. Cicero, Chic and Sandra Tabatha (editors). *The Golden Dawn Journal: Book II — Qubalah: Theory and Magic.* St. Paul, MN: Llewellyn Publications, 1994, pages 165–6.

Chapter Sixteen

1. *New Millennium Magic*, pages 71–5.

Chapter Seventeen

1. *Psychology and Alchemy*, page 10.

2. Shakespeare, William. *Macbeth*, Act IV, Scene 1, lines 44–5.

Chapter Eighteen

1. *Occult Philosophy*, page 711.

Chapter Nineteen

1. Tyson, Donald. *Enochian Magic For Beginners.* Saint Paul, MN: Llewellyn Publications, 1997, pages 29–32. Also see Casaubon for the text of the covenant agreed to between Dee, Kelley, their wives, and the Enochian angels.

Bibliography

Ashmole, Elias. *Theatrum Chemicum Britannicum*. London: 1652. Photocopy facsimile reprint by Kessinger Publishing Company, Kila, MT, 1991.

Bardon, Franz. *Initiation into Hermetics* [1956]. Translated from the German by A. Radspieler. Wuppertal, Germany: Dieter Ruggeberg, 1971.

———. *The Practice of Magical Evocation* [1956]. Translated from the German by Peter Dimai. Wuppertal, Germany: Dieter Ruggeberg, 1975.

Betz, Hans Deiter (editor). *The Greek Magical Papyri in Translation: Including the Demotic Spells—Volume One: Texts* (second edition). Chicago and London: University of Chicago Press, 1992.

Beyer, Stephan. *The Cult of Tara: Magic and Ritual in Tibet* [1973]. Berkeley: University of California Press, 1978.

Blofeld, John. *The Tantric Mysticism of Tibet* [1970]. New York: Causeway Books, 1974.

Budge, E. A. Wallis. *The Book of the Dead* [1890]. New York: University Books, 1960.

Burckhardt, Titus. *Alchemy: Science of the Cosmos, Science of the Soul* [1960]. Translated from the German by William Stoddart. Baltimore, MD: Penguin Books Inc., 1971.

Burton, Richard F. *The Kama Sutra of Vatsyayana* [1883]. New York: E. P. Dutton and Co., 1964.

Burton, Richard F. and F. F. Arbuthnot. *The Ananga Ranga of Kalyana Malla: or, The Hindu Art of Love* [1885]. New York: Lancer Books, 1964.

Casaubon, Meric. *A True and Faithful Relation of What passed for many Yeers Between Dr. John Dee . . . and Some Spirits* [1659]. Glasgow: The Antonine Publishing Company, 1974. Facsimile edition.

Charles, R. H. *1 Enoch. The Apocrypha and Pseudepigrapha of the Old Testament: Volume II*, pages 163-281. Oxford: Clarendon Press, 1913.

Chinmayananda, Swami. *Discourses on Taittiriya Upanishad*. Madras, India: Chinmaya Publication Trust, 1962.

Crowley, Aleister. *De Arte Magica: Secundum ritum Gradus Nonae O.T.O.* [1914]. San Francisco: Level Press, no date.

————. *Book Four*. Dallas: Sangreal Foundation, 1972.

————. *Liber Aleph: The Book of Wisdom or Folly*. West Point, CA: Thelema Publishing, 1962.

————. *Magick in Theory and Practice* [1929]. New York: Dover Publications Inc., 1976.

————. *Moonchild* [1929]. New York: Samuel Weiser Inc., 1973.

————. *The Book of Lies* [1913]. New York: Samuel Weiser Inc., 1974.

———. *The Holy Books of Thelema* (The Equinox: Volume Three, Number Nine). York Beach, ME: Samuel Weiser Inc., 1983.

———. *The Vision and the Voice*. Dallas: Sangreal Foundation Inc., 1972.

David-Neel, Alexandra. *Initiations and Initiates in Tibet*. Translated from the French by Fred Rothwell. New York: University Books, 1959.

———. *Magic and Mystery in Tibet* [First French edition: 1929; English edition: 1932]. New York: Dover Publications Inc., 1971.

Deren, Maya. *Divine Horsemen: the Voodoo Gods of Haiti* [1952]. New York: Chelsea House Publishers, 1970.

Edwardes, Allen. *The Jewel in the Lotus: A Historical Survey of the Sexual Culture of the East* [1959]. New York: Lancer Books, 1965.

Eliade, Mircea. *Rites and Symbols of Initiation: the Mysteries of Birth and Rebirth* [1958]. Translated from the French by William R. Trask. New York: Harper Torchbooks, 1965.

———. *Shamanism: Archaic Techniques of Ecstasy* [1951]. Translated from the French by Willard R. Trask. Princeton: Princeton University Press, 1972.

———. *Yoga: Immortality and Freedom* [1954]. Translated from the French by Willard R. Trask. New York: Pantheon Books, 1958.

Evans-Wentz, W. Y. *The Tibetan Book of the Dead* [1927]. New York: Causeway Books, 1973.

———. *Tibetan Yoga and Secret Doctrines* [1935]. Oxford and London: Oxford University Press, 1967.

Flammel, Nicholas. *Alchemical Hieroglyphics*. Translated from the French by Eirenaeus Orandus [1624]. Gillette, New Jersey: Heptangle Books, 1980.

Fortune, Dion. *The Sea Priestess* [1938]. New York: Samuel Weiser Inc., 1978.

————. *Psychic Self-Defence* [1930]. New York: Samuel Weiser, Inc., 1979.

Garrison, Omar. *Tantra: the Yoga of Sex* [1964]. New York: Avon Books, 1973.

Grant, Kenneth. *Cults of the Shadow*. New York: Samuel Weiser Inc., 1976.

Guazzo, Francesco Maria. *Compendium Maleficarum* [1608]. Translated from the Latin by E. A. Ashwin [1929]. New York: Dover Publications, 1988.

Guenther, Herbert V. *The Tantric View of Life*. Berkeley and London: Shambala, 1972.

Humana, Charles and Wang Wu. *The Ying-Yang: the Chinese Way of Love*. London: Tandem, 1971.

Iyengar, B. K. S. *Light on Pranayama: the Yogic Art of Breathing*. New York: Crossroad Publishing Company, 1985.

————. *Light on Yoga* [1966]. London: Unwin Paperbacks, 1976.

Jung, Carl G. *Psychology and Alchemy* [1944]. Translated from the German by R. F. C. Hull. Princeton, NJ: Princeton University Press, 1980.

King, Francis and Isabel Sutherland. *The Rebirth of Magic*. London: Corgi Books, 1982.

King, Francis. *The Rites of Modern Occult Magic*. New York: The Macmillan Company, 1970.

————. *The Secret Rituals of the O.T.O.* New York: Samuel Weiser Inc., 1973.

————. *Sexuality, Magic and Perversion*. Secaucus, NJ: The Citadel Press, 1972.

Kramer, Heinrich and James Sprenger. *The Malleus Maleficarum* [1486]. Translated from the Latin by Montague Summers. New York: Dover Publications Inc., 1971.

Lal, Kanwar. *The Cult of Desire: An Interpretation of Erotic Sculpture of India.* New York: University Books, 1967.

Lauf, Detlef Ingo. *Secret Doctrines of the Tibetan Books of the Dead* [1975]. Translated from the German by Graham Parks. Boulder and London: Shambhala, 1977.

Leacock, Seth and Ruth. *Spirits of the Deep: A Study of an Afro-Brazilian Cult* [1972]. New York: Anchor Books, 1975.

Levi-Strauss, Claude. *Totemism* [1962]. Translated from the French by Rodney Needham. Boston: Beacon Press, 1963.

Lewinsohn, Richard. *A History of Sexual Customs From Earliest Times to the Present* [1956]. Translated from the German by Alexander Mayce [1958]. New York: Harper and Row, 1971.

Legeza, Laszlo. *Tao Magic: The Chinese Art of the Occult.* New York: Pantheon Books, 1975.

Lewis, I. M. *Ecstatic Religion: An Anthropological Study of Spirit Possession and Shamanism.* Harmondsworth, Middlesex: Penguin Books, 1971.

Lounsbery, G. Constant. *Buddhist Meditation in the Southern School: Theory and Practice for Westerners.* New York: Alfred A. Knopf, 1936.

Masters, R. E. L. *Eros and Evil: The Sexual Psychopathology of Witchcraft* [1962]. Baltimore, MD: Penguin Books Inc., 1974.

Mathers, S. L. MacGregor. *The Book of the Sacred Magic of Abramelin the Mage* [1900]. New York: Dover Publications Inc., 1975.

Nagarjuna and the Seventh Dalai Lama. *The Precious Garland and the Song of the Four Mindfulnesses*. Translated by Jeffrey Hopkins and Lati Rimpoche with Anne Klein. London: Goerge Allen and Unwin Ltd., 1975.

Nauman Jr., St. Elmo (editor). *Exorcism Through the Ages*. Secaucus, NJ: The Citadel Press, 1974.

Oesterreich, Traugott K. *Possession and Exorcism* [1921] (originally titled *Possession: Demoniacal and Other*). Translated from the German by D. Ibberson. New York: Causeway Books, 1974.

Pandit, M. P. *Kundalini Yoga* [1959]. Madras, India: Ganesh and Co., 1968.

Pernety, Antoine-Joseph. *An Alchemical Treatise On the Great Art* [1898]. New York: Samuel Weiser Inc., 1976.

Radha, Swami Sivananda. *Kundalini: Yoga for the West*. Boulder and London: Shambhala, 1981.

Rama, Swami. *Path of Fire and Light: Advanced Practices of Yoga*. Honesdale, PA: The Himalayan International Institute of Yoga Science and Philosophy of the USA, 1986.

Rawson, Philip. *Tantra: the Indian Cult of Ecstasy*. London: Thames and Hudson, 1973.

Sadhu, Mouni. *Concentration* [1959]. London: Unwin Paperbacks, 1977.

———. *Samadhi: The Superconsciousness of the Future* [1962]. London: Unwin Paperbacks, 1976.

Scot, Reginald. *The Discoverie of Witchcraft* [1584]. New York: Dover Publications, Inc., 1972.

Scott, Sir Walter. *Demonology and Witchcraft* [2nd edition: 1830]. New York: Bell Publishing Company, 1970.

Taimni, I. K. *Glimpses into the Psychology of Yoga*. Madras, India: Theosophical Publishing House, 1973.

———. *The Science of Yoga: A Commentary On the Yoga-Sutras of Patanjali in the Light of Modern Thought*. Wheaton, IL: Quest Book/Theosophical Publishing House, 1967.

Taylor, Thomas. *The Eleusinian and Bacchic Mysteries*. New York: J. W. Bouton, 1875. Photocopy reprint by Health Research, California, 1971.

Tyson, Donald. *Enochian Magic for Beginners*. St. Paul, MN: Llewellyn Publications, 1997.

———. *New Millennium Magic*. St. Paul, MN: Llewellyn Publications, 1996.

———. *Tetragrammaton*. St. Paul, MN: Llewellyn Publications, 1995.

Tyson, Donald (editor). *Three Books of Occult Philosophy Written by Henry Cornelius Agrippa of Nettesheim*. St. Paul, MN: Llewellyn Publications, 1993.

Tucci, Giuseppe. *The Theory and Practice of the Mandala*. Translated from the Italian by Alan Houghton Brodrick. London: Rider and Company, 1969.

Waite, Arthur Edward. *Alchemists Through the Ages* [1888]. New York: Rudolph Steiner Publications, 1970.

——— (translator). *The Alchemical Writings of Edward Kelly* [1893]. New York: Samuel Weiser Inc., 1970.

——— (editor). *The Magical Writings of Thomas Vaughan*. London: George Redway, 1888.

——— (tanslator). *The Turba Philosophorum* [1896]. New York: Samuel Weiser Inc., 1970.

Wilhelm, Richard (translator). *The Secret of the Golden Flower: A Chinese Book of Life* [1931]. London: Routledge and Kegan Paul, (new revised and augmented edition) 1962.

Woodroffe, Sir John (Arthur Avalon). *Principles of Tanta* [1914]. Madras, India: Ganesh and Co., 1952 (2nd edition).

———. *Tantra of the Great Liberation* [1913]. New York: Dover Publications, 1972.

———. *The Garland of Letters: Studies in the Mantra-Sastra* [1922]. Madras, India: Ganesh and Company (6th edition), 1974.

———. *Sakti and Sakta* [1918]. Madras, India: Ganesh and Co. (7th edition), 1969.

Yü, Lu K'Uan. *Taoist Yoga: Alchemy and Immortality*. London: Rider and Company, 1970.

Index

341